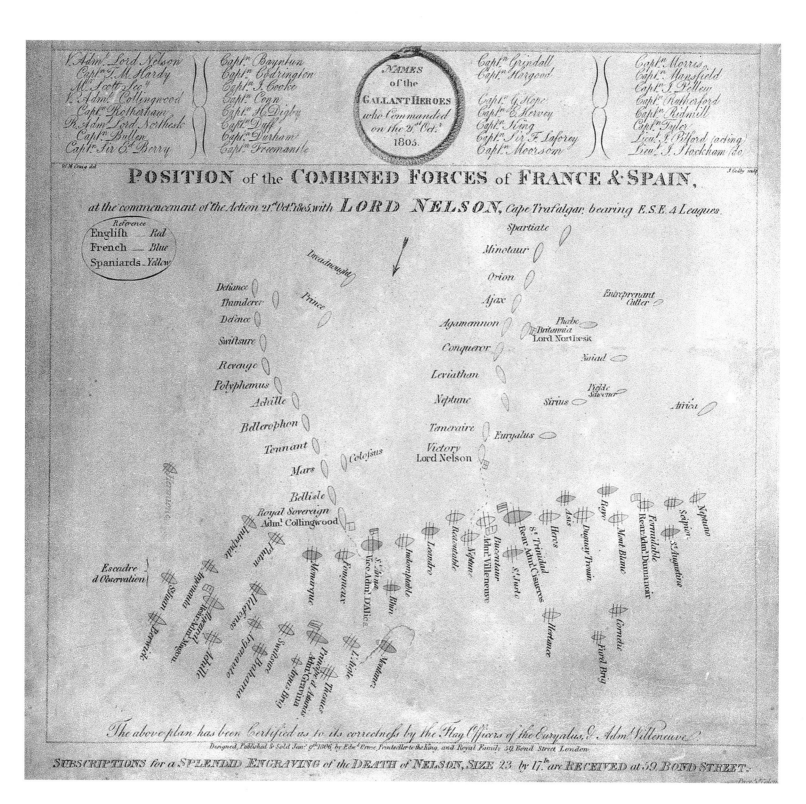

NAMES of the GALLANT HEROES who Commanded on the 21.st Oct.r 1805.

V. Adm.l Lord Nelson
Capt.r T. M. Hardy
M.r Scott Sec.y
V. Adm.l Collingwood
Capt.r Rotherham
R. Adm.l Lord Northesk
Capt.r Bullen
Capt.r Sir Ed. Berry

Capt.r Bayntun
Capt.r Codrington
Capt.r J. Cooke
Capt.r Conn
Capt.r H. Digby
Capt.r Duff
Capt.r Durham
Capt.r Freemantle

Capt.r Grindall
Capt.r Hargood
Capt.r G. Hope
Capt.r E. Harvey
Capt.r King
Capt.r Sir F. Laforey
Capt.r Moorsom

Capt.r Morris
Capt.r Mansfield
Capt.r J. Pellew
Capt.r Rutherford
Capt.r Redmill
Capt.r Tyler
Lieu.t J. Pilford (acting)
Lieu.t J. Stockham (do

W. M. Craig del.   J. Godby sculp.

POSITION of the COMBINED FORCES of FRANCE & SPAIN,

at the commencement of the Action 21.st Oct.r 1805, with LORD NELSON, Cape Trafalgar, bearing E.S.E. 4 Leagues.

Reference
English — Red
French — Blue
Spaniards — Yellow

The above plan has been Certified as to its correctness by the Flag Officers of the Euryalus, & Adm.l Villeneuve.

Designed, Published & Sold Jan.r 9.th 1806, by Edw.d Orme, Printseller to the King, and Royal Family, 59 Bond Street London.

SUBSCRIPTIONS for a SPLENDID ENGRAVING of the DEATH of NELSON, SIZE 23 by 17.th are RECEIVED at 59 BOND STREET.

Nelson & Napoléon

EDITED BY
Margarette Lincoln

*This catalogue and the audio-visual interpretation of the Battle of Trafalgar
have been generously sponsored by the*
ZVI AND OFRA MEITAR FAMILY FUND

First published in 2005
by the National Maritime Museum, Greenwich, London, SE10 9NF
www.nmm.ac.uk

ISBN 0 948065 59 1
LEATHER-BOUND EDITION ISBN 0 948065 66 4

Text © National Maritime Museum, London, 2005
Illustrations © as listed on page 280

1 2 3 4 5 6 7 8 9

A CIP catalogue record for this book
is available from the British Library.

Catalogue design by Peter Ward
Jacket design by Head Design

Printed and bound in the UK by Bath Press Limited

List of Contents

THE THREAT AND THE DEFENCE OF ENGLAND

Simon Burrows
British Propaganda and Anti-Napoleonic Feeling in the Invasion Crisis of 1803
125

Catalogue Entries 133–162
131

N. A. M. Rodger
The Royal Navy in 1803
149

Catalogue Entries 163–192
153

THE THREAT: THE 1805 CAMPAIGN

Margarette Lincoln
The Impact of Nelson and Naval Warfare on Women in Britain, 1795–1805
173

Catalogue Entries 193–212
179

TRAFALGAR

Colin White
Trafalgar
189

Catalogue Entries 213–278
197

LAST JOURNEYS

Timothy Jenks
Commemorating Trafalgar: Politics and Naval Patriotism
231

Christopher Woodward
Napoleon's Last Journey
237

Catalogue Entries 278–323
245

Sponsor's Foreword

I FEEL GREATLY HONOURED to be able to contribute to this outstanding exhibition commemorating the bicentenary of Vice-Admiral Viscount Horatio Nelson's victory at the Battle of Trafalgar.

Millions of words have been written about Nelson as a naval strategist, commander in battle, leader, and as a romantic person. English naval heroes have long captured my interest and admiration; I have a statue of Sir Francis Drake on my table. I was especially intrigued by the personality of Nelson, realizing that although he was disappointed by the politicians of the day – who he believed did not adequately recognize his leadership and genius in battle or the personal sacrifices he made – he did not grow bitter, but carried on undaunted.

Aware of Nelson's tremendous popularity and the esteem in which the public held him, politicians relied upon him to persuade Parliament that the Amiens Peace Treaty of 1801, practically dictated by Napoleon, was not as bad as it seemed. Yet even though Nelson was the victor of the Battles of St Vincent, the Nile, Copenhagen and, the greatest of all, Trafalgar,

politicians bestowed upon him only the lowest ranks of Baron and Viscount. Ferdinand, King of Naples, mitigated this surprising treatment by granting Nelson the highest title he could bestow, that of Duke of Bronte. It was obvious that Nelson was extremely gratified, since after being granted the Dukedom he signed every document 'Bronte and Nelson' (later 'Nelson and Bronte'). Nelson was always short of funds to maintain his lifestyle, so he was delighted that the Dukedom also provided a modest source of income enabling an annual allowance of £500 to his father.

Even after Nelson's glorious victory and heroic death the politicians' attitude did not change: his last request in what amounted to his will, that the state might take care of and support his daughter, was discarded and she was left to endure difficult times.

But Nelson's achievements proved stronger than the politicians' attitude; he is regarded as England's greatest naval hero and his popularity has not waned in 200 years.

Zvi Meitar

Director's Foreword

ARMED CONFLICT persists despite well-intentioned efforts by successive generations to end war and its consequences. Looking back two hundred years it is easy to underestimate the fear prompted by the risk of invasion from across the Channel. A grim determination to fight for national independence led to the mobilization of the Navy, a vigorous and bloody campaign and the creation of military heroes. As we ponder Nelson's record it is sobering to realize how little distance humankind has travelled since his time.

The National Maritime Museum usually has the key objects relating to Nelson and Trafalgar on permanent display, so fresh interpretation of them demands particular effort. *SeaBritain 2005*, this Museum's year-long initiative to promote Britain's enduring relationship with the sea, provides a compelling backdrop to this important bicentenary exhibition that presents new insights into Nelson's outstanding achievement and offers an objective interpretation of the wider historical context.

Nelson & Napoléon places our collections alongside exceptional loan material from private collections and national and international institutions. Focusing on the years 1789–1806, it offers material chosen both for its historical interest and for its aesthetic quality. We have been rigorous and selective in bringing together an extraordinary range of material that offers a rare opportunity to explore in detail the circumstances surrounding Trafalgar, a battle that remains one of the most significant in British history.

The exhibition focuses on personal stories as a way of promoting understanding of a complex period in European history. By bringing Nelson and Napoleon together, we avoid a purely Anglo-centric view and consider the impact that the French Wars had on societies at the time. Napoleon's influence on France and the rest of Europe was on a scale that permits us to offer only modest insights; necessarily, the exhibition has rather more to say about the impact of the war in Britain. However, we are able to begin to decode the meanings and messages inherent in everyday objects that contemporaries would have recognized but which are now less obvious. Better understanding of the period deepens perceptions of the realities of Europe today.

Nicholas Rodger has helped to scope the exhibition. Colin White has been a source of expert advice on Nelson and Trafalgar. Holger Hoock has acted as Research Curator, while Brian Lavery has given advice on the operation of Nelson's navy and Peter Hicks has helped with research in France. Luisa Cale's research in Italy was vital, as was Eleanor Tollfree's generous sharing of her knowledge of Napoleonic collections.

Many organizations and individuals have loaned generously to the exhibition. The National Maritime Museum is grateful to them all, but I would particularly like to thank Her Majesty The Queen and the staff of the Royal Collection, the British Museum and the British Library, the Fondation Napoléon, Lloyd's of London, Musée du Louvre, Musée Carnavalet, Musée de l'Armée, the Museum of London, the National Archives, the National Army Museum, the National Portrait Gallery, Tate and the Victoria and Albert Museum. We have welcomed our partnership with the Musée de la Marine, Paris, and the assistance of Bruno Ponsonnet, Bernard Chevallier and the Director of the Musée National du Château de Malmaison. Private collectors Pierre-Jean Chalençon, Clive Richards, John Goldstein, Jean-Louis de Talencé and Shortall of Ballylorcan have been generous in lending material, and we also extend our gratitude to others who prefer to remain anonymous.

I would like to thank Sian Flynn who headed the exhibition team, Claire Warrior, principal in-house exhibition curator and numerous other staff from across the Museum who helped to put this exhibition together. Thanks are also due to Margarette Lincoln, who edited this catalogue, the publishing team under Rachel Giles, and particularly Fiona Renkin who project managed the publication. We thank David Quarmby (Chairman), Stephen Riley, Deirdre Livingstone and their teams for making *SeaBritain 2005* a most rewarding programme.

Finally, the Trustees and staff of the Museum would like to record their gratitude to those who have sponsored the show. BP Shipping generously agreed to sponsor the Special Exhibitions Gallery, Morgan Stanley backed *Leading Lives*, a programme in leadership for sixth-form students, and many individuals and organizations have contributed to 'Nelson's Fleet'.

Most substantial has been the personal commitment and sponsorship of Mr Zvi Meitar. He shares a passion for Nelson and we have welcomed his attentive, thoughtful interest to our plans. We are grateful for his confidence and we acknowledge his loans to the show and the generous support of the Zvi and Ofra Meitar Family Fund for the catalogue and for the audio-visual interpretation of the Battle of Trafalgar.

Roy Clare
Director, National Maritime Museum
Greenwich
2005

Acknowledgements

MANY PEOPLE have helped to make this exhibition possible. In addition to Nicholas Rodger, Colin White and Holger Hoock, the Museum particularly thanks Roger Knight, Andrew Lambert and Christopher Woodward who all gave valuable advice at various stages in exhibition planning. David Spence (formerly Director of Exhibitions at the National Maritime Museum) also provided important input at the critical early stages of the project.

An exhibition on this scale is always a museum-wide effort. I am grateful to Claire Warrior, to Kristian Martin, the interpretation curator; to Maria Blyzinsky, who managed the exhibition production; to Valérie Didier and Zoe Kahr, who helped with research in France, and to Sabine Panneau for liaising with French lenders. Many curators have been directly involved, giving generously of their time over a long period; special thanks are due to Janet Owen, who coordinated their effort, and to Amy Miller, Curator of Decorative Arts, for her work as a member of the extended exhibition team. The Museum is grateful to Angela Doane and to her expert staff in Registration, Storage & Movement, Display Care, and Conservation & Preservation, to Liz Smith and her education team, and to Phil Pain and John Malone, who have worked hard to coordinate resources across the Museum. We warmly thank Lucy Cooke, Head of Corporate Development, who coordinated the input of sponsors; Michael Barrett, former Head of Corporate Communications, and also their respective teams. Finally, the Museum thanks Phillip Tefft and his team at Ralph Appelbaum Associates for the exhibition design.

Sian Flynn
Head of Exhibitions

I SHOULD LIKE to record my thanks to everybody in the National Maritime Museum who made working on this catalogue such a pleasure. Special thanks are due to Gloria Clifton, Andrew Davis, Daphne Knott, Douglas Hamilton, Gillian Hutchinson, Jeremy Michell, Roger Quarm, Geoff Quilley, Hellen Pethers, Rina Prentice, David Rooney, Simon Stephens, Barbara Tomlinson, Liza Verity, Emily Winterburn and Gwen Yarker. In particular, I would like to thank Pieter van der Merwe, who read the entire manuscript, Brian Lavery, who provided expert help with technical detail, and Colin White, who offered invaluable assistance with Nelson's biography. Grateful thanks are also due to those external contributors not yet mentioned above, to Simon Burrows, John Cardwell, Timothy Jenks, Annie Jourdan, Helen Weston, Barry Langridge, Vaughan Hart, Joe Robson and Peter Hicks, all of whom provided valuable specialist input and helped to ensure that for this complex project we captured a range of expertise and scholarship.

The catalogue has been ably produced by NMM Publishing. I should like to add my personal thanks to Rachel Giles, Head of Publishing, Eleanor Dryden, Project Editor, and most particularly Fiona Renkin, Project Manager. Many of the objects in the exhibition have been specifically photographed for this book by Ken Hickey and the Museum's photographic team: Tina Warner, Josh Akin, Enzo di Cosmo and Sarah Laker. Thanks are also due to copy editor Richard Collins, picture researcher Sara Ayad and catalogue designer Peter Ward.

Margarette Lincoln
Editor

List of Lenders

Her Majesty The Queen
Ashmolean Museum, University of Oxford
Bank of England Museum, London
Bodleian Library, University of Oxford
The Borough of Lymington
The British Library, London
The British Museum, London
Centre historique des archives nationales, Paris
Pierre-Jean Chalençon
Chequers Trust, UK
The Council of the National Army Museum, London
The Drapers' Company, London
Fitzwilliam Museum, Cambridge
Fondation Napoléon, Paris
Gesellschaft der Musikfreunde, Vienna
John Goldstein
Sir John Soane's Museum, London
Lloyd's of London
Madame Tussaud's, London
Manchester Art Gallery, Gallery of Costume, Platt Hall, Manchester
Zvi Meitar
Musée Carnavalet, Paris
Musée d'Armes, Liège
Musée d'Art Moderne et d'Art Contemporain de la Ville de Liège
Musée de l'Armée, Paris

Musée du Louvre, Paris
Musée national de la Legion d'Honneur et des Ordres de Chevalerie, Paris
Musée national des châteaux de Malmaison et Bois-Préau
Musée nationale de la Marine, Paris
Musée de la Révolution française, Vizille
Museo del Tessuto di Prato
Museo Napoleonico, Rome
Museum of London, London
The National Archives, Kew
National Portrait Gallery, London
Nelson Museum and Local History Centre, Monmouth
Österreichische Nationalbibliothek, Vienna
Clive Richards
Royal Astronomical Society, London
Royal College of Physicians and Surgeons, Glasgow
Royal Naval Museum, Portsmouth
Earl and Countess of Rosebery
Jean-Louis de Talancé
Victoria and Albert Museum (Apsley House), London
Wellcome Library, London
The Science Museum, London
Shortall of Ballylorcan
Spode Museum Trust, Stoke-on-Trent
Tate, London
All generous private lenders

Catalogue Contributors

Note: each catalogue entry is followed by the initials of its author

Simon Burrows, Lecturer in Modern History, University of Leeds (SB)

John Cardwell, Researcher, Modern History Faculty, University of Oxford (JC)

Gloria Clifton, Curator of Navigational Instruments, National Maritime Museum, and Head of the Royal Observatory Greenwich (GC)

Andrew Davis, Curator of Manuscripts, National Maritime Museum (AD)

Douglas Hamilton, Curator of Eighteenth-Century Maritime and Imperial History, National Maritime Museum (DH)

Peter Hicks, Historian, Fondation Napoléon, Paris (PH)

Holger Hoock, British Academy Postdoctoral Fellow, Selwyn College, University of Cambridge (HH)

Gillian Hutchinson, Curator of the History of Cartography, National Maritime Museum (GH)

Timothy Jenks, Assistant Professor of History, East Carolina University (TJ)

Annie Jourdan, Associate Professor, European Studies, University of Amsterdam

Daphne Knott, Manuscripts Archivist, National Maritime Museum (DK)

Brian Lavery, Curator of Naval History, National Maritime Museum (BL)

Margarette Lincoln, Director of Research & Collections, National Maritime Museum

Pieter van der Merwe, General Editor, National Maritime Museum (PvdM)

Jeremy Michell, Curator, Historic Photographs and Ships, National Maritime Museum (JM)

Amy Miller, Curator, Decorative Arts & Material Culture, National Maritime Museum (AM)

Hellen Pethers, Librarian, National Maritime Museum (HP)

Rina Prentice, Curator of Antiquities, National Maritime Museum (RP)

Roger Quarm, Curator of Pictures, National Maritime Museum (RQ)

Geoff Quilley, Curator of Maritime Art, National Maritime Museum (GQ)

N. A. M. Rodger, Professor in Naval History, University of Exeter

David Rooney, Curator of Timekeeping, National Maritime Museum (DR)

Simon Stephens, Curator of Ship Model and Boat Collections, National Maritime Museum (SS)

Barbara Tomlinson, Curator of Antiquities, National Maritime Museum (BT)

Liza Verity, Information Specialist, National Maritime Museum (LV)

Claire Warrior, Curator of Exhibitions, National Maritime Museum (CLW)

Helen Weston, Professor in History of Art, University College London

Colin White, Director, Trafalgar 200, National Maritime Museum and Deputy Director, Royal Naval Museum, Portsmouth (CSW)

Emily Winterburn, Curator of Astronomy, National Maritime Museum (EW)

Christopher Woodward, Director, Holburne Museum of Art

Gwen Yarker, Curator, Art, National Maritime Museum

Notes on Conventions

The information in the catalogue has been given as accurately as possible but areas of uncertainty remain. Catalogue entries have been compiled in the following order:

— Title and date of object. Square brackets indicate date is uncertain. * before the catalogue number indicates that the item does not feature in the exhibition itself, sometimes on grounds of its size. If on display elsewhere in the Museum the location is given in brackets at the end of this section.
— Artist/maker/author and his/her dates or school.
— Media, and publisher of printed books or prints.
— Dimensions in mm(height x width): with few exceptions, measurements have only been provided for paintings, single-leaf prints and drawings, and medals (diameter). Some objects have depth as a third measurement.
— Inscriptions on paintings and medals, or where they add to the meaning of the object.
— Immediate provenance where known.
— Location and reference number where documented.
— Text: spelling has been modernized, except for long quotations.
— Literature: up to three works have been selected. Full details are provided for works that appear only once. Otherwise, the full reference appears in the bibliography.
— Authorship: abbreviations are explained on the previous page.

Nelson and Napoleon: A Personal Rivalry

COLIN WHITE

EARLY IN APRIL 1804 the Royal Navy cutter *Swift* was captured by the French. She was carrying long-awaited mail from home to the British Mediterranean Fleet: not only secret official dispatches, but private correspondence as well – including a thick packet of letters to Vice-Admiral Lord Nelson from his mistress, Emma, Lady Hamilton. When Nelson learned of their loss he did all he could to retrieve them – even, at one point, sending his chaplain and unofficial intelligence agent, the Revd Alexander Scott, on shore to buy them back. To his dismay, he learned that they had already been forwarded to Paris, to the Emperor Napoleon.

In the following weeks, Nelson tortured himself with the thought of Napoleon reading Emma's indiscreet outpourings. As well he might – for, five years earlier, their roles had been reversed. In the autumn of 1798, shortly after his victory at the Battle of the Nile, Nelson had intercepted letters from General Bonaparte, then stranded in Egypt. In one, Napoleon expressed his anguish at the news that his wife Josephine was being unfaithful to him. Having enjoyed his opponent's discomfiture, Nelson sent the letters home to England where they were published, thus parading Napoleon's private pain for all to see.

Napoleon never published Emma Hamilton's letters: possibly, he never saw them. But Nelson's emotional reaction to their capture highlights the degree to which he had come to see Napoleon as a personal adversary. By the time of their greatest contest, in 1805, his letters were full of dismissive references to 'the Corsican tyrant', whose surname he always spelt with the Italian 'u' : 'Buonaparte'. There is evidence that Napoleon viewed their rivalry in a similar personalized way. British visitors to the Tuileries during the Peace of Amiens noticed a bust of Nelson in the First Consul's dressing-room. During the extensive fleet movements of the 1805 campaign, Napoleon often mentioned Nelson in his letters, speculating on what he was doing and fantasizing that he had succeeded in outwitting him. So, by 1805, each had become for the other the personification of the enemy.

Although Nelson and Napoleon never actually met in battle, they came close to doing so twice. During the Italian campaign of 1796 Nelson, then a commodore, commanded a squadron that disrupted the transport by sea of General Bonaparte's supplies, on one occasion capturing his entire siege train. There was an even closer encounter in 1798, some weeks before Nelson's extraordinary victory at the Nile effectively ended Napoleon's eastern adventure. On 22 June, Nelson's fleet, scouring the Mediterranean for the great armada bearing Napoleon's expedition, sighted sails on the distant horizon. At about the same time, Nelson received intelligence that the French were already some days ahead of him – so he recalled his scouts and sailed hurriedly eastwards in pursuit.

In fact, the intelligence was wrong: the French were just over the horizon and it was their outlying frigates that Nelson's ships had seen. If he had investigated more closely, there might have been a battle on 22 June between his highly trained squadron and Napoleon's large, unwieldy force of warships and troop transports.

In death, they drew even closer. In January 1806, Nelson was given a state funeral, with the elaborate ceremonial usually reserved for royalty. He was laid to rest in St Paul's Cathedral, the British Pantheon, occupying the place of honour, directly beneath the great dome. Napoleon's funeral on St Helena in 1821 was considerably less elaborate; but he had his share of royal-style ceremonial later, in 1840, when his body was brought home to France. Like Nelson, he was buried beneath the dome of the national pantheon – in his case Les Invalides.

Two hundred years later both are the subject of extensive cults. Societies are devoted to their memory; museums display their possessions and re-enactors recreate their battles. Books about them are bestsellers; their letters and relics fetch high prices in sale rooms. Each has become a powerful talismanic figure, a symbol of their respective nation's struggle for power and supremacy.

In July 1815, following Waterloo, Napoleon arrived at Rochefort, hoping to escape to America. He found his way blocked by the battleship *Bellerophon*, a veteran of both the Nile and Trafalgar. Eventually, he gave himself up to her captain, Frederick Maitland, and, clearly appreciating the symbolism of his action, remarked that the Royal Navy had consistently thwarted his ambitions.

In fact, Napoleon's act was even more symbolically appropriate than he realized, for it has recently been established that, for a brief period in February 1799, the *Bellerophon* served as Nelson's flagship. So, as he stepped on to her quarter-deck to make his formal surrender, Napoleon was walking directly in his former antagonist's footsteps.

REVOLUTION

Nelson and Napoleon: An Introduction

N. A. M. RODGER

WHAT DID they have in common, Nelson and Napoleon? They were more or less contemporaries (born in 1758 and 1769 respectively) who rose to become public heroes in two countries which confronted one another in a war of unprecedented length and ferocity. Each made his career in war and through war, conspicuous for courage and skill at a time when both were very much in demand. Both died young (Nelson killed in action at forty-seven, Napoleon probably of natural causes at fifty-two), and both might be described as icons of the Romantic era who have never ceased to fascinate succeeding generations, and whose public images have been and are still continuously reshaped. Both were themselves very much aware of their own reputations and took steps to form them, Nelson by 'feeding' the press with suitable material about himself, Napoleon by extensive manipulation of all sorts of media for political as well as personal motives, and eventually by the totalitarian control of all possible sources of information and opinion. Both were distinguished by supreme professional gifts, as leaders, organizers and tacticians, but both had a conspicuous personal weakness. Nelson betrayed both his wife and his duty, effectively allowing the squadron under his command to come under the control of a foreign power during 1799 and 1800 as Maria Carolina, Queen of Naples and Sicily, manipulated the admiral via Emma Hamilton (cat. no. 100). Officers who loved and admired him were appalled at the visible change in his personality and behaviour in her company, and ministers spent the remainder of his career trying to keep them apart. Nelson himself, conspicuous in his generation for public piety, calmed his conscience with easy phrases, but the haggard look of his later portraits reveals the inner cost of betrayed ideals

Emma, Lady Hamilton, by Johann Heinrich Schmidt (cat. no. 100).
Opposite: Rear-Admiral Sir Horatio Nelson, by Johann Heinrich Schmidt (cat. no. 100).

(cat. no. 100). Napoleon never suffered from moral scruples, however far behind he left the idealism of the early French Revolution in his ruthless drive for power, but the more he used the men and women about his throne, the less he commanded their loyalty. One who habitually distorted the truth for his own ends was increasingly the prisoner of those who told him only what he wanted to hear. Only in the field did he still have capable followers, some of whom remained loyal to the end.

This is the fundamental difference between the two men. The great dictator, absolutely corrupted by absolute power, demanding, as one enemy remarked, an income of 10,000 men a month,[1] ruthlessly throwing away the lives of his soldiers and consuming the resources of his adopted country, France, and much of Western Europe with it, to sustain his limitless ambitions – all this is as far removed as it could be on one planet from the career of Nelson. Morally and politically, the two men inhabited different worlds. Loyal subject of a parliamentary monarchy ruled by law, Nelson never for a moment contemplated breaking out of the legal and conventional limits of a naval career. Extraordinary as a man, extraordinarily successful as an officer, he lived his whole life in a very ordinary and traditional society, albeit in extraordinary times. The internal stability and external defences of Britain repelled the forces of revolution. Britain never suffered the violent anarchy, the totalitarian idealism decaying into greed and cynicism which wracked France and destroyed half Europe. It would have been absurd and unthinkable to imagine Nelson mounting a *coup d'état* in Britain, and the limit of his political activity was a passing idea of entering the House of Commons, and a handful of speeches in the Lords after he was ennobled. His moral failures were in his private life, and they chiefly hurt his wife, himself, his friends and his reputation. His king and country had nothing to fear from him, and only a little to regret.

Both Nelson and Napoleon owe much of their fame to the fact that they have come to epitomize national triumphs, at sea and on land respectively. Napoleon rose to fame and power as one of the most brilliant of the many brilliant generals who led the French Revolutionary armies to conquer much of Europe (cat. no. 41). They represented a new and devastating way of war in the service of a new and revolutionary political order, the fascination and terror of the world. Though in reality many of the tactical novelties of the French Revolutionary armies had been developed before the Revolution, and much of their success depended on the reckless expenditure of superior resources of manpower, they carried France to a pinnacle of glory and an extent of empire which has distracted Frenchmen ever since. In civil government, moreover, he imposed forms and structures which mark the society of much of Europe today. There are still many enthusiasts for this legacy of Napoleonic government – usually the same who embrace the Enlightenment as an uncomplicated benefit to mankind – and even those who have misgivings on both scores do not deny the importance of Napoleon's civil reforms in shaping modern Europe.

Napoleon as a young man,
by Francesco Cossia [?] (cat. no. 41).

Nothing like this can be claimed for Nelson, who was never a dictator or a conqueror, whose achievements were strictly personal and confined to the Royal Navy at war. He was the most brilliant of a talented generation of senior officers, the heirs of much thought and effort applied over several generations to the improvement of naval tactics. Under his command British fleets achieved the same sort of crushing, annihilating victories at sea as the French Revolutionary armies were winning on land. At sea, as on land, the new era of total victory is often perceived as the product of the new age of total war and total ideology, but it was in many ways the logical culmination of purely technical and professional developments which had made all European navies, not only the British, steadily more effective during the course of the eighteenth century. There was a real political transformation in the French navy, which was severely disrupted by the Revolution, and

lost most of its officers, but went to sea with a new generation of promising young commanders, and a new determination to fight and win, which surprised and impressed the British when they encountered it at the Battle of the Glorious First of June in 1794 (cat. no. 32). These French officers neither surrendered nor ran away when their situation was hopeless, which encouraged British officers to adopt yet more bloody and decisive fighting tactics. But Napoleon, who knew how to use talented young generals, was frightened by admirals with minds of their own and made sure to get rid of the promising republicans of the 1790s. By the time of Trafalgar the French navy was in the hands of former noble officers of the old navy, experienced but cynical and demoralized men like Villeneuve, Decrès and Bruix, who could be relied upon not to offend the imperial ears with unwelcome truths. Under their command French naval morale and discipline – still relatively high at Trafalgar – progressively collapsed.

Behind morale, discipline and professional skill lay the essential 'sinews of war': money, and the capacity to deploy money in effective systems of administration and logistics. One of the greatest strengths, but also the greatest weaknesses of the French Revolutionary armies, was that they lived off the conquered countryside, which both permitted and enforced rapid movement. It also enforced a policy of continual conquest, in order to feed the armies and satisfy the generals' need for loot and power. In this way the French armies of the late 1790s effectively took over French foreign policy, forcing aggressive war on politicians who were weary of it and would have bought peace by surrendering their conquests had they not feared their own armies and generals more than the enemy. They were right to do so, as Napoleon's rise to power proved, but he in turn was the willing prisoner of the same strategic logic. Although in public Napoleon embraced a conservative financial system, in practice he only once balanced his budget, in the peace year of 1802, and the Napoleonic empire demanded unceasing expansion to feed the armies and endow the new military aristocracy which he erected to guard his throne. The system was incapable of peace and stability. It was also incapable of supporting a major navy, which cannot live off the country, and cannot be improvised, but requires long years of heavy investment in capital and technology.

It was precisely such long-sustained investment which allowed the British to overcome the greatest difficulties in the way of long-range naval operations, which were victualling and health. The ability to remain at sea for long periods obviously depended on the capacity to supply large quantities of reliable preserved foods, while armies and navies, crowding large numbers of men together for long periods, had always been extremely vulnerable to epidemic illness. By the late 1790s, after more than a century of effort, the British had effectively solved both problems. The very high quality of the preserved food packed and issued by the Victualling Board, the great effort and expense applied to providing fresh food to ships at sea all over the world, and the general issue of lemon juice had virtually eliminated dietary disease. Rigorous attention to the cleanliness of men, clothes and ships, and a campaign of inoculation against smallpox, had contained most infectious diseases. Only landing operations in tropical climates still presented insoluble medical challenges. In the Mediter-

French republican banner captured during the Battle of the Glorious First of June, 1794 (cat. no. 32).

ranean between 1803 and 1805, Nelson, who was a gifted administrator as well as a great leader, devoted enormous energy to the victualling of his ships. 'The great thing in all Military Service is health,' he wrote, 'and you will agree with me, that it is easier for an Officer to keep men healthy, than for a physician to cure them.'[2] In the first three years of the Napoleonic War, there were only 110 deaths from all causes in a squadron of 6500 men. When Dr Leonard Gillespie joined the *Victory* as Physician to the Mediterranean Fleet in January 1805, when most of the ships had been twenty months at sea, he found almost nothing to do. There was one man in the flagship's sick berth, and only a handful ill in the whole fleet. Presently the squadron moved rapidly to Alexandria, back the whole length of the Mediterranean, chased to the West Indies and back across the Atlantic, arriving after two years at sea and a voyage of almost 10,000 miles, as Nelson reported, 'in the most perfect health, and only require some vegetables and other refreshments to remove the scurvy'.

These achievements were expensive. The British war effort, unlike Napoleon's, depended on orthodox finance – but for a century British financial orthodoxy had involved spreading the cost of war by borrowing. In the 1690s the English government was paying for almost half the cost of the war from current income, but by the time of the American War of Independence eighty years later this proportion had fallen below one-fifth. In the late 1790s the financial markets finally grew restless at the mounting proportion of government debt to income. The response was a real financial revolution: income tax, first imposed in 1799. Throughout the eighteenth century most British tax revenue had come from indirect taxes paid by the whole population. The only significant direct tax, the Land Tax, was levied on an assessment fixed in 1692, so that income from land was grossly underestimated, and no other income was taxed at all. Now, for the first time, the monied classes of Britain paid heavy direct taxation, and the finances of war were transformed. Between 1800 and 1815 current income from taxation paid for not less than 70 per cent of the cost of the war.

The sources of Britain's wealth, from which taxes were paid and government loans purchased, were the two principal economic activities of the British Isles: agriculture and foreign trade. It is a common misconception that the Industrial Revolution made Britain a great economic power: chronology alone makes it clear that Britain was already a great power before she was an industrial power. By 1815, when her main commercial rival, France, had destroyed herself and much of Europe with her, Britain was incontestably the dominant world trading power – but the Industrial Revolution was still in its early stages, and only water-powered cotton mills were as yet making a major contribution to the economy. In the period in which Britain rose to greatness, the only significant generators of wealth in the British Isles were agriculture and foreign trade. The Navy was essential to both, for only naval protection made it possible to sustain foreign trade in wartime (and in peacetime, too, in many parts of the world), while the existence of a national agricultural market depended on coastal shipping: before the railway age land transport was completely inadequate. The Royal Navy was therefore essential to Britain's economic as well as military survival. It not only guarded the Channel against the Grand Army at Boulogne, it guarded the trade without which no war effort could have been sustained.

It is necessary to bear in mind the economic as well as the military factors in order to understand the significance of the Battle of Trafalgar in which Nelson lost his life. Napoleon's invasion plans provided the immediate strategic context. The number of French and Spanish ships of the line available to Napoleon was sufficient, on paper, to overwhelm the British Channel Fleet off Brest and enter the Channel in overwhelming force to cover the Grand Army's invasion. The difficulty was that the ships were divided among half a dozen different ports, all under British blockade or observation. Napoleon therefore produced a succession of complex and increasingly muddled plans, which were supposed to allow all his squadrons to escape and unite by decoying British ships away to the West Indies or somewhere else. These plans depended on the assumption that winds and tides would obey his requirements, and that the enemy would do nothing and understand nothing except what suited his purpose. By the end of August 1805 they had collapsed so completely that even the Emperor had noticed. Moreover his gamble that he could knock Britain out of the war before any other enemy attacked had failed, for the Austrian and Russian armies were on the march. The Grand Army therefore abandoned its camp at Boulogne and marched off towards the Rhine. Napoleon now ordered his Combined Fleet to sea from Cadiz, where it had taken refuge, in support of troop movements in southern Italy which formed a minor part of his plans against Austria. He knew that the British blockade had been reinforced, and that there was a very high risk of battle and defeat. To endanger his fleet for so trivial an objective can only be explained, in the opinion of recent French scholars, by wounded vanity, a subconscious desire to punish the hated navy for failing to contribute to his glory.[3]

He had no sooner thrown away the Combined Fleet than he began to realize how much he needed it, not only to cover a cross-Channel invasion but to break out of his strategic situation in any direction. It is often remarked that for want of a major field army Britain was condemned to indirect and indecisive, or at least slow, strategies against a dominant continental military power. This was true, but so was the reverse: for want of a fleet Napoleon was now condemned to an indirect strategy against Britain. His political situation and his personal ambition made it unthinkable for him to make lasting peace, but the only way he could make lasting war against Britain was by attacking the British economy. Napoleon never understood Britain's economic strength. He remained all his life wedded to the orthodox economics of mid-eighteenth-century France, which held that real wealth was the product of land and people, agriculture and domestic industries producing for home consumption. All trade, and even more finance, was essentially parasitic, and any economy which depended on them (the British economy in particular) was fundamentally flimsy, exploitative and vulnerable. He therefore determined to ruin the British economy by shutting it out of all European trade. He was indifferent to the fate of the merchants, especially the non-French merchants, of his own empire. Napoleon's 'Continental Blockade' did indeed do real damage to the British economy, but it did much more damage to the Napoleonic empire. Everywhere in Europe merchants whose livelihoods were at risk penetrated the system with every kind of false flags and papers, while the British established commercial depots at Malta, Gibraltar, Heligoland (a small island in the North Sea), Lissa (a large island in the central Adriatic) and elsewhere from which a flourishing clandestine trade passed into Europe. Soldiers and officials even at the highest levels of the Napoleonic system were eminently corruptible, and many honest men, not otherwise disloyal, had no patience with measures openly designed to support Napoleon's ambitions by beggaring his subjects, and particularly his non-French subjects. Behind the official façade, the Continental System was dissolving the political glue of the Napoleonic regime. Moreover it depended on the whole of Europe being united under Napoleon's command, and required him to conquer any country, friendly or neutral, which did not choose to sacrifice its trade to his ambitions. But Portugal and Sweden resisted, Spain rebelled and Russia changed sides. The Peninsular and Russian campaigns which destroyed Napoleon's armies and his regime were necessary only to support the Continental Blockade against Britain: they had no other strategic logic.

The only answer to this dilemma would have been a navy capable of challenging Britain, as Napoleon soon realized. Throughout the years after Trafalgar, he was pouring large resources into a new battle fleet to replace the one he had thrown away. Brest was virtually abandoned in 1810 because of the British blockade, but a new building yard was established at Antwerp. British governments watched Napoleon's efforts warily, as they were prudent to do, and maintained the operational strength of the Royal Navy at rather more than one hundred ships of the line, but they did not divert money or manpower from the frigates and other cruisers whose numbers continued to increase. Some modern historians have been impressed by Napoleon's efforts, and have taken his claims and ambitions much more seriously than they deserve. In fact much of the building effort, like all Napoleon's naval plans, was based on fantasy. Hastily constructed of green timber to obsolete designs, many of these ships were rotten before they were ever commissioned. Shipwrights were scarce and scarcely paid, so the building quality was poor. A number of the ships constructed at Antwerp proved to be either unstable or too big to get through the lock gates, and had to be broken up in the basin where they had been launched. In 1811 the French empire had seventy-two ships of the line on paper, but at best only fifty-five might have been made seaworthy, and perhaps thirty were of some military value. Eleven were built at Venice and Trieste, but the only one which actually put to sea, the *Rivoli*, was captured within thirty-six hours, and there is little reason to expect that the others would have fared much better. Morale and discipline were very poor, especially among the officers, and the remaining seamen hated Napoleon's solution, which was to dress them as soldiers and drill them in 'naval battalions'. Much as an efficient fleet would have done to increase Napoleon's strategic options, there is nothing to suggest that he ever had any realistic idea how to obtain one.

At the peace settlement of 1814 and then 1815, the British government devoted much care to ensuring that post-war France would never again have the chance to become a dangerous naval rival. To keep the French out of Antwerp, a powerful new Kingdom of the Netherlands was fashioned from the old Dutch Republic and Austrian Netherlands. When Napoleon escaped from his exile on Elba in March 1815 to re-establish his rule, his first move was to march on Antwerp. Barring his way was the Prussian army under Marshal Blücher, and a Dutch–British army under the Duke of Wellington. When they defeated him at Waterloo outside Brussels on 18 June 1815, he had no options left, and a month later he surrendered to the Royal Navy.

By the time Napoleon sailed aboard the *Bellerophon* for England then to final exile on St Helena, Nelson had been dead almost ten years (cat. no. 310). His contribution at Trafalgar to Napoleon's final defeat had been to wreck his most promising hope of breaking out of the strategic limitations of European military power, into the trade and wealth of the world on which Britain depended. In 1805, with the Royal Navy enfeebled by St Vincent's reforms and the Franco-Spanish fleets at their maximum strength, Napoleon had his best chance and he was never offered another.

Genius, luck and lack of scruples made Napoleon the supreme symbol and exponent of French conquests, and the object of nostalgia to this day among those who regret them, but his legacy, like so much of French history, continues to divide France. The upholders of republican ideals prefer to remember the author of the Napoleonic Code rather than the vulgar military dictator. The French army prefers to remember the young general leading his armies to victory rather than the old egotist throwing away his soldiers' lives to feed his insensate

ambitions. Catholic France has never been wholly reconciled to an atheist state and its children. Only by cultivating a myth of glory as far removed as possible from divisive truths can Napoleon be made into some sort of national symbol.

Nelson's posthumous fate was rather different. He did not live to participate in ultimate victory, and in the age of the Evangelical revival which followed it his very public moral failings were something of an embarrassment. The national memorial to him in Trafalgar Square (largely paid for by subscriptions from the Navy) was not finished until 1843, by which time many other Nelson monuments already existed throughout the English-speaking world. The 'immortal memory' began to revive in the middle years of the century, and reached its apogee in the years before the First World War, when the Navy League promoted the cult of Trafalgar Day as a central part of its campaigns, and the Navy itself adopted the celebration as part of its traditions. Nelson was now a symbol of imperial Britain and its overarching sea power, and a talisman against anxiety. Whatever strengths other imperial and naval powers might gain, they could not have Nelson – though they tried, for the Nelson cult was strongly promoted in both the Japanese and German navies. By this time Nelson the man and leader of men had largely been forgotten in Nelson the hero, and his heroism was looked for, not in his humanity, but in formulas. Admirals (the majority) who knew nothing of naval history, justified their views with half-remembered quotations from the great man. The Admiralty demonstrated to the public how well prepared the Navy was for future war by publishing, in 1913, the report of a weighty official committee on Nelson's tactics at Trafalgar.

In spite of this preparation the First World War failed to yield the second Trafalgar which the Royal Navy, and the public, expected, but the disappointment did not cause a turning away from Nelson, as it might so easily have done. Instead the late Victorian Nelson was dismantled, and behind the façade new biographers began to discover the human figure as well as the hero. Dramatists and film-makers presented his life (usually his life with Emma Hamilton) in vivid, not to say garish, colours. In the 1920s the Society for Nautical Research led a successful campaign to preserve and reconstruct the *Victory*, which has ever since presented a powerful physical and visual image of Nelson and the Navy of his day. During the Second World War Nelson was a real, and in many ways a realistic inspiration to his countrymen: Churchill reckoned Alexander Korda's 1942 film *Lady Hamilton* was worth four divisions in morale. Since then Nelson has never ceased to fascinate and he remains a lively subject of historical research, a perennial favourite of biographers, an inspiration for the Royal Navy and an icon of popular culture.

DÉCLARATION DES DROITS DE L'HOMME ET DU CITOYEN,

Décretés par l'Assemblée Nationale dans les séances des 20, 21, 23, 24 et 26 août 1789, acceptés par le Roi.

PRÉAMBULE

Les representans du peuple François, constitués en assemblée nationale, considerant que l'ignorance, l'oubli ou le mépris des droits de l'homme sont les seules causes des malheurs publics et de la corruption des gouvernemens, ont résolu d'exposer, dans une déclaration solennelle, les droits naturels, inalienables et sacrés de l'homme, afin que cette déclaration, constamment présente à tous les membres du corps social, leur rappelle sans cesse leurs droits et leurs devoirs; afin que les actes du pouvoir législatif et ceux du pouvoir exécutif, pouvant être à chaque instant comparés avec le but de toute institution politique, en soient plus respectés; afin que les réclamations des citoyens, fondées désormais sur des principes simples et incontestables, tournent toujours au maintien de la constitution et du bonheur de tous.

En conséquence, l'assemblée nationale reconnoît et declare, en présence et sous les auspices de l'Être suprême, les droits suivans de l'homme et du citoyen.

ARTICLE PREMIER.

Les hommes naissent et demeurent libres et égaux en droits; les distinctions sociales ne peuvent être fondées que sur l'utilité commune.

II

Le but de toute association politique est la conservation des droits naturels et imprescriptibles de l'homme; ces droits sont la liberté, la propriété, la sûreté, et la résistance à l'oppression.

III.

Le principe de toute souveraineté réside essentiellement dans la nation, nul corps, nul individu ne peut exercer d'autorité qui n'en émane expressément.

IV.

La liberté consiste à pouvoir faire tout ce qui ne nuit pas à autrui. Ainsi, l'exercice des droits naturels de chaque homme, n'a de bornes que celles qui assurent aux autres membres de la société la jouissance de ces mêmes droits; ces bornes ne peuvent être déterminées que par la loi.

V.

La loi n'a le droit de défendre que les actions nuisibles à la société. Tout ce qui n'est pas défendu par la loi ne peut être empêché, et nul ne peut être contraint à faire ce qu'elle n'ordonne pas.

VI.

La loi est l'expression de la volonté générale; tous les citoyens ont droit de concourir personnellement, ou par leurs représentans, à sa formation; elle doit être la même pour tous, soit qu'elle protege, soit qu'elle punisse. Tous les citoyens étant égaux à ses yeux, sont également admissibles à toutes dignités, places et emplois publics, selon leur capacité, et sans autres distinctions que celles de leurs vertus et de leurs talens.

VII.

Nul homme ne peut être accusé, arrêté, ni détenu que dans les cas déterminés par la loi, et selon les formes qu'elle a prescrites. Ceux qui sollicitent, expédient, exécutent ou font exécuter des ordres arbitraires, doivent être punis; mais tout citoyen appelé ou saisi en vertu de la loi, doit obéir à l'instant; il se rend coupable par la résistance.

VIII.

La loi ne doit établir que des peines strictement et évidemment nécessaires, et nul ne peut être puni qu'en vertu d'une loi établie et promulguée antérieurement au délit, et légalement appliquée.

IX

Tout homme étant présumé innocent, jusqu'à ce qu'il ait été déclaré coupable, s'il est jugé indispensable de l'arrêter, toute rigueur qui ne seroit pas nécessaire pour s'assurer de sa personne doit être sévèrement réprimée par la loi.

X.

Nul ne doit être inquiété pour ses opinions, mêmes réligieuses, pourvu que leur manifestation ne trouble pas l'ordre public établi par la loi.

XI.

La libre communication des pensées et des opinions est un des droits les plus précieux de l'homme; tout citoyen peut donc parler, écrire, imprimer librement; sauf à répondre de l'abus de cette liberté dans les cas déterminés par la loi.

XII.

La garantie des droits de l'homme et du citoyen nécessite une force publique; cette force est donc instituée pour l'avantage de tous, et non pour l'utilité particulière de ceux à qui elle est confiée.

XIII.

Pour l'entretien de la force publique, et pour les dépenses d'administration, une contribution commune est indispensable; elle doit être également répartie entre tous les citoyens, en raison de leurs facultés.

XIV.

Les citoyens ont le droit de constater par eux-mêmes ou par leurs représentans, la nécessité de la contribution publique, de la consentir librement, d'en suivre l'emploi, et d'en déterminer la quotité, l'assiette, le recouvrement et la durée.

XV.

La société a le droit de demander compte à tout agent public de son administration.

XVI.

Toute société, dans laquelle la garantie des droits n'est pas assurée, ni la séparation des pouvoirs déterminée, n'a point de constitution.

XVII.

Les propriétés étant un droit inviolable et sacré, nul ne peut en être privé, si ce n'est lorsque la nécessité publique, légalement constatée, l'exige évidemment, et sous la condition d'une juste et préalable indemnité.

AUX REPRÉSENTANS DU PEUPLE FRANÇOIS.

Le Barbier l'ainé inv.

I. Laurent sculp.

EXPLICATION DE L'ALLÉGORIE.

Sur un large pied destal, surmonté d'un socle, où est inscrite la déclaration des droits, apparoît, sur son plinthe, d'un côté la France ayant brisé ses fers, de l'autre la loi, indiquant du doigt les droits de l'homme, et montrant avec son sceptre l'œil suprême de la raison qui vient de dissiper les nuages de l'erreur qui l'obscurcissoient.

Les tables des droits de l'homme attachées et contenues sur ce pied destal, par une lance en faisceau surmontée d'un bonnet, d'un serpent et le tout orné d'une guirlande de chêne tombant de chaque côté en pendentif, offrent tout à la réunion l'union des Departemens du Royaume, la liberté, le civisme, la prudence et la sagesse du gouvernement. Dieu françois.

Se vend, à Paris, chez Amfret, Md d'Estampes, au Palais Royal, N.º 146, et chez M. Linguet, Rue Philipponeau, N.º 15.

1. *Déclaration des Droits de l'Homme et du Citoyen, 1789* / Declaration of the Rights of Man and the Citizen
L. Laurent after Jean-Jacques François Le Barbier the Elder
Etching and engraving
648 x 500mm
Musée Carnavalet, Paris; Histoire LCXXII

The representatives of the French people, constituted in National Assembly . . . have resolved to express in a solemn declaration, the natural, inalienable and sacred rights of man . . . [Article 1] Men are born and live free and with equal rights.

Six weeks after the fall of the Bastille launched the French Revolution, the new National Constituent Assembly passed the Declaration of the Rights of Man, which Louis XVI was obliged to accept. With only the American Declaration of Independence as a precedent, the concept struck at the aristocratic heart of existing European political systems: the first sentence of Article 1 is essentially that of Article 1 of the UN Universal Declaration of Human Rights today. At the top, under the eye of the 'Supreme Being', France looses her shackles while a figure representing the Law points to the Declaration inscribed below on tablets like those on which Western art usually shows the biblical Ten Commandments. The design also incorporates allusions to liberty, unity, strength, civic virtue, prudence and governmental wisdom.   PvdM

2. Phrygian cap, late eighteenth century
Wool and linen
225 x 230 x 180mm
John Goldstein, private collection

The image of the cap of liberty was drawn from Roman coins on which freed slaves were shown being given a cap at the moment of liberation. Its use as a graphic symbol went back at least as far as the Dutch revolt of the sixteenth century. From 1792, these caps (now based on the ancient Phrygian type) were worn by the most active supporters of the Revolution, particularly Jacobins. This example is made of red wool cloth with a white linen lining and brim edged with kid. It is embroidered on the front with the slogan 'LA NATION LIBERTE'. The tricolour cockade is made of leather. A linen loop at the back indicates that it had a ceremonial use and was most likely carried in a procession.   BT

LITERATURE: Schama, *Citizens*, p. 603.

3. Revolutionary cup and saucer, *c.* 1793–96
Sèvres, France
Porcelain
Musée Carnavalet, Paris; C2077

This painted porcelain cup and saucer, of Etruscan shape, incorporates Revolutionary symbols in its design, including red caps of liberty and oak wreaths on spears. Borders of blue and gilt, with another of green leaves, enclose a central panel of yellow ground on which the devices are painted. The makers' marks on the base indicate that this cup and saucer were painted by Jean-Jacques Pierre, who produced other Revolutionary designs for porcelain at this period, and that they were gilded by another master craftsman, Henry-François Vincent.   RP

4. The *San Culote*, *c.* 1795
Anonymous, French, eighteenth century
Pen, wash and watercolour
267 x 327mm
National Maritime Museum, London; PAH0129

It was usual for ships to bear figureheads with political or ideological meanings. This is one of two drawings of the French Revolutionary ship *San Culote*, the other of which shows the stern. Here the starboard profile view of the prow focuses on the figurehead, the icon of the Revolutionary ideal, the Jacobin *sans-culotte*. He is, however, a fusion of various Revolutionary iconographies. The Republic took as its political model the *polis* of the classical Greek republic, and openly adopted severely rational, neo-classical cultural ideals in emulation of the classical past. The mythological hero Hercules was also adopted, along with the female icon Marianne, as the incarnation of French Revolutionary principles. Here, therefore, the *sans-culotte*'s dress is transformed into a classicized toga, and, while clutching the *fasces* (the bound rods and axe that represented Roman justice) with his left hand, he holds in his right a Herculean club. Meanwhile, his contemporary identity is also represented, somewhat incongruously, by his wearing typical French eighteenth-century footwear and the obligatory *bonnet rouge*. GQ

5. Portrait miniature of a man, thought to be Jérôme Pétion de Villeneuve, late eighteenth century
Artist unknown
Gouache on ivory
Musée Carnavalet, Paris; OM3013

Pétion, then a Jacobin, was one of the commissioners who brought the King back from Varennes after the royal family escaped from Paris in June 1791. He became a popular hero and his reputation in Paris was such that he was elected as its second mayor in November 1791, with almost twice the votes of his nearest rival, the Marquis de La Fayette. This miniature is thought to depict him at around this time. He was suspended from office by the *département* of Paris for dereliction of duty after a crowd of armed demonstrators stormed into the Tuileries in June 1792, humiliating Louis XVI and undermining his authority. He was reinstated in July and became a member of the Convention. No longer such a radical, and increasingly estranged from his former friend Robespierre, he allied himself with the Girondin party and was one of the twenty-two deputies expelled from the Convention in June 1793 and placed under house arrest. Some of them managed to escape, fleeing first to Caen, which rose against the government, and then to Saint-Émilion. He committed suicide some time after, his body later being found half-eaten by wolves. CLW

LITERATURE: Doyle, *The Oxford History of the French Revolution*; Hibbert, *The French Revolution*; Schama, *Citizens*; Soboul, *The French Revolution 1787–1799*.

6. Enamel pendant with Revolutionary symbols, c. 1789–90

Gold, enamel
Musée Carnavalet, Paris; FL II 42

Gold pendant, decorated in blue enamel with a monogram, sword, two fleurs-de-lis, cap of liberty and the motto 'VIVRE LIBRE' (Long live liberty). The whole is surrounded by a palm branch, representing victory, and an olive branch, representing peace. The gentleman in the miniature (cat. no. 5) wears a similar pendant on a tricolour ribbon round his neck. BT

7. Metal pendants of Phrygian bonnets, c. 1791–93

(1) White metal and silk ribbon
(2) Gilt metal and insc. J. Chal. [Joseph Chalier ?]
Musée Carnavalet, Paris; inv. FL II 74 (1) and
FL II 74 (3)

The tricolour first appeared as the cockade of the Paris Militia (later the National Guard). Red and blue were the colours of the House of Orléans and City of Paris, to which the Marquis de La Fayette added the white of the Bourbons, actively promoting the cockade as a patriotic symbol. It became a badge of solidarity with Paris and the Assembly in 1789 and tricolour ribbons were worn by individuals as sashes and watch fobs. A rectangular tricolour was placed in the corner of the white French naval ensign in 1790 and in 1794 it became the ensign and national flag, filling the whole of the design. BT

LITERATURE: Schama, *Citizens*, p. 454.

8. Painted plate, c. 1791–92

French faience
Painted inscription
Musée Carnavalet, Paris; C757

This tin-glazed earthenware plate was probably made in the South of France at Moustiers, which specialized in this type of ware. Part of the painted inscription has been deliberately obliterated: Vive la nation La loi Le [Roi] [La Reine?]. The plate would have been defaced at the time of the execution of Louis XVI. RP

9. Badge of a *commissaire national*, 1795–98

Gilt bronze, enamel
Musée Carnavalet, Paris; inv. FL II 36 (1)

Badge of a *commissaire*, a locally elected agent who represented and reported to the central state. The badge dates from the period of the Directory (the executive of the legislature established in 1795). It is inscribed in gold letters on the obverse: 'RÉPUBLIQUE FRANÇAISE COMMISSAIRE NATIONAL'. Reverse: 'PAIX, SECOURS, LIBERTÉ, EGALITÉ ET FRATERNITÉ À TOUS LES PEUPLES NOS AMIS'. BT

10. Buttons with Revolutionary symbols, before 1793

Ceramic, silver, copper alloy and glass
Musée Carnavalet, Paris; (1) B1939, (2) B1954,
(3) B1989, (4) B1921, (5) B1963, (6) B1891

(5) Button with the design reverse-painted on glass in a copper alloy setting. It depicts a crosier, hay rake and sword representing the three estates of the realm – the clergy, peasantry and aristocracy: 'ÉGALITÉ' is inscribed below (the tax burden traditionally fell upon the peasantry).

(3) is of similar construction, captioned 'Prise de la Bastille', and showing the capture of the fortress. This is shown partially demolished on (2) with the caption 'LIBERTÉ'. (1) 'W. [Vive] la République Française 1793' shows the *bonnet rouge* between tricolour pennants. This year saw the execution of the King, federalist uprisings in the French regions and the declaration of war with Great Britain and the Dutch Republic. The symbol of the *fasces* represented the unity of France in the face of internal divisions and external threats. This is shown on (4), a biscuit porcelain button inscribed 'VIVRE LIBRE OU MOURIR' with the *fasces* between three fleurs-de-lis. This last symbol, latterly more associated with the French monarchy, is engraved on a silver button (6) with the caption 'VIVRE LIBRE OU MOURIR'. BT

11. Key to the Bastille, 1789

Madame Tussaud's, London

The prison of the Bastille in Paris became the symbol of political oppression in France. When it fell on 14 July 1789, Edward Rigby, an English physician in the Paris crowd, reported, 'We saw a flag, some large keys, and a paper

elevated on a pole above the crowd in which was inscribed "*La Bastille est prise et les portes sont ouvertes*".' In fact, there were hardly any prisoners in the Bastille by this time.

This key, thought likely to be an authentic relic of the Bastille, was sold to Madame Tussaud's waxworks in June 1860 at a sale of items previously exhibited at John Sainsbury's Napoleon Museum in the Egyptian Hall, Piccadilly, London. At that time it was attached to a carved stone from the dungeons of the Bastille, with an inscription stating that it was a presentation made in the Revolutionary Year IV (1795–96) by '*le patriot Palloy*', who had the contract for the demolition of the Bastille after its fall. Palloy made other presentations of keys and stones from the Bastille, and even medals said to be made from manacles found in the cells.

Madame Tussaud's Napoleon collection was destroyed with other relics in a fire of 1925. The key then appears to have become separated from the stone on which it was mounted. Other keys said to have come from the Bastille also exist but with less good provenance. RP

LITERATURE: Bindman, *Shadow of the Guillotine*, p. 212.

13. Cap, late eighteenth century
France
Wool, silk thread
Musée de l'Armée, Paris; inv. GB 20448

A symbol of liberty, the plain red Phrygian cap was emblematic of the French Revolution. It was also an essential element of the costume of the *sans-culotte*. Versions of the cap, such as this one of blue wool faced with red, were worn by patriotic members of the neighbourhood constabulary and other local officials. It has been heavily embroidered with silk threads featuring the symbols of revolution including a Phrygian cap on the tip of a pike and a tricolour cockade. AM

12. Carmagnole, late eighteenth century
France
Wool
Musée de l'Armée, Paris; inv. 19864

At the outbreak of the French Revolution, many of the rioters and leaders were known as *sans-culottes* because of their distinctive clothing – almost a type of unofficial uniform. They wore Phrygian caps, trousers instead of knee breeches, and short jackets called *carmagnoles* made of a rough, heavy-grade wool. Antoine-François Momoro, credited with devising the slogan 'Liberty, Equality, Fraternity', described a *sans-culotte* as 'someone who goes everywhere on foot, who isn't loaded with money like the rest of you, but lives quietly with his wife and children … on the fourth or fifth floor' – alluding to the fact that the poor tended to live on the higher floors. However, many were in fact middle-class shopkeepers or highly skilled workers. AM

14. Portrait miniature of a young boy, thought to be Joseph Bara, late eighteenth century
Artist unknown
Gouache on paper
59mm diam., frame 91 x 72mm
Musée de l'Armée, Paris; EA 35'

In 1794, at the age of thirteen, Joseph Bara had been too young to join the French Revolutionary army. Managing to attach himself to a regiment of hussars fighting counter-revolution in the Vendée, he was killed by rebels, whom he called 'brigands', when he refused to give them the horses he was minding. A myth was spread that he died for his refusal to utter '*Vive le Roi!*', instead crying, '*Vive la République!*'. Because of his youth and perceived martyrdom for the Republic he became a powerful political symbol. Maximilien de Robespierre planned a festival to commemorate such young martyrs in order to distract potential political dissent. Robespierre fell from power before the festival could happen but Bara was immortalized and his story romanticized by the painter Jacques-Louis David in a painting that now hangs in Avignon.   CLW

LITERATURE: Thomas Crow, *Emulation: Making Artists for Revolutionary France* (New Haven, Conn., 1995); Schama, *Citizens*.

15.   Revolutionary drum

Musée de l'Armée, Paris; inv. GE 21

This drum of the 16th Brigade of Infantry was later repainted with crossed sabres and the Revolutionary slogan '*Liberté Égalité*'.   RP

16.   Wedgwood medallions of Louis XVI and Revolutionary leaders, 1789–92

Jasper ware (stoneware)
Josiah Wedgwood (impressed mark)
Each 60mm diam.
British Museum, London

Five circular plaques – the portrait of La Fayette is applied to a scent bottle, made of white jasper ware dipped in dark blue, with applied white reliefs.

(1)   **Louis XVI (1754–93)**
      After a medal by Pierre-Simon-Benjamin Duvivier
      (1730–1819); 1853, 11-4, 8

The monarchy's financial difficulties, and popular resentment against taxation, created an impetus for reform that was to trigger revolution. The monarchy fell in 1792, following the royal family's attempt to leave the country. Louis was executed on 21 January 1793.

(3)   **Honoré-Gabriel de Riqueti, Comte de Mirabeau (1749–91)**
      1853, 11-4, 9

An extravagant younger son, Mirabeau had made a precarious living as a radical pamphleteer and writer. Although an inflammatory popular orator, he advocated an English-style constitution and later made attempts to save the King and Queen. He was made President of the National Assembly in 1791 but died the same year.

(2)   **Jacques Necker (1732–1804)**
      After Joseph-Siffred Duplessis (1725–1802); 1853,
      11-4, 11

Necker was Director of the Treasury and Director-General of Finance, between 1776 and 1781. During this time he attempted to grapple with the financial deficit. Recalled from Geneva in 1788, he recommended the summoning of the States-General. Wedgwood's medallion was in production by 1789. During that year Necker's dismissal and exile by the King led to the storming of the Bastille.

(4)   **Jean-Sylvain Bailly (1736–93)**
      After a medal by Pierre-Simon-Benjamin Duvivier
      (1730–1819); 1853, 11-4, 10

An Enlightenment intellectual of broad interests, Bailly was President of the National Assembly and Mayor of Paris. He is the central figure in Jacques-Louis David's famous picture *The Oath of the Tennis Court*. He was executed during the Terror in 1793.

(5) Louis-Philippe-Joseph, Duc d'Orléans
(Philippe Égalité) (1747–93)
Pot. Cat. I.48

A distant cousin of Louis XVI, the Duc d'Orléans was a
liberal and a member of the National Assembly. He also
pursued his own ambitions during the Revolution at the
expense of the monarchy. His former popularity with the
English dissipated when he voted in favour of the death of
the French King. He was executed in 1793.   BT

17. Two ceramic medallions celebrating
the fall of the Bastille, 1789

Jasper ware (stoneware)
Wedgwood, Staffordshire
Impressed 'Wedgwood'
British Museum, London (Franks Collection); 1853,
  11-4, 12 and Pot. Cat. I.674

Josiah Wedgwood, the renowned Staffordshire potter, along
with other British radicals, sympathized with the French
Revolution and celebrated the storming of the Bastille on 14
July 1789. Wedgwood wrote to Erasmus Darwin (1731–
1802, physician, poet, radical thinker, grandfather of Charles),
'I know you will rejoice with me in the glorious revolution
which has taken place in France. The politicians tell me that as
a manufacturer I shall be ruined if France has her liberty, but I
am willing to take my chance in that respect.' Although
Wedgwood later modified his opinions, he immediately issued
a number of medallions to commemorate the fall of the
Bastille, and these were being manufactured within fifteen
weeks of the announcement of the event in the London press.

The medallions were produced primarily for export
but are also known to have been sold in England. They are

of Wedgwood's white jasper ware, dipped dark blue, with
applied white reliefs:

(a) A figure of Public Faith, holding a cornucopia and a
sheaf of corn, stands on an altar inscribed '*Fidei Publ.*', while
Liberty with her cap on a pole clasps the hand of France,
who wears a helmet and holds a shield.

(b) A figure of Liberty, holding a cornucopia and a cap of
liberty on a pole, stands beneath a pillared arch, on which
rests a shield with three fleurs-de-lis. The Latin inscription
'*En quam saepe optastis libertas*' can be translated as 'Behold!
The liberty which you have often wished.'   RP

LITERATURE: Bindman, *Shadow of the Guillotine*, pp. 97–8;
  Reilly and Savage, *The Dictionary of Wedgwood*, p. 36.

18. Miniature portrait supposedly
representing Charles-Maurice de
Talleyrand (1754–1838), late
eighteenth century

Anonymous, French
Ivory in metal frame with forty-two turquoises
56 x 47mm
Chequers Trust UK, 930

The sitter's proposed identity as Napoleon's Minister of
Foreign Affairs from 1799 to 1807 and Grand Chamberlain
from 1804 to 1809 is given on a label on the back, which
reads 'Taleyrand'. However, this miniature does not resemble any of the other well-known portraits of Talleyrand, in

particular the official portraits by Pierre-Paul Prud'hon. The man in the portrait has pale grey eyes, Talleyrand's were dark brown. This man has an oval face and pointed chin, Talleyrand had a fuller face and square chin. This man has a long nose, Talleyrand had a relatively broad nose. Talleyrand wore his hair loosely falling over his ears down to the neck; this man's is raised above the ears and tightly rolled. The features do, however, fit those of Napoleon's formidable Minister of Police, Joseph Fouché (1758–1820). Fouché is often represented with a smile on his thin lips. During the early 1790s (from which period this portrait probably dates) Fouché had been a much feared Jacobin and regicide and supporter of the systematic measures of dechristianization. It is understandable that Talleyrand and Fouché might be confused. Of all Napoleon's statesmen, they were the only two who retained a degree of independence after the reorganization of the Council of Ministers. This was largely due to the extraordinary personalities of both men.   HW

LITERATURE: Exhibition catalogue *Napoléon*, Grand Palais, June–Dec. (Réunion des Musées Nationaux, 1969) pp. 74–5; Herold, *The Age of Napoleon*.

19. **Register of the decisions of the Committee of Public Safety, [22] October 1793**
Ink on paper
Pierre-Jean Chalençon, private collection

The Committee of Public Safety was formed in April 1793, replacing the earlier larger Committee of General Defence, a coordinating body for the work of several committees of the governing National Convention. Although initially established to oversee the government and the running of the war effort, by December 1794 it had become the effective government of France. Its members acted to enforce the Reign of Terror that had been declared necessary to overcome the Republic's enemies and ensure its survival. Maximilien de Robespierre, elected to the Committee in July 1793, had become an ideological leader. The horrific results of the Terror are well known: an estimated 16,000 people are thought to have died under the guillotine blade in about nine months. After Robespierre's fall, in July 1794, the power of the Committee of Public Safety waned.

The signatories on this manuscript include Jacques-Nicolas Billaud-Varennes; Lazare Carnot, an army engineer; the playwright and actor Jean-Marie Collot d'Herbois; the lawyer Betrand Barère; and Robespierre himself. Collot d'Herbois and Billaud-Varennes had particularly bloody

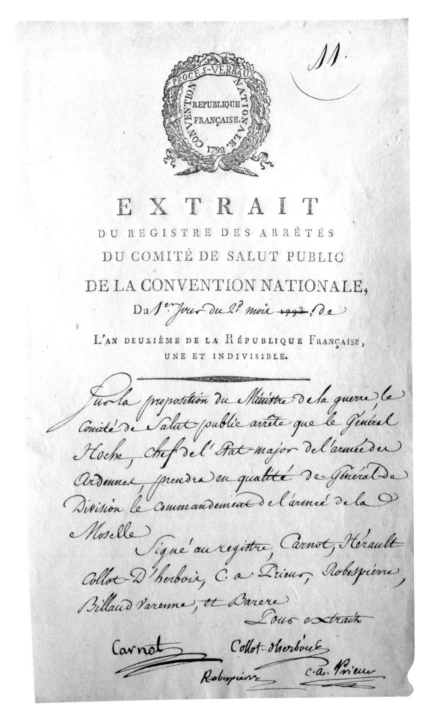

and radical reputations, the latter insisting that 'either the revolution will triumph or we will all die'.   CLW

LITERATURE: David Andress, *French Society in Revolution, 1789–1799* (Manchester and New York, 1999); Doyle, *The Oxford History of the French Revolution*; Schama, *Citizens*.

by the second executioner. Below the image a key to the scene points out the guillotine and its blade, the dead King and the executioners, and the different sized baskets for the head and the body. The caption describes the execution as 'An Event most Wonderfull [*sic*] in the History of the World'. RP

LITERATURE: Bindman, *Shadow of the Guillotine*, pp. 140–41; Drakard, *Printed English Pottery*, p. 171.

21.   'Massacre of the French King!'
        Published by William Lane, early 1793
        Woodcut
        468 x 309mm
        British Museum, London; 1856-7-12-1101

William Lane rushed into print with this broadsheet depiction of the execution of Louis XVI on 21 January 1793, using an existing woodcut. This helps to explain the rather curious contrast between the horrific title of the print and its lifeless and technical draughtsmanship. The print's original purpose was to explain the guillotine as a 'modern' and more humane instrument of execution. In January 1793, the Terror lay in the future, so Dr Guillotine's device was not yet associated with cold-blooded mass-killing. For all its limitations, this first British visual representation of Louis XVI's death sold well and was recycled for other purposes. The text below the image offers a number of documents associated with the King's death and a narrative of his final hours, together with a description of the guillotine and anecdotes from his captivity. The final section of the broadsheet is highly sympathetic to the King, describing him as 'THE FRIEND OF THE PEOPLE' and 'RESTORER OF THEIR LIBERTIES'. It adds that not even these virtues could 'save him from this CRUEL SACRIFICE'. At a later date the memoirs of persons attached to the 'martyred' Louis XVI and Marie-Antoinette in their final years and hours also sold very well in Britain.   SB

20.   Mug commemorating the
        execution of Louis XVI, *c.* 1793
        Staffordshire
        Creamware
        Inscription: 'MASSACRE & EXECUTION of LOUIS XVI,
            KING of FRANCE'
        British Museum, London; 1988, 12-1, 1

The execution of Louis XVI in Paris on 21 January 1793 crucially undermined British sympathies with the French Revolution. The wares produced by the English pottery manufacturers now presented scenes demonstrating the worst of the French excesses. The black transfer print signed by John Aynsley of Lane End, which appears on this creamware mug, shows the head of Louis XVI being held up

22.   *The Contrast 1792*
        Thomas Rowlandson after Lord George Murray
            [December 1792]
        Engraving
        305 x 470mm
        British Museum, London (Banks Collection); J 4-50

A simple propaganda device that was commonly used throughout the 1790s to extol the virtues and liberties of Britain over the French Republic was the pairing, as here, of contrasting images and values. This is one of several

MASSACRE OF THE FRENCH KING!

VIEW OF | MODERN

La Guillotine; | Beheading Machine,

OR THE | AT PARIS.

By which the unfortunate LOUIS XVI. (late King of France) ſuffered on the Scaffold, January 21ſt, 1793.

Decree of the National Convention of the 15th, 17th, 19th, and 20th of January, 1793.

ARTICLE I.

THE National Convention declares LOUIS CAPET, laſt King of the French, guilty of a conſpiracy againſt the Liberty of the Nation, and of a crime againſt the general ſafety of the State.

II. The National Convention declares, that LOUIS CAPET ſhall undergo the puniſhment of DEATH.

III. The National Convention declares, that the act of LOUIS CAPET, brought to the bar by his Counſel, and termed an Appeal to the Nation on the Sentence paſſed againſt him in the Convention, is null; and forbids every perſon from giving it authority, on pain of being proſecuted, and puniſhed as guilty of a crime againſt the general ſafety of the Republic.

IV. The Temporal Executive Council ſhall notify the preſent Decree, within the Day, to LOUIS CAPET, and ſhall take the neceſſary meaſures of police and ſafety to ſecure its execution within *twenty-four hours,* reckoning from the notification, and ſhall render an account of the whole to the National Convention immediately after its execution.

Report of the Council who communicated the Decree to LOUIS.

The Executive Council was convoked and aſſembled at a very early hour this morning, in order to conſult on the execution of a decree relative to LOUIS CAPET.

The Council then ſent for the Mayor of Paris, the Commandant General, the Preſident, and the Accuſateur Public of the Criminal Tribunal: After having conſulted with theſe conſtituted authorities, the Miniſter of Juſtice, the Preſident of the Executive Council, a Member of the Council, the Secretary of the Council, and two Members of the Department repaired to the Tower in the Temple.

At two o'clock they were conducted before LOUIS, to whom the Miniſter of Juſtice, as Preſident of the Executive Council, ſpoke as follows:

LOUIS, the Executive Council hath charged us to notify to you the Extracts of the *Proces-Verbal* of the National Convention of the 15th, 17th, and 19th of the preſent month: the Secretary will now read them.—[On this the Secretary of the Executive Council read the three above Articles.]

Louis then obſerved, that he had ſomething to ſay; on which he took out the following requiſition, written with, and ſigned by his own hand.

"I demand a delay of three days, in order to enable me to appear in the preſence of Almighty God; and the better to effect this, I requeſt leave to call to my aid the Ex-Biſhop of Fermont, who lodges at No. 483, *Rue de Bacq.*

"I demand that his perſon be protected from all manner of inſult, in order that he may be enabled to deliver himſelf up without fear to the work of charity which he is about to be employed in, with reſpect to me.

"I demand to be freed from the perpetual inſpection which the General Council of the Commons has made uſe of towards me for ſome time paſt.

"I demand, that during this interval, I may be permitted to ſee my Family, without any witneſs, every time that I ſolicit this permiſſion.

"I deſire that the National Convention may deliberate immediately about the fate of my Family, and that they may be permitted to retire wherever they pleaſe.

"I recommend all the perſons who were attached to me to the care and protection of the Nation. There are many of them who have expended the whole of their fortunes in order to purchaſe their places, and muſt conſequently be in great diſtreſs.

"Among my penſioners are a great number of old men, and of poor people burthened with large families, who have not any thing to ſubſiſt on but the allowance which I paid them.

"*Given at the Tower in the Temple.*

January 20, 1793.

(Signed) "LOUIS."

The Convention having heard the Report of the Miniſter decrees,

That the *reſpite* demanded by LOUIS *ſhall not be granted.*

That the vigilance of the Municipality ſhall be continued in the chamber adjoining that of LOUIS. Reſpecting the other points, the Convention paſſes to the order of the day, conſidering that the Committee of Legiſlation is competent thereto.

ORDERS FOR THE DAY.

January 20, 1793.—*Second Year of the Republic.*

The Proviſional Executive Council, after deliberating on the meaſures to be taken, in order to execute the decrees of the National Convention of the 15th, 17th, 19th and 20th of January, 1793, has ordered as follows:

I. That the Execution of the Judgment of LOUIS CAPET ſhall take place to-morrow, Monday the 21ſt.

II. The place of Execution ſhall be *La Place de la Revolution, ci-devant Louis XV.* between the Pedeſtal and the Elyſian Fields.

III. LOUIS CAPET ſhall leave the Temple by eight o'clock in the morning, and the Execution ſhall take place at noon.

IV. Commiſſaries from the department of Paris, Commiſſaries from the Municipality, and two Members of the *Tribunal Criminel,* ſhall aſſiſt at the Execution. The Secretary of the Tribunal ſhall draw up the *proces-verbal*; and the ſaid Commiſſaries and Members of the Tribunal, immediately after the Execution, ſhall render an account of it to the Council, who will remain in permanent during the whole day.

V. LOUIS CAPET ſhall paſs by the *Boulevards* to the Place of Execution.

By the Executive Proviſional Council,

ROLAND, | MONGE, | GARAT,
CLAVIERE, | LEBRUN, | PACHE.

By order of the Council,
GRONVILLE, Secretary.

On which the Period of his Fate, and the Day of Execution, took Place, and was as follows:

At ſix o'clock in the morning he took his laſt farewel of the Queen and Royal Family, and was with them ſome time; the parting was affecting to the laſt degree; the diſtreſs of the Queen paſſed all deſcription. He left the Temple agreeable to the Inſtructions from the Provincial Council, at eight o'clock, at which time the mournful proceſſion ſet out from the Temple. The Royal Victim ſat in the Mayor's Carriage, with his Confeſſor by his ſide, praying very fervently, and two Captains of National Light Horſe on the front ſeat. The carriage was drawn by two black horſes, preceded by the Mayor, General Santerre, and other Municipal Officers. One ſquadron of horſe, with trumpeters and kettle-drums, led the van of this melancholy convoy; three heavy pieces of ordnance, with proper implements, and cannoneers, with lighted matches, went before the vehicle, which was eſcorted on both ſides by a treble row of troopers.

The train moved on with a ſlow pace from the Temple to the *Boulevards,* which was planted with cannon, and beſet with National Guards, drums beating, trumpets ſounding, and colours flying. The *Guillotine* † was erected in the middle of the ſquare, directly facing the gate of the garden of the *Tuileries,* between the Pedeſtal on which the Grandfather of LOUIS was ſtanding, before the 10th of Auguſt, and the avenues which lead to the groves, called the *Elyſian Fields.* The trotting and neighing of horſes, the ſhrill ſound of the trumpet, and the continual beating of drums, pierced the ears of every beholder, and heightened the terrors of the awful ſcene.

† A more particular account of this machine may be ſeen in TWISS's TRIP to PARIS, lately publiſhed.

The ſcaffold was high and conſpicuous, and the houſes ſurrounding the place of Execution were full of women, who looked through the windows. The very ſlates which covered the roofs were raiſed for the curious and intereſted to peep through.

The King alighted from the carriage at twenty minutes paſt ten. His hair was dreſſed in curls, his beard ſhaved; he wore a clean ſhirt and ſtock, a white waiſtcoat, black florentine ſilk breeches, black ſilk ſtockings, and his ſhoes were tied with black ſilk ſtrings. At the foot of the ſcaffold he threw off his coat himſelf, and finding ſome difficulty in unbuckling his ſtock, he calmly thanked a by-ſtander, who aſſiſted him.—His hair was then cut off, when he took leave of his confeſſor, who ſhed a thouſand tears on this mournful occaſion; but rouſed the King with theſe animating expreſſions: "FAREWELL LOUIS! *aſcend the Scaffold and go to heaven.*"—He then aſcended the ſteps of the ſcaffold with heroic aſſurance, and every feature of his majeſtic countenance beſpoke the calm ſerenity of conſcious innocence, and the heroic fortitude of a Chriſtian. Having walked half round the horrid preparations, he then beckoned with his hand to be heard; the noiſe of the warlike inſtruments ceaſed for a moment; but ſoon after a thouſand voices vociferated, with deteſtable ferocity, "*No ſpeeches! No harangues!*" The unfortunate Monarch wrung his hands—lifted them up towards heaven—and with agony in his eye and geſture, exclaimed, diſtinctly enough to be heard by thoſe perſons who were next to the ſcaffold, "*To thee, O God, do I commend my ſoul! I forgive my enemies! I die innocent!*"

He was then ſeized by the Executioners, dreſſed in black, who directly laid him upon his belly on the bench, and lifted up the upper part of the board which was to receive his neck, adjuſted to his head properly, then ſhut the board and pulled the ſtring which is faſtened to the peg at the top of the machine, which lifted up a latch, and down came the axe; [See the annexed plate.] the head was off in a moment, and fell into a baſket which was ready to receive it; the executioner took it out by the hair, to ſhow the populace, and then put it into another baſket along with the body.—The final part of his execution was exactly twenty-two minutes paſt ten.

After his head was cut off, the *Sans Culottes* and *Jacobines* waved their hats in the air, exclaiming, *Vive la Nation! Vive la Republique!* The muſic ſtruck up *Ca Ira,* and the body was immediately removed in a black coffin.—The proceſſion returned to the Temple in full gallop, and the ſworn Deputies went to make their report.

DESCRIPTION OF LA GUILLOTINE.

This deſtructive inſtrument is in the form of a Painter's Eaſel; about ten or twelve feet high. At two feet from the bottom is a croſs bar, on which the head is placed, in a circular opening, to contain the neck, in the form of the Engliſh pillory, which is kept down by another placed above. In the inner edge of the frame are grooves, on the top of which is placed a ſharp axe, with a heavy weight of lead ſuſpended to the top by cords through a block, and which axe is kept up by being faſtened to a peg, about four feet from the bottom of the machine, which the executioner taking out, the axe falls and beheads the criminal.

He is firſt tied to a plank of about eighteen inches broad, and an inch thick, ſtanding upright, faſtened with cords about the arms, body, and legs; this plank is about four feet long, and comes almoſt up to the chin; the executioner then lays him on his belly on the bench, lifts up the upper part of the board which receives his neck, adjuſts his head, then ſhuts the board, and pulls the ſtring faſtened to the peg at the top of the machine, which lifts up a catch. The axe falls down, and the head, which is off in a moment, is received in a baſket ready for that purpoſe, as is the body in another baſket. This preparation was omitted in the Execution of this unfortunate Monarch, he being immediately placed at length under the machine.

LOUIS made a will, in which he aſked pardon of God, for having ſanctioned the Decree upon the Civil Conſtitution of the Clergy, although this ſanction was extorted by violence; and was contrary to his ſolemn proteſt.

In this teſtament, LOUIS acknowledges his having freely accepted all the other parts of the Conſtitution; and having neglected nothing to remove from his dominions the ſcourge of War, and prevent the invaſion of the Pruſſians.

In a previous Decree made by the National Convention, the place for putting their inhuman ſentence into execution was to have been the Carouſel, fronting the Palace of the Tuileries. This was changed by the Miniſters, to whom all the arrangements were confided, to the Place de la Revolution, heretofore the Place LOUIS XV.

This City yeſterday reſembled an immenſe Camp; the Sections and Federates were marching and counter-marching through the different diſtricts;—they had their watch word;—they wheeled round wherever one corps met the other. They carried with them upwards of 153 pieces of heavy artillery, and it made a moſt impoſing ſpectacle. They were conſtantly in motion, and could not ſtand ſtill five minutes.

During the exhibition of this horrid ſcene, all Paris was in conſternation.

The Commiſſaries of the Temple found in the King's deſk ſome gold coin, to the amount of about 3000 livres. It was done up in rouleaus, and on them was written, "to M. Malaſherbes." This grateful bequeſt of the deceaſed Monarch was not complied with—the money was depoſited in the Secretary's Office.

The following Anecdotes ſhew that for ſome Time he had been expecting his Fate.

LOUIS ſaw his laſt moment approaching with coolneſs and tranquillity. It is long ſince he reſolved to ſacrifice life, if we may judge from the two following anecdotes.

Two years ago, M. de Liancourt repreſenting to LOUIS, that the modifications and the *veto* which he oppoſed to certain Decrees might be dangerous—"What can they do?" replied LOUIS, "They will put me to death—well, I ſhall obtain an immortal for a mortal crown."

The other Anecdote is more recent, and proves, like the former, that LOUIS never feared death.—On the day that Deſeze made his defence in the Convention, Malaſherbes, in a converſation which he had with LOUIS in the evening, wiſhed to prepare him for the event by hinting that his defence might not be attended with the deſired effect, and that the iſſue of the trial was uncertain. "I underſtand you," replied LOUIS; "but my reſolution is already taken. I ſee, without fear, my laſt hour approaching; and I ſhall lay my head on the block without uneaſineſs. You will perhaps be ſurpriſed when I tell you that my wife and my ſiſter think exactly as I do."

The laſt requeſts of the unfortunate LOUIS breathes the ſoul of magnanimity, and a mind enlightened with the fineſt ideas of human virtue. He appears not to be that man which his enemies reported.—His heart was ſound, his head was clear, and he would have reigned with glory, had he but poſſeſſed thoſe faults which his aſſaſſins laid to his charge.—His mind poſſeſſed the ſuggeſtions of wiſdom; and even in his laſt moments, when the ſpirit of life was winged for another world, his lips gave utterance to them, and he ſpoke with firmneſs and reſignation.

Thus has ended the life of LOUIS XVI. after a period of four years detention; during which he experienced from his ſubjects every ſpecies of ignominy and cruelty which a people could inflict on the moſt ſanguinary tyrant.—LOUIS XVI. who was proclaimed at the commencement of his reign, THE FRIEND OF THE PEOPLE; and by the Conſtituent Aſſembly, THE RESTORER OF THEIR LIBERTIES.—LOUIS, who but a few years ſince was the moſt powerful monarch in Europe, has at laſt periſhed on a ſcaffold. Neither his own natural goodneſs of heart—his deſire to procure the happineſs of his ſubjects—nor that ancient love which the French entertained for their monarch, has been ſufficient to ſave him from this CRUEL SACRIFICE.

London: Printed at the MINERVA OFFICE, for WILLIAM LANE, Leadenhall-Street, and ſold Wholeſale at One Guinea per Hundred.

And Retail by every Bookſeller, Stationer, &c. in England, Scotland and Ireland.

PRICE THREE-PENCE.

Where may be had an exact and authenticated Copy of his Will, Price One-Penny.

demented Medusa-like harridan, running and open-mouthed: the complete opposite of the sedate, feminine politeness and propriety of Britannia. The French emblem tramples over a decapitated corpse and is a grotesque parody of the French Revolutionary icon of Marianne, the female personification of the Revolutionary ideal. The inscriptions beneath each roundel make clear the political and social values to be ascribed to them, and finally ask the spectator 'WHICH IS BEST'. It was not unusual for artists and engravers to work from ideas or designs proposed by other non-artists, and here Rowlandson has worked to the specifications of the Revd Lord George Murray, Bishop of St David's in South Wales.

GQ

prints, made on this specific theme in the wake of the French Revolution and the execution of Louis XVI, contrasting British liberty and French liberty. The engraving is presented as two roundels, recalling the format of coins or medals. In one is Britannia, seated under an oak tree with the British lion at her feet. She has her typical emblems of shield, staff and cap of liberty, and holds the 'Magna Charta' and the scales of justice. The open sea with a ship in full sail behind indicates the peace and commercial prosperity ensuing from 'British Liberty'. By contrast, the emblem of France is a

23. Covered cup and saucer, 1793–94

Wallendorf, Germany
Porcelain
Musée Carnavalet, Paris; C1492

The hand-painted cup, cover and saucer are painted *en grisaille* with scenes of the guillotine in Paris. The two scenes are different and probably derived from prints on paper. On the saucer, the executioner shows the severed head of Louis XVI to the crowd; on the cup, Marie-Antoinette awaits her execution. The King was executed on 21 January 1793 and the Queen on 16 October 1793.

RP

24. Guillotine blade, 1792

Steel, lead, wood
Weight 63lb (28kg)
National Maritime Museum, London (Royal United
Service Museum Collection); TOA0079

This guillotine blade, still mounted with rivets to its original lead-weighted wooden block, was used on the West Indian island of Guadeloupe by French republicans. It is said to have been used to execute more than fifty royalists. This guillotine is likely to have been taken to the Americas by the French Revolutionary commissar Victor Hugues, when he was sent to Martinique and Guadeloupe to purge the royalists. In 1794 the British occupied Guadeloupe and Captain Matthew Scott of HMS *Rose* brought back the guillotine blade as a war trophy.

Madame Tussaud's waxworks in London has a guillotine blade said to be the one used to execute Louis XVI and Marie-Antoinette in Paris in 1793.   RP

25. Mould for wax head of Louis XVI and wax head of Louis XVI

Wax (head) and plaster of Paris (mould)
Madame Tussaud's, London

Marie Grosholz, who became Madame Tussaud, was an eyewitness to many of the events of the French Revolution which she recorded in her *Memoirs*. An art tutor to Louis XVI's sister Elizabeth from 1780, she had lived at the royal court in Versailles until the outbreak of Revolution in 1789. Returning to Paris, she apparently worked with her uncle, Dr Curtius, from whom she learnt the art of wax modelling at his thriving waxworks display. It is not certain that she was forced to make moulds of freshly decapitated heads while herself in prison under threat of death – as was later claimed; she does not mention this in her reminiscences. Nevertheless, when she arrived in England in 1802, she undoubtedly brought with her the moulds for many prominent victims of the Terror. Waxworks made from these became one of the main attractions of her show. By 1822 she was displaying these wax heads and other relics of the French Revolution in a separate room from other historical figures, which became known as the Chamber of Horrors. Thus Tussaud continued to influence British perceptions of the Revolution throughout the nineteenth century.

Many of the Tussaud relics were destroyed in a fire in 1925 but, fortunately, the head moulds were saved and the collection could be rebuilt. This head was specially commissioned from Madame Tussaud's for this exhibition. Marie Tussaud, who had been in close contact with the royal family during her time at court, claimed that Louis XVI was

'one of the most amiable men, perhaps, who ever graced a throne . . . his heart was kind in the extreme and tender to a fault'. The King's death by guillotine, on 21 January 1793, was, to the British people, one of the most shocking events of the Revolution and helped precipitate a lengthy period of conflict. In fact, war broke out ten days after it.　　CLW

LITERATURE: Bindman, *Shadow of the Guillotine*; Tussaud, *Memoirs of Madame Tussaud*; 'The full history of Madame Tussauds', www.madame-tussauds.co.uk/aboutus_history_fullhistory.asp.

26.　The Edict of Fraternity, issued by the National Convention, 19 November 1792 / *Décret de la Convention nationale du 19 novembre 1792*

Bill poster printed in Pau

Musée de la Révolution française, Vizille, France, Fonds Estampe; MRF 1989–138

In the wake of General Dumouriez's victory at Jemmapes (6 November 1792), republicans at the National Convention (the Revolutionary government of the time) excitedly trumpeted their success. On 16 November, Chaumette (a

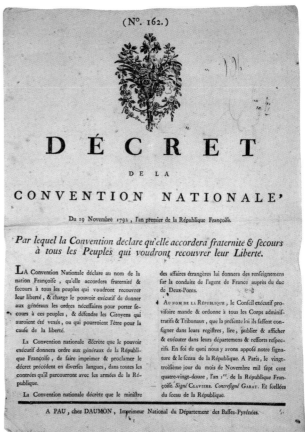

member of the extreme Jacobin club, the Cordeliers) harangued the chamber: 'The territory which separates Paris from Petersburg and from Moscow will soon be "Frenchified", "municipalized", "Jacobinised".' Since technically non-French regions such as Savoy and Belgium (previously the Austrian Netherlands) were now under French control, it was necessary to decide what to do with them: whether to occupy them with arms, to turn them into sister republics or simply to annex them. The debate resulted in the Edict of Fraternity of 19 November 1792, and Cambon's Proclamation of the Convention dated 15 December of the same year. The first (shown here) promised military 'aid' to 'peoples who wished to recover their liberty' and enabled French generals to 'give the orders necessary for the provision of aid to those peoples'. The second, a proclamation to foreign peoples, offered them the possibility of 'enjoying the inestimable good' of the Revolution and incited them to 'show themselves free men', promising protection from the vengeance of men who had previously oppressed them with impunity. The Revolutionary War, which up to that point had been defensive, was becoming a war of conquest.   PH

27. Wine canteen with Revolutionary symbols

Painted wood, iron bound
Inscription: *Armée des Alpes*
John Goldstein, private collection

This *tonnelet*, or small cask, is the type carried by *cantinières*, women who were commissioned by French army units to sell food or drink to soldiers, over and above that provided as rations. The *tonnelet* was carried across the chest with a strap, and would contain wine or brandy, which was served in small metal cups which the women also carried. This example is painted red, white and blue, and decorated with sprays of oak and laurel and a depiction of *fasces*. This is a symbolic reference to the bundle of wooden rods and axe, bound with a strap, which was originally carried before the consul or magistrate in ancient Rome, as a symbol of civic authority and unity.

Cantinières had to be wives of soldiers, and some even took their children with them on campaign. They received no pay but had to live off their husbands' wages and what they could earn by selling their provisions at a fair price. Although they did not wear uniform, other than a badge or medallion, they were subject to military discipline. They might also be paid to do additional duties such as cooking, laundry, sewing or fetching firewood. In the heat of battle they often helped to tend the wounded and offered free drinks to soldiers under fire. Although noncombatants, many went armed for their own protection.   RP

29. Medal commemorating the Battle of the Glorious First of June, 1794

W. Barnett
Silver, 36mm diam.
Signed
National Maritime Museum, London; MEC1318

Obverse: bust of Admiral of the Fleet Richard, Earl Howe (1726–99) shown in profile wearing a tie-wig, uniform and cloak. Legend: 'RIC : COMES HOWE VICE-ADMIRALLUS ANGLI-AE &c'. Reverse: Neptune standing in his sea-car drawn by two horses, pointing with his right hand to a distant action (one vessel sinking), and with his left giving his trident to Britannia seated (right) with shield and trophies; a winged Victory above inscribing an obelisk with the names of the admirals who took part in the battle: 'HOWE GRAVES BRIDPORT BOWYER CALDWELL GARDNER PASLEY'. Legend: 'NON NOBIS SED PATRIAE' (Not for us but for our country). Exergue: 'MDCCXCIIII 1ST JUNE'. The maker's signature 'BARNETT' is on the obverse and below Britannia on the reverse. This is a commercial not a state production.   BT

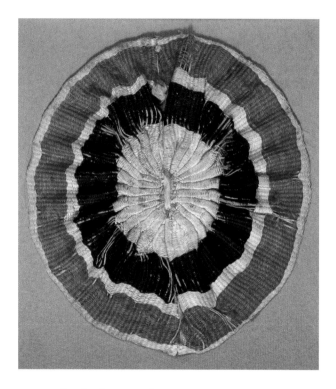

28. Cockade, 1796

France
Grosgrain (grogram)
Musée de l'Armée, Paris; inv. 2351

The cockade was a rosette or ribbon generally worn as a hat badge. In the early days of the French Revolution a green cockade, symbolizing hope, was worn, while monarchists wore a white cockade. However, the tricolour was adopted which paired the colours of Paris, red and blue, with the white of the monarchy. Although worn to demonstrate patriotic sympathies, the cockade was also a feature of eighteenth-century military uniform. This tricolour cockade was part of the uniform of the army of Republican France; it was worn by Colonel Lobreau, commandant of the 3rd Regiment of Artillery in the Army of Italy.   AM

30. Soup tureen commemorating the 'Glorious First of June', 1794

John Schofield, London, 1795
Silver
Inscription
Lloyd's of London; Nelson Collection, inv. 118

This silver soup tureen, with cover and stand, was awarded posthumously to Captain John Harvey (1740–94) of the *Brunswick* by the Committee of Lloyd's. The body of this large tureen of oval form has handles cast with mermen blowing on shells and rests on four intertwined dolphins. The stand and cover are decorated with palm fronds and a pineapple finial. An inscription on the side in an oval escutcheon surrounded by naval trophies reads: 'Lloyds Coffee House. A Tribute of Gratitude and respect from his Country to the Memory of Captain John Harvey of his Majesty's ship, the Brunswick, who gloriously fell in the Important Action of the 1st of June 1794 when the French Fleet was defeated by the British Fleet under Command of Admiral Earl Howe. John Julius Angerstein Chairman.'

In February 1793 John Harvey was appointed to the *Brunswick*, 74 guns, in the Channel Fleet under Admiral Howe. The *Brunswick* was severely damaged at the Battle of the Glorious First of June, having become entangled early in the action with the French *Vengeur*, which eventually sank with half her crew. Forty-four of the *Brunswick*'s men were killed and 114 wounded, including Captain Harvey, who received a number of injuries during the battle from which he died afterwards at Portsmouth. He shares a monument in Westminster Abbey with Captain John Hutt of the *Queen*, who also died from his wounds and was awarded a matching tureen by Lloyd's.   RP

31. *Promis'd Horrors of the French INVASION. – or – Forcible Reasons for negotiating a Regicide PEACE. Vide, The Authority of Edmund Burke*

James Gillray, published 20 October 1796
Hand-coloured etching and aquatint
325 x 437mm
National Portrait Gallery, London; NPG D12579

This complex satire refers to Edmund Burke's pamphlet *Reflections on a Regicide Peace*, which denounced plans to make peace with Revolutionary France. It also refers more immediately to the King's speech of 6 October, in which the threat of invasion was raised. This threat was dismissed by the Opposition, who were unaware of French plans to invade, but was in fact a very real possibility. Gillray's vision of London overrun with French troops appears to be compositionally based on Hogarth's *The March to Finchley* and is remarkable for its gory, bloodthirsty documentation of torture and killing. In this respect, it recalls Gillray's earlier anti-Jacobin print *Un petit Souper a la Parisienne; – or – A Family of Sans Culottes refreshing after the fatigues of the day* (published September 1792), which shows French Revolutionaries gorging on the flesh of their executed victims in the early days of the Terror. In this print, how-ever, the scene of mutilation is instead transferred to the

Promis'd Horrors of the French INVASION, – or – Forcible Reasons for negociating a Regicide PEACE. Vide. The Authority of Edmund Burke

most exclusive English abodes of elite dining and consumption, outside Brooks's and White's clubs in St James's. A tree of liberty has been planted in the centre foreground, against which Pitt is being scourged by Fox, and in the distance St James's Palace is on fire. Burke, the Duke of York and Grenville are all victims to the tide of carnage sweeping down the street in the form of serried ranks of French soldiers. In line with Burke's rhetoric, Gillray offers an apocalyptic vision of French occupation as a consequence of a 'regicide peace'.   GQ

32. **French republican banner captured during the Battle of the Glorious First of June, 1794**

Linen, gold thread

686 x 660mm

National Maritime Museum, London; AAA0564

This banner belonged to the boarding division of *L'America*, 74 guns, engaged and taken by the *Leviathan*, commanded by Lord Hugh Seymour (1759–1801). It is made of white linen, hand-sewn with a gold fringe on three sides and embroidered in yellow with the battle cry 'MARINS LA REPUBLIQUE OU LA MORT' (Sailors, the Republic or Death). There is fainter, illegible lettering in ink underneath: 'BATAILLON DE PARAI[. . .]OU COMPAGNIE'. The banner shows the attempts by the French fleet to carry out the ideas of political commissioner, Jeanbon Saint-André – 'Distaining skilful evolution . . . perhaps our seamen will think it more fitting and useful to try those boarding actions in which the Frenchman was always a conqueror.'   BT

33. *The DELEGATES in COUNCIL or BEGGARS on HORSEBACK*

Isaac Cruikshank, published 9 June 1797

Hand-coloured etching

274 x 372mm

National Maritime Museum, London; PAF3899

French Revolutionary principles spread even to the Royal Navy. Published at the critical moment of the naval mutiny at the Nore, led by Richard Parker, this print represents the events of 20 May, when Admiral Buckner, the Admiralty's negotiator, went on board the mutineers' ship *Sandwich* to be presented with their demands. He stands to the left, before a motley group of grotesquely brutal figures (who resemble contemporary caricatures of French Revolutionary *sans-culottes*) seated around a table, in a composition that might almost be a travesty of the Last Supper. Certainly, the scene casts the mutiny as an inversion of all natural and social order, with Buckner standing before the seated mutineers, men of irredeemably inferior status (hence the title reference to 'beggars on horseback'). Britannia, in the print on the rear wall, is overturned. Yet the mutineers are also shown as the simple, unthinking

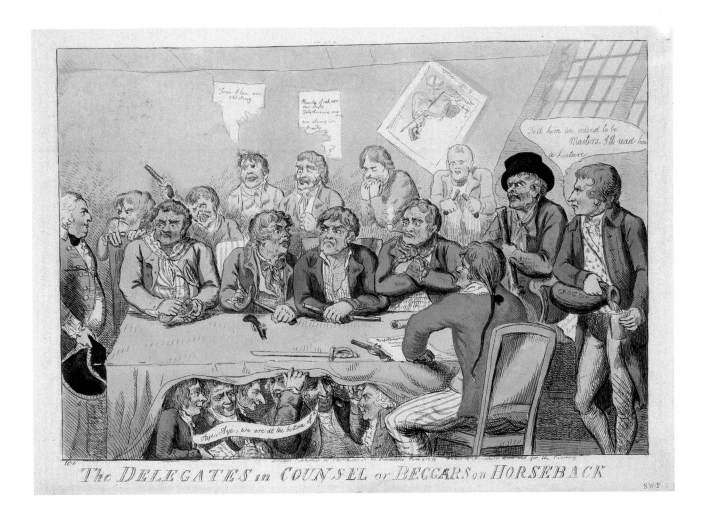

stooges of the Whig Opposition: below the table are concealed Horne, Tooke, Stanhope, Grey, Fox and Sheridan, who admit 'Aye, Aye, we are at the bottom of it', to imply that the mutiny was the product not so much of genuine lower-deck grievances but of republican and French Revolutionary sympathizers, encouraged by these leading politicians, who were widely derided by government supporters as Francophile 'democrats'.   GQ

34. Drum used to beat to quarters in the *St Fiorenzo* during the Nore mutiny, May 1797

Leather, wood

Provenance: on loan from the Borough of Lymington

National Maritime Museum, London; AAB0233

The mutineers had ordered the *St Fiorenzo*, anchored off Sheerness, to join the rest of the ships under their control off the Nore. Her crew remained loyal and her captain – Sir Harry Burrard Neale (1765–1840) – was eventually able to get her away into the Channel on the 31 May. The drum was

presented to the Borough of Lymington by one of his descendants. The Hanoverian royal arms are painted in full colour on a blue background.   BT

LITERATURE: Lieutenant's log, National Maritime Museum, London; ADM/L/S/100.

35. *RICHARD PARKER. PRESIDENT of the DELEGATES in the late MUTINY in his MAJESTY'S FLEET at the NORE. For which he suffered DEATH on board the SANDWICH the 30th of June 1797*
Harrison after William Chamberlain; published 8 July 1797 by J. Harrison and Co.
Hand-coloured etching
510 x 327mm
National Maritime Museum, London; PAH5441

Richard Parker, as the caption states, was the leader of the naval mutiny at the Nore in May and June 1797. Following swiftly on from the major, and seemingly entirely unanticipated, mutiny of the fleet at Spithead, the Nore mutiny presented a potentially disastrous crisis to the government at a very difficult time in the war against France. The anxiety was compounded by the widespread belief that the mutiny was caused by radical democratic and republican lower-deck elements in the Navy. Certainly, due to the increasing demand for manpower, a greater proportion of unskilled landsmen, Irishmen and potential radicals had been absorbed into the lower deck, and some of the sailors were members of the Corresponding Societies. The use of methods such as the 'round-robin' petition also indicated the mutineers' familiarity and presumably sympathy with methods adopted by American and French revolutionaries. However, it is unclear to what extent such political sympathies extended through the lower-deck population: the grievances of the majority were directed principally against poor pay and conditions. The crisis was averted when, after lengthy negotiations, the first ships broke away from the mutiny on 9 June, after which its leaders rapidly capitulated. Parker was court-martialled and hanged on his ship, the *Sandwich*, on 30 June, 'for having been the Principal in a most daring Mutiny on board several of his Majesty's Ships at the Nore, & which created a dreadful alarm through the whole Nation'. The political message of this print is underscored by

RICHARD PARKER.
PRESIDENT of the DELEGATES in the late MUTINY in his MAJESTY'S FLEET at the NORE For which he suffered DEATH on board the SANDWICH the 30th of June 1797
York Published as the act directs July 8th 1797 by J. Harrison. & Cº

the fact that, though titled 'Richard Parker', he is not the principal figure, as we might expect. Instead it is Parker's fate that is the main subject, as the heroically posed officer points with his drawn sword to Parker hanging from the yardarm in the background, as a warning to other possible lower-deck subversives.   GQ

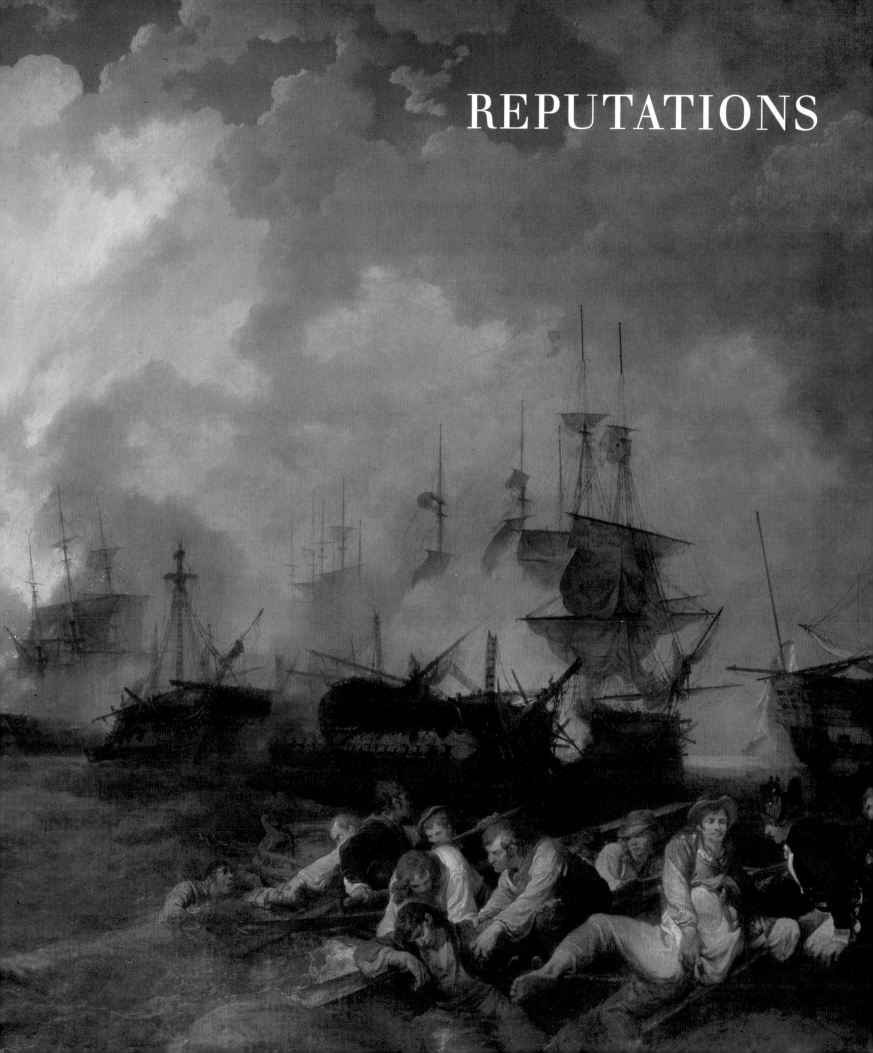

REPUTATIONS

Images of Napoleon:
A National Hero for France?

ANNIE JOURDAN

INTRODUCTION

A CAREER SOLDIER, Napoleon Bonaparte was above all a man of his time in that he realized the importance of civilization to the development of modern society. An assiduous reader and aspiring writer, he discovered during the Italian campaign of 1796–97 the prestige that great works of art and scientific discoveries brought to a nation. He also discovered the importance of the press and engraving. From this point on, and more precisely after the victory at Lodi (May 1796), he realized that he could take his place in history and began to do everything in his power to achieve this aim. As general commanding the Army of Italy, in his quarters at the castle of Mombello, near Milan, he not only received artists and sculptors but also men of letters and science. It was to all of these that he soon became indebted for the fame that he enjoyed until he came to power in Paris. And it was from this time that he conceived a strategy of seducing public opinion that did not cease until his death.

FRENCH HERO

F RESH FROM his victory in the peninsula but already celebrated by several artists, both more and less well known, Bonaparte encouraged them to engrave portraits that physically replicated aspects of the mental picture which he created of himself in his two Italian journals– *Le Courrier de l'Armée d'Italie* and *La France vue de l'Armée d'Italie* – and in his many proclamations to the army. These first portraits by Italian artists, which did not bear a particularly good likeness to their subject, were subsequently joined by portraits by Bacler d'Albe, Laffitte, Guérin, Appiani and Gros. The most famous is *Bonaparte au pont d'Arcole* (*Bonaparte at the Bridge of Arcole*) – the portrait by Gros, a young pupil of David, which was started in 1797 and portrays the general as a republican hero, in a forceful pose, a tricolour in one hand and a sword in the other. Other artists and engravers portrayed a rather more classic image: hair dishevelled by the wind, emaciated face, hook nose, keen eyes, thin lips and a firm chin, which denote courage, tenacity, virtue and authority. All of them portray a hero: the 'Italian hero', as he soon became known as a result of his prestigious victories, because Bonaparte conquered a large part of Italy in the space of a few months.

As a war hero, Bonaparte subsequently became a peacemaker, thanks to his involvement in the peace treaty of Campo Formio (October 1797). This was how David wanted to portray him in 1797, if we are to believe his pupil, Delécluze. On his return to Paris, Bonaparte was invited by France's leading painter of the time to come and pose in his studio, where the latter claimed he could 'reproduce this image that everyone wanted to see and own'.[1] We know about the artist's enthusiasm for the hero's beautiful 'classical-style' head, but in 1797 he had not finished his portrait, which was only begun when Bonaparte left for Egypt. Meanwhile, engravings by the above artists circulated around Revolutionary France, just like Sèvres porcelain, of which according to the historian, Dayot, 385 busts and 1242 medallions were sold between 1797 and 1800.[2]

The Egyptian campaign (1798–99), which took the hero to distant shores, could have damaged his growing popularity but did nothing of the kind. Not only did the press reverberate with his far-off adventures but the Egyptian Institute, which he set up there to study the Egyptian world, also published details of his discoveries and work. These served to fill the columns of the journal *La Décade philosophique* (1794–1807), published by a group of intellectuals, known as the ideologues, who sought to relaunch the spirit of Enlightenment liberalism in republican France. The journal's authors were fervent supporters of the enlightened general, who had become a member of the French Institute in 1797, in the mathematics section. In Egypt, Bonaparte displayed talents in civil administration and continued to surprise everybody by his intelligence, vivacity, curiosity and vast knowledge. Thus the general enthusiasm that met his return can be better understood, particularly since the French defeats against the Second Coalition (Britain, Austria and their allies) in the spring and summer of 1799 contributed to discrediting the Directory even more.

On *18 brumaire an VIII* [3] – 9–10 November 1799 – the Directory was overthrown. Sieyès, the most powerful of the ruling executives, who was responsible for a conspiracy aimed primarily at amending the Constitution in an authoritarian (and not dictatorial) sense, made the mistake of forming an alliance with Bonaparte. The latter did not waste any time in assuming the top position as Consul in the new government. Whether he used his charisma, intimidation, blackmail or promises, we simply do not know. However, within one month Bonaparte was appointed First Consul. In the meantime, he had adopted a Titus hairstyle, which emphasized his resemblance to the great men of ancient Rome and which gave him an air of maturity more in keeping with the role of supreme magistrate. New job, new image: Bonaparte was soon sporting the consular uniform and adopting a posture appropriate to public office. Several official portraits were completed to reflect this role, which were modelled on the Gros portrait and destined for Lille. The intention was that they would gradually adorn town halls across France and new *départements*, which, if we are to believe minister Chaptal, would have demonstrated the desire of each to own a portrait of the head of state. Greuze, Robert Lefebvre, Meynier, Mme Benoit and Ingres were consequently invited to paint a portrait of the First Consul. Destined for Antwerp, Dunkirk, Brussels, Ghent and Liège (since the Belgians had been reunited with France), these portraits were required to mention the names of the decrees issued in favour of the respective towns. In this way, they testify to consular achievements at the same time as depicting the young magistrate in his scarlet velvet suit, standing in his office where he has just completed his umpteenth piece of work. These portraits therefore emphasize Bonaparte's administrative achievement and no longer highlight the heroism of the protagonist, but rather his devotion to the public realm, his concern for the well-being of French citizens (both old and new), his flair as a statesman and his republican virtue. In the meantime, the face of Bonaparte has filled out and softened, while the body language is self-assured and dignified.

This is, however, not the only iconography relating to his

Bonaparte as First Consul,
by Jean-Auguste-Dominique Ingres (cat. no. 56).

time as Consul. On his return from Marengo (1800), where he claimed a great victory against the Austrians in retaking possession of Italy, Bonaparte was depicted in the famous painting by David, *Bonaparte au Grand-Saint-Bernard* (*Bonaparte Crossing the Saint Bernard*) (1801). Here the war hero image resurfaces as portrayed by the young Gros. Depicted on a rearing charger, Bonaparte, wrapped in a red cloak (or yellow cloak in the version given to the King of Spain), is climbing a steep snow-capped summit. The posture is assertive; his right hand is indicating to his soldiers the place to be reached and his gaze is fixed on an undefined distance: 'impassive and calm, he is completely engrossed in his great purposes,' concluded the *Journal des Arts*. Composed and sitting astride a spirited charger is how Bonaparte would have wished to be represented and how David painted him. This is where, above all, it differs from the Gros portrait, in which the hero, armed with a sword, appears to enter the heat of the action. In fact, the battle scenes ordered in 1800 for Malmaison, Napoleon's house just outside Paris, generally adopt David's angle. The point seems to be to depict Bonaparte engaged in combat. He sits imposingly in the foreground or in the centre from where he supervises the action, directs it or spurs it on. The First Consul remains the head of the armies, the Great Commander, but he no longer allows himself to take up arms and hurl himself into the fray.

If one is to believe the French intellectuals of the time, the hero had to be characterized by 'animated gestures that conjure up the grandeur and heroism of his thoughts and actions' (*La Décade philosophique*). He displayed a boldness that incorporated tranquillity of soul, self-confidence and laconic detachment. It is in the paintings of Gros and David that the critic sees this image, because the contrast between the calm of Bonaparte's expression, which denotes great character, and the physical effort made, which denotes his courage, is particularly successful. Not all artists could achieve the required standard, however. There is nothing of this in *The Battle of Marengo* (1801) by Lejeune, which

Napoleon Bonaparte Visiting the Plague-Stricken at Jaffa, March 11, 1799,
by Auguste-Hyacinthe Debay (1804–65), 1823, after Antoine-Jean, Baron Gros (1771–1835), 1804.
Museum of Fine Arts, Boston; 47.1059.

is too broad and too anecdotal, and where Bonaparte does not feature enough in the foreground. Consequently, the *Journal des bâtiments et des arts* regretted that the First Consul did not look like 'enough of a hero' here.

On the other hand, there are heroes galore in the two paintings commissioned by Bonaparte for Malmaison in 1800, the subjects of which were borrowed from Ossian and were entitled 'Ossian on the banks of the Lora invoking the gods to the strains of a harp' (Gérard) and 'The apotheosis of French heroes who died for their country during the war for freedom' (Girodet).[4] We know how fond the young Bonaparte was of the pseudo-Celtic bard. In his St Helena memoirs, Napoleon confessed to having discovered in Ossian the great, the sentimental and the

sublime to which he had aspired during his youth, and to which he continued to aspire. These two paintings by Gérard and Girodet portray a different image to the public at large, that of a sensitive and melancholy Bonaparte. They reveal his human side and his loathing of war and consequently provide an emotional counterbalance to the battle scenes and official portraits. Perhaps they also contribute towards emphasizing the hidden qualities of the enigmatic man whom France chose as its lord and master.[5]

It was after the *coup d'état* of 9–10 November 1799 that Bonaparte also began to encourage representations (mental and pictorial) that elevated him to an unprecedented level. He accentuated the supernatural nature of his exploits. This is how the famous *Pestiférés de Jaffa* (*Napoleon Bonaparte Visiting the Plague-Stricken at*

Jaffa) (1804), by Gros could be perceived, though one critic qualified its portrayal of 'a heroism of benevolence'. Designed in some degree to counter the rumours, spread particularly in England, that General Bonaparte had poisoned the casualties in question, the painting celebrates the courage and bravery of the commander, who risked his life to comfort his men, and accords with the mental image disseminated by the press of a man protected by the gods and Fate. This new inspiration was to reach its peak under the empire. Its aim was to elevate the Great Man to a divine status.

After this initial phase, images of Napoleon proliferated. From simple portraits to action or allegorical portraits that glorified the hero of Italy or the conqueror of Egypt and, after the Peace of Amiens in 1802, the peacemaker and restorer; from battle scenes where the protagonists are rather indeterminate to pictures of the Consulate, in which Bonaparte oversees from centre stage as the Great Commander; from portraits of the hero and those of the hard-working and tireless magistrate, a shift takes place in which Bonaparte quits the arena of war heroism and enters the pantheon of 'Great Men'. This is how his contemporaries described him. Friends and enemies alike concurred in giving him the label of 'most extraordinary' man. Bonaparte himself did not want to be or be seen in any other way.

Imperator

Now at the mercy of the advancing years and putting on weight, but borne along by his increasing power, nothing diminished his tyranny – quite the opposite, since he began to act more independently and refused the advice of his ministers and state advisers. It was this man who, in 1804, was proclaimed Emperor of France. The shift towards empire happened gradually. Being made Consul for life (1802–4) had already conferred greater power on Bonaparte than had been bestowed on Louis XVI under the Constituent Assembly. But this power was vested solely in his person; it was not hereditary. In 1804, following the royalist plot by Georges Cadoudal and Charles Pichegru which sought to assassinate Napoleon, voices were raised across virtually the whole of France demanding that consular power be made hereditary. Whether it was spontaneous or manipulated, public opinion seemed to want a new dynasty. This was how the constituted powers – the Tribunate, Senate, Legislature and the Council of State – interpreted it in the hope that the benefits of the French Revolution would be safeguarded and that there would be a better counterbalance to Bonaparte's dictatorship. A decision was also made to call the regime an empire, not only so as to distinguish it from the Bourbon monarchy and create a dynasty better adapted to the new order, but also because the word 'empire' more realistically defined the natural borders of France. Had France not, after all, restored the former borders of the Gallic Empire?[6] Two arguments merged in favour of this exalted term: the empire was perceived as conferring non-absolute power, and therefore viewed as totally compatible with the earlier Republic, but it also reflected the reality of French hegemony in Europe. However, it was essential that the empire should be founded on the basis of a social pact – a contract – that restricted the powers of the head of state.

At the time of his Anointing on 2 December 1804, which Napoleon imposed against the wishes of the legislators, the social pact was still on the agenda in the form of a constitutional oath that the Emperor of the French people took on behalf of the nation and their representatives – at the end of the religious ceremony and in the absence of the Pope. At the same time as he was working on his depiction of the coronation (1806), David was also commissioned to paint this scene. The project was subsequently abandoned at Napoleon's behest. But that means that both these portrayals briefly coexisted: Napoleon the *imperator*, being anointed by the Pope and crowning himself Emperor, and Napoleon the constitutional monarch, vowing to respect the Constitutions of the empire and national civil and political liberties. However, considering the official paintings completed subsequently by Gérard (1805), David (1805), Ingres (1806) and Robert Lefebvre (1806, 1807 and 1811), the *imperator* wins hands down. In the imperial portraits the signs of power and regalia are predominant, not the tables of the law. Here the Emperor is portrayed in majesty – a symbol of power and sovereignty. Only Girodet's official portrait (1811) depicts Napoleon taking an oath, not on the Constitution, however, but on the Napoleonic Code – which was quite different.[7] The constitutional oath was actually very quickly forgotten. Proud of both his popular and divine legitimacy, Napoleon soon showed that he cared little for what the Senate thought and he constantly flouted the famous oath.

The imperial portraits did not replace the battle paintings where Napoleon continued to sit imposingly in the centre of the picture. Dressed in his grey frock coat, his famous tricorn hat and his simple blue or green suit, the military commander scrutinizes the battlefield, directs and inspires his generals, enters a conquered city, sympathizes with the pain suffered by the wounded, comforts the dying or even uses his genius to spur the armies forward. More than an image of the majestic and dignified sovereign, which borrows both from the Holy Roman Empire and the ancient Roman Empire; it is this image of *Le Petit Caporal* (the nickname by which Napoleon was later known), of the

Une illustration sur la prestation du Serment from *Le Livre du Sacre*. Drawing by Jean-Baptiste Isabey (1767–1855).
Château de Fontainebleau; GM Bibl. 3502

'monarch of the people and father of the soldiers', which would remain in the memory of the French nation. Less popular are pictures of the court, where Napoleon, in Renaissance-style dress, sits resplendent in the midst of the imperial family, foreign princes and important dignitaries.

TRIUMPHALIST PATRIOTISM

THERE IS NO QUESTION that the imperial saga revived the national pride of the French, who believed they were reliving the triumphs of Julius Caesar and the exploits of Charlemagne. Though at the time of the Anointing, the Parisian public casually scoffed at the event, 'after a month had passed, France was on its knees, Europe fell silent and the fourth dynasty created',[8] how many were there during the first few years of the great adventure who did not congratulate themselves for conquests that increased the nation's territory, bringing it new glory? How many who did not brag about the masterpieces painted by the geniuses of the century, who offered them subjects of national importance? The first setbacks were necessary for triumphalist patriotism to be tempered by a more peaceful emphasis and so that the French could admit to their own yearning for peace and quiet.

At the same time the images depicting the Emperor in his office lived on and replaced the consular portraits. In addition to little known works by Garnier (1808) and Lefebvre (1809), which emphasized the hard work carried out by the great man, the portrait by David for Alexandre Douglas (1812) shows

The Emperor Napoleon in His Study at the Tuileries, 1812, by Jacques-Louis David. Kress Collection, National Gallery of Art, Washington DC; 1961.9.15.

Napoleon at the end of a long night spent drafting the Civil Code. He realizes that it is four o'clock in the morning and rises from his desk to take up his sword and go out to inspect the troops. This portrait is a wonderful representation of the image that most French people had of their Emperor and King: a great man concerned about the happiness and prosperity of his subjects; an austere and hard-working magistrate; an extraordinary man on account of his talents, energy and genius. In this sense, but in this sense only, he remained a republican emperor.

A CONFLICTING IMAGE

THIS PERCEPTION did not exist elsewhere, however, notably in England where the caricaturists began to launch their attack on Napoleon from 1798 onwards. Gillray set the tone when he transformed the hero of Italy and Egypt into a bellicose but puny character, a depiction that was hugely successful. In the English caricatures, the only ones to dominate the market until 1812–13, Bonaparte's qualities were assiduously and systematically reversed. The hero's courage was called into question. In *Buonaparte leaving Egypt* (1800) by Gillray, for example, which, in contrast to the official line, depicts a hypocritical and cowardly general who deserts his men on the quiet and who, obsessed by his own ambitions, abandons them to their sad fate. Gillray, also the first to reveal the truth of the *18 brumaire*, offers a snapshot of Bonaparte's life in *Democracy or a Sketch of the Life of Bonaparte* (1800), where he emphasizes the hero's wretched background, his ingratitude, cowardice, usurpation of power and the harmful consequences arising from this. We could cite endless examples. In addition to Gillray, many others including Rowlandson, Cruikshank and Williams mocked Bonaparte incessantly. Each in his own inimitable fashion laid bare the faults, mistakes, pretences and crimes of the great man, whom France had chosen as its lord and master, and tore down the sublime image created by the great artists of the Consulate and the empire. They depicted Napoleon as a vulgar usurper, an heir of the Revolution, a bloodthirsty Jacobin. They refused to confer any qualities on the diminutive Corsican – neither as a hero, great man, great commander, a brilliant magistrate, nor, above all, as legitimate emperor. The Corsican was indeed diminutive and diminutive he remained, in both a figurative and literal sense, in most British satirical drawings, as General Bonaparte remained *Little Boney*, *Bonaparte*, *Boney*, *Bone Part*. The maestros from across the Channel took issue with any other title. And although in *The Grand Coronation Procession of NAPOLEONE the 1st Emperor of France* (cat. no. 64), Gillray acknowledged the change that came about in 1804, it was simply in order to transform the scene into a grotesque parody, which emphasized with caustic irony the pedigree of the new sovereigns: Josephine as a coarse and portly matron figure and Bonaparte, bloated and shrouded in showy imperial rags; the Pope hunched over and diffident, and the court of the *nouveaux riches* dripping with gold and finery. Once again, Gillray returns to the illegitimacy of the new Caesar and his appetite and desire for power – subjects that are taken up, but less skilfully, by his successors both in England and on the Continent.

CONCLUSION: MAN OF THE NATION

PATRIOTIC SENSITIVITIES clashed in what became a genuine war of images and this enables us to understand why, on the one hand, countries that had been occupied, overthrown and plundered by Napoleon's armies applauded Britain's calculated campaign of defamation; and why, on the other, many French people tried to discredit it or prevent its dissemination on the Continent, at least until the Restoration, for the caricatures ridiculed not only the head of the empire, his generals and dignitaries, but also his armies and ultimately the French people themselves. Metamorphosed continuously into sheep, hares, crocodiles, rats or bloodthirsty Jacobins, some felt hurt, and even humiliated, and there is nothing like humiliation to make national feelings run higher.

At the time of the fall of Paris in 1814 and Napoleon's abdication, attacks by foreign and royalist lampoonists and caricaturists increased, becoming so outrageous that they shocked the population. The French people – the middle and working classes and the common soldiery – began, as a reaction against this, to identify Napoleon *with* the Revolution; Napoleon *with* the Nation. At the end of the modern Odyssey, disappointed by the Restoration and with their patriotism wounded by the sheer impertinence of the caricaturists, the French gradually began to forgive the Ogre who had devoured their children and saw in him a genuine father of the Nation, king of the people and heir of the Revolution. *Le Petit Caporal* definitely prevailed over the enthroned *imperator*. From that moment onwards, myth and legend could gradually be born. No one could have foreseen this surprising but logical conclusion; neither the caricaturists nor the great painters of the period.

36. *Plan de la Rade et du Port de Toulon avec la Position des Postes Extèrieurs de Cette Place, Occupés Par les troupes des Puissances Coalisées en Décembre de l'Année 1793* / Plan of the Anchorage and Port of Toulon with the Position of the External Outposts of That Place Occupied By the troops of the Coalition Powers in December 1793

Anonymous French cartographer, 1793 or 1794
Manuscript: ink and watercolour
850 x 640mm
National Maritime Museum, London; G231: 6/30

This plan shows the scene of Napoleon's early rise to prominence as a military commander at Toulon, France's principal Mediterranean naval port.

The population of the southern French cities resisted the domination of the Jacobins. As a captain of artillery, aged twenty-three, Napoleon helped crush rebellions in Avignon and Marseilles. Realizing that Toulon would be next, in desperation the people of Toulon called on the Coalition forces (Britain, Spain and the Kingdom of Naples) for assistance. After extracting reluctant promises to support the restoration of the monarchy, Admiral Lord Hood sailed the fleet into the anchorage on 27 August. The Jacobin siege began in early September and the plan shows the fortifications held by the attackers and the defending forces. Napoleon, now promoted to major, recognized that Fort l'Éguillette, marked N on the plan, on the headland opposite the port, was

of key importance. Guns mounted there could destroy ships in the inner and outer anchorages. Following his plan, on 17 and 18 December the republicans destroyed Fort Mulgrave (XX on the plan), a redoubt built by the English to protect the landward side of the headland. Napoleon captured l'Éguillette and began bombardment of the fleet.

Hood ordered an immediate evacuation. Before sailing, the Coalition blew up the arsenal and burnt all the French ships in the Port Neuf but only some of those in the Port Vieux. (The ships are listed in the key.) The people of Toulon were left to face the revenge of the Republic. Two days later, Napoleon was promoted to brigadier-general. He later used Toulon as the base for the 1798 expedition to Egypt.

The plan is drawn over a faint pencil grid, indicating that it is a copy of another document. The scale is in *toises*, the standard French distance unit until the republicans introduced the metric system in 1795. GH

37. Manuscript 'map' of the siege of Toulon, 1793

Ink on paper
Napoleon Bonaparte and Jean-Andoche Junot
Pierre-Jean Chalençon, private collection

An eight-side description of the military dispositions at Toulon in 1793, where French republican forces besieged and finally defeated royalist counter-revolutionaries. The royalists were supported by Admiral Lord Hood's British expeditionary force, which included Nelson, commanding

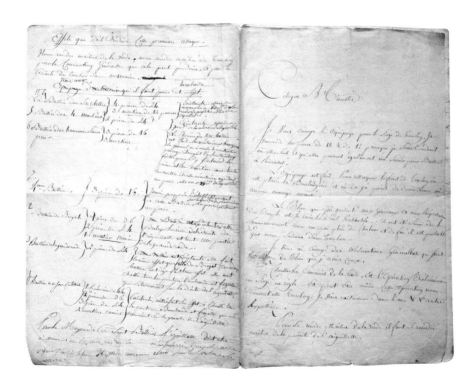

the *Agamemnon*. The description was dictated by Bonaparte, who first came to prominence at Toulon as republican artillery commander, and written out by his aide-de-camp, Junot – himself later a Marshal of France. Bonaparte has added various annotations and corrections in his own hand.

PvdM

38. Portrait of the Empress Josephine, 1805

Robert Lefebvre (1755–1830)
Oil on canvas, oval
635 x 533mm
Signed and dated *Robert Lefebvre/ft* [fecit] 1805
From the collection of Dalmeny House; P 604

In this portrait, of which there is a full-length version at Versailles, the Empress is shown half-length, wearing a white dress with a blue shawl.

Lefebvre was the son of a Bayeux draper who, after training and establishing a practice in Normandy, moved to Paris in about 1784 and entered the studio of Jean-Baptiste Regnault. He made a name with mythological subjects, which invited comparison with Jacques-Louis David and François-Pascal-Simon Gérard, and was employed to paint state portraits of the Emperor and his family.

The portrait is inscribed on the reverse: *Painted by Robert Lefevre* [sic] *of whom I Purchased it at Paris in September 1818. George Watson Taylor.* The portrait was subsequently acquired by the 5th Earl of Rosebery, historian as well as politician, whose lifelong interest in Napoleon resulted in his collection of Napoleon memorabilia as well as a biography which dealt with the Emperor's last years. RQ

39. Malachite jewellery set, Empire period

Unknown jeweller
Gold, malachite and pearls
Red morocco case bearing inscription *A* (surmounted
    by a crown), *n°50, PARURE MALACHITES ENTOUREE
    DE PERLES*
Fondation Napoléon, Paris; inv. 973 (donation Lapeyre)

This exceptional ensemble – comprising two necklaces (one large, one small), bracelets, a diadem, a brooch, a pendant, a pin with small cameos, a pin with large cameos and a pin with pearls – dates from the beginning of the nineteenth century. The decorative scheme is themed, with variations, on antique-style female and male profiles (one of which is Apollo) and face-on views. Of particular interest is this set's remarkable closeness in style to the 'gothic chain' necklace held at the Musée de Malmaison. The latter piece (whose

case is marked with the same crowned initial A, the no. 42, and the name of the piece), was given by Hortense de Beauharnais, Josephine's daughter, to her niece, Amélie (1812–73), the future Empress of Brazil. Since we know from inventory of Josephine's possessions made after her death that the Empress of the French possessed such malachite jewellery, it is possible that the set here was once owned either by the Empress Josephine or by her daughter-in-law, Auguste-Amélie, Vice-Queen of Italy, from whom it passed to the Empress of Brazil.
PH

LITERATURE: B.Chevallier, K. Huguenaud, *Trésors de la Fondation Napoléon, Dans l'intimité de la Cour impériale* (Paris, 2004), pp. 104–5.

40. Letter from Napoleon to Josephine, 1796

Signed and dated [*an V* (1796)] *3 frimaire* (23 November 1796), from Verona

Archives Nationales, France; 400 AP 6, vol. 1, no. 16

Josephine was the love of Napoleon's life. Yet, had it not been for her son Eugène de Beauharnais, the tremendous affair might never have happened. In the aftermath of General Bonaparte's suppression of the *coup d'état of 13 vendémaire an IV* (5 October 1795), and the infamous 'whiff of grapeshot', Parisians were banned from carrying arms. Eugène, however, wished to continue wearing the sword he had inherited from his father Alexandre, executed in 1794. His application to do so brought Bonaparte to the Beauharnais household and into the presence of Eugène's widowed mother, the 'graceful' and 'irresistibly sweet' Marie-Josèphe Rose. Bonaparte was well aware of the rumour that she had been the lover of (and was to remain close friends with) his patron, the powerful libertine politician Paul Barras, soon to become chief of France's national governing body, the Directory. But even that charmed him – he was bewitched. A whirlwind courtship in which Bonaparte was 'sultan' and 'Rose' became 'Josephine' led to a civil marriage on 9 March 1796. Bonaparte's career entered a new phase: he found himself wedded to a woman with free access to the highest echelons, and also appointed commander-in-chief of the Army of Italy – and consequently off on campaign merely three days after his wedding! Deeply in love (and lust) with his 'sweet and incomparable', Napoleon in his personal letters reveals his literary power. He begins by lambasting Josephine in mock fury, criticizing her for a) never writing, and b) sending only 'six lines, thrown down at random' when she did write. 'What do you do all day?' exclaims the jealous, frustrated husband. Watch out, he warns, or one night he will break down the doors, appear in her bed and stab her 'with his little sword', as

Othello did Desdemona. 'But seriously,' he continues, 'send me just four pages of those lovely things that fill my heart with love.' The penultimate, intimate paragraph, with its kisses 'as hot as at the equator' to be given to Josephine's 'little scamp' and 'all over' was, for reasons of decorum, to remain unpublished until 1981.
PH

LITERATURE: J. Tulard, *Napoléon: Lettres d'amour à Josephine* (Paris, 1981), pp. 124–5.

41. Napoleon as a young man, 1797

Francesco Cossia [?]

Oil on canvas laid down on panel

180 x 149mm

Sir John Soane's Museum, London

This is a rare portrait of Napoleon as a young man. Recent research by Xavier Solomon has identified the artist as Francesco Cossia who in a letter concerning the portrait dated 17 March 1797 refers to himself as a Venetian painter, but nothing further is known of him. In his letter the artist boasts of having achieved 'a very good likeness' and states that Napoleon posed for him in his camp at Verona for half an hour before and after lunch, and that he followed him to complete the portrait on his way to Bassano. He had another opportunity after breakfast at San Bonifazio but afterwards had to

return to Verona. Although Sir John Soane considered that the portrait was commissioned by 'Madame Beauharnais, afterwards the Empress Josephine', a letter of 26 March 1797 from Francesco Ricardi in Milan to the painter and miniaturist Maria Cosway (1759–1838) in London clearly states that it was she who commissioned it. Maria Cosway was a friend of Sir John Soane and it is therefore almost certain that Soane acquired the portrait from her. The letters are now in the archive of the Sir John Soane's Museum.

RQ

42. Standard carried by the *escadron des guides*, late eighteenth century

Painted silk banner, gold fringe

540 x 540mm (banner)

Musée de l'Armée, Paris; inv. Ba 68

In 1792, small companies of *guides* (guides) were permitted by the French government for each of its armies as security detachments, to be picked by the army commanders who could then choose their uniforms according to their own tastes. The guides for Napoleon's Army of Italy were formed from a foot company, brought together by General Kellermann from the Army of the Alps, and comprising former poachers and smugglers. These were to guard the rear of the headquarters in Milan, and went on to become the *chausseurs à pied* of Bonaparte's guard. The duties of *guides* included maintaining the personal security of the commanding general, his headquarters and baggage. They might also undertake short-range reconnaissance work and act as a small force to be used in moments of crisis. The mounted guides that Bonaparte took with him to Italy were brave but notorious for their indiscipline and carelessness. When Bonaparte became First Consul, he abolished all existing guide organizations, as their loyalty to their commanders was seen as potentially dangerous.

This standard was carried by the *escadron des guides* that accompanied Bonaparte on the Italian campaign of 1796–97 and the Egyptian campaign of 1798–99. It displays the familiar emblems of the Revolution, including the Phrygian cap. Before the Revolution, each regiment had had a different flag but after 1791 some attempts were made to make them more uniform.

CLW

LITERATURE: Bertaud, *The Army of the French Revolution*; Elting, *Swords around a Throne*.

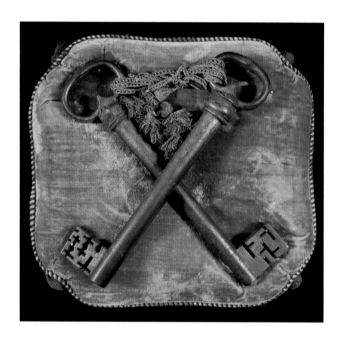

43. Keys to the castle of Milan, 1796

Gilded iron

Musée de l'Armée, Paris; inv. Cd 64

These huge keys to the castle of Milan were taken during Napoleon's Italian campaign of 1796–97. They were handed over to General Despinay on 29 June 1796 by the defenders. The French had invaded Italy in April 1796 as a means of striking at its Austrian rulers. Napoleon entered Milan in triumph on 15 May and the old aristocratic government was replaced with a new regime. Italian radicals originally welcomed the French as liberators, believing that their action would lead to Italian unity, but the reality of military occupation soon turned the Italians against the French. RP

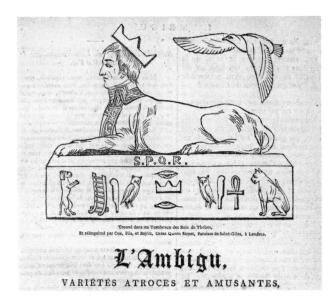

44. Frontispiece to *L'Ambigu* by Jean-Gabriel Peltier
Published in London, by Cox, Son and Baylis, 1802
Woodcut
British Library, London; P.P. 3612.C.

The émigré journalist Peltier was Napoleon's most vocal critic in the British press, especially after the launch of his satirical and political journal *L'Ambigu* in mid-1802. This vignette of Napoleon as a sphinx adorned the earliest numbers of the journal, during 1802 and 1803. It was among the pieces cited when, following French diplomatic pressure, Peltier was brought before the court of King's Bench on 21 February 1803 charged with criminal libels inciting the assassination of the First Consul. The use of a sphinx was an allusion to Napoleon's Egyptian expedition, a favourite topic for caricaturists at the time. Peltier uses the image to denounce Napoleon's despotism and predict his elevation to Emperor in 1804, represented by the inscription SPQR on the plinth. *The Trial of John Peltier* explained the image's full symbolism as follows. The sphinx's lion-like body symbolizes Napoleon's 'power', the tail between his legs 'dissimulation' and the outstretched paws 'ambition, ready to pounce on everything within his reach'. The crown on his 'Brutus-like head' represents 'the anti-republican intrigues at his court to have him named king or emperor, consul for a term or for life, hereditarily or nominating his successor'. The 'Egyptian spirit', with one wing pointing to his head

and the other to his tail, symbolizes the vigilance with which 'every pen' should expose his designs and methods. The hieroglyph of a crown between two eyes indicates the object of his gaze. On either side of the crown were two sparrow-hawks, or *chouans* (a word used for the royalist rebels in the west of France during the Revolutionary period), representing 'its imperturbable guardians'. Meanwhile the ladder and the axe 'indicate the punishments awaiting regicides, rebels and thieves'. Finally, the dog and the cat at the outer extremes represent 'the concord and unity that reign far from the crown'. The trial was a political one and it was widely rumoured that if Peltier were found innocent the result would be war. In the event, he was found guilty and retaliated by decapitating the sphinx. However, he was never punished for his libels as war broke out prior to his sentencing hearing. He made a small fortune by publishing an account of his trial. SB

45. Order sentencing those involved in the Cairo rebellion to death, *13 brumaire an VII* (3 November 1798)
Ink on paper
Pierre-Jean Chalençon, private collection

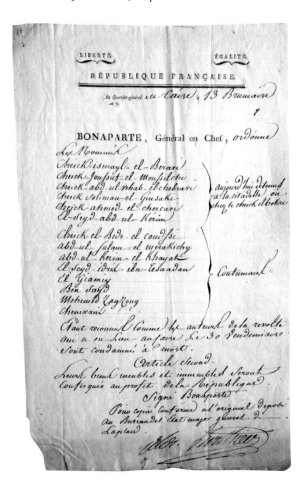

Bonaparte had an early triumph in his Egyptian campaign: victory over the Mameluke rulers of Egypt at the Battle of the Pyramids on 21 July 1798 allowed him to take Cairo, which he entered several days later. However, the campaign was not to go entirely his way, particularly after Nelson destroyed the French fleet in Aboukir Bay. The loss of bullion caused by this action necessitated the raising of taxes in Egypt and imposition of forced loans, which were inevitably unpopular, while the declaration of war by Turkey destabilized the situation further. On 21 October, matters came to a head and, beginning at the University of El Azhar, Cairo rose in revolt. After two days of fighting, Bonaparte regained control but some 2000 Arabs and 300 Frenchmen, including General Dupuy and Bonaparte's favourite aide-de-camp, Sulkowski, had been killed. Although subsequent French propaganda stated that Napoleon had pardoned the ringleaders of the revolt, this manuscript shows otherwise: it contains Bonaparte's orders, signed by Berthier, condemning them to death and seizing their property for the profit of the Republic. CLW

LITERATURE: Frank McLynn, *Napoleon: A Biography* (London, 1998); Tulard, *Napoleon: The Myth of the Saviour*.

46. Diary of John Tillery
an American prisoner of war,
March 1790–February 1800
Ink on paper; bound volume
National Maritime Museum, London; X2003.30

John Tillery, an American sailor, served on board the *Tigre* under Sir Sidney Smith, a charismatic commander. Nelson had worked with Smith earlier in his career but unlike others remained unimpressed by his flamboyant manner. Tillery and eighteen shipmates were captured by the French at Acre on 21 March 1799. Initially, they were well treated – Napoleon even sent them a bottle of Jew's Brandy and a share of his provisions. Tillery was interrogated by Napoleon himself and asked to identify the body of a dead marine. However, after Napoleon's failure at Acre, the prisoners were marched to Egypt and kept in appalling conditions. Tillery wrote personally to Napoleon to ask for mats to sleep on but his request was ignored. The prisoners were released on 22 December and returned to England on the *Theseus*. DK

47. Presentation sabre, *c.* 1800
Gold, silver and steel
Inscribed in Arabic: You will annihilate your enemies
and protect the Muslims
Musée de l'Armée, Paris; inv. Ca 12

This sabre, probably presented to Napoleon when First Consul, was taken with him to St Helena, where he was exiled after his defeat at the Battle of Waterloo. After Napoleon's death, General Bertrand returned the sword to King Louis-Philippe on 4 June 1840. LV

48. *BUONAPARTE, hearing of Nelson's Victory, swears by his Sword, to Extirpate the English from off the Earth. See, Buonaparte's Speech to the French Army at Cairo; publish'd by authority of the Directory, in Volney's Letters,* 8 December 1798
James Gillray, published by H. Humphrey
Hand-coloured etching
370 x 279mm
National Maritime Museum, London; PAF3964

This is effectively a triumphalist mocking satire of Napoleon in Egypt, through celebratory reference to the resounding victory over the French fleet at the Battle of the Nile some four months earlier. The French leader is ridiculed as a set of contradictions. Gillray plays principally upon Napoleon's stature, for which he is shown attempting to compensate by the extraordinary and extravagant uniform he wears, which is in marked contrast to that of the dispatch rider beyond. The latter (whose mount in the Egyptian context is transformed from a horse to a camel) looks on frozen in astonishment and fear at the uncontrolled outpouring his message has provoked in his leader, his leaden pose pointing up the overblown theatricality of Napoleon's. The latter unleashes his sabre marked '*Egalité*', but it is dripping with blood, like the dagger tucked into the fulsome tricolour sash around his waist. His 'Muslim pose', by which he tramples the report of Nelson's victory, at the same time recalls David's celebrated painting *The Oath of the Horatii*. In short, Napoleon is burlesqued as a contradictory combination of the personification of French Revolutionary principles and an orientalized despot, marked most clearly by the crescent

What? our Fleet capturd & destroyd, by the Slaves of Britain?—
"by my Sword & by holy Mahomet, I swear, eternal Vengeance!—yes,
"when I have subjected Egypt, subdued the Arabs, the Druses & the Maronites;
"become master of Syria,—turn'd the great River Euphrates,& saild upon it through
"the sandy Deserts; compel'd to my assitance, the Beduins, Tuscomans, Kurds
"Armenians, & Persians; form'd a Million of Cavalry, & pass'd them upon Rafts
"six or seven Hundred Miles over the Bosphorus, I shall enter Constantinople—
"—Now I enter the Theatre of Europe, I establish the Republic of Greece,
"I raise Poland from its ruins, I make Prussia bend ÿ knee to France;
"I chain up the Russian Bear;—I cut the Head from ÿ Imperial Eagle;
"I drive the ferocious English from the Archipelago—I hunt them
"from the Mediterranean,—& blot them out from the catalogue of
"Nations!—Then shall the conquer'd Earth sue for Peace,
"& an Obelisk be erected at Constantinople, inscribed
"To Buonaparte, Conquerer of the World,
"& extirpater of the
"ENGLISH NATION"

BUONAPARTE, hearing of Nelson's Victory, swears by his Sword, to Extirpate the English from off the Earth.
See, Buonapartes Speech to the French Army at Cairo; publish'd by authority of the Directory, in Volney's Letters.

moon on his enormous hat, the camel and the oriental tent in the background. The satire's ridicule resides finally in the play of word and image that is typical of Gillray. Matching the swaggering pose and excessive costume of Napoleon is the unchecked stream of words he utters. The English viewer is invited to regard both his gestures and words as hollow and empty in the face of the victory at the Nile. GQ

Menou had 'completely trounced the English and the remains of their army' and looks forward to confirmation. It was written when he was French governor in northern Italy. He later became King of Naples and was executed by the restored Bourbon king, Ferdinand, in 1815 after a failed attempt to regain the throne. PvdM

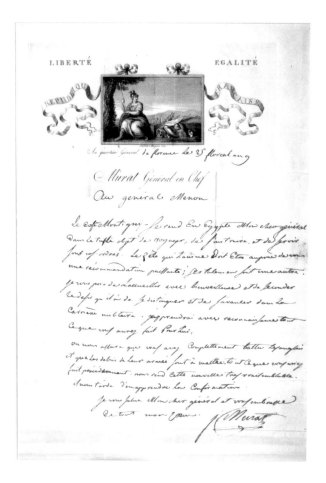

49. Letter from Joachim Murat in Florence to General Jacques-François Menou in Egypt, 15 May 1801 (*25 floréal an IX*)

Ink on paper

John Goldstein, private collection

Menou became French commander in Egypt on the assassination of General Kléber by a Muslim fanatic in 1800. His defeat by a British army at the Battle of Aboukir on 22 March 1801 sealed the fate of Napoleon's expeditionary force, which surrendered in August and was repatriated to France. Murat had been one of Napoleon's cavalry commanders in Egypt, and accompanied him home in 1799 and married his youngest sister in 1800. This letter of introduction for a Captain Montigny asserts his belief that

50. Drawing of Bonaparte, Commander of the Army of Egypt, 1798

André Dutertre (?1753–1842)

Pencil on paper

100 x 120mm

Musée de Malmaison, France; MM 40.47.4678

This small portrait of Napoleon was drawn on board *L'Orient*, the flagship of the French fleet on the Egyptian campaign, during its voyage out to Egypt. Bonaparte had spent two months planning this expedition to take Malta and then Egypt, apparently to block British trade interests in India. He was in supreme command of both the troops and the fleet. His plan was both to conquer and, in his view, to civilize: he took with him a team of 167 learned men who would not only study Egypt but also help to exploit its resources to the full, particularly as it was potentially valuable as a colony. Dutertre, an artist, was one of the members of this team, the 'Committee of Arts and Sciences'. The results of his work, and of the rest of the group, can be seen in the magnificent *Description de l'Égypte*, published in some ten folio volumes and with more than 3000 illustrations between 1809 and 1828.   CLW

LITERATURE: Humbert *et al.*, *Egyptomania*; Humbert and Ponsonnet, eds, *Napoléon et la mer*; Thompson, *Napoleon Bonaparte*.

51.   Textile, *c.* 1799
France
Roller-printed cotton
Museo del Tessuto di Prato

Roller-printed textiles, a manufacturing innovation of the mid-eighteenth century, often featured designs that reflected political or cultural events. This 'toile de Jouy', named after the French town where they were produced, illustrates the initial popularity of the Egyptian campaign among the French public. The image shows Napoleon after the victory of the Battle of the Pyramids, crowned by Fame. At his feet are the weapons of war and before him are three turbaned figures to whom he extends the tricolour sash of office. In the background the newly liberated Egyptian populace can be seen. This illustrates not only the French victory but also the perception that France was bringing both liberty and good government to Egypt. Many of these textiles could be produced quite cheaply and so were available to a large part of the population.   AM

ARRIVÉE DE BONAPARTE, EN EGYPTE.
Général en Chef des Armées de Terre et de Mer de la République Française.

52.   *Arrival of Bonaparte in Egypt*, late eighteenth century
Anonymous, French
Engraving
263 x 388mm
Inscribed bottom right: 'Chez Bonneville, rue Jacques no. 195'
Musée de Malmaison, France; MM 40.47.4353

Bonaparte is represented as the victorious general-in-chief of the land and sea armies of the French Republic. The date of the print is probably 1799, shortly after his return to Paris. An allegorical winged figure of Victory holds a crown of laurels over Bonaparte's head. She wears a halo of five-pointed stars of immortality. Bonaparte also holds branches of laurel and oak for enduring conquest.

Following his successes in Italy, Bonaparte was given the command of the Army of England by government of the Directory. The plan was to force England to make peace by damaging her commercial ventures (by preventing her traders from passing through Egypt to and from India). Bonaparte set sail for Egypt on 19 May 1798. This was firstly a military expedition to strike at the Ottoman Empire; secondly, a diversion tactic that attempted to quell internal divisions between royalists and Jacobins in France through imperial expansion; and thirdly, a bid to set up a new French territory – for which purpose scientists, archaeologists, architects, mathematicians, astronomers, linguists and engineers all joined forces. The troops arrived on 2 July, took Alexandria then marched on to Cairo with great loss of life. Here they defeated the Turkish rulers and Albanian armies in Egypt at the Battle of the Pyramids on 21 July. On 1 August Nelson destroyed the French fleet in Aboukir Bay but Bonaparte stayed on in Egypt until 24 August 1799, when he returned to France as a hero. The army he left behind eventually surrendered to the British in August 1801. Only when the French had evacuated Egypt did England sign the Peace of London.

This print is related to a painting of *Napoleon after the Battle of Lodi* by Andrea Appiani (1799), which referred to Bonaparte's entry into Milan in May that year. There the winged Victory, placed in front of a large palm tree, engraves the names of the locations of Bonaparte's Italian victories on to a shield. The pose of Bonaparte, his uniform, facial expression and hair in this print all appear to be derived from this painting. HW

LITERATURE: Milan, Academia di Belle Arte di Brera. See exhibition catalogue, *1769–1797 Da Montenotte a Campoformio: la rapida marcia di Napoleone Bonaparte*, Museo Napolonico, Rome ('L'Erma' di Bretschneider, 1997), pp. 64–6, no. 37.

BUONAPARTÉ *leaving EGYPT.*
For an illustration of the above, see the Intercepted Letters from the Republican General Kleber, to the French Directory respecting the Courage, Honor & Patriotic-Views, of 'the Deserter of the Army of Egypt.'

53. *BUONAPARTÉ leaving EGYPT*

[James Gillray], published 8 March 1800 by
    H. Humphrey
Hand-coloured etching
418 x 301mm
National Maritime Museum, London; PAF3965

Another satire on Napoleon in Egypt, ridiculing the French leader's campaign there. Napoleon departed secretly on 23 August 1799 on the *Muiron*. The caption refers to a group of 'Intercepted Letters from the Republican General Kléber, to the French Directory' and denounces Napoleon as 'the Deserter of the Army of Egypt'. This refers to a batch of letters between Bonaparte and Kléber that was intercepted by the British in the Mediterranean and, as a propaganda ploy, published by the government to great acclaim. They contained Kléber's account of Napoleon's sudden departure from Egypt: 'Bonaparte quitted this country for France . . . without saying a word of his intention to any person whatsoever. He had appointed me to meet him at Rosetta on the subsequent day!' Gillray reinforces the propaganda value of the letters by taking as the basis for his print Napoleon's duplicity, which is everywhere signified: the figurehead on the boat he is about to embark is a crowned Janus. Similarly, while he adopts a heroic pose (based loosely on the Apollo Belvedere), in a conventional gesture of military prowess, he looks back to his abandoned ragbag of an army, whose few tents are lined up against a seemingly limitless Turkish camp. While his gesture points in the direction of the open sea, as though to further, future campaigns, it also points to a vision in the clouds of the Revolutionary symbols of the fasces and axe overlaid with the imperial crown and sceptre, again stressing the idea of doubleness. Meanwhile, the figure of Fame, above, looks and points down at Napoleon and laughs. GQ

54. The *Muiron*, French 18-pounder frigate, launched 1797

Jean Lille and Claude Meirier, residents at the Arsenal,
  Toulon, 1803–5
Scale 1:72
Musée de la Marine, Paris; 17 MG 7

The frigate and the two-decker 74s were the most numerous ships of all major navies during the late eighteenth century. Known as the 'eyes and ears' of a fleet, frigates were heavily armed and fast, which enabled them to carry out a variety of roles including reconnaissance, cruising on a station and acting as messengers between ships in the fleet. This is a contemporary model of the *Muiron*, a 44-gun, 18-pounder frigate built at the Arsenal in Venice in 1797. The *Muiron* was taken back to Toulon for fitting out before joining Admiral de Brueys's squadron in the Mediterranean. In 1798, at Alexandria, the hull was copper-sheathed (an idea copied from the Royal Navy) to prevent weed growth and damage from the marine boring mollusc *teredo navalis*. The *Muiron* is probably best known for transporting Napoleon back to France from Egypt in 1799. Because of the blockade of the French fleet in Alexandria by the British squadron under Captain Samuel Hood, Napoleon's departure was delayed by several months. Eventually, on 22 August, Napoleon set sail on board the *Muiron* under the flag of Rear-Admiral Ganteaume, arriving at the port of Fréjus on 9 October. Afterwards, Napoleon ordered this model for his study at Malmaison, his residence outside Paris. The *Muiron* was clearly a talismanic ship for him. Built at a slightly smaller scale than usual of 1:72, the model is complete with a full suit of sails, cannon and boats, which are stored in the waist. The starboard side below the waterline lifts away to reveal the construction and internal layout of the hull. SS

55. State chair of First Consul, 1803

France
Mahogany, silk velvet and metal thread
From the collection of Dalmeny House

In November 1799 the Directory was abolished in a coup engineered by Bonaparte, Talleyrand, Sieyès and others. The new government, the Consulate, was loosely based on that of ancient Rome, with Napoleon as First Consul. Much of the iconography utilized by the new government drew on both Imperial Rome and Pharaonic Egypt. The throne-like chair of the First Consul has the Egyptian papyrus motif, a symbol of immortality, on both the arms and legs. The embroidery on the front of the cushion replicates the double papyrus motif, while at the centre is an embroidered palmette surrounded by laurels. The chair is also military in style (it lacks arm rests, making it easier for the sitter to sit or stand up without entangling his sword). Although the decoration is sparing, the chair is made of lavish materials and features a flame-grained mahogany back, crimson velvet cushion with metal thread embroidery.   AM

56. Bonaparte as First Consul, 1804

Jean-Auguste-Dominique Ingres (1780–1867)
Oil on canvas
2270 x 1470mm
Musée d'Art Moderne et d'Art Contemporain de la
    Ville de Liège, on deposit at the Musée d'Armes, Liège

After Napoleon and Josephine toured the northern *départements* of France in 1803, five full-length portraits of the First Consul were commissioned to be sent to towns in the region to remind citizens of their loyalty to the new regime. The other artists were Marie-Guilhemine Benoit, Jean-Baptiste Greuze, Robert Lefebvre and Charles Meynier. Ingres' portrait was to go to Liège in present-day Belgium. It shows the First Consul pointing to a decree of August 1803 that designated 300,000 francs for the reconstruction of the city, which had been partially destroyed by Austrian troops nine years earlier.   RQ

57. Uniform of a divisional general, worn by Napoleon at Marengo, 1800

France
Wool, metal thread
Musée de l'Armée, Paris; inv. Ca 14

French and Austrian troops clashed in a gruelling twelve-hour battle at Marengo on 14 June 1800. By the late afternoon it was thought that the French had lost the battle, but

Napoleon launched a last counter-attack with reinforcements, which broke Austrian ranks and secured a French victory. His general's uniform worn at the battle was the blue of the Republic; it had been changed in 1793 from the traditional white of the French monarchy. The colours of the Republic also feature in the mariner's cuff which is faced with white and red. This colour scheme is echoed in the red collar. The collar, revers and cuffs are heavily embroidered in gold thread with oak leaf and acorn motifs, as an indication of rank. The buttons are reproductions.   AM

58. Briefcase, c. 1799–1804
Leather and brass
Musée de l'Armée, Paris; inv. Cc 80

Leather travel briefcase decorated with gold tooling and lettering: '*Premier Consul*'. This lockable briefcase was used by Agathon-Jean-François Fain, a close associate of Napoleon's, who later became his secretary. On 12 December 1799 Napoleon was nominated as First Consul, with Jean-Jacques

Cambacérès and Charles Lebrun as Second and Third Consuls, with advisory powers, intended in theory to provide some balance of power. Napoleon's powers were increased after August 1802, when he was made First Consul for life, and again on 2 December 1804 when he was crowned as Emperor of the French.   RP

59. *The Corsican Crocodile dissolving the Council of Frogs!!!*

Anonymous
Published November 1799 by W. Holland
Hand-coloured etching
255 x 346mm
British Museum, London; 1868-8-8-12565

This print satirizes the clearing of the legislative Council of Five Hundred by Napoleon's grenadiers during the *brumaire* coup that bought him to power. As Napoleon storms the building, the deputies, represented by frogs, many still sporting *bonnets rouges* and revolutionary cockades, hurl themselves through the windows to escape. However, one brave frog, representing Napoleon's Corsican compatriot Barthélemy Aréna, attempts to play the role of Brutus, and makes futile attempts to stab the scaly would-be dictator, who already wears a crown. It is probable that the stabbing incident was invented by apologists for the coup. The depiction of Napoleon as a crocodile is an allusion to his recent return from Egypt, the overwhelming power of military force, and possibly his hypocrisy. However, the portrayal of Napoleon leading the other crocodiles is misleading. The troops who intervened were rallied by his brother Lucien after Napoleon's attempts to address the Council were drowned out by neo-Jacobin deputies calling for him to be outlawed. This use of force destroyed any pretence that the coup was constitutionally legal. The depiction of a bespectacled frog presiding over the Council is also inaccurate. The president on the day of the coup was Lucien Bonaparte, whose initiative on his brother's behalf left the Council without a chairman, causing chaos and paralysis at a decisive moment. The incident did not happen on *18 brumaire*/9 November, the date given on the caption, but the following day at Saint-Cloud. SB

61. Decree of the French Republic, *département du Rhône*, November 1799

Printed sheet, published in Lyon
Pierre-Jean Chalençon, private collection

Napoleon returned to France from Egypt in October 1799 to discover the Directory in chaos. Sieyès had recognized that the situation was untenable and had begun plotting both a regime change and the revision of the constitution but he needed the support of a reliable general to aid him in his

60. Bicorn hat, worn by Napoleon, 1799

France
Musée de l'Armée, Paris

In the early nineteenth century the painter Jacques-Louis David designed the official costumes worn by both the Directory and Consulate governments. The designs drew heavily on the imagery of ancient Rome and included white togas and sashes of office. Unusually, the black bicorn hat of beaver felt, worn by Napoleon as First Consul, was firmly within the lines of contemporary fashion. AM

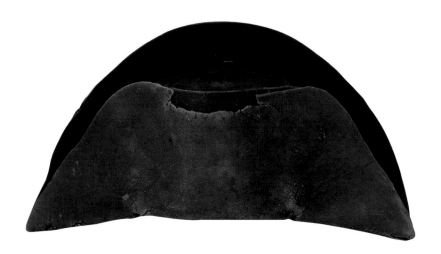

attempts to mount a coup. Napoleon's return placed him in the right place at the right time, his position further strengthened as his brother Lucien was president of the Council of Five Hundred, the lower house of the legislature. The coup took place on 9 and 10 November 1799, *18 brumaire* according to the Revolutionary calendar. Sieyès and Duclos resigned as directors and Barras was persuaded to do the same. As the executive needed at least three members to function, the government was therefore effectively frozen. The upper house, the Council of the Ancients, then agreed that the government should be moved out of Paris to Saint-Cloud, to avoid civil disturbances, and despite initial opposition by the Council of Five Hundred, Bonaparte, Sieyès and Duclos were named as provisional consuls. Bonaparte, as First Consul, had effectively seized power.

This decree announces the decisions taken by the Council of the Ancients and the Council of Five Hundred, and also contains reassurances from Bonaparte to the army and to the national guard. CLW

LITERATURE: William Doyle, *The French Revolution: A Very Short Introduction* (Oxford, 2001); Ellis, *Napoleon*; Frank McLynn, *Napoleon: A Biography* (London, 1998).

62. Ceremonial sword, 1804

Jacques-Louis David (1748–1825) and N. N. Boutet (1761–1833)
Gilt metal, silver, bronze, ebony, velvet and steel
Pierre-Jean Chalençon, private collection

A special workshop was established at Versailles for the manufacture of presentation weapons under the directorship of Nicolas-Noël Boutet. Designed by the French artist Jacques-Louis David, this sword was used by the Chief Heralds to proclaim Napoleon Emperor of the French at his coronation on 2 December 1804. LV

63. Coronation of the Emperor Napoleon I, *c.* 1808

Jacques-Louis David (1748–1825)
Oil on canvas
275 x 425mm
Signed bottom left, *David faciebat*
Louvre, Paris; R. F. 2510

David's huge painting representing the coronation of Napoleon and Josephine in Notre-Dame Cathedral was triumphantly received at the 1808 Salon in Paris. This little sketch might not be a preparatory study for the monumental

work but could have been executed by David as a model for the replica at Versailles. The act officially proclaiming Napoleon as Emperor was made on 18 May 1804. The day before the coronation the Pope had married Napoleon and Josephine in the Chapel of the Tuileries. In this sketch we see Notre-Dame, richly decorated with velvet fabric featuring golden bees – the emblem chosen to replace the royal fleur-de-lis (being of a similar size and conveniently representing collective work and obedience to the sovereign). Members of the imperial family are recognizable, including Madame Laetitia, Napoleon's mother. In fact, she was in Rome on the day of the ceremony but Napoleon wanted her included in this family picture. The sketch captures the moment when Napoleon, having crowned himself, turns his back on the Pope to crown Josephine who kneels before him. She is dressed in a gown and long train that her envious sisters-in-law hold with visible repugnance. GQ

64. *The Grand Coronation Procession of NAPOLEONE the 1st Emperor of France, from the Church of Notre-Dame, Decr 2d 1804*

James Gillray, published 1 January 1805
Hand-coloured engraving
249 x 778mm
British Museum, London; 1868-8-8-7312

Published on New Year's Day 1805, this is a brilliantly savage lampoon against the excesses and hypocrisies of the coronation of Napoleon as Emperor on 2 December 1804, which would be officially commemorated in Jacques-Louis David's monumental painting of the subject completed in 1807. In a densely complex and inventive composition, Gillray depicts the event in the form of a panorama, pointing it up as spectacular, hyperbolic theatre. Leading the procession on the far right is a mincing Louis Bonaparte, termed 'High Constable of the Empire', followed by the 'Three Imperial Graces', the Princesses Borghese, posed in an overt parody of Canova's celebrated contemporary sculpture made for Pauline Borghese. At the centre is the bathetically diminutive figure of Napoleon, engulfed in his too-large robes, next to a gross Josephine. They follow Talleyrand, who carries Bonaparte's family tree (surely a gesture on Gillray's part back to the bogus family tree of Lord Squanderfield in Hogarth's *Marriage-A-la-Mode*), and the Pope, summoned from Rome to conduct the ceremony. He looks back over his shoulder in alarm and apprehension. Beside him, tellingly, is the devil in disguise. Gillray here summons all his artistic and satirical genius on behalf of the British anti-Napoleonic position, to deride the apparent pretensions and delusions of Napoleon's claims to imperial authority. GQ

65. **Symphony no. 3, 'Eroica',**
    op. 55, E Flat; composed 1803,
    first performed 1805

Ludwig van Beethoven (1770–1827)

Autograph manuscript

Gesellschaft der Musikfreunde, Vienna; Archiv,
no. 61.407

The 'Eroica' – written during a brief period of rapproche-
ment between Austria and France in 1803 – was originally
entitled 'Bonaparte'. The work was conceived in homage to
Napoleon, after he had brought a degree of order to
Europe. Through the symphony, Beethoven also gave
expression to his vision of a peaceful alliance between
Austria and France and probably hoped to cultivate an
audience for a projected visit to Paris. However, relations
between the two countries degenerated during 1804. It
was when the First Consul proclaimed himself Emperor
that the disillusioned Beethoven erased the words 'Intitulata
Bonaparte'. On its publication in 1806, the symphony was
finally entitled 'heroic symphony', with the subtitle '*composta
per festiggiare il sovvenire di un grand Uomo*' (composed to
celebrate the memory of a great man). This possibly was an

allusion to Prince Louis Ferdinand of Prussia, who had died
a heroic death that year. One of the most influential
symphonies ever composed, Napoleonic connections in the
'Eroica' can be seen in the epic, battle-like opening movement, the French Revolutionary celebrations echoing in the
funeral march, the soldier's song quoted in the scherzo and
in references to the ballet *The Creatures of Prometheus*.   HH

66. **Cushion, 1804**

France

Silk velvet, gold thread

Pierre-Jean Chalençon, private collection

Much of the visual imagery at Napoleon's coronation
evoked the *ancien régime* of pre-Revolutionary France, in
part to foster a sense of legitimacy. At his coronation
Napoleon carried the Hand of Justice, Charlemagne's
sceptre, traditionally associated with Bourbon ceremonies.
The silk velvet cushion used at his coronation features a
heavily embroidered golden bee at the centre. Adopted by
Napoleon as a badge, the bee had been traditionally linked

to the sovereigns of France and was considered one of the oldest heraldic emblems associated with a royal house as its use on a coat of arms dates to the fifth-century reign of Clovis. As a symbol it represents resurrection and immortality.   AM

67.   *The Emperor arriving at Notre-Dame*
      Charles Percier, published 1807
      Hand-coloured engraving
      640 x 490mm
      Pierre-Jean Chalençon, private collection

This engraving, from a book describing the coronation of Napoleon and Josephine on Sunday 2 December 1804, conveys something of the magnificence of that day. Charles Percier and Pierre-François-Léonard Fontaine had worked together as designers since the 1790s, first collaborating on

the design of scenery for the Opéra in Paris. Together, they were to contribute to the development of the Empire style, a reinterpretation of classicism for which the late eighteenth and early nineteenth centuries are known. The pair, as the Emperor's architects, were responsible for decorating Paris for the coronation. Buildings were demolished around the Cathedral Church of Notre-Dame, an annexe attached to its west front and a covered way erected along its south side. Inside, the choir screen and two altars were removed and the church was bedecked with rich swathes of luxurious textiles (the ancient French royal symbol of the bee, the imperial and military symbol of the eagle and Napoleon's

initial 'N' all much in evidence). The coronation in 1804 is thought to have cost about £250,000, in today's money nearly £12 million. Fragments of the original decorations from the ceremony can still be seen in the Musée de l'Armée, Paris.

This set of engravings originally belonged to Napoleon and was given by him to his Foreign Minister, Talleyrand.

CLW

LITERATURE: Thompson, *Napoleon Bonaparte*; Percier and Fontaine, *Description des cérémonies et des fêtes* . . .

The Battle of the Nile and its Cultural Aftermath

HOLGER HOOCK

IN EARLY 1798, France, her allies and satellites dominated Spain, northern Italy and the Netherlands. After Prussia and Austria had concluded peace with France, only Britain, with the lukewarm support of Portugal, was still fighting the Republic. Strategic attention in both France and Britain was on the Mediterranean. Napoleon decided to postpone the invasion of Britain and – always searching for new theatres in which to fight for more glory – proposed an eastern expedition instead. The Directory's Foreign Minister Talleyrand, who saw colonial wealth as a key to French economic growth, supported Napoleon's scheme. The Directory agreed, mainly in order to remove the hero of Italy from France before he could mount a political challenge to them. Napoleon was consequently given command of an expeditionary force – thirteen ships of the line, a number of frigates, a nearly 31,000-strong army and a supply convoy consisting of some 280 vessels. Its mission – initially unknown to the British – was to conquer Egypt, drive the British from all possessions it could reach, secure exclusive use of the Red Sea and prepare the way for a possible later advance to India.

The British government was aware of an impending French expedition but lacked adequate information as to its destination. At first only Henry Dundas, Secretary for War, took intelligence pointing to the Levant seriously. In late April 1798, Nelson rejoined St Vincent off Cadiz who detached him with three ships of the line and three frigates to watch Toulon. When the government decided to restation a fleet in the Mediterranean, primarily to give Britain access to the southern flank of France, protect the friendly Kingdom of Naples and Sicily, and fulfil Austria's demand for the renewal of an anti-French coalition, St Vincent detached part of his newly reinforced fleet to join Nelson. The latter now had a task force – twelve ships of the line, three frigates but no supply organization – to find and destroy the French fleet, which many still suspected to be heading for Sicily or Malta.

The Battle of the Nile, fought after a two-month chase on 1 August 1798, was one of the most complete victories in the Age of Sail and the beginning of the end of French dreams of empire in the East. 'Nelson of the Nile' was fêted across Britain as well as continental Europe. The battle was instantly presented as a visual spectacle in London theatres and exhibitions. British naval and subsequent military superiority over Napoleon's Egyptian forces also secured outstanding archaeological trophies for the British.

HOURS AFTER Napoleon had sailed with part of his expeditionary force from Toulon on 19 May (the other ports of embarkation were Marseilles, Genoa, Civitavecchia and Ajaccio) Nelson, who had taken up position to intercept ships bound into Toulon and Marseilles, was fighting a storm just north of Cape Sicie. His flagship – the two-decker, 74-gun ship of the line *Vanguard* – was severely damaged, and when the squadron dispersed Nelson lost his reconnaissance screen of frigates. One of Nelson's greatest problems throughout the following two months would be how to gather reliable, up-to-date intelligence of the enemy's movements from diplomats, intercepted ships at sea, and in ports (cat. no. 75).

The Nile campaign raises some of naval history's greatest 'what-ifs?'. If Nelson had retained his frigates; if he had used some of his thirteen 74-gun ships as frigates to restore his reconnaissance screen; if intelligence received from intercepted ships had been more accurate; if the information that Sir William Hamilton, British Ambassador at Naples, received about Napoleon's Egyptian destination had reached him; or if Nelson – who apparently knew from mid-July that Napoleon's ultimate destination was Egypt – had waited for one more day when he first arrived off Alexandria at the end of July, he might have fought Napoleon at sea, possibly ended his enemy's career and saved Europe from another two decades of war.

The two months spent searching the Mediterranean were among of the most anxious periods in Nelson's professional career. Having twice missed the enemy very narrowly – once near Malta, once off Egypt – Nelson finally sighted the French fleet on 1 August in Aboukir Bay, at the mouth of the Nile.

Bonaparte had arrived off Alexandria within a day of Nelson's departure on 30 June, taken the city by 3 July, spectacularly defeated an army of Mamelukes, Bedouin and Fellahin at the

Prayer at Sea. Nelson at a service of thanksgiving on *Vanguard* after the Battle of the Nile. National Maritime Museum, London; PAD3879.

Battle of the Pyramids on 21 July, entered Cairo the following day and effectively secured the country. Much seemed at stake. Napoleon hoped, and parts of the British government feared, that a successful Egyptian expedition might threaten British lines of communication and trade with India, and might compensate the French for the recent loss to the British of their Caribbean empire and the Cape of Good Hope.

Conscious of the need for fleet protection for troops on land, though without much caring what happened to the fleet, Napoleon had first ordered the French ships into Alexandria's Old Port. When Vice-Admiral F. P. de Brueys protested that the port could be blocked by a single enemy ship, Napoleon permitted the French fleet to move into Aboukir Bay. There it anchored in a supposedly secure position, in a long crescent in the sandy bay, stretching south from the shallows just inside the fortified Aboukir Island. The ships were lying at single anchor, mostly without springs. The spring was a cable attached from the stern of the ship to the main anchor cable, which was let out from the bows. Hauling on the spring would turn the ship round, allowing the broadside to be aimed in different directions. The French were therefore more vulnerable to attack.

With his squadron spread over some ten miles and the French fleet nine miles away at the first sighting, around 2.30 in the afternoon of 1 August, Nelson decided on immediate attack. He was thus taking advantage of a favourable wind and the lower risk of friendly fire in a battle fought inshore, albeit in shoal water, expecting the better trained British fleet to have even more of an edge over their opponents. At 5.30 p.m. Nelson signalled to form line of battle 'as convenient' and to concentrate attack on the French van and centre, though he was unaware that the French van ships were short of their complement of troops.

Brueys had not taken sufficient care to position the ships at the head of his line close enough to the shoals. The leading British ship, the *Goliath*, Captain Foley, daringly edged between the shore and the front of the first French ship, the *Guerrier*. Foley most probably acted on his own initiative rather than on a preconceived tactical plan, but Nelson's captains knew they would be supported if they exploited a weakness in the enemy's position. As Nelson wrote to Lord Howe in January 1799, 'I had the happiness to command a Band of Brothers; therefore, night was to my advantage. Each knew his duty, and I was sure each would feel for a French ship'.[1]

The French had not even cleared for action on the shoreward side and five French ships surrendered within less than three hours. With Nelson taking the *Vanguard* on the outside of the line, British ships then 'doubled' the enemy and worked down the line to *L'Orient*.

Contemporary and historical written accounts as well as visual representations of the battle have always focused on the following several key moments. Nelson was wounded on the quarter-deck of the *Vanguard* at around 8.30 p.m. by a piece of flying debris, and morbidly assumed his imminent death when a flap of skin, torn from his forehead, fell over his one good eye and blinded him temporarily. Below deck, the surgeon saw to the

Extirpation of the Plagues of Egypt; — Destruction of Revolutionary Crocodiles; — or — The British Hero cleansing ye Mouth of ye Nile, by James Gillray (cat. no. 87).

7- or 8-centimetre wound, Nelson dictated a letter to the Admiralty, asked the chaplain to convey his last remembrance to his wife and was then left to rest. He was back on deck to witness the battle's climactic moment, the explosion of the 120-gun, three-decker French flagship *L'Orient*. The *Alexander*'s raking shots had started a fire in *L'Orient*'s stern cabin which was soon out of control and burned so brightly that it could be seen twelve miles away in the tower of Rosetta. British and French ships around *L'Orient* tried to move away, others took precautions by closing ports and hatches, removing cartridges from their upper decks, wetting sails and organizing bucket brigades. Contemporary accounts stress how Nelson, in a stereotypical display of humane British conduct in war, 'forgetting his own suffering' and 'impelled by the purest humanity', ordered the *Vanguard*'s last remaining boat to save as many lives as possible.[2] Between 9.37 p.m. and 11.30 p.m., but probably much closer to the later time, the flames reached *L'Orient*'s magazines and blew up the huge ship in an explosion which could be seen nine miles away by the French army staff at Alexandria, and stunned both fleets into suspending their action for several minutes.

By dawn it was apparent that British victory was almost total. Although the French fleet had been superior in numbers of guns and men, the British had destroyed, immobilized or captured eleven French ships of the line with the loss of some 1700 French officers and sailors and 1500 wounded, compared to 218 British killed and 678 wounded, with losses more severe on ships which had attacked the outside of the French line. Some 3300 French prisoners were taken on board the prizes. The French Admiral Villeneuve escaped with four ships, including two ships of the line, in the direction of Malta. In the attempt to shift blame on to others, Napoleon later criticized Villeneuve for failing to move up to the head of line in the earlier stages of the battle, and for being indecisive about an early retreat which could have salvaged several more ships. As it was, all four escaping ships later fell into British hands.

With clearing-up operations still continuing, on 2 August Nelson issued several memoranda to the fleet. He first promoted his image as a Christian hero by announcing his intention to return public thanksgiving to God for having 'blessed His Majesty's Arms with victory'. That afternoon, a service was performed on the quarter-deck of the *Vanguard* and on other ships of the fleet at similar times, in those days a highly unusual public display of religion in a battle fleet. Later in the afternoon of 2 August, Nelson wrote to his captains that '[i]t must strike forcibly every British Seaman, how superior their conduct is, when in discipline and good order, to the riotous behaviour of lawless Frenchmen.'[3] Sermons preached at thanksgiving services around Britain during the weeks following the reception of the news echoed Nelson in interpreting total British victory as divine punishment of an oppressive enemy. The victory at the Nile, delivered by a wise king and good government under divine protection, was seen to have defended British liberties, religion and the monarchy against French atheism and regicidal republicanism (cat. no. 87).

CONQUEST AND COLLECTING

DESPITE WIDESPREAD celebration in Britain of the battle and its heroes, there was some partisan debate about the strategic significance of the Nile victory. For loyalists it facilitated the renewal of a Europe-wide anti-French coalition and possibly spelled the end of the French Revolution itself. For the opposition the victory ought to have ended the campaign and war altogether. In the short term, Nelson's victory promised to isolate Napoleon and hand Britain control of the Mediterranean. Yet, after the only partial success of his Egyptian and Syrian campaigns, Napoleon abandoned his shrinking army and sailed for France in August 1799. Despite his retreat, which was characterized by many as desertion, and in the face of news circulating about atrocities he had committed during the Syrian campaign, Napoleon had sufficient support in France to carry off the coup of *18 brumaire an VII* (9–10 November 1799) and become First Consul (cat. nos 53, 59 and 56).

After the Royal Navy had repeatedly thwarted French attempts to reinforce their troops bottled up in Egypt, a British army strike force of 15,000 troops under General Sir Ralph Abercromby was dispatched in 1801 to conquer Egypt and thereby to remove the French threat to India and hand the British a bargaining counter in forthcoming peace negotiations. But in the Peace of Amiens (March 1802), Britain negotiated away not only most of her recent conquests in the West Indies and the Cape, but also Malta, Minorca and Egypt itself. Napoleon, but not the British government, was aware of the French surrender in Egypt when the Preliminaries were signed on 1 October 1802; Britain, however, needed a breathing space and the government had to sign a peace after news of an imminent victory, yet before news of the victory itself arrived (the following day), otherwise parliamentary and public opinion would have demanded better terms.

FOR BOTH the French and the British, the Egyptian campaign had cultural as well as strategic repercussions. Napoleon's Egyptian expedition was one of scientific exploration and collecting as well as one of conquest. His army was accompanied by a 167-strong Commission on the Sciences and Arts. Under the leadership of Dominique-Vivant Denon, an artist, diplomat, Egyptologist and later museum director, they established the Egyptian Institute on the outskirts of Cairo complete with a printing press, library, observatory, laboratories, aviary, zoological garden and museums of natural history and antiquities.

Napoleon used the Institute for an Enlightenment project: to map the Egyptian world, both past and present, and as a brains trust to advise on administrative matters. The savants' labour was later published in the monumental *Description de l'Égypte*.

The defeat of the French fleet and army between 1798 and 1801 led to the surrender to the British expeditionary force of all the antiquities collected by Napoleon's savants (cat. no. 131). Upon their arrival in England in 1802 these trophies formed the basis of the British Museum's first sculpture collection. They included the famous Rosetta Stone which led to the deciphering of hieroglyphs (cat. no. 129). While lying in temporary accommodation at the Museum, the monuments were described and reproduced in magazines. In the House of Commons the foundation of the British Museum's Egyptian collection was discussed as entailing the acquisition of 'memorable Trophies of National Glory' 'by His Majesty's victorious Arms'.[4] After British cultural and political figures had seen Napoleon's new antique galleries in Paris during 1802–3, the Department of Antiquities was founded at the British Museum in 1803. In 1808, the Navy helped install what were the first large Egyptian sculptures to be acquired by the British Museum in their purpose-built gallery. Thus was started the first of many antique galleries charting the progress of civilization from primitive to the ideal of Greek art in the form of the Parthenon, or Elgin, Marbles. It is worth noting that the surrender of Cairo by the French to the British in 1801 also led directly to Lord Elgin obtaining the Ottoman firman (an official permit) which allowed him to work on the Parthenon site in Athens and eventually resulted in the acquisition of what became known as the Elgin Marbles by the British Museum.

Egypt continued to occupy both military strategists and the builders of national collections. The British prevented Napoleon from regaining a foothold in Egypt: they retained Malta in defiance of the Peace of Amiens, risking renewed war, and they reoccupied Alexandria in 1807 when the Turks aligned with France. Pharaonic antiquity had not been the highest priority of the Napoleonic expedition itself, but the surrender of the monuments, subsequent competition of antique displays between Paris and London and the opening up of Egypt to diplomatic missions sustained Anglo-French scrambling for Egyptian antiquities well into the 1820s. Nelson and Abercromby had conclusively won the war over Napoleon's forces in Egypt, but the war by cultural means, which they had helped trigger, continued well beyond the departure of their forces.

'NELSON OF THE NILE'

THE BATTLE OF THE NILE immediately and definitively established Nelson's reputation as Britain's pre-eminent naval hero. Some contemporary debate over the wider strategic significance of the battle notwithstanding, his astonishing victory earned Nelson a barony, the respect and gratitude of allied nations, and the adulation of the British public.

While news of the victory was spreading across Europe in the autumn of 1798, Nelson was being fêted in Naples. By defeating the 'regicide Fleet', the Queen of the Two Sicilies wrote, Nelson had 'raised in the Italians an enthusiastic reverence for the English nation'. 'All here are frantic with excess of joy.'5 In Naples, Nelson began to appreciate the charms of Lady Hamilton, who jocosely created him 'Marquis Nile, Earl Alexandria, Viscount Pyramid, Baron Crocodile'. Infatuated with Emma, and his vanity and egotism indulged by the Neapolitan court, Nelson interfered in the military-political affairs of that kingdom. As an admiral promoted solely on professional ability, but lacking a broad education and adequate political and strategic awareness, Nelson allowed himself to be manipulated into supporting the Queen's aggressive foreign policy, which was aimed at provoking a French attack, forcing Austria into war and thus eventually at overthrowing the French republicans who had murdered her sister Marie-Antoinette. Leghorn surrendered to Nelson's ships in November 1798. Yet, before the end of the year the French counterattack had forced the evacuation of the Neapolitan court to Palermo: a French satellite republic was established in Naples. Over the following months, Nelson first disobeyed orders by staying with King Ferdinand instead of taking a substantial part of his force to protect Minorca, and then helped restore the monarchy at Naples, in the process involving himself in the persecution of Neapolitan rebels (cat. no. 113).

After this stressful period, which ever since has left a stain on Nelson's name, in mid-1800 Nelson and the Hamiltons left Naples. During a four-month triumphal progress across Europe – which took in Trieste, Laibach (modern Ljubljana, Slovenia), Vienna (cat. no. 101), Prague, Dresden, Magdeburg and Hamburg – the Hero of the Nile was greeted everywhere by illuminations, concerts and dinners. Wherever he went, Nelson had his portrait painted: he sat for artists in Naples, Vienna and Dresden, and for at least seven portraits during his few weeks of leave in England before his departure for the Baltic campaign in 1800–01. Two very different types of portrait emerged of Nelson in this period: the swashbuckling, conquering hero (cat. no. 102) and the emaciated, battered, haunted Nelson, sick in body as well as guilt-ridden after his Sicilian adventures and with Emma (cat. no. 100).

By the time he arrived in Britain – on the *King George* packet rather than on a British frigate – to a hero's welcome, first in Great Yarmouth, where he landed on 6 November 1800, and then in London, Nelson and the Nile had been celebrated and commemorated for more than two years. News of Nelson's victory had been confirmed on 2 October 1798, when Captain Capel brought Nelson's letter to the Admiralty at 11.15 a.m. By the evening the news had spread all over the capital. Spontaneous fireworks and illuminations in London were echoed by local celebrations across the country. *The Times* on 3 and 4 October pronounced that 'all ranks of people seemed to participate in the glorious news' of a victory which was 'unexampled in its kind'. Nelson's victory dispatch with the line of battle and return of casualties was printed in the *London Gazette Extraordinary* and soon reprinted in national and local newspapers, magazines and special publications.

Partly due to the lack of specific information, after the first few days the press gave more space to how Nelson was being celebrated and honoured, both across Europe and by his own country, than to the battle itself. Nelson received honours and presents not only from the King of the Two Sicilies, including the Dukedom of Bronte, but also from the King of Sardinia, the island of Zante, the city of Palermo and the Tsar. The Sultan of Turkey, Selim III, presented him with a variety of precious objects, including the *chelengk*, an aigrette or ornament of Brazilian diamonds with a central star, taken from the Sultan's turban, which turned on its centre by means of a clockwork mechanism. In Britain, Nelson received the thanks of both Houses of Parliament as well as a pension of £2000 a year, with the Irish Parliament granting a further £1000. Nelson was raised to the British peerage as Baron Nelson of the Nile and Burnham Thorpe, his Norfolk birthplace, and adopted the motto '*Palmam qui meruit ferat*' (Let he who has earned it bear the Palm). He received a king's naval medal in gold, a sword from the City of London in a ceremony on Lord Mayor's Day, the freedom of many other cities, as well as gifts in money and plate from the East India Company, the Levant Company and Lloyd's.

Biographical sketches of the decorated hero began to be published in magazines, some apparently drawing on information solicited from Lady Nelson. The *Naval Chronicle* in 1799–1800 printed a 'Biographical Memoir', partly based on an autobiographical sketch procured from Nelson. It promoted the image of the dashing warrior hero who, with superhuman strength, wrote letters moments after receiving hideous wounds. The memoir equally emphasized Nelson's piety and the more reflective aspects of his character.

The Battle of the Nile, by Philippe-Jacques de Loutherbourg, 1800 (cat. no. 77).

RE-ENACTING THE BATTLE

WITHIN WEEKS of the news of Nelson's victory at the Nile arriving in London on 2 October 1798, commemorative pottery was being mass-produced, decorated with portraits, ships, plans and scenes of the battle, trophies such as cannon or flags, coats of arms, or symbolic items such as crocodiles, and often also carrying Nelson's name and a short motto or piece of verse. Moreover, cultural entrepreneurs began to exploit the battle as popular entertainment. As the *Monthly Mirror*'s theatrical column noted in 1799, the public seemed to demand that every naval event 'receive due honour from the conductors of our theatrical amusements'.[6] In October 1798, the French invasion of Egypt and the Battle of the Nile were the subject of dramatic

entertainments at Astley's Amphitheatre, the Royal Circus and the Royal Covent Garden Theatre. Versions of the battle ran for another year and dominated the 1799 exhibition season. Like many official and personal accounts of the battle, as well as poems and sonatas for pianoforte, most of the visual spectacles prompted by the Nile focused on the explosion of *L'Orient*: several of the paintings at the summer exhibition of the Royal Academy of Arts at Somerset House; William Turner's private, commercial show of *The Battle of the Nile by Fire Light* at the Historic Gallery; the Naumachia, the first panoramic show on the Battle of the Nile which offered pictures under the title 'BLOWING UP OF L'ORIENT'; Barker's 360-degree panorama in Leicester Square; and, one year on, in spring 1800, Royal Academician Philippe-Jacques de Loutherbourg's spectacular *The Battle of the Nile* (cat. no. 77). In reviews of these shows, appearing in London, provincial English newspapers and international magazines, as well as in poems and dramatic entertainment, contemporary writers compared the explosion of *L'Orient* to natural disasters such as volcanic eruptions and earthquakes, shaking 'air, earth, and sea', making the tower of Rosetta, the pyramids and Cairo's mosques tremble, and the 'wild Arabs leap from their couch'.[7]

REMEMBERING THE NILE

THE BATTLE OF THE NILE also produced more durable material culture and prompted official acts of commemoration. Sailing into battle Nelson had allegedly pronounced: 'Before this time tomorrow, I shall have gained a Peerage or Westminster Abbey.' Surviving the night, he did indeed gain a peerage; he was also famously presented by Captain Hallowell of the *Swiftsure* with a coffin made from a chunk of *L'Orient*'s mainmast, which had landed on board his ship during the massive explosion: 'that when you are tired of this Life you may be buried in one of your own Trophies'.[8]

Nelson later visited a monument to Captain Westcott of the *Majestic*, the highest ranking casualty of the Battle of the Nile, in Westcott's birthplace of Honiton, Devon, where he handed his own Nile medal to Westcott's widow (cat. no. 81). Nelson also saw the 'naval' temple on the Kymin above Monmouth, built by locals after the Battle of the Nile to commemorate Britain's recent naval victories. Nelson himself asked that John Flaxman (1755–1826) be commissioned to execute a monument of his former flag-captain Captain Miller of the *Theseus*, who had been wounded at the Nile and died during the accidental explosion of some shells on board his ship during the defence of Acre, Syria, in 1799. It is not known whether Nelson was aware of a Nile pyramid commissioned in 1801 by Charles Herbert, Earl Manvers, a naval captain and heir to the estate of Thoresby Hall,

Davison's Nile medal, reverse (cat. no. 81).

near Mansfield, Nottinghamshire. The pyramid, on a 28ft-square base (8.5m) with a Georgian porch, carried an inscription based on the defeat of Pharaoh's host and chariot in Exodus. It was surrounded by the Union Plantation: clumps of trees named after naval captains or ships. In 1806, Nelson was indeed buried in the coffin from *L'Orient*, though not in Westminster Abbey but in St Paul's Cathedral, the nation's new naval and military pantheon, where Captains Westcott and Miller already had their monuments. On Flaxman's Nelson monument in St Paul's, as in Nelson monuments from Liverpool to Montreal, the Nile features as one of the key battles which made Nelson's reputation and redefined the naval balance during Britain's epic struggle with Revolutionary and Napoleonic France.

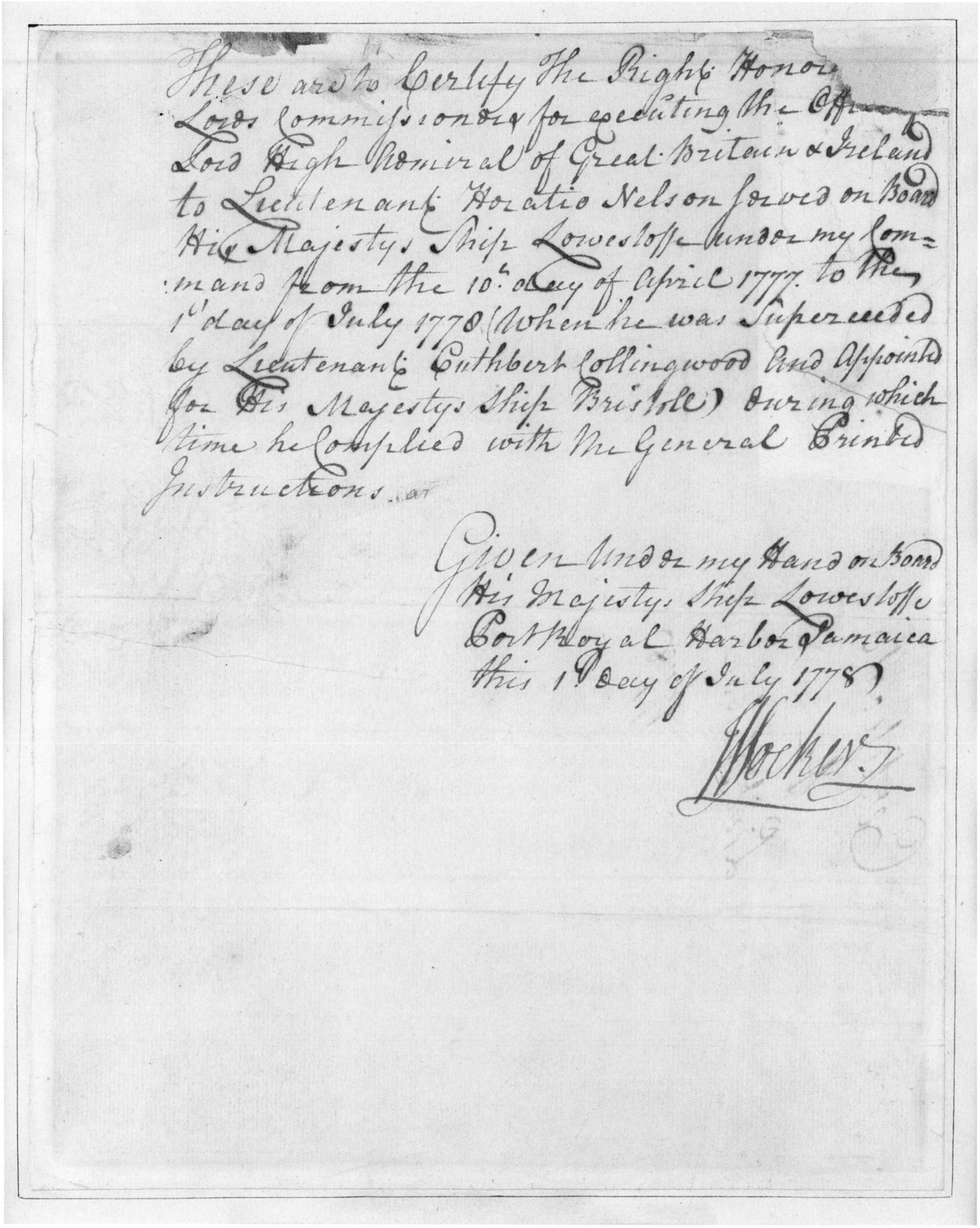

These are to Certify the Right Hono[r]
Lords Commissioners for executing the Offi[ce]
Lord High Admiral of Great Britain & Ireland
to Lieutenant Horatio Nelson served on Board
His Majestys Ship Lowestoffe under my Com=
=mand from the 10th day of April 1777 to the
1st day of July 1778 (When he was Superseeded
by Lieutenant Cuthbert Collingwood And Appointed
for His Majestys Ship Bristoll) during which
time he Complied with the General Printed
Instructions

Given Under my Hand on Board
His Majestys Ship Lowestoffe
Port Royal Harbor Jamaica
this 1st Day of July 1778

Locker

68. Document certifying to the good conduct of Lieutenant Nelson, 1778

Ink on paper
Lloyd's of London (Nelson Collection)

The *Lowestoffe*, which Nelson joined in 1777, was his first appointment as a lieutenant. She served in the Caribbean, where Britain's wealthy sugar-producing islands were constantly in danger of attack from American privateers. Nelson saw plenty of action on this cruise: the *Lowestoffe* chased and captured an American privateer, which Nelson volunteered to board and take to Jamaica as a prize. A further experience of command came when the *Lowestoffe* captured a small schooner and Captain Locker gave the command of it to Nelson. In 1778 Nelson was transferred to the *Bristol* under Sir Peter Parker, which was the occasion for this letter of recommendation. William Locker was a friend of Captain Maurice Suckling, Nelson's uncle.　　DK

69. Captain Horatio Nelson

John Francis Rigaud (1742–1810)
Oil on canvas
120 x 1015mm
Signed and dated 1781
National Maritime Museum, London (Caird Collection
　　presented in 1948, from the collection of Earl
　　Nelson); BHC2901
See page 150

A native of Turin, Rigaud trained in Italy and came from Rome to London with James Barry in 1771. Begun in 1777, when Nelson was a lieutenant, but not finished until 1781, the portrait is one of a group of three painted for William Locker of officers who had served under him, the other two being Captain Pole and Captain Peacock. X-rays show the portrait began with Nelson more round-faced and his hat tucked under his arm. The background, possibly painted by Dominic Serres, is Fort Juan, Nicaragua, which Nelson helped to capture in 1780. The captain's barge in the background refers to his new rank.　　RQ

70. Book of Common Prayer, *c.* 1760–70

Printed book, leather-bound
Royal Naval Museum, Portsmouth; 91/267

This prayer book belonged originally to Captain William Locker. In August 1777, he presented it to his young friend and protégé Horatio Nelson, then serving as a lieutenant in Locker's frigate the *Lowestoffe*. Locker had been seriously ill and Nelson had looked after him, so it seems likely that the book was given as a token of gratitude. The date of the presentation on the flyleaf is in Nelson's right-handed writing.

Later, on 19 May 1799, Nelson presented the book to Emma Hamilton, as recorded by Emma herself on the flyleaf. Nelson was sailing that day from Palermo, expecting to meet the French fleet in battle. Emma wrote, 'God protect this great & Brave man.'　　CSW

71. French small-sword, *c.* 1789

Gilt brass, wood, copper wire and steel
Inscribed on blade: obverse: VIVRE. LIBRE. OU.
　　MOURIR. POUR. LA. LOI. & LE [ROI?] (last word
　　is defaced); reverse: VIGELANCIE
Museum of London; sword no. 7790

This sword was surrendered to Lord Nelson by Rear-Admiral Blanquet du Chayla after the capture of his flagship the *Franklin*, 80 guns, at Aboukir Bay. Du Chayla was made a scapegoat for the defeat at the Nile. Taken prisoner by

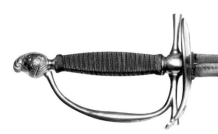

the British, he was exchanged at the Peace of Amiens and retired in disgrace in 1803. With the restoration of the

French monarchy, he was reinstated as a vice-admiral in 1816. Nelson sent the sword to the Lord Mayor of London, requesting that 'the City of London will honour me by the acceptance of it, as a remembrance that Britannia still rules the waves'.   LV

72. Letter from Napoleon to Admiral Ganteaume, 29 November 1798
Ink on paper
National Maritime Museum, London; COP/3A

This document (and the next) was intercepted by Nelson's ships and gave the British valuable information. In Egypt Napoleon was anxious to hear news of events in Europe. He therefore orders boats to be sent to the main possible areas of attack by the British: Corfu, Ancona and Toulon. Captains of the boats are to gather as much information as possible and pass it on to him at pre-arranged points he expected to reach with his army. Napoleon's great need of news is shown by the fact that captains who return with news are to be well rewarded. He is also concerned by the possible activities of Villeneuve, who had taken refuge in Malta after the Battle of the Nile. He thinks it possible that Villeneuve might be able to break the English blockade and land newspapers and other intelligence material at Damietta. This is an opportunity not to be missed, and Ganteaume is ordered

to intercept any such information lest it fall into English hands. The letter is signed 'Bonaparte'.   DK

73. Letter from Napoleon to Admiral Ganteaume regarding operations against the English fleet, 7 December 1798
Ink on paper
National Maritime Museum, London; COP/3B

Written to Ganteaume from Egypt, after Napoleon's defeat at the Battle of the Nile, this letter considers the blockade of Brest and possible tactics to deal with the situation. Napoleon has framed the letter as a series of questions, giving possible alternative scenarios and asking Ganteaume to give his opinion on the best solution. The questions mostly deal with the availability of ships and their battle capabilities.   DK

74. Sketch by Nelson of the Battle of the Nile, 1803
Ink on paper
British Library, London; Add. MS 18676

Nelson was often asked by admirers to demonstrate his battles. As the written inscription indicates, he made this

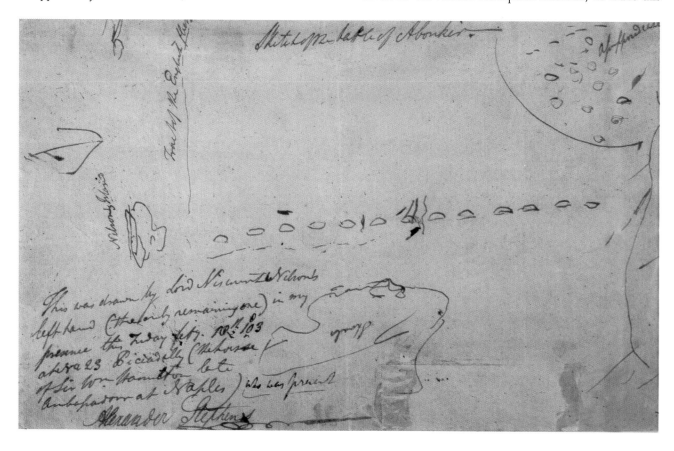

sketch of the Battle of the Nile (1 August 1798) for the author Alexander Stephens on 18 February 1803 at Sir William Hamilton's house in Piccadilly, London. Clearly, it was drawn to illustrate a verbal description – the explanatory notes were added later by Stephens.

In the centre of the diagram, Nelson shows the French fleet moored close to the shoals, with his own fleet approaching from the left around 'Nelson's Island'. The arrow on the extreme left indicates the wind direction. Dark lines show the positions of some of the key British ships, including Nelson's flagship the *Vanguard* (third from left). Vertical lines above the central French ship indicate the huge explosion that destroyed the French flagship *L'Orient* at the height of the battle.

Other rough sketches by Nelson have survived of the actions at St Vincent (14 February 1797) and Tenerife (25 July 1797) and also of his 1805 battle plan of Trafalgar (cat. no. 235).

CSW

75. Nelson's questions to his captains during the Nile campaign, 22 June 1798

Ink on paper. One quarto sheet

National Maritime Museum, London (Croker
    Collection); CRK/14

The Battle of the Nile, fought on 1 August 1798, was preceded by a long chase when Nelson and his squadron searched for Napoleon's large flotilla of troop-ships and warship escorts. At one point, on 22 June 1798, the two fleets passed within a few miles of each other.

The main reason why Nelson missed the French was that he had just received intelligence which suggested that they were already some days ahead of him, to the east.

He called a conference of 'those captains in whom I place great confidence' and these documents were written at that meeting, in the early morning of 22 June. In the first, Nelson outlines the information he has received and asks his colleagues what course they think the squadron should follow. The replies – from Captains Alexander Ball (*Alexander*), Edward Berry (*Vanguard*), Henry Darby (*Bellerophon*), James Saumerez (*Orion*) and Thomas Troubridge (*Culloden*) – agree that they should sail at once for Alexandria.

These documents demonstrate Nelson's collegiate style of leadership – he was prepared to involve his subordinates in decision-making, and made it clear that he valued their opinions.

CSW

LITERATURE: B. Lavery, *Nelson and the Nile: The Naval War
    against Bonaparte, 1798* (London, 1998).

76. Nelson's Public Order Book, 1798–99

Vellum-bound volume

British Library, London; Add. MS 30260

Nelson worked closely with his captains and used a number of methods to keep in regular touch with them. Whenever possible, he held briefings on board his flagship. For daily contact, he employed a 'Public Order Book', such as this one. His orders would be written in the book, sometimes in his own hand, sometimes by a secretary. Each ship in the fleet would then be ordered to send an officer to the flagship to make a copy of the order.

These were 'working' books, not formal documents, and only three examples have survived. This one covers the build-up to, and the aftermath of, the Battle of the Nile in 1798. The others cover the Battle of Copenhagen in April 1801 (State Archive, Copenhagen: D/173) and the Channel campaign of July–October 1801 (Admiralty Library, Royal Naval Museum: MS200).

The book is open at the page where Nelson describes the tactics he expects to use in the event of a battle. Note that he plans to divide his fleet into three divisions – this foreshadows his famous battle plan at Trafalgar seven years later. Note, too, that he has ordered the words 'The Destruction of the Enemys Armament is the Sole Object' to be emphasized. This highlights his aggressive spirit and single-minded search for decisive results in battle.

CSW

LITERATURE: White, *Nelson: The New Letters*.

77. *The Battle of the Nile, 1800*
   Philippe-Jacques de Loutherbourg (1740–1812)
   Oil on canvas
   1524 x 2140mm
   Provenance: purchased with assistance from the Friends
      of the Tate Gallery, 1971
   Tate, London; T01452

The Battle of the Nile in 1798 was Nelson's decisive victory over the French off the coast of Egypt and isolated Napoleon's army there. It secured British control of the Mediterranean and ensured the retaking of Malta from the French. The battle was fought at night in Aboukir Bay, near Alexandria, when Nelson found and attacked the anchored French fleet. The climax of the battle came when the French flagship of Admiral Brueys, *L'Orient*, exploded. This is the moment de Loutherbourg shows in the painting. The explosion killed most of the crew and caused sails and masts to fly into the air with considerable danger to the surrounding ships.

The exploding French ship on the central horizon dominates the scene. In a painting packed with dramatic effect, ships of the line stand out as dark silhouettes against the vivid orange glow lighting up the night. The drama is continued through brilliant white, yellow, orange, pink and red effects of the explosion as the smoke of battle rises into the sky. Using man's heroic struggle against the sea to enhance the conflict of the opposing fleets, de Loutherbourg's interpretation is in the Romantic tradition, depicting both the drama and nature of the event. The desperate exertions of the sailors shown in the foreground on the right emphasize human suffering.   GY

78. **Nelson's undress coat worn at the Battle of the Nile, 1798**
Wool, linen, brass, gold and silver alloy
National Maritime Museum, London (Greenwich
    Hospital Collection); UNI0022

A rear-admiral's undress wool coat. It is entirely lined with white linen, except for the collar, which is lined with silk twill, and the unlined right sleeve. A black silk loop secures the cuff of the right sleeve to the front buttons of the lapels. The back of the collar and shoulders are stained with pomatum (pomade) or pigtail grease. The 1795 regulations distinguished the ranks of flag officers by the number of stars on the epaulettes and the rows of gold lace on the sleeves. Rear-admirals had one silver star on each epaulette and one row of sleeve lace. In the course of the seven years between the Nile and Trafalgar, Nelson gained a little weight, noticeable in the cut of his uniforms.   BT & AM

79. *Nelson wounded at the Nile,*
    1 August 1798
    Attributed to Guy Head (d. 1800)
    Oil on canvas
    840 x 650mm
    National Maritime Museum, London (Greenwich
        Hospital Collection); BHC2903
    See page 80

At the Battle of the Nile, Nelson narrowly escaped death from a piece of langridge, rough metal fired as anti-personnel shot. It tore open his forehead leaving a large flap of skin hanging down over his (good) left eye. He was taken below to have it dressed and while this was being done was told that the French flagship *L'Orient* was on fire. In great pain and probably badly concussed, he went back on deck in time to see *L'Orient* explode, as shown here in the background. Despite its theatricality, this is an unusually intimate portrait which is thought to have belonged to Nelson and may thus be fairly accurate. The artist is possibly Guy Head, an English portraitist and copyist working in Naples at the time Nelson was recovering there after the battle and beginning his affair with Lady Hamilton. The hand-on-heart gesture may reflect her famous 'attitudes' or indicate that the portrait was painted for her as a love token to Nelson's order, or vice versa. Head also painted a formal portrait of Nelson for King Ferdinand of Naples (now in the National Portrait Gallery, London).   PvdM

the British ensign flying above the French. On the grip, in ovals surrounded with brilliants, are the arms of the City of London on the obverse and the arms of Nelson on the reverse. Nelson had written in reply to Sir William Anderson, from Palermo, 31 January 1799, 'I am truly sensible of your politeness, in desiring me to say what particular devices I should wish on the Sword which is to be presented to me by the City of London; but I beg to leave that to the better judgment of my Fellow-Citizens.'   LV

81. Davison's Nile Medal, awarded to Sir Edward Berry

Conrad Heinrich Küchler (*c.* 1740–1810) and Matthew
    Boulton (1728–1809)
Gold, 47mm diam.
Signed
National Maritime Museum, London; MED0971

Alexander Davison was appointed by Nelson as sole prize agent for the captured ships after the Battle of the Nile. He had this medal struck at Matthew Boulton's Birmingham mint and presented it to all who took part in the action – in gold to Nelson and his captains, in silver to lieutenants and warrant officers, in gilt metal to petty officers, and to seamen and marines in copper. This gold example was presented to Nelson's flag-captain, Sir Edward Berry (1768–1831).

Obverse: on a rock near the sea, Peace is standing holding in her right hand an olive branch and supporting with her left hand a medallion of Nelson, an anchor behind her.

80. City of London presentation sword presented to Nelson after the Battle of the Nile, 1798

J. Morisset (1738–1815) and R. Makepeace
    (1761–1827)
Gold, brilliants, enamel, steel and leather
Inscribed: ANDERSON MAYOR / A Common Council
    holden in the Chamber of / the GUILDHALL of the
    CITY of LONDON / on Tuesday the 16 Day of October
    1798 / RESOLVED UNANIMOUSLY / that a Sword of /
    the Value of / Two Hundred Guineas be presented to
    / REAR ADMIRAL LORD NELSON / OF THE NILE / by
    this Court as a testimony of the HIGH ESTEEM / they
    entertain of his Public Services / and of the eminent
    advantages he has / RENDERED HIS COUNTRY
Museum of London, sword no. 11952

The hilt is of chased and embossed gold and polychrome enamel decorated with brilliants. The enamels show Britannia in front of a pyramid and the British lion trampling on a French ensign before the stern of a ship with

Legend: 'REAR-ADMIRAL LORD NELSON OF THE NILE'. Inscription: 'EUROPE'S HOPE AND BRITAIN'S GLORY'. Below: 'C.H.K.' (C. H. Küchler). Reverse: view of Aboukir Bay, the English fleet going into action, the French at anchor. Legend: 'ALMIGHTY GOD HAS BLESSED HIS MAJESTY'S ARMS'. Exergue: 'VICTORY OF THE NILE AUGUST 1 1798'. Above (left) 'M . B . SOHO' (right) 'C . H . KUCHLER . FEC'. Edge: 'FROM ALEXR DAVISON, ESQR. ST. JAMES'S SQUARE = A TRIBUTE OF REGARD'. It is fitted with a ring.

The topography on the reverse of the medal shows the Aboukir promontory on the eastern rather than the western side of the bay.   BT

LITERATURE: Marquis of Milford Haven, *Naval Medals*,
        p. 482.

82.   Lloyd's Nile silver
        Entrée dish: Paul Storr, London, 1800
        Vegetable dish: Timothy Renou, London, 1801
        Silver
        Lloyd's of London; ZBA1341 (entrée dish)

Since 1794, the underwriters and merchants at Lloyd's Coffee House had subscribed to funds for those wounded in naval battles and the relatives of those killed. The Committee also made awards of merit to particular naval officers for their services. Following the Battle of the Nile in August 1798, the sum of £38,436 was raised, and Nelson

was voted £500 by the Committee to purchase a service of silver. A second grant of £500 was made to Nelson after the Battle of Copenhagen, which could be used to order additional items of silver of his own choice to supplement the Nile pieces. It appears that the Nile silver was not delivered until April 1801. The service became dispersed after Nelson's death but many pieces, including wine coolers, meat dishes, sauce tureens and plates, have found their way back to Lloyd's, the National Maritime Museum and other museum collections.

This oblong covered entrée dish is part of the Nile service. It has a detachable finial representing Nelson's *chelengk* crest issuing from a naval crown. This crest was added to his coat of arms after the Battle of the Nile as a reference to his gift of a diamond aigrette from the Sultan of Turkey. The cover is engraved with Nelson's coat of arms as a viscount and has an inscription. The inscription on all the Nile items reads: 'Lloyd's 1800. Presented by the Committee for managing a Subscription made for the Wounded & Relatives of the Killed at the Battle of the Nile to Vice Admiral Lord Nelson and Duke of Bronti [*sic*] KB etc etc who was there wounded. As a testimony of the sense they entertain of his Brilliant Services on the first of August 1798 when a British Fleet under his Command obtained a most decisive Victory over a Superior French Force. J J Angerstein, Chairman.'   RP

LITERATURE: Dawson, *The Nelson Collection at Lloyd's*,
        pp. 1–11.

83. Fan commemorating the Battle of the Nile, 1798

Wood, paper

National Maritime Museum, London; OBJ0422

A paper fan on wooden sticks printed in monochrome with a half-length portrait of Nelson surrounded by naval trophies, between two scrolls inscribed: 'GLORIOUS VICTORY', 'OF THE NILE, 1ST AUGUST 1798'. A third scroll below identifies the sitter: 'ADML LORD NELSON'. The portrait is flanked by a patriotic verse within two star-shaped borders: 'Another conquest swells Britannia's Fame / Let gratefull memory wait on Nelson's name / In distant Seas the conquering Hero shows / How vain the projects of

our Gallic foes / When the glad tidings reached the public ears / From Beauties eye distilled the joyous tears / Down Manhood's cheek the tide of rapture flow'd / And every breast with kindling transports glow'd / Nelson, thy praise from shore to shore shall ring', 'Joy to the Nation, joy to England's King / Such prowess every tribute justly craves / E'en Arabs shout, Britannia rules the waves / With well earned Laurels grace the Victors brow / Recall the deeds of Vincent, Duncan, Howe / Illustrious names to every Briton dear / Here then, the Altar of our thanks we'll rear / Fleets led to battle by such Men as these / Shall fix on Brunswick's hand the trident of the seas.' 'Brunswick' probably refers to George III who succeeded to the title of Electoral Prince of Brunswick-Lüneburg. Admirals John Jervis, 1st Earl St

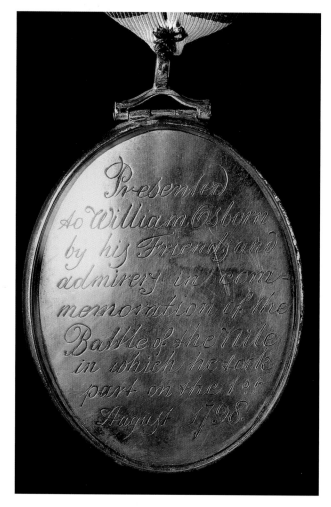

Vincent (1735–1823), Adam Duncan, 1st Viscount Duncan (1731–1804) and Richard Howe, 1st Earl Howe (1726–99) were the commanders of the earlier naval victories of the war – St Vincent and Camperdown (1797) and the Glorious First of June (1794).   BT

84. Badge commemorating the Battle of the Nile, 1798
Gold
National Maritime Museum, London; MEC1156

Badge commemorating the Battle of the Nile, 1798, in the shape of a foul anchor within a circle. An inscription is engraved on the latter – above: 'ADMIRAL NELSON', below: 'THE BRITISH TARS & GLORIUS . 1 . AUG . 1798'. [sic]. Reverse: Inscription engraved on the circle: 'THANKS BE TO GOD WHO HATH GIVEN US THE VICTORY'. These anchors were originally worn on the coat in the centre of a patriotic 'favour', or ribbon rosette. Emma Hamilton wrote to Nelson on 8 September 1798, 'My dress from head to foot is *alla Nelson*. Even my shawl is in Blue with gold anchors all over. My ear-rings are Nelson's anchors: in short, we are all be-Nelsoned.'   BT

LITERATURE: Colin White, *The Nelson Companion* (Stroud, 1995), p. 92; Warner, *A Portrait of Lord Nelson*, p. 168.

85. Locket commemorating the Battle of the Nile, 1798
Silver-gilt, ivory and glass
National Maritime Museum, London; MEC1157

The locket contains a painted ivory plaque depicting an oval shield, a trophy of arms and flags behind it, under glass with a blue- and gold-scalloped border. On the shield is the inscription: 'NELSONS VICTORY'. A silver-gilt plaque on the back is inscribed 'Presented to William Osborn by his Friends and admirers in commemoration of the Battle of the Nile, in which he took part on the 1st August, 1798.' The locket has a glazed, gilt setting and is fitted with a suspension loop and blue-edged white ribbon. William Osborn(e) served as an able seaman in *Minotaur* during the battle. He was born in north Buckinghamshire in late 1754, entering the Navy as a volunteer in HMS *Dictator* from Chatham. Details of his career after 1802 are unknown.   BT

86. *The HERO of the NILE*
James Gillray, published 1 December 1798 by
    H. Humphrey
Hand-coloured etching
341 x 226mm
National Maritime Museum, London; PAF3888

In contrast to other unquestioningly adulatory prints of Nelson's victory at the Battle of the Nile, Gillray here sardonically points to the very large material rewards heaped upon Nelson as a result. Burlesquing the genre of heroic portraiture, he presents Nelson in solitary full-length, on deck and enveloped in smoke. Gillray draws attention to the diamond *chelengk* in Nelson's hat, presented to him by the Sultan of Turkey, and in the adapted coat of arms below the main image satirizes his recent baronetcy. In November Nelson was created Baron Nelson of the Nile and Burnham Thorpe and was awarded a pension of £2000 a year. Gillray substitutes for the correct arms on the original shield a bulging purse and scroll inscribed '£2000 pr Ann'. Placed alongside Nelson's motto '*Palmam qui meruit ferat*' (Let he who has earned it bear the Palm), Gillray undermines the motto's meaning, to question whether such a large material reward really is merited. GQ

87. *Extirpation of the Plagues of Egypt; – Destruction of Revolutionary Crocodiles; – or – The British Hero cleansing ye Mouth of ye Nile*

James Gillray, published 6 October 1798 by
    H. Humphrey
Hand-coloured etching
180 x 227mm
National Maritime Museum, London; PAF3893
See page 67

This is a simple but effective celebration of Nelson's resounding victory over the French fleet at the Battle of the Nile on 1 August 1798. A colossal Nelson stands in the mouth of the river capturing and culling tricoloured crocodiles. The biblical plagues of Egypt of the title are transformed into crocodiles, which stand in turn for the French ships taken or destroyed during the battle: one with flames issuing from its jaws evidently represents *L'Orient*, whose dramatic explosion was the focus of many contemporary paintings and prints of the battle. Unlike Gillray's satire of Nelson as *The Hero of the Nile* (cat. no. 86), published a few weeks later, this print shows him, in line with contemporary newspaper reports, as the unqualified British hero, a modern demi-god, combining Moses with Hercules. GQ

88. Nile frog mug, *c.* 1798

Staffordshire earthenware
National Maritime Museum, London; AAA4751

This earthenware mug is transfer-printed with a scene of warships in action inscribed 'Lord Nelson engaging the Toulon Fleet of the mouth of the Nile' and a verse. Inside is a pottery frog, a ceramic joke of the period, intended to surprise the unwary by coming into view and gurgling as the ale is drunk. Many cheap pottery items like this were sold to

commemorate Nelson's popular victory at the Battle of the Nile.

This same engraved naval action was used as decoration on earthenware mugs produced to commemorate both the Battle of the Nile and the Battle of Trafalgar, the caption being adjusted to suit the event. In fact the scene is neither of these, but is taken from an engraving dating from forty years earlier. The design actually depicts the *Buckingham*, 66 guns, Captain Tyrrell RN, defeating *Florissant*, *Aigrette* and *Atalante* on 3 November 1758, as engraved by Robert Sayer after Swaine. RP

89. *'Emma Hamilton as a bacchante', from* Drawings faithfully copied from Nature at Naples and with permission dedicated to the Right Honourable Sir William Hamilton

Tommaso Piroli after Friedrich Rehberg, 1794
Engraving
264 x 206mm
National Maritime Museum, London; PAD3221

This is plate VI of a set of twelve engravings by Piroli after the German artist Rehberg, published in 1794. All are of the 'attitudes' for which Emma Hamilton was celebrated throughout Europe. In her performances of these, which

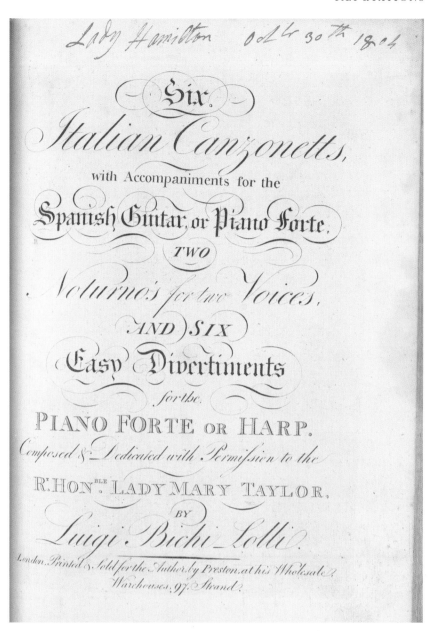

she first began about 1786, Emma adopted poses taken from classical sculpture or Renaissance painting: at one point Sir William Hamilton even constructed a special box with a black border for her to pose in, to imitate more closely the appearance of a framed painting. She was certainly encouraged by her husband's love of the antique, and performed the 'attitudes' not just in Naples, where Rehberg made his drawings for these plates, but throughout the courts of Europe. Numerous contemporary descriptions praise both her skill at adopting poses that would have been easily recognizable to connoisseurs steeped in a classical education and her own naturally 'classical' beauty. Rehberg's publication was highly popular, running to several editions: so much so that it was lampooned in 1807 by (probably) James Gillray, who substituted for the graceful, classically proportioned body of Rehberg's prints a 'considerably enlarged' figure, truer to the by then excessively fat Lady Hamilton, in what was termed a 'new edition . . . humbly dedicated to all admirers of the grand and sublime'.   GQ

90. **Emma, Lady Hamilton's, songs, early nineteenth century**

A collection of patriotic songs, operatic arias and romantic ballads in modern half-calf and marbled binding

Inscribed: 'Lady Hamilton' on some of the song sheets

National Maritime Museum, London; PBE6757

Nelson's mistress was celebrated in eighteenth-century society for her classical 'attitudes'. Her singing, however, was not to everyone's taste. Goethe, who visited the Hamiltons in Naples in 1787, remarked, 'I must confess that our fair entertainer seems to me, frankly, a dull creature . . . even her singing is neither full throated nor agreeable', and Lady Holland, the wife of the Whig politician, is said to have described it as 'vile discordant screaming'.   LV

91. **Ring with an intaglio of Emma, and impression, *c.* 1795**
Teresa Talani (*fl.* 1797–after 1800)
Gold, bloodstone (ring), shellac and cardboard
(impression)
33 x 25 x 22mm
Signed
National Maritime Museum, London; JEW0161 (ring),
JEW0022 (impression)

Gold ring belonging to Nelson. The bloodstone is set with a large bloodstone intaglio depicting Emma, Lady Hamilton (*c.* 1761–1815) as a bacchante – a votary of the Roman wine god Bacchus. Roman engraved gems were keenly collected at this time and contemporary works were produced in imitation of them. This is an example of particularly fine quality. The artist originated in Rome but worked in Naples during the late eighteenth and early nineteenth centuries. If the ring were used as a seal, the impression would show the portrait the right way round in relief. BT

92. **Emma Hart (*c.* 1761–1815) in a cavern**
George Romney (1734–1802)
Oil on canvas
1270 x 1015mm
National Maritime Museum, London (Caird Collection,
from L. W. Neeld, presented in 1944); BHC2736

The young Emma was one of Romney's favourite models and this portrait of her has been called *Lady Emma Hamilton as Ariadne*. This seems to be an invention in the late nineteenth century as there is no evidence that she ever sat to Romney as Ariadne. Although it is clearly intended to be Emma, it is possible that it was painted after her departure for Naples in 1786, seven years before she and Nelson met there. RQ

93. **Dress flounce, *c.* 1799**
Embroidered silk muslin
National Maritime Museum, London (Nelson-Ward
Collection); TXT0304

This embroidered panel is part of the border of a dress worn by Emma Hamilton at the fête of Palermo to commemorate Nelson's victory at the Nile. Three other pieces of this embroidery are known, another at Greenwich and two at the Royal Naval Museum, Portsmouth.

The panel is decorated in coloured silks and gold thread and sequins, with oak leaves, acorns, anchors and coronets and the words 'Nelson' and 'Bronte', in reference to his new

dukedom. In 1799 Ferdinand IV, King of Naples, in gratitude bestowed on Nelson the Sicilian duchy of Bronte.
Nelson used the title and included Bronte in his signature,
finally settling on the form 'Nelson and Bronte'. After the
death of his brother William, 1st Earl Nelson, the earldom
and this dukedom were divided between different branches
of the family. The Bronte estate descended through the
Viscounts Bridport until 1981, when it was sold to the local
authority, the Commune di Bronte.   RP

94. *Sketches of the State of Manners and Opinions in the French Republic, towards the Close of the Eighteenth Century*, by Helen Maria Williams (London, 1801)

Printed book, leather-bound
British Library, London; Add. MS 34991

Nelson's involvement with the restoration of the monarchy
in Naples in 1799, and the brutal suppression by King
Ferdinand of the Parthenopean Republic, was controversial
at the time and remains so today.

This book, by a passionate supporter of republican
ideals, Helen Maria Williams, was published in Britain in
1801 and is highly critical of Nelson's actions in Naples. She
even suggested that his judgement had been clouded by his
passion for Emma Hamilton. This is Nelson's own copy and
he has added a number of marginal notes angrily refuting
some of Mrs Williams's claims.

On the pages shown, he marks her eulogy (p. 222) of
the republican 'martyrs' and comments, 'Mrs Williams has
in my opinion completely proved that the Persons she
has named deserved Death from the Monarchy'. He also
dismisses her claim (p. 223) that 'The attempt was sublime'
with the words, 'They fail'd and got hanged or beheaded'.

CSW

95. *A COGNOCENTI contemplating ye Beauties of ye Antique*

James Gillray, published 11 February 1801 by
   H. Humphrey
Etching
370 x 263mm
National Maritime Museum, London; PAF3876

A complex and extremely pointed satire on Sir William
Hamilton and his wife Emma's notorious relationship with
Nelson. Ostensibly adopting the long-established comic
iconography of the old man cuckolded by a young wife, it
represents Hamilton as the great classicist and antiquary

89

A COGNOCENTI contemplating ỹ Beauties of ỹ Antique.

antiquity. Finally, to the right is a portrait of Hamilton as the Roman emperor Claudius, deceived by his young wife Messalina: it is in a frame surmounted by stag's or cuckold's horns. Similarly, the objects ranged around the room allude in various ways to the same subject. The bust of Lais, a celebrated Greek courtesan, again takes the form of Emma, but minus her nose, possibly a reference to the effects of venereal disease, and the headless statue of a Bacchante to the left assumes the pose of one of Emma's 'Attitudes'. On the far right, below the picture of Claudius, is a full-length statue of Midas, but with ass's ears: clearly a symbol for Hamilton himself, signifying that his ability to turn objects into gold will not stop him being a fool. Beneath this barbed visual commentary is a larger moral point, to do with the relationship of public to private life, the value of learning, and the diversion of military leaders such as Nelson from performing their duty to the nation at time of war.   GQ

96. Letter from Lady Nelson to Alexander Davison, 1 May 1801

Ink on paper
National Maritime Museum, London; DAV/2/41

Davison was Nelson's prize agent and banker and served as a confidant to Lady Nelson for several years while her husband was away at sea. Her letters to Davison display her concern at the breakdown of her marriage, which was effectively over when Nelson returned to sea in January 1801. They were never to see each other again. This letter was written when preparations were under way for the funeral of Maurice Nelson, Horatio's older brother. Lady Nelson expresses her desire to 'please my Lord Nelson', explains that in the past she has unwittingly angered her husband and asks Davison to help her avoid this in future. She lives a retired life to avoid censure: 'I am more circumspect and cautious than any young miss of 16.'

Lady Nelson often appears paranoid about a faction forming against her, even among her in-laws, and here begs Davison to 'consider my enemies'. Further letters from this collection refer with hostility to Lady Hamilton, and particularly to William Nelson, Horatio's surviving brother.   AD

scrutinizing his motley and bizarre collection of objects, but blind to their real significance: he even contemplates them the wrong way through his glasses. Everywhere they disclose his cuckoldry at the expense of Nelson and Emma. The bull Apis protects and points with his horns to two of the paintings on the wall, one of Emma as Cleopatra, bare-breasted and clutching a gin bottle, the other of Nelson as Mark Antony: these refer both to the great classical and Shakespearean love story and to Nelson's Egyptian campaign, but also raise a question about Nelson in the comparison with Mark Antony, concerning his commitment to put his public duty before his private desires. In the next painting, above Hamilton's head, Vesuvius erupts, a blunt sexual innuendo and also a reference to the Hamiltons' home at Naples, site of classical

97. Frances, Viscountess Nelson, 1761–1831

Daniell Orme (*c. 1766–c. 1832*)

Watercolour on paper

113 x 88mm (sight)

Inscribed in back of frame in a contemporary hand
Ladie Nelson / 1798 with Orme's printed label
*MR ORME / PAINTER AND ENGRAVER / TO / HIS
MAJESTY . . .*

National Maritime Museum, London; MNT0047

Orme was a portrait painter, engraver and miniaturist. His drawing of Lady Nelson was made while Nelson was away in 1798, the year of the Battle of the Nile and of Nelson's subsequent stay with Sir William and Lady Hamilton at Naples. In the previous year, however, Fanny had nursed her husband back to health after the loss of his arm, during what was possibly their happiest time together.   RQ

98. Maria Carolina, Queen of the Two Sicilies

Miniature by an unidentified artist

69 x 58mm

National Maritime Museum, London (Nelson-Ward
    Collection); MNT0152

The Kingdom of the Two Sicilies comprised Naples and the island of Sicily. Under the 'Golden Monarch', King Ferdinand IV, and Queen Maria Carolina it proved a valuable foothold for British Mediterranean operations until it was annexed by Napoleon in 1806. Maria Carolina was a daughter of the Empress Maria Theresa of Austria and sister of Queen Marie-Antoinette of France, who had been beheaded in 1793. The court at Naples and at their Sicilian capital, Palermo, was characterized by display and extravagance.   RQ

99. Life mask of Nelson, *c.* 1800

Plaster

National Maritime Museum, London (Nelson-Ward
    Collection); SCU0106

This cast of Nelson's face, one of three similar examples in existence, was for many years believed to be a death mask. However, in all the detailed descriptions of the events following Nelson's death, there is no contemporary reference to a death mask having been taken.

It is now thought almost certain that this is a cast of Nelson's face taken during his lifetime, probably as a part

of the process of sculpting one of the life-sized portrait busts. During this uncomfortable procedure, the subject would have to breathe through straws or quills inserted in the nostrils, until the plaster was set hard enough to remove in sections. It is recorded that when Nelson was in Vienna in the autumn of 1800 he permitted a cast of his face to be taken by the sculptor Franz Thaller and it is therefore likely that the life masks are related to the marble bust completed by Thaller and Ranson in 1801. Nelson does not appear to have mentioned undergoing this process, but Sir William Beechey referred to one occasion when Nelson's face was being cast and 'he pursed up his chin and screwed up his features when the Plaster was poured on it'.

This mask shows the eyes open, as does one of the other versions, while the one at the Royal Naval Museum, Portsmouth, has them closed. In both masks the hair has been added by modelling. The matrix of the Greenwich mask, in two sections, also exists.   RP

LITERATURE: Nash, ed., *The Nelson Masks*; Richard Walker, 'Nelson's masks – life or death', *Mariner's Mirror* (Nov. 1980), 319–27; Walker, *The Nelson Portraits*, pp. 107–12, 232–3.

100.

(1) **Rear-Admiral Sir Horatio Nelson, 1800**
(2) **Emma, Lady Hamilton, 1800**

Johann Heinrich Schmidt (1749–1829)

Pastel

Each 290 x 237mm approx.

(1) Signed and dated upper right *Schmidt / F. 1800*

(2) Signed and dated lower left *Schmidt / 1800*

National Maritime Museum, London; PAJ3939 and
    PAJ3940

After visiting Vienna on their way home to England, Nelson and his party travelled to Prague and then to Dresden where the court painter Schmidt produced these pastel drawings of Emma and Nelson, commissioned by Hugh Elliot, the British minister in Dresden.

These two pastels by Schmidt were favourites of Nelson. Although now together they were separated for 150 years. Nelson's portrait descended through Elliot's family until purchased from Lord Minto by the National Maritime Museum in 1955. Emma's hung in Nelson's cabin during his later campaigns, referred to as his 'Guardian Angel'. On the backboard of the frame is an inscription in Emma's handwriting – 'This Portrait of Emma Hamilton was in all the battles with the virtuous, gallant and heroic Nelson. He called it his Guardian Angel and thought he could not be victorious if he did not see it in the midst of Battle. He used to say under his banner. I grieve (or lament) the fatal 21st

October when he gloriously fell and ordered captain Hardy to bring it to me.'

Schmidt had already drawn Napoleon, among other famous people. His portrait of Nelson agrees with contemporary accounts of Nelson's appearance at this time, notably that by the Lutheran pastor Thomas Kosegarten who wrote,

'Nelson is one of the most insignificant figures I ever saw. His weight cannot be more than 70lbs. A more miserable collection of bones and wizened frame cannot be imagined. His bold nose, steady eye and the solid worth revealed in the whole face betray in some measure the great conqueror. He speaks little, and then only in English, and he hardly ever smiles.'

RQ

101. *Missa in Angustiis,* 'Nelson Mass', in D minor and major, Hob. XXII: 11 (1798)

Joseph Haydn (1732–1809)

Autograph manuscript

Österreichische Nationalbibliothek, Vienna; Cod. 16.478

This dramatic musical work is an indicator of the international fame Nelson won with the Battle of the Nile. Haydn entitled it *Missa in Angustiis* (Mass in [times of] tribulation), but it has become known as the 'Nelson Mass'. One of Haydn's three great late masses, it was most likely intended for the name day of Princess Esterházy, the wife of Haydn's patron Prince Nikolaus II. Haydn composed the mass between 10 July and 31 August 1798, just after completing the *Creation*. It was first performed shortly after news of Nelson's triumph at the Nile reached Vienna in mid-September 1798 and probably again in honour of Nelson's visit to the Prince in Eisenstadt in 1800, which was part of the admiral's four-month triumphal progress home across Europe. The mass was originally scored only for three trumpets, timpani, strings and organ, though later the organ part was supplemented with woodwind. A dramatic,

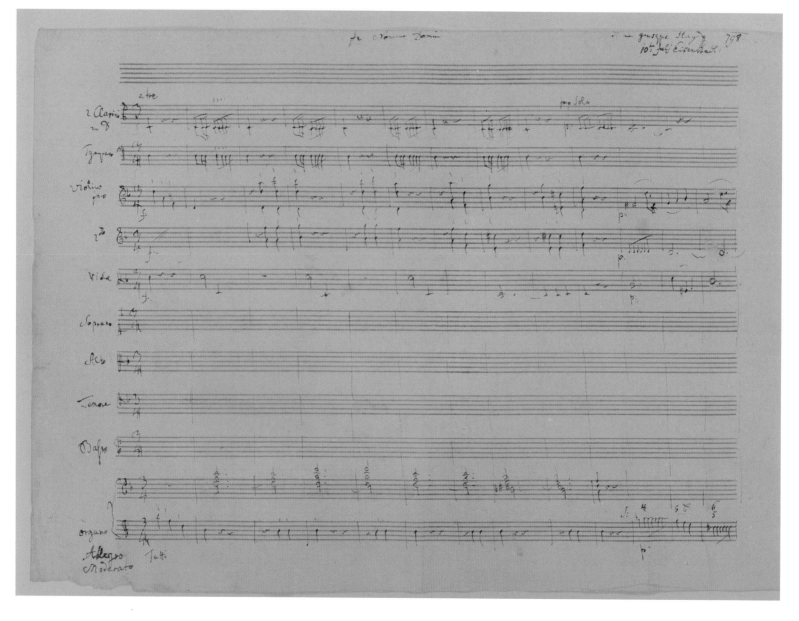

emotional work, it starts with a sombre Kyrie, with drums and threatening trumpets in the lowest registers. It has been suggested that Haydn added a trumpet call in the Benedictus, recalling the courier's own trumpet call when news of the battle was brought to Prince Esterházy.   HH

102.   **Horatio Nelson, 1800**
Sir William Beechey (1753–1839)
Oil on canvas
623 x 483mm
Inscribed on the reverse of the original canvas:
   'WB. pinx^t. / Presented to his / beloved son /
   Cap^tn. Beechey. / 1830'
Provenance: purchased with help from the National
   Heritage Memorial Fund, 1985
National Portrait Gallery, London; NPG5798

The immediacy of Beechey's portrait is particularly notice-able in this sketch of the head. The artist kept it in his studio and eventually gave it to his son, Captain William Beechey, who was Nelson's godson, although in the intervening period it may have belonged to Earl St Vincent. The hair has been altered and coincides with the finished version at Norwich.   RQ

103.   **Horatio Nelson, 1807**
Sir William Beechey (1753–1839)
Oil on canvas
2610 x 1820mm approx.
The Draper's Company, London
See page 96

The Draper's Company commissioned this copy of Beechey's full-length portrait of Nelson as a rear-admiral after Trafalgar. It is noted in Beechey's account book for 13 June 1807 as the 'large picture of Lord Nelson 200 guineas'. Nelson's return from the Mediterranean late in 1800 had prompted a spate of portrait painting. The city of Norwich at last ordered a portrait of Norfolk's most distinguished man who had presented the city with the Spanish admiral's sword surrendered at St Vincent in 1797 and had in return been awarded the freedom of the city. The portrait was commissioned by the chamberlain of Norwich and presented to the city 'in Remembrance of the signal services to his King and Country, and the Splendid Victories obtained under his Command'.

Nelson is shown standing on deck in rear-admiral's full-dress uniform, ribands of the Bath and St Vincent, stars of the Bath (above), St Ferdinand and the Crescent; badge

of St Ferdinand fastened at the waist, two naval gold medals (St Vincent and the Nile). The full-dress cocked hat with the *chelengk* is on the sable-lined pelisse to his left, his sword leaning against a carronade draped with a Spanish standard to his right. The portrait is perhaps the most intense and penetrating of all Nelson's portraits, suggesting the ruthless side of his character. When exhibited at the Royal Academy, however, it was the subject of criticism – the colouring of the face considered too high and the whole effect too much like a caricature. The *Quarterly Review* commented, 'The pencil of Sir William Beechey was, however, altogether unequal to the man of Trafalgar . . . the spare war and weather Admiral is swelled into an overgrown figurehead. The burning fire which animated his fragile frame is extinguished in the painting of the feeble academical knight.'   RQ

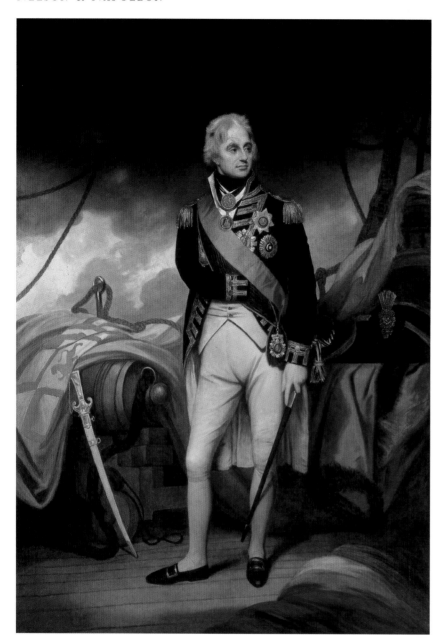

of a sailor and a lion tearing a Spanish flag. Following the Battle of the Nile, Nelson's arms were augmented by a chief to the shield depicting a palm tree, disabled ship and ruined fort; the sailor now held a palm branch and the lion has a French flag added to the Spanish. Nelson also received the *chelengk* crest which appears on this Grant of Arms above the Baron's coronet surmounting the coat of arms, as well as a new motto '*Palmam qui meruit ferat*' (Let he who has earned it take the Palm).   RP

104.   Nelson's Grant of Arms
       as a Baron, 1798
Vellum
Lloyd's of London (Nelson Collection)

Following the victory of the Battle of the Nile, Nelson was created Baron Nelson of the Nile. This illuminated Grant of Arms, issued on 20 December 1798, shows Nelson's new coat of arms as a Baron. The parchment was signed and sealed by Sir Isaac Heard, Garter King of Arms.

Nelson's naval successes can be traced through the changes to his original family coat of arms. After the Battle of St Vincent in 1797 he was created a Knight of the Bath and acquired the *San Josef* crest and supporters to his arms

105.   Deed of title for the
       Dukedom of Bronte, 1799
Moroccan leather-bound volume
Zvi Meitar, private collection

On 10 October 1799, Ferdinand the Bourbon king of Naples and Sicily created Nelson Duke of Bronte as a reward for putting him back on his throne. The dukedom came with an estate at Bronte, in eastern Sicily, on the slopes of Mount Etna. The title was of special importance to Nelson who, for the rest of his life, used it in conjunction with Nelson when signing every document he wrote.

In Greek mythology Bronte, like Nelson, is one-eyed – a Cyclops serving Jupiter as well as Thunder. Emma Hamilton called Nelson 'Lord Thunder'.

The six pages of Latin text are illuminated in red, blue and gold with decorative coloured borders and marbled end pages. The Italian binding comprises inlays in tan, yellow, green and red leathers embossed with the Royal Arms of the Kingdom of the Two Sicilies. A fine wax impression of Ferdinand's Great Seal is attached to the document by golden-coloured thread cords and tassels.

As recorded at the end of the deed, Nelson applied to the College of Arms and on 9 January 1801 obtained a Royal Warrant authorizing him to use the title of Bronte.

This is the first time the deed has been exhibited.

CSW

106. Letter with enclosures from Nelson to Lord Spencer, 1797

Ink on paper
British Library, London; Add. MS 75808

In 1797 Nelson returned to England to recover from the loss of his arm. He also took the opportunity to apply for a pension for the loss of the sight of his right eye, which had been injured during the siege of Calvi, Corsica, in June 1794.

Outwardly, the eye appeared perfectly normal, so Nelson had to submit doctors' certificates to confirm that he had no vision in it. It is interesting to note that each certificate uses different phrases to describe the disability. The first, by Dr Harness, says there is 'a material defect of sight'. The second, three days later, says, 'he will never recover perfect use of it again'. By September 1797, the doctors are saying, 'we found the sight entirely lost'.

The three certificates have recently been located in the papers of Lord Spencer, the First Lord of the Admiralty in 1797, in the British Library and are displayed here for the first time. With them is a covering letter from Nelson to Lord Spencer. A naturally right-handed man, he was still learning to write left-handed, as the writing clearly shows.

CSW

LITERATURE: White, *Nelson: The New Letters*.

107. Nelson's combined knife and fork, 1797–1805
Silver, unmarked
National Maritime Museum, London; REL0115

Nelson used this combined knife and fork after the loss of his right arm at Santa Cruz, Tenerife, on 25 July 1797. The silver three-pronged fork has a separate steel blade attached alongside the prongs by a screw. There is a ducal coronet and initials *N B* engraved on the back of the fork; the silver head is mounted in an ivory handle. Captain Hardy is said to have given it around 1820 as a memento to his friend Henning of Dorchester, whose grandson Colonel Henning sold it to the Museum in 1945.

Evidently Nelson was in the habit of using such devices after he lost his arm, and two other well-authenticated combined knife and fork sets of slightly different designs are known. Lloyd's of London has a gold example, said to have been used on special occasions, which came from the Bridport sale of Nelson relics in 1895. Another silver set is owned by descendants of Nelson's sister, Catherine Matcham.　　　　　　　　　　　　　　　　　RP

108. Tourniquet used at Tenerife, 1797
Science Museum, London (Wellcome Collection);
ZBA2220

This is a Petit-type tourniquet, believed to have been used when Nelson's right arm was amputated at Tenerife. The screw tightens a linen strop fastened around the limb to restrict the flow of blood during the operation.

Nelson was wounded in the arm while stepping out of the boat to land on the beach during the attack on the mole at Santa Cruz. He was rowed out to the *Theseus*, where he was attended by the ship's surgeons Thomas Eshelby and Louis Remonier. Eshelby's fee was £36 and his assistant Remonier's was twenty-four guineas. Eshelby's journal entry reads: 'Compound fracture of the right arm by a musket ball passing through a little above the elbow, an artery divided: The arm was immediately amputated and opium afterwards given.' Nelson suffered phantom pains in his arm throughout his life following the amputation.　　RP

LITERATURE: Pugh, *Nelson and his Surgeons*.

109. Nelson's collar of the Order of the Bath, 1797
Unmarked
Gold and enamel
Lloyd's of London; ZBA1342

Nelson received the insignia of a Knight of the Order of the Bath from George III in September 1797 while convalescing in England following the loss of his arm. The gold collar is composed of nine imperial crowns and eight enamelled roses, thistles and shamrocks, linked together with seventeen gold knots enamelled white. The plain gold badge pendant from the collar is of the 1797–1814 design and has the motto of the Bath, '*Tria iuncta in uno*'.　　RP

110.   Order of St Ferdinand, 1800
Gold and enamel
National Maritime Museum, London (Greenwich
 Hospital Collection); REL0783

The Grand Cross of the Order of St Ferdinand and of Merit, conferred on Nelson in 1800 by Ferdinand IV, King of Naples and Sicily, to mark the restoration of his kingdom, is seen here on its original ribbon. It survived the theft of the Nelson relics from the Painted Hall of Greenwich Hospital in 1900. The Star of the Order shows St Ferdinand in regal robe and mantle and is surrounded by six bundles of golden rays and six Bourbon lilies surmounted by a royal crown. The sash, which was worn across the right shoulder, has faded in colour from its original dark blue with red borders, the colours of the royal house.   RP

111.   Nelson's orders of chivalry, 1797–1805
Gold and silver wire
National Maritime Museum, London (Greenwich
 Hospital Collection); REL0119 (Bath), REL0121
 (Crescent), REL0123 (St Joachim)

These three embroidered stars of Nelson's orders, worked in gold and silver wire, were the versions he always wore on his uniform coats. All four of his orders can also be seen on the Trafalgar undress uniform coat in which he was shot at Trafalgar. Most of the original jewels of Nelson's orders were stolen from the Painted Hall at Greenwich in 1900; only the Order of St Ferdinand (REL0783) and the Collar of the Order of the Bath (ZBA1342) have survived.

   Nelson's services were rewarded by the granting of four Orders of Chivalry. After the Battle of St Vincent, in

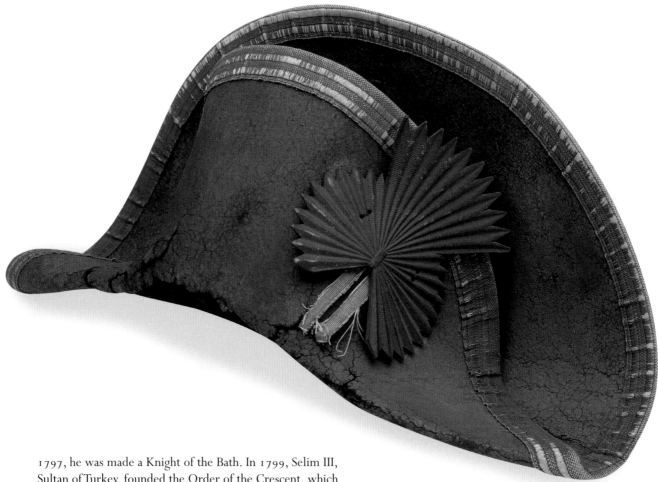

1797, he was made a Knight of the Bath. In 1799, Selim III, Sultan of Turkey, founded the Order of the Crescent, which Nelson was the first person to receive, as a tribute for his victory at the Nile the previous year. Ferdinand IV, King of Naples and Sicily, made him a Knight Grand Cross of the Sicilian Order of St Ferdinand and of Merit in 1800, and two years later he became a Knight Grand Commander of the German Order of St Joachim. Mrs St George described Nelson in Dresden in October 1800 as being 'a perfect constellation of stars and orders'.

Nelson constantly wore the gold and silver thread stars on his uniform, as was the custom at that time, and consequently they became worn and had to be replaced. A bill, which survives in the collection of Monmouth Museum, records that between October 1803 and August 1805 Nelson purchased five replacement sets of stars from Barrett & Corney of the Strand at about four guineas a set.   RP

LITERATURE: Burke, *Book of Orders of Knighthood &
     Decorations of Honour*; Risk, *History of the Order of the
     Bath & its Insignia*; 'The Order of St Joachim', *Journal
     of the Orders & Medals Research Society*, 12.4 (1973),
     196–202.

112.   Bicorn hat, *c.* 1801
          Britain
          Beaver felt, gold alloy lace, leather and painted card
          National Maritime Museum, London; UNI0058

Although the Battle of Copenhagen was a victory, it did not achieve the same level of popularity with the British public as the Battle of the Nile. However, Nelson's reputation remained undiminished and objects associated with him, such as this hat which he wore at Copenhagen, attained the status of relic within his lifetime. This hat, given by Nelson to his sword cutler, Mr Salter of 73 The Strand, was displayed in the shop window with a black card cut out, which indicated where the *chelengk*, a gift from the Ottoman sultan, was worn.   AM

113. List of prisoners executed at Naples, 1798

Ink on paper
National Maritime Museum, London; GIR/3

After the Battle of the Nile, Nelson sailed to Naples where he recuperated at the home of Sir William Hamilton, the British Ambassador, and his wife Emma. He became an intimate of the Neapolitan court and grew to identify with their political battles. During his stay, the crown was threatened by a Jacobin uprising. Nelson remained in Naples to help suppress the revolt, despite Admiralty orders sending him to Minorca. His involvement in the affair was much criticized. In particular, his treatment of Commodore Francesco Caracciolo, the commander of the Neapolitan Navy, who was court-martialled on the *Foudroyant* and hanged from the yardarm, caused some outcry and raised doubts about Nelson's political judgement.

This list of prisoners is enclosed in an envelope with the inscription, probably in Emma Hamilton's hand: 'Some <u>very private</u> Papers of importance respecting Naples – List of Jacobins 1799 only.' The list has appended to it, in Emma's handwriting, the names of three additional prisoners who were executed, including Dr Cottone Cirillio, physician to both the Royal family and the Hamiltons.   DK

PEACE
AND THE
SPOILS OF WAR

Egyptomania: The Impact of Nelson, Napoleon and the Nile on Material Culture in France and Britain

AMY MILLER

THE CONFLICT between France and Britain in Egypt at the turn of the nineteenth century fired the public imagination and left an indelible imprint on the popular culture of both countries. In part this was because the campaigns reflected certain political and military aspirations of each country: France had ambitions to extend its sphere of influence across Europe to the east; Britain was determined to protect trade interests; both wished to reinforce international perceptions of their military power. For those in command, Napoleon Bonaparte and Horatio Nelson, the success of engagements such as the Battle of the Pyramids and the Battle of the Nile served to advance their reputations as men of tactical genius. Further, the state-sponsored acquisition of such iconic antiquities as the Rosetta Stone enhanced the collections of both the Louvre and the British Museum. Egypt had long been a popular subject in material culture, yet it was propelled to new heights in both France and Britain as clothing, textiles, porcelain and furniture lent themselves to visual representations of victory. The early nineteenth-century fad, Egyptomania, and, specifically in Britain, the vogue for naval styles, illustrates the underlying patriotism in the public consumption of images of Egypt, Nelson and Bonaparte. Yet patterns of consumption also reveal a cross-cultural interest and influence because British designers and consumers often tended to follow French fashions and trends.

The French had long held ambitions with regard to Egypt; from as early as the mid-seventeenth century various plans towards its colonization had been suggested at court. By the late eighteenth century it was thought that Egypt could potentially be a profitable colony where a French presence would secure the eastern Mediterranean and strike at British trade interests in India. French trade would be enriched through control of the ports of Cairo and Alexandria.

In addition, the Directory government was concerned about the nature and extent of Napoleon Bonaparte's political ambitions and deemed it convenient to distance him from Paris by appointing him Commander-in-Chief of the Army of the Orient. As Egypt was part of the deteriorating Ottoman Empire, the pretext given for an unprovoked invasion of the province was that local rulers, the Mamelukes, were pursuing particularly vicious policies in dealing with the populace and were in collusion with the British. These policies allegedly resulted in both unpardonable atrocities and, more tellingly, a threat to France.

The French army was accompanied by between 150 and 200 civilian scholars or savants. They were to research and compile information on society, government and resources so that with such knowledge the French might effectively colonize Egypt. They were also to study the culture and artefacts of ancient Egypt – the lost civilization of the Pharaohs, viewed romantically by Europeans as one of unparalleled splendour and power. The latter aim had a more propagandistic use, for by recording and disseminating information and images of ancient monuments it would be seen that the French had restored the ancient culture of Egypt and the cultural cachet gained by this would enhance France and, more specifically, Napoleon. The 'Scientific and Artistic Commission' of savants included such luminaries as former diplomat, artist and historian Dominique-Vivant Denon, zoologist Etienne Geoffry Saint-Hilaire, mathematician Joseph Fourier and mineralogist Guy-Sylvain Dolomieu (after whom the mineral was named). Their contributions were both unique and invaluable as they provided the first systematic study of antiquity, which in turn laid the foundations for archaeology and Egyptology in the nineteenth century.

The first French troops landed in Alexandria on 1 July 1798. Bonaparte assured the populace that they had come 'to restore your rights and to punish the usurpers'.[1] They met with initial success, as on 4 July the officials of Alexandria signed a declaration agreeing to support the French regime. As part of this support, all Muslim high officials were to wear the French tricolour sash of office. The first military clash with the Mamelukes took place on 13 July at Shubrakhit and was easily won by the French. As Bonaparte's troops advanced towards Cairo, they encountered the waiting armies of Mameluke co-rulers Murad Bey and Ibrahim Bey within sight of Giza and the famed pyramids. On 21 July the French army defeated superior numbers of Mameluke cavalry in the scorching heat. The victory, at what became known as the Battle of the Pyramids, contributed to Bonaparte's already not inconsiderable reputation as a brilliant military tactician. However, the reality was that the French were poorly provisioned and relying on faulty intelligence reports – victims of Bonaparte's haste and impatience to conquer Egypt. In addition, the French never really gained the support of the populace and were, throughout the period of their occupation, continually harassed by small units of Mameluke cavalry.

During this time, the French fleet remained at anchor at Aboukir Bay. On 1 August they were discovered by the British under the command of Horatio Nelson. The British attacked almost immediately, taking the French by surprise. The Battle of the Nile was fought as night fell and the outcome saw the French fleet devastated, effectively stranding Napoleon and his troops in a rapidly deteriorating situation. The victorious Nelson was cast as the hero of the Nile and immediately linked to Egyptian motifs, as Emma Hamilton declared, 'If I was King of England I would make you the most puissant Duke Nelson, Marquis Nile, Earl Alexandria, Viscount Pyramid, Baron Crocodile, and Prince Victory that posterity might have you in all forms.'[2]

The French were defeated in Egypt and withdrew in 1801, when the savants returned to Paris to compile and publish their work. Much of this had been generated at the Egyptian Institute, which was established in late August 1798 on the outskirts of Cairo. While the French army was in Egypt, it served not only as a valuable centre with regard to colonial development and occupation, but also as a centre for study of the monuments, private tombs and artefacts of Pharaonic Egypt. It was largely through these scholarly efforts that the Egyptian campaign, though a military failure, was celebrated in France with the same fervour that Britain greeted the outcome of the Battle of the Nile.

The public taste for objects in the Egyptian style can be seen in France through such products as roller printed textiles or 'toiles de Jouy', named after the town in which they were produced. The designs produced in the late eighteenth and early nineteenth centuries reveal the extent to which the public were

Roller-printed textile celebrating the French expedition to Egypt, *c.* 1799 (cat. no. 51).

caught up in the celebration of both French victories and Egyptian culture. It should be noted that many of the toiles were relatively inexpensive to produce and therefore economically available to a large part of the population. They were used as both furnishing and dress fabrics. One toile produced at the end of the eighteenth century depicts Napoleon as the victor of the Battle of the Pyramids (cat. no. 51). Shown as the conqueror, crowned by Fame and against the backdrop of the pyramids, he is wearing the French tricolour cockade in his hat. At his feet are the weapons of war and bowing before him are three turbaned figures to whom he extends the tricolour sash of office – thus bringing liberty and good government to Egypt in one stroke. French roller- and plate-printed textiles featuring Egyptian themes remained a popular subject throughout the first part of the nineteenth century. *Les Monuments d'Égypte*, with illustrations of obelisks, sphinxes and temples, was produced in 1808. The political aspect of these objects cannot be ignored, as another popular toile, *Scènes d'Égypte*, was produced in 1820, near the end of Napoleon's life. It illustrates one of the more disastrous events of the French occupation of Egypt: the assassination of Napoleon's governor, Kléber.

In Britain the impact of the Battle of the Nile went further than a taste for the Egyptian. It also led to a fashion for all things naval, which had a particular impact on costume. There had long been a crossover between male fashion and naval uniform. The first naval uniforms drew on contemporary fashion, and by the late eighteenth and early nineteenth centuries British fashion magazines featuring male costume highlighted this vogue for naval-influenced styles. This made a further crossover into the realm of feminine clothing. A new design for a staple of the female wardrobe, the riding habit – which had copied male costume since the late seventeenth century – was featured in the July 1799 issue of the *The Lady's Monthly Museum*. Clearly derived from naval uniform, it features a blue jacket with double rows of small gilt buttons, the style of which was named after Horatio Nelson.

Accessories also feature in the celebration of the Navy in the wake of the Battle of the Nile. Such examples included commemorative fans with poems praising the heroes of the Nile (cat. no. 83), and small pieces of jewellery with naval emblems (cat. no. 85). Further, this predilection for naval styles reflects not only the popularity of the Navy engendered by victory at the Nile, but also the way in which the Navy was viewed by British society. An article in the *The Lady's Monthly Museum* offers comment on the role of local volunteer forces formed to defend Britain from a French invasion in comparison to that of the Navy: 'the first wish I can form in their favour, is, that – protected as we are by the wooden walls of old England – they may never be called upon to prove their skill and courage in any real engagement'.[3]

The British public was not immune to the lure and mystery of Egypt. The victory of the Nile and its exotic location were seized upon and celebrated in myriad Egyptian styles. These were lampooned by one satiric print, *Dresses a la Nile, respectfully dedicated to the Fashion Mongers of the day* (cat. no. 126). It depicted both male and female fashions made ridiculous by the liberal application of crocodile motifs, boots with webbed toes and beribboned headdresses with the inscription 'Nelson and Victory'. The fad for all things Egyptian permeated almost every aspect of daily life: Wedgwood produced tea services, canopic jar garnitures and a blancmange mould that imprinted a canopic jar on to the pudding. Egyptomania reached such a level that future Poet Laureate Robert Southey complained in his correspondence, 'the ladies wear crocodile ornaments, and you sit upon a sphinx in a room hung round with mummies, and the long black lean-armed long-nosed hieroglyphical men . . . are enough to make children afraid to go to bed. The very shop boards must

Dresses a la Nile, respectfully dedicated to the Fashion Mongers of the day, anonymous (cat. no. 126).

be metamorphosed into the mode and painted in Egyptian letters, which, as the Egyptians had no letters, you will doubtless conceive must be curious'.[4] Egyptian styles were retained in costume far past the first flush of the Nile victory, in 1803 women's costumes included 'sleeves à la Mameluc', while dresses were described as having a 'long train of Egyptian earth colour'.[5]

It should be noted that the representation of Egyptian motifs and architectural styles was not new, but part of what had been termed a 'rediscovery' of the ancient world that enjoyed periods of popularity from the medieval period through to the eighteenth century. In the mid-eighteenth century, Britain contributed to the scholarly study and advancement of knowledge about Egypt through the Egyptian Society, founded in 1741 under the presidency of the Earl of Sandwich. In addition, the British Museum, founded in 1753, included a collection of Egyptian artefacts from Sir Hans Sloane. The vogue for things Egyptian was also in evidence in the work of designer and architect William

Illustration from Dominique-Vivant Denon's *Voyage dans la Basse et la Haute Égypte* (cat. no. 128).

Kent who created furniture for both Wilton House, Wiltshire, and Houghton Hall, Norfolk, with sphinx motifs. Publications on the antiquities of the ancient world including those of Egypt, such as *L'Antiquité Expliquée* (1719) by Bernard de Montfaucon and *A Plan of Civil and Historical Architecture* (1721) by the Viennese architect Johann Bernard Fischer von Erlach, were sources for both designers and architects.

While Britain contributed a great deal to furthering the understanding of Egypt, popular designs that triggered the first fad for all things Egyptian came out of Rome. Italy was a fixture on the Grand Tour as the sons of wealthy families and artists and writers made their pilgrimages across Europe to view famous art and antiquities in some of the great collections on the Continent as well as in the continuing excavations at the ancient sites of Pompeii and Herculaneum. With regard to Egyptian objects, these included sculpture in the Barbarini and Borghese collections, and the Canopus gallery in the Capitoline Museum, which was dedicated to Egyptian and Egyptianized artefacts from

excavations on the site of Hadrian's Villa at Tivoli. These in turn influenced designers and architects who created an Egyptian style that featured motifs such as sphinxes and sarcophagi grafted on to popular forms of furniture, ceramics and other objects.

One Italian designer, Giovanni Battista Piranesi (1720–78), was a pivotal figure in the interpretation and dissemination of the Egyptian style. His publications and engravings of the antiquities of ancient Rome were popular souvenirs of the Grand Tour. His 1769 publication, *Diverse maniere d'adornare i cammini*, included plates of designs for fireplaces and room interiors that owed more to the fantasy of imagination than anything that could realistically be carried out. However, among the designs were those for an interior that had actually been executed: the Caffè degli Inglesi, or English Coffee House, in Rome. It featured *trompe-l'œil* paintings of fantastic Egyptian landscapes bordered by architectural elements incorporating scarabs, hieroglyphs, crocodiles, locusts and myriad Egyptian gods and goddesses. Although the interior of Caffè degli Inglesi was derided by the painter Thomas Jones (1742–83) as 'a filthy vaulted room, the walls of which were painted with sphinxes, obelisks and Pyramids, from capricious designs of Piranesi, and fitter to adorn the inside of an Egyptian-Sepulchre, than a room for social conversation',[6] *Diverse maniere* was to prove one of the most influential publications of the late eighteenth century, appearing in Italian, French and English. It is worth noting that the potter and entrepreneur Josiah Wedgwood (1730–95) owned a copy, which was one of the sources used for his basaltware.

Although an interest in Egypt was not new in Britain, the success of the Nile catapulted this interest into a craze for the Egyptian. It is ironic that one particular publication which fuelled this trend came from a French source. When Denon returned to France in August 1799, after just over a year in Egypt, he set about preparing his notes and drawings for what would be his celebrated publication *Voyage dans la Basse et la Haute Égypte* (1802). The book was dedicated to Bonaparte: 'To associate the glory of your name with the splendours of the monuments of Egypt is to combine the grandeur of our century with the mythical eras of history.'[7] Denon gained a great deal of favour by associating Bonaparte's name with one of the more successful aspects of the Egyptian campaign and was eventually appointed Director of the Museum Central des Arts. His *Voyage* appealed to the general reader as it was not written from a scientific or academic standpoint but provided an engaging and exciting narrative. The entry of the French army into the fabled ancient capital Thebes, for example, is evocatively described: 'This forsaken city, which our imagination can only conjure up through the mists of time, so haunted our imagination that, at the sight of these scattered ruins, the army came to a halt and spontaneously began to applaud as if occupying the ruins of this capital had been the purpose of this glorious enterprise, thus completing the conquest of Egypt'.[8] *Voyage* was published throughout Europe and appeared in Britain in 1802 as *Travels in Upper and Lower Egypt*, where it ran to forty editions (cat. no. 127). It was reviewed in the popular press as 'one of the most important accessions to science that has yet been made, even in this enlightened century'.[9] The illustrated plates of Egyptian monuments were used as a direct source for the decorative arts, such as the Egyptian service commissioned from Sèvres by Napoleon as a gift for Josephine when they divorced.

They also provided inspiration for British designer Thomas Hope (1768–1831) in his book illustrating the interiors of his London house, *Household furniture and interior decoration executed from designs by T.H.* (1807). The rooms in his Duchess Street home were executed in styles taken from the ancient world and included an Egyptian Room complete with a small mummy in a 'pyramidal glazed case'.[10] The colours, designs and motifs used

Chair by Thomas Hope for his Duchess Street home. His Egyptian Room was heavily influenced by the work of Napoleon's favoured architects. Buscot Park, Faringdon Collection.

were taken from 'Egyptian scrolls of papyrus' and mummy cases.[11] He cites as his greatest influences publications by Norden (a founding member of the Egyptian Society), Piranesi, Denon, and by Percier and Fontaine, Napoleon's favoured architects. Although the French and Italian sources influenced Hope, he stressed that he was not slavishly copying their work. In fact, he decried the liberal application of hieroglyphics, seen in both Percier's and Piranesi's designs as 'a mere aim at novelty'.[12] Further, Hope sought to avoid some of the more excessive Egyptian-inspired designs, noting on the same page that they were 'composed of lath and plaster, of calico and paper, offer no one attribute of solidity or grandeur . . . and can only excite ridicule and contempt'. In his introduction to *Household furniture*, Hope ultimately urges economic patriotism, speaking out against the trend of 'disadvantageous importation' and consumption of foreign goods from 'repulsive and unpatriotic shops'.[13]

Public taste for the Egyptian style would outlive its patriotic associations. It was used for designs like the Egyptian Hall at Piccadilly (1811), and was deemed particularly appropriate for funerary architecture – an example of which can be seen in the Egyptian Avenue at Highgate Cemetery in north London, built in the mid-nineteenth century. However, those objects produced at the height of Egyptomania, while capitalizing on an already existing interest in aspects of the ancient world, also served to underscore the relationship between France and Britain – one that was by turns combative and amicable. Ironically, in terms of material culture it was France that was the dominant partner, and the work of French designers and scholars was widely disseminated in Britain, shaping its material culture at home, even as Britain claimed military victory over France at the Nile.

État des Monuments D'art qui se trouvent à Alexandrie avec l'indication des proprietaires et des lieux ou se trouvent ces Monuments.

Indication Des Monuments	Noms des proprietaires	Lieux ou se trouvent les Monuments.
1° Un sarcophage Egyptien chargé d'hyeroglyphes, de Breche Verte, qui etait Placé dans la Mosquée, D° S° athanase,	Le Gouvernement.	à Bord du Vaisseau le Causse.
2° Un sarcophage Egyptien, de granite Noir orné d'hyero-glyphes apporté du Kaire.	Le Gouvernement	Sur le rivage du Port Vieux
3° un troisième sarcophage de Trapp Noir, Orné d'hyero-glyphes, Apporté de Menouf.	Le Général Lanusse.	Près de l'embarcadaire.
4° Le Poignet d'une statue Colossale, de granite rouge, decouvert dans les ruines de Memphis. Vulcain	Le Général Dugua	Idem.
5° Cinq fragmens de statue à tête de lion, de granite Noir rapportés des ruines de Thebes.	Le Gouvernement.	dans le Mag° de la Marine N° 24
6° un fragment Mutilé de figure de femme accroupie, en Granite Noir.	Le Gouvernement	Idem.
7° Deux statues Antiques de Marbre Blanc trouvées dans des fouilles faites à Alexandrie, en arm	Le Général Friant	Chez le Général Friant
8° Une Pierre de granite Noir chargée de trois Bandes de caracteres, hyeroglyphiques, Grecs Et Egyptiens, trouvée à Rozette	Le Général Menou.	Chez le Général Menou
9° Une figure Assise representant une femme, à tête de lion, trouvée dans la haute Egypte de Granite Noir.		
10° deux fragmens de tête de lion trouvés dans la haute Egypte de Granite Noir		
11° Une petite figure à genoux mutilée ornée d'hyeroglyphes trouvée dans la haute Egypte, de granite Noir	Les Citoyens Hamelin	Dans le Magasin °
12° une tête mutilée, de granite Noir, trouvée dans la haute Egypte	Et Liveron.	La Marine N° 24
13° Un fragment de sarcophage, de Granite Noir trouvé dans la haute Egypte.		

CATALOGUE
ENTRIES
114–132

114. Peace of Amiens mug, *c.* 1802

Bristol earthenware
National Maritime Museum, London (Sutcliffe-Smith
    Collection); AAA4471

Earthenware mug, transfer-printed in brown and hand-coloured. This mug, made in 1802 by Bristol Pottery, is inscribed, 'PEACE Signed at AMIENS between ENGLAND FRANCE SPAIN and HOLLAND March 27, 1802'.

  The brief Peace of Amiens inspired only a few commemorative items, unlike contemporary battles and victories which were always popular with the public and souvenir manufacturers. The design of this mug shows two female figures in classical dress standing before the flags of the signing nations, holding a laurel branch and a cornucopia. The monument at which they stand is surmounted by palm and laurel sprays, and the background depicts peaceful scenes of docks and commerce.   RP

115. Court dress, 1805–10

Britain
Muslin, metal thread and spangles
Gallery of Costume, Platt Hall, Manchester; 1947.1738

Although the relationship between Britain and France was one of combative competition, there was also an element of cultural exchange. The influence of French fashion is apparent in this muslin court dress embroidered with silver thread and further embellished with spangles. Sheer muslins were immensely popular and meant to approximate classical draperies, but some considered them risqué as dresses were cut to expose the arms and bosom and the lightweight muslin fabric clung to the body. It was such a dress that prompted Jane Austen to comment in her correspondence that an acquaintance was both 'expensively and nakedly dressed'. AM

116. Fashion plate illustrating 'Paris Dress', *Lady's Magazine*, October 1800

Britain
Printed paper
171 X 126mm
Gallery of Costume, Platt Hall, Manchester; 19877

The neo-classical style, popular in the late eighteenth and early nineteenth centuries, drew on images and artefacts of antiquity. Inspiration came from excavations of Pompeii and Herculaneum as well as from artefacts in public and private collections across Europe. In Paris, women like Madame Récamier and Josephine de Beauharnais set trends with clothing that imitated the dress of the ancient world. This style featured sheer muslin dresses that approximated the

Engraved for the Ladies Magazine.

PARIS DRESS.
Straw-Hat trimmed with Crape.

Mutlow. *sculp.*

draperies seen on classical statues, sandal-like shoes that tied around the ankles and legs with ribbons, and wigs or curls resembling the cropped styles seen on antique portrait busts. Fashion plates illustrating Parisian styles were widely published in Britain. This example, from the *Lady's Magazine* from October 1800, illustrates 'Paris dress' and the image bears a resemblance to Josephine herself.   AM

The first Kiſs this Ten Years! — or — the meeting of Britannia & Citizen François

117. *The first Kiss this Ten Years! – or – the meeting of Britannia & Citizen François*
James Gillray, published 1 January 1803 by
    H. Humphrey
Hand-coloured etching
368 x 268mm
British Museum, London; 1868-8-8-7071

This print treats the insecure Peace of Amiens sceptically and with suspicion. Gillray sums it up brilliantly by conceiving the Peace as a form of entirely incongruous and ill-matched marriage. Britannia, short and excessively fat, is embraced by 'Citizen François', tall and thin, who leans down to kiss her. They conform again to national stereotypes established in eighteenth-century satire. Britannia is a version of Mrs John Bull, and 'Citizen François' combines the two characterizations of the French popularized by Hogarth: on the one hand the emaciated, sabot-wearing peasant; on the other the unctuous and duplicitous sophisticate. On the wall above these two figures two roundels show profiles of Napoleon and George III, in stature echoing their allegorical counterparts below who regard each other (more realistically, we are led to suppose) with mutual suspicion and antagonism.   GQ

118. Diary of a trip to Paris in 1802
    William Herschel (1738–1822)
Manuscript
Royal Astronomical Society, London; WH.7/15

Many travellers took advantage of the Peace of Amiens to visit Paris. One of them was the astronomer William Herschel, famous throughout Europe for his discovery of the planet Uranus, who travelled with his wife, son and niece. They visited and dined with numerous mathematicians, philosophers, astronomers, chemists, ministers and 'other persons of eminence in literature'. They were introduced to Madame Bonaparte, whom they met first at the home of M. Chaptal, the Minister of the Interior, on 8 August 1802, and then to Napoleon ('the first Consul', as he is referred to throughout the diary). Herschel's political allegiance is difficult to determine. He never talked to anyone about politics and, although funded by George III, had friends on both sides of the Channel with outspoken views in favour of the French Revolution. Whatever Herschel's opinion of Napoleon's politics, he was clearly impressed by his scientific knowledge. In describing the meeting he remarks, 'he entered into conversation with them [some other gentlemen in the room] on the subject of a Canal which is to be made in France. The Consul seemed to be perfectly acquainted with the subject . . . [he] then asked

[Herschel] a few questions relating to Astronomy and the construction of the heavens to which I made such answers as seemed to give him satisfaction. He also addressed himself to M. Laplace on the same subject, and held a considerable argument with him in which he differed from that eminent mathematician.' EW

LITERATURE: Constance A. Lubbock, *The Herschel Chronicle* (Cambridge University Press, 1933).

119. *A TRIP to PARIS or JOHN BULL and his SPOUSE Invited to the Honors of the SITTING!!*
[C. Williams], published 14 May 1802 by S. W. Fores
Hand-coloured etching
252 x 368mm
Bodleian Library, Oxford (John Johnson Collection); French Wars and Revolutions folder 6(26)

After the Peace of Amiens was signed in March 1802, Britons flocked across the Channel as tourists to see Bonaparte's Paris, and in particular his accumulated collections of art and antiquities in the Louvre. This gentle satire lampoons as misplaced such cultural aspirations among the British middling sort by representing John Bull, the personification of down-to-earth Englishness, and his wife Hibernia (Ireland) as country bumpkins. They are shown as woefully out of place in the refined environment of Napoleonic Paris. Bonaparte welcomes them, however, saying, 'Indeed Mr Bull I am quite charmed with you – there is something so easy and polite in Your manners', to which John denies knowing anything of politeness. This print follows in a long tradition of eighteenth-century satirical prints in which John Bull is represented positively as the epitome of simple and honest English values in the face of French over-sophistication. GQ

120. 'Mars and Venus' in the 'Studies in the Louvre' sketchbook, 1802
Joseph Mallord William Turner (1775–1851)
129 x 114mm
Provenance: bequeathed by the artist, 1856
Tate, London; D04319 (Finberg LXXII. 35)

The brief Peace of Amiens (1802–3) allowed British travellers to visit the Continent for the first time in nearly ten years. Turner was among many artists who went, on his first European tour, to Switzerland in 1802. On the way home in

September–October he visited Paris, where the contents of the Louvre had swelled with the cultural booty of French conquests since 1793. This pocket book of notes and sketches of eighteen Old Masters and other paintings which he examined closely there is open at his study of Guercino's *Mars and Venus* (1633). The painting was one of the many items looted from the ducal collection of the Este family of Modena in 1796. It was returned in 1815 on the intercession of the great Italian sculptor Antonio Canova. PvdM

121.   Medal commemorating
        the Peace of Amiens, 1802

Conrad Heinrich Küchler (c. 1740–1810)
Signed
Bronze, 48mm diam.
National Maritime Museum, London; MEC1546

Britain gave up most of the overseas territory it had conquered during the war in this peace treaty. Captured enemy weapons representing the gains of victory are shown being destroyed by Peace in favour of the commercial benefits symbolized by her traditional attributes – the cornucopia of agriculture and the staff of Mercury signifying trade. Obverse: bust of King George III in a tie-wig, uniform and order (left), 'GEORGIUS III . D : G . BRITANNIARUM REX . FID . DEF. &c'. Signed 'C.H.K.' below truncation. Reverse: Peace standing on the seashore raising an olive branch in her left hand, a caduceus and fruit (right), she is putting a lighted torch to a fallen trophy (left); sea and shipping in the distance. Legend: 'TRIUMPHIS POTIOR' (To possess [peace] by victories). Exergue: 'PAX UBIQUE MDCCCII' (Peace everywhere). Signed 'C. H. KUCHLER' above exergue.   BT

122.   *PROCLAMATION OF PEACE AT*
        THE ROYAL EXCHANGE, LONDON,
        APRIL 29, 1802

Anonymous, British, nineteenth century, published
    1 June 1802 by P. W. Tomkins
Hand-coloured etching
395 x 405mm
Royal Library, Windsor Castle; 750616

This is a highly elaborate and accomplished print issued to commemorate the conclusion of the Peace of Amiens on 27 March 1802. It celebrates the official royal proclamation of the peace on 26 April, which was publicly honoured by holiday festivities and a grand ceremonial procession through

London on 29 April. The image shows the culmination of the procession at the Royal Exchange in the City: in the right foreground, in profile on horseback directly before the Exchange's main entrance, is Edmund Lodge, the Lancaster Herald, who gave the final reading of the proclamation there.

Besides evoking the bustling crowds and the sense of public jubilation at the peace between the two countries, the print also represents the harmonious meeting of the City of Westminster and the City of London, respectively the royal and commercial centres of the metropolis, in the persons of Sir James Bland Burges, Knight Marshal (just to the right of centre, on horseback), and the Lord Mayor of London (also on horseback, to the left). The lengthy accompanying description gives both the text of the King's proclamation, which was read by different heralds at various stations on the procession, and also an account of the procession itself, from its starting point at 10.30 a.m. in the Stable Yard, St James's, then via Charing Cross to the City. Much attention is given to the formal ritual by which the Knight Marshal and the Westminster Officers at Arms were granted permission to enter the City through the gates at Temple Bar.

Though skilfully evoking the spontaneity and confused atmosphere of such a public occasion, the image is carefully composed to register the order of the crowd (this is no Hogarthian mêlée) and the social proprieties and hierarchies of the ceremony. Though set in the City, the central and principal figure is the King's representative, the Knight Marshal, whose horse rears in a pose conventionally associated with equestrian royal portraits. This raises him slightly above his counterpart, the Lord Mayor, at whom he looks with an attitude of superiority. The fact that the print was not published until 1 June indicates both the labour involved in its preparation (not least in the elaborate hand-colouring) and the degree of prestige it was intended to have as a commemoration of this significant event. Nonetheless, in spite of being welcomed across the country and celebrated in public festivities and prints such as this, the Peace of Amiens was always an uneasy one and lasted barely a year; hostilities were recommenced in spring 1803.   GQ

123.   Autograph speech written by
        Charles-Maurice de Talleyrand-
        Périgord, 1802

Ink on paper
Pierre-Jean Chalençon, private collection

In this toast, written on the night of the signing of the Peace of Amiens, Napoleon's Foreign Minister Talleyrand asks his audience to drink to the long-lasting union of two great nations in an advantageous peace. In fact, the Peace was to be

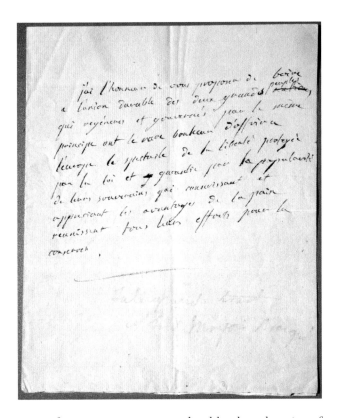

These boxes became fashionable during the 1780s, although it is unlikely that they were commonly used to hold patches. Those commemorating contemporary personalities and events were probably collected as small ornaments and put on display within the home. The manufacture of these items was centred on Birmingham and its neighbouring towns, most notably Bilston, the name most associated with this type of enamel work.   BT

more of a transitory truce, stimulated by the exhaustion of the lengthy preceding period of conflict and a desire to return to economic prosperity. In Britain, although news of the Peace was generally greeted positively, there was dissatisfaction at the relinquishing of recently conquered territories, coupled with a sense that Bonaparte's expansionist aims were unlikely to have been satisfied. Ratified in March 1802, the Peace of Amiens lasted only until May 1803, whereupon French intervention in Switzerland and Piedmont and the British failure to evacuate Malta and Alexandria signalled the outbreak of war once more.   CLW

LITERATURE: Alexandra Franklin and Mark Philp, *Napoleon and the Invasion of Britain* (Oxford, 2003); Lefebvre, *Napoleon: From 18 Brumaire to Tilsit, 1799–1807*; Frank McLynn, *Napoleon: A Biography* (London, 1998).

124. **Oval patch box commemorating the Peace of Amiens, 1802**
Enamel, metal and glass
43 x 37 x 23mm
National Maritime Museum, London (Walter Collection; OBJ0027

The surface is enamelled with a white base, pink sides and lid with a black-painted inscription: 'IN PEACE rejoice, AND WAR no more'. There is a mirror inside the lid.

125. **Medal commemorating the Peace of Amiens, 1802**
Rambert Dumarest (1760–1806) after Antoine-Denis Chaudet (1763–1810)
Bronze, 49.5mm diam.
Signed
Provenance: Sir W. Calverley Trevelyan, 1879
Ashmolean Museum, Oxford; ASH.MUS.1879.445

The portrait of Napoleon is based on a bust by Chaudet now in the Louvre. The reverse implies a certain French military superiority, her continental power represented by the standing warrior. The date is given in both the Revolutionary and pre-Revolutionary calendars.

Obverse: laureate bust of Napoleon (right). Legend: 'NAPOLEON BONAPARTE PREMIER CONSUL'. Signed 'DUMAREST F.' below truncation. Reverse: a standing, helmeted Greek warrior, holding in his left hand a statuette of Victory standing on a globe. With his right he offers an olive branch to Britain – a semi-nude, reclining female figure wearing a mural crown and supported by a lion. Legend: 'PAIX D'AMIENS'. Exergue: 'VI GERMINAL AN X XXVII MARS MDCCCII' (27 March 1802). Signed 'DUMAREST F.' towards the edge. BT

LITERATURE: Bramsen, *Médailler Napoléon le Grand*, I.

126. *Dresses a la Nile, respectfully dedicated to the Fashion Mongers of the day*
Anonymous, British, eighteenth century, published by
    W. Holland, 24 October 1798
Hand-coloured etching
335 x 238mm
National Maritime Museum, London; PAF3864
See page 107

A gentle lampoon against British fashionable society, making facetious suggestions for ways to incorporate the topical news of Nelson's victory over the French fleet at the Battle of the Nile on 1 August into the latest fashions. It was commonplace for people to display patriotic sentiment or

political opinions (for example, for the campaign for the abolition of the slave trade) through dress or other accoutrements, but this satire takes this trend to ridiculous extremes, with its overabundant and absurd Egyptian references. It also maintains a staple iconography of satirical prints, treating the excesses of fashion. On the left, the woman is virtually mummified in her white dress decorated with crocodiles. Opposite her, the man's costume is even more extravagant, consisting of crocodile skin coat, waistcoat and reptilian boots. His hat also sports a bright yellow crocodile. They stare at each other in mutual astonishment at the other's appearance. To complete the topical references, and by way of explanation of the outfits, both wear hats with the motto 'Nelson and Victory'. GQ

127. *Travels in Upper and Lower Egypt in company with several divisions of the French Army . . . Embellished with maps, plates, vignettes, &c.* Translated from the original folio edition by Francis Blagdon, 2 vols, London, 1802
[Baron Dominique-Vivant Denon]
Printed book
British Library, London; 1424.b.21

Although the two-volume London publication of the Paris edition of Denon's *Voyage* (cat. no. 128) was an instant success, translations soon appeared to satisfy a still larger market. English editions, in various formats, mostly with integrated plates, some re-engraved at a reduced size and with some of the modern subjects omitted to reduce the price, were published from 1802 onwards. In the course of the nineteenth century, forty-two translations and adaptations appeared in English, German, Dutch, Danish and Italian.   HH

128. *Voyage dans la Basse et la Haute Égypte pendant les campagnes du général Bonaparte*, 2 vols, Paris, 1802
Baron Dominique-Vivant Denon (1747–1825)
Printed book
British Library, London; 458.h.11

Denon joined Napoleon's Egyptian expedition as the leader of the Commission on the Sciences and Arts. He travelled with General Desaix's forces through the desert in pursuit of the Mamelukes to Upper Egypt. His movements dictated by military needs, Denon was incessantly sketching ancient sites in hurried conditions, occasionally having to be rescued by patrols: 'If a fondness for antiquities has frequently made me a soldier, on the other hand, the kindness of the soldiers, in aiding me in my researches, has often made antiquaries out of them.' Denon accompanied Napoleon back to Paris where in 1802 he hastened to publish his personal account of the expedition, the *Voyage*. Dedicated to the 'Hero' Bonaparte, it was issued in two

immense elephant-folio volumes, one of text and one of plates depicting pyramids, sphinxes, ruins, architectural fragments and towns and settlements, and describing local customs and manners along the way. Denon later became the first Director of the Central Museum of Art and founded the Louvre's Egyptian collections.   HH

129. Cast (between 1803 and 1855) of the Rosetta Stone, original 196 BC
Plaster (with frame)
900 x 785mm
Provenance: given by Sir G. Scharf (1820–95), 1855
Fitzwilliam Museum, Cambridge; E.1.1855

The Rosetta Stone is the surviving part of an irregularly shaped slab of a dark hard rock, a stela bearing an inscription dated to the year 9 of Ptolemy V (196 BC). It is the Memphis Decree, a priestly decree affirming the royal cult of the thirteen-year-old Ptolemy V Epiphanes (205–180 BC). The decree is repeated in Egyptian, in both the hieroglyphic script (suitable for a priestly decree, originally twenty-nine lines) and the demotic, or native, everyday script (thirty-two lines), as well as in Greek, the language of the administration under the Macedonian dynasty (fifty-four lines). The stela, originally around 149cm (58.5 inches) in height, and of a dark grey colour, and most probably with a rounded top headed by a winged sun disc, would have been placed in a temple. It was found in 1799 during works on defences at Fort St Julien near the town of el-Rashid (Rosetta). Soldiers and savants recognized the stone's significance as a possible key to hieroglyphs. In keeping with the enlightened mission of

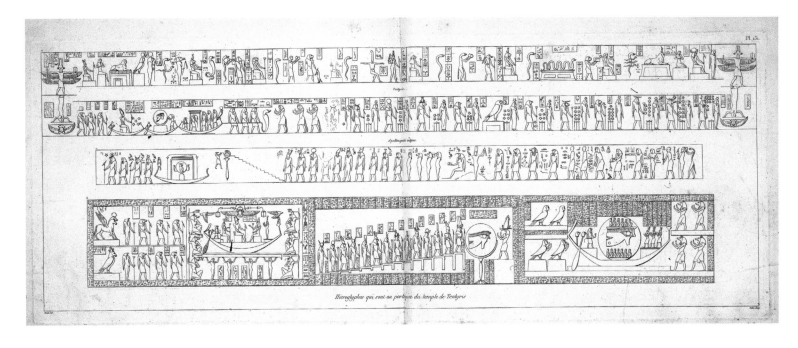

Hieroglyphes qui sont au portique du temple de Tentyris

and engraved copies, Champollion expanded Young's list of individual hieroglyphs and deduced the grammatical and syntactical nature of the language. The decipherment helped to unlock the numerous surviving Egyptian texts on papyri and inscribed objects and with them a long-lost ancient culture. HH

LITERATURE: Parkinson *et al.*, *Cracking Codes*.

130. **Egyptian service, 1810–12**
Sèvres, France
Hard-paste porcelain
Victoria and Albert Museum, on loan to Apsley House,
London; C.124:1-132P-1979

This service is based on drawings made by Dominique-Vivant Denon as official artist during Napoleon's Egyptian campaign of 1798–9, which had been published in 1802

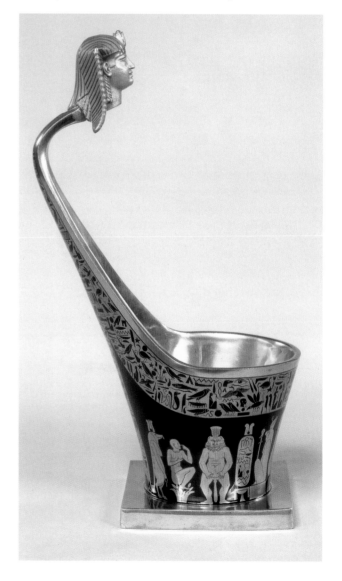

Napoleon's scholarly expedition under arms, the stone was discussed in a session of the Egyptian Institute and copies of the inscriptions were made. In 1801, the stone was surrendered, along with other antiquities, to the British forces at Alexandria (cat. no. 131). After the French had been allowed to make a cast, the stone was conveyed to England separately on board the frigate *L'Égyptienne* and delivered first to the Society of Antiquaries. They sent plaster casts of the monument to Oxford, Cambridge, Edinburgh and Dublin. The present exhibit is another early cast. The earliest attempts at deciphering were hampered by long-held, false premises that hieroglyphs represented pictures rather than sounds. The English polymath Thomas Young (1773–1829) in 1814–18 identified a remarkable number of hieroglyphic word groups and proposed that foreign names such as Ptolemy were written 'alphabetically', but he maintained the flawed tradition that hieroglyphs were symbolic. It was the brilliant French linguist Jean-François Champollion (1790–1829) who in the 1820s realized that hieroglyphs predominantly recorded the sound of the Egyptian language, although they also contained logograms. Working from casts

as *Voyage dans la Basse et la Haute Égypte*. He became director of the Musée Napoléon (now the Louvre), and was artistic adviser both to Napoleon and to the Sèvres porcelain factory. Denon supervised the production of this dinner service comprising sixty-six plates, a dozen comports, a pair of ice pails, four figures supporting bowls, a pair of sugar bowls and a pair of *confituriers* (jam dishes). The plates have sepia hand-painted scenes of temples and other monuments of Egypt, views of the Nile and scenes of contemporary Egyptian life. The rims are richly decorated with ancient symbols and figures in gilt on a blue ground. Decoration on other pieces of the service includes signs of the zodiac, Egyptian bas-reliefs, hieroglyphs and masks, which were painted and gilded by a number of different craftsmen.

This Egyptian dessert service was originally made as a divorce gift from Napoleon to the Empress Josephine. She refused to accept the service, which remained in the Sèvres factory until 1818 when Louis XVIII of France presented it to the Duke of Wellington.   RP

131. **Inventory of Egyptian antiquities in the possession of the French authorities at Alexandria, certified by Jean Baptiste Joseph Fourier, Secretary of the Egyptian Institute, *c.* 1801**

Ink on paper

Provenance: presented by A. F. Loveday, who found the inventory among papers of General Sir T. H. Turner

British Library, London; Add. MS 46839 F

Under article 16 of the capitulation of Alexandria, 31 August 1801, the British demanded that the French should surrender everything they had collected in Egypt. After protests by the French savants, they were allowed to keep personal property, including their natural history collections and scientific papers, but surrendered all antiquities to the British forces. This list gives fifteen monumental items which George III presented to the British Museum in 1802. They formed part of the founding collection of the Department of Antiquities. The list, handed by Fourier's deputy to Colonel Tomkyns Hilgrove Turner, describes the items, complete with those who claimed to possess them when they were seized (the French government, General Menou, etc.) and the places where they were found. As no. 8 it includes, most famously, the Rosetta Stone (cat. no. 129).   HH

LITERATURE: Loveday, *Sir Hilgrove Turner, 1764–1843.*

132. **Teapot and incense burner in the Egyptian style**, *c.* 1805

Spode, Staffordshire

Teapot: red stoneware (*rosso antico*)

Incense burner: black basalt

Spode Museum Trust, Stoke-on-Trent; WTC3017 (teapot), WTC3006 (incense burner)

In the early nineteenth century the publication of the archaeological discoveries in Egypt gave additional impetus to public interest in ancient Egyptian design, which for some twenty years became fashionable source material for painting, architecture, interior design, furniture and the decorative arts. As early as 1773, Wedgwood's catalogue had included sphinxes and other Egyptian symbols, but it was only after 1798 that the military campaign in Egypt prompted a wave of Egyptomania to sweep through Europe. While Napoleon's objective was a military one, he had been accompanied on the campaign by artists, scholars and architects to record everything about Egyptian life, history and antiquities.

The Spode teapot shows a typical use of ancient Egyptian motifs on ceramics. The body and stand of red stoneware are decorated with black basalt reliefs representing gods, hieroglyphs and other Egyptian decoration, and the finial of the lid is modelled as a crocodile. Very similar pieces were produced by Wedgwood. The pyramid incense burner is of black basalt decorated with white Egyptian motifs.

RP

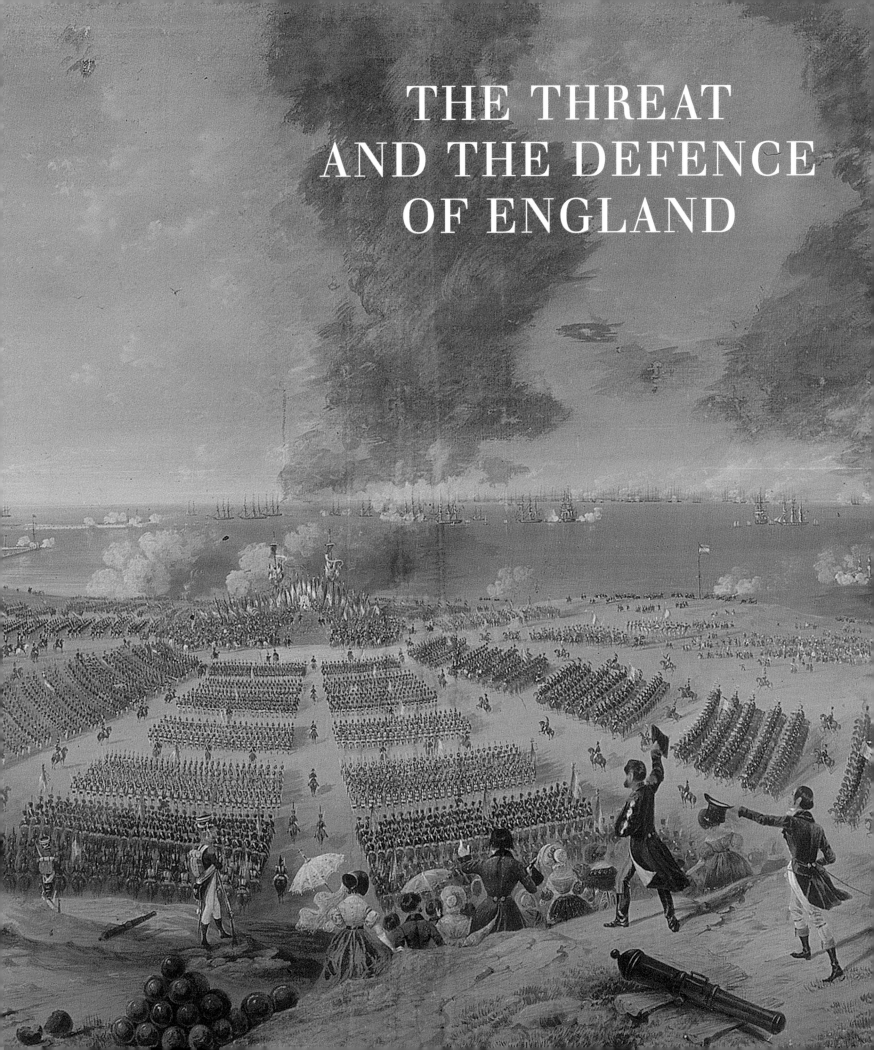

THE THREAT
AND THE DEFENCE
OF ENGLAND

British Propaganda
and Anti-Napoleonic Feeling
in the Invasion Crisis of 1803

SIMON BURROWS

THE RENEWAL OF WAR with France in May 1803 unleashed a wave of British government-inspired propaganda unprecedented in volume, intensity, nationalistic rhetoric and social reach. This chapter sets out to explain this material within the context of developing British views of Napoleon and the politics and propaganda warfare of the period. There were three reasons for the deluge of British propaganda, each of which helped to define its aims, means, messages and limitations. First, it responded to domestic and international propaganda campaigns by Napoleon, including attempts during and after the Peace of Amiens to direct and contain public opinion across Europe. Second, the ideological debates of the 1790s between radical and loyalist publicists had massively increased the audience for political publications. Finally, the imminent threat of invasion compelled the British government to resort to mass mobilization on a scale previously unimagined. By 1804, perhaps 25 per cent of adult males were enrolled in local volunteer forces. The creation of this mass popular force was a calculated risk, and one that the Prime Minister William Pitt had refused to countenance, fearing rebellion, as recently as 1792–93.

In Napoleon, Britain faced a master propagandist. Since taking command of the French army in Italy in 1796, he had nurtured his reputation through carefully crafted military bulletins, which were republished across Europe. After seizing power in November 1799, he employed a full range of media for propaganda purposes, including print, art, monumental architecture, pageantry, proclamations and decrees, coins and medals and the pulpit, as many items in this exhibition

Bonaparte as First Consul,
by Antoine-Jean, Baron Gros.
Pierre-Jean Chalençon, private collection.

demonstrate. Nevertheless, in his propaganda efforts as much as his military campaigns, Napoleon was less an innovator than a brilliant systematic organizer and master of improvisation. He had no ministry of propaganda. Instead he sought to bring cultural media throughout France's empire and client states under his exclusive control by tight supervision and calculated patronage. Architects and leading artists, including David and Ingres, were employed by the state on major commissions, many of which celebrated the First Consul's achievements, and authors were paid to write in the service of the state. Most important of all, the tumultuous Revolutionary press was brought under control. The number of newspapers in France was limited, and it was decreed that all political news should be taken from the official *Moniteur* newspaper. A decree of 17 January 1800 reduced the Parisian press from some sixty titles to thirteen, and by 1810 forced mergers and closures left only four Parisian papers, and no more than one closely supervised local paper per *département*. This press model resembled the policy of the Bourbon monarchy before the French Revolution. However, whereas Bourbon news policy had been undermined by a foreign-produced international French-language press, Napoleon sought to dominate the press throughout the whole of Europe. His aim was not simply to manipulate his image: he also wanted to control the flow of complex agenda-setting information upon which the decisions of foreign governments were made.

The Napoleonic government adopted a three-pronged approach to the foreign press. First, it dispatched agents such as Joseph Fievée to buy the support of proprietors and editors of foreign papers, particularly the most vociferous émigré journals. Pamphleteers were also bought over with pensions and bribes. Second, French diplomatic agents and spies watched foreign papers closely, and extracts from the British press were read to Napoleon by his secretaries while he took his daily bath. The purpose of this surveillance was both to monitor individual newspapers and glean snippets of information about British intentions. Thirdly, Napoleon campaigned against hostile papers, using diplomatic pressure to close them down and silence his critics. During the Peace of Amiens, he launched a sustained offensive against the British press. After concerted pressure on the British government, his most vociferous émigré detractor, the seasoned counter-revolutionary journalist Jean-Gabriel Peltier, was charged with criminal libel, having persistently calumniated Napoleon and incited his assassination. Peltier was found guilty before the court of King's Bench on 21 February 1803, but escaped punishment because war broke out before he could be sentenced. Napoleon's campaign attenuated criticism in the London press and briefly silenced the émigrés altogether. This, in turn, limited the repertoire of anti-Napoleonic material in which British propagandists could find inspiration in 1803. Nevertheless, British propaganda did not emerge in a total vacuum: it drew both on earlier anti-Napoleonic materials and the pro-government propaganda networks that had first emerged during the Revolutionary War.

In the 1790s, the British government and loyalist propagandists had developed a well-oiled propaganda machine to help overturn residual pro-Revolutionary sympathies among the population. Even those Britons who later became its implacable opponents had been almost unanimous in their initial enthusiastic response to the French Revolution. France appeared set to enjoy a 'Glorious Revolution' and to become Europe's second great constitutional monarchy. In *The Prelude*, William Wordsworth summarized the mood of the moment: 'Bliss was it in that dawn to be alive / But to be young was very heaven'. Britain's Whigs, in particular, fanned the enthusiasm, while popular Corresponding Societies sprang up all over the country to discuss politics and write letters of encouragement to the French Constituent Assembly. Edmund Burke's grimly prophetic *Reflections on the Revolution in France*, published in November 1790, initially did little to dent this ardour. Whig friends wondered if he had gone mad, and sales of Burke's treatise were massively outstripped by Thomas Paine's *Rights of Man*, which sold between 100,000 and 200,000 copies. Allowing for several readers per copy, this implies that Paine's work reached a substantial proportion of the adult population, yet *Rights of Man* was only the most popular of some 200 replies to Burke's *Reflections*.[1]

However, in 1791, as Louis XVI was sidelined and the Revolutionary assemblies passed ever-more draconian laws against émigrés and refractory priests, many Britons began to grow alarmed by Jacobin egalitarianism and violence. The fall of the French monarchy in August 1792 and promulgation of a republic in September exacerbated this concern, as did French calls for continental radicals to join the Revolutionary War against Prussia and Austria. The British government now began to consider contacts between French and British radicals problematic and became increasingly worried by the subversive potential of radical societies. In late 1792, Pitt's ministry was terrified into repressive measures by alarmist reports from self-serving spies, and these efforts intensified following the French declaration of war on Britain in February 1793. Habeas Corpus was suspended, 'seditious meetings' banned and leading radicals charged with treason, although in England at least it proved impossible to secure convictions.

Loyalists responded to the sense of crisis in imaginative ways. Their efforts were spearheaded by John Reeves's 'Association for the Preservation of Liberty and Property against Republicans and Levellers', founded in November 1792. Reeves's Association pamphleteered vigorously and stimulated the creation of a network of loyalist associations run by local notables. Its propaganda efforts stigmatized British radicals, suggesting that they were infected by French egalitarianism and atheism, and tried to detect and root out radical activists while warning the lower orders of the dangers of associating with incendiaries. Pitt's government encouraged these efforts. Between 1795 and 1798, they also supported Hannah More and her collaborators to deliver similar, simplified moral messages to counteract the French contagion to the labouring poor in a series of more than 100 *Cheap Repository Tracts*. In total, over 2,000,000 copies of these tracts were sold, often to local patricians who distributed them free to labourers. The political and intellectual elite were not forgotten either. They were served by the *Anti-Jacobin; or, Weekly Examiner*, produced in 1797–98 by the ambitious young Pittite Member of Parliament and future Prime Minister, George Canning, in collaboration with leading Tory politicians. The *Anti-Jacobin*'s contributors apparently included both Pitt and James Gillray, the leading caricaturist of the day. The paper's successor was John Gifford's long-running *Anti-Jacobin Review* (1798–1821), whose early contributors included William Cobbett, Isaac Disraeli, John Reeves, the conspiracy theorist John Robison, and the proscribed moderate revolutionaries Mounier and Montlosier. Overall, these propagandizing efforts were so successful that historians now consider loyalism rather than radicalism to have been the true popular political movement of the 1790s.[2] Nevertheless, by

1801 much of the population was tired of war. The powerful London merchant lobby opposed it and in 1801 and 1802 rioters demanded food and peace.

It is hardly surprising, therefore, that in 1803 government propaganda attempted to revive the loyalist enthusiasm of the mid-1790s. However, the propaganda campaign of 1803 threw up a new set of problems, not least because British attitudes to Napoleon had not solidified. Many of the achievements to which Napoleon pointed, literally, in Ingres's propagandist portrait *The First Consul in his Study* had been welcomed or admired in Britain. The *coup d'état* of *18 brumaire* (9–10 November 1799), which brought Napoleon to power, had destroyed Jacobinism as a political force. His Concordat with the Pope had formally restored the French Church and recognized Christianity's importance in national life. The decisive victories over the Austrians by Moreau at Hohenlinden and Napoleon at Marengo had forced the Austrian and British governments to the negotiating table after they spurned his initial peace offers, and secured the peace treaties of Lunéville and Amiens. In October 1801, when Anglo-French peace preliminaries were signed, jubilant crowds pulled the French diplomatic envoy General Lavriston through the streets of London, hailing Bonaparte as a peacemaker. The Amiens treaty was welcomed by Britain's mercantile and financial interests, who expected a trading agreement along the lines of the 1786 Eden treaty to follow, and by a nation tired of war. The Addington ministry viewed Amiens as an experimental peace, but it enjoyed the support of most of the political elite, with the exception of a few hard-line Tories led by William Windham. Moreover, the peace settlement was not fundamentally unjust, unbalanced or unstable. It recognized geopolitical realities by accepting Britain's maritime hegemony, French preponderance in Western Europe and Russian dominance in the East. Thus, until Napoleon began abrogating the spirit, if not the letter, of the peace treaty by his political interventions in Switzerland, Italy and Germany from mid-1802, the British had little reason to be dissatisfied. In fact, the British elite was so fascinated by Bonaparte that, once a definitive peace treaty was signed on 25 March 1802, they flocked to Paris in droves to see the hero up close.

There were, of course, some negative images of Napoleon available, particularly in the cartoons of Gillray, which, though purchased only by the wealthy, were viewed avidly by curious crowds through print-shop windows. The first satirical representation of Bonaparte, Isaac Cruikshank's *Buonaparte at Rome giving Audience in State*, appeared as early as March 1797, and to judge from its accuracy was drawn from a French print. However, prior to *brumaire*, caricatures are relatively limited and many offer only allegorical representations of the Jacobin general. Satirical or derogatory verbal portraits of the First Consul were also available to a French-speaking elite through French émigré periodicals, particularly Peltier's spirited *L'Ambigu* (1802–18), an anthological arsenal of anti-Bonaparte materials, and Jacques Regnier's vitriolic *Courier de Londres* (1802–5) and *Courier d'Angleterre* (1805–15). Elements of the British press were also hostile to Bonaparte, especially *The Times*. Although the paper briefly supported peace in the autumn of 1801 and extolled the Foreign Minister Hawkesbury, by the end of the year it had changed position, perhaps for commercial reasons. Throughout 1802, it launched numerous attacks on the French government, some of them penned by émigré journalists. French agents suspected that editorial policy was intended to manipulate the stock exchange by creating rumours of imminent war, but it also seems to have been an attempt to provoke Napoleon, encouraged by Windham and the pro-war party. In the wake of Peltier's trial, *The Times* denounced Napoleon's attempts to suborn British press liberty and ridiculed French claims that the British government had a duty to ensure that other governments were treated with respect. *The Times* retorted that this was not the case with regimes based on disloyalty, terror, usurpation and despotism. During 1802 and early 1803, more papers turned against the peace, perhaps provoked by the apparent threat to press freedom, but also as a reflection of growing public disillusionment with the Amiens treaty. From the autumn of 1802, disquiet grew over Napoleon's actions on the Continent, and his failure to renew the Eden trade treaty, which was perceived to have been highly favourable to Britain on both sides of the Channel.

Prior to 1803, the range of anti-Napoleonic materials was still relatively limited. Nevertheless, several key themes had already emerged, including irreverent allusions to Napoleon's Jacobin past, as in Gillray's *Democracy; — or — a sketch of the Life of Napoleon Buonaparte*. Likewise, as Gillray's title indicates, writers and caricaturists persisted in spelling his surname 'Buonaparte' or 'Buonaparté', as a reminder of Napoleon's Corsican-Italian ancestry. Moreover, émigré publicists were well informed about Napoleon's early life due to the presence in London of General Paoli and his Corsican nationalist supporters. The Paolists provided details of how the Bonapartes had been driven from the island in the civil strife of the early 1790s and fled to Marseilles. They probably also provided Peltier's journal with fabricated accounts of how Bonaparte's mother and sisters survived there by fraternizing with French soldiers. These tales are the first examples of the legend of the sexual promiscuity of Napoleon's sister, Pauline Bonaparte-Borghese.

However, the event from Napoleon's early career that most

Democracy; – or – a Sketch of the Life of Buonaparte, by James Gillray, published by Hannah Humphrey, 12 May 1800.
National Portrait Gallery, London; D12735.

captured the imagination of the European public, cartoonists and writers was the Egyptian expedition of 1798–99. Much of this fascination was aroused by the scholars and artists who accompanied Napoleon to Egypt and provided the European public with the first systematic and detailed descriptions of Egyptian antiquities. Thus the expedition was represented in numerous ways including the cryptic vignette in Peltier's *L'Ambigu* depicting Napoleon as a sphinx (cat. no. 44). The expedition was also a staple of satirists and propagandists because it had tarnished Napoleon's military reputation. After a spectacular victory over the Egyptian beys at the Battle of the Pyramids, Nelson destroyed Napoleon's fleet at the Battle of the Nile; an advance into Syria ended in precipitate retreat; and Napoleon eventually returned to France furtively – an action that could be, and was, portrayed as desertion (cat. no. 53). The Syrian campaign also gave rise to the two most serious atrocity stories in the entire anti-Napoleonic Black Legend. These were endorsed by Colonel Robert Wilson's *History of the British*

Expedition to Egypt published in 1802. Wilson alleged that at the capture of and retreat from Jaffa, Napoleon had ordered that Turkish prisoners be massacred and plague-ridden French soldiers poisoned. Both stories had a factual basis, but they ignored key mitigating factors. His army lacked supplies, was weakened by plague and in a desperate plight. He could not afford to take prisoners, and some of his victims seem to have already been captured once before, then released having given their word of honour not to fight on. By the standards of the day, their execution, given that they had broken their word, was justifiable if harsh. Likewise, his abandoned, plague-ridden troops could expect a slow agonizing natural death, or worse, at the hands of the Turks. Wilson's work infuriated Napoleon, whose visit to the plague-house in Jaffa is celebrated in a famous propaganda painting by Antoine-Jean, Baron Gros (see p.37). It is probable that he ordered the publication of the notorious Sébastiani memorandum – which recommended a new French invasion of Egypt – in retaliation. This was a grave miscalculation, for it pursuaded the British of France's hostile intent and helped propel them into declaring war pre-emptively. Napoleon's time in the Near East also gave initial impetus to the charge that he was a religious cynic, hypocrite and serial apostate. His assiduous attempts to woo the Egyptian population included the notorious propagandist proclamation to the Egyptians of 12 July 1798 (*24 messidor an VI* by the Revolutionary calendar). It declared that the French were children of the prophet, and made a virtue of the Revolution's persecution of the Pope and Church.

Nevertheless, a couple of unsubstantiated atrocity stories, defeat in a sideshow campaign far from Europe, a youthful flirtation with Jacobinism and suspicion of his motives in religious policy probably counted for little in British eyes in comparison with the Napoleon's other military and civic achievements. This ambiguous attitude is exemplified in James Gillray's *Exit Libertè a la Francois! Or Buonaparte closing the Farce of Egalitè at St. Cloud near Paris, November 10th 1799*. In this print Bonaparte's bearing, posture and firmness are almost heroic, in marked contrast to the cowardly and grotesque Revolutionary deputies who scatter before him in this final confrontation of the *brumaire coup d'état*. Thus, prior to late 1802, British images of Napoleon were characterized by ambiguity and generally quite positive. No overriding image predominates and the range of anti-Napoleonic materials was limited. Many of the most enduring images of the Corsican Ogre only developed later. In the interim, the most diverse, dynamic and vitriolic aspects of the anti-Napoleonic Black Legend had been developed among Corsican exiles and in French émigré publications. Thus, in 1803, British propagandists were faced with an urgent need to develop an effective message in the face of imminent invasion.

The result was an outpouring of anti-Napoleonic propaganda exclusively intended for domestic consumption. As in the 1790s, most of this propaganda received official encouragement and elite backing rather than direct government funding. It is true that there was an international dimension to British propaganda warfare. The government hired émigré papers to carry information and opinion to francophone elites across Europe, but such papers were not intended for domestic consumption. From about 1810, caricature images also crossed linguistic borders and carried anti-Napoleonic messages around Europe. However, the international propaganda potential of cartoon images remained largely unrealized until relatively late in the struggle against Napoleon, perhaps in part due to the complex texts that accompanied many British cartoons. Thus, the themes and ideas conveyed by anti-Napoleonic propaganda in 1803–4 tend to be both immediate and peculiarly British in nature, as shown by many of the prints in this exhibition. Its purpose was to stiffen popular resolve to fight, sometimes by

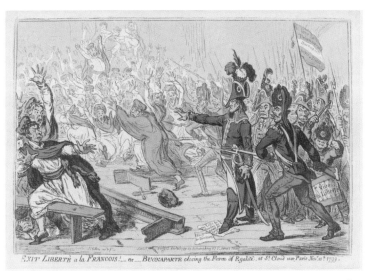

Exit Libertè a la Francois! — or — Buonaparte closing the Farce of Egalitè, at St. Cloud near Paris Nov. 10th 1799, by James Gillray, published by Hannah Humphrey, 21 November 1799. National Portrait Gallery, London; D12714.

presenting the war as one of national survival, and to destroy any inclination to accept a French invasion, whether with passivity or enthusiasm. These imperatives betray both the strength of British national feeling by 1803 and contemporary suspicions that there remained widespread sympathy for 'French principles'.

British propaganda in and after 1803 thus continued many earlier themes and developed new ones. One major tactic was to belittle the French invaders both to inspire contempt and raise morale. Perhaps the most enduring aspect of this campaign was the creation of the myth of Napoleon's diminutive stature. Its most striking recent manifestation was a scene in the film *Time Bandits* in which a morose, inebriated Napoleon, on campaign in Italy, comforts himself by reciting the heights of other celebrated generals who were vertically challenged. The creation of 'Little Boney' was a propaganda master stroke, allowing cartoonists to portray him as a petulant child, a toy soldier, an absurd Lilliputian, a dwarf attempting to play the role of a giant (cat. no. 159). They also sought to suggest that Napoleon, like the Jacobins before him, was driven by an almost insane and implacable hatred of England. This theme dated back at least to Gillray's *Buonaparte, hearing of Nelson's Victory, swears by his Sword to Extirpate the British from off the Earth*', published on 8 December 1798 (cat. no. 48). French invasion plans were also belittled, albeit in a less literal sense. Cartoons such as *The COFFIN EXPEDITION or BONEY's Invincible Armada* and *THE UPSHOT OF THE INVASION, or BONY in a Fair Way for Davey's Locker* (cat. no. 151) relied for their effectiveness on the dismal military record of the French Revolutionary navy. In contrast, *FRENCH INVASION —*

or – *BUONAPARTÉ Landing in Great-Britain* (cat. no. 160), which depicts an invading French army led by Bonaparte fleeing before the first whiff of British shot, was little more than morale-boosting bravado pandering to popular prejudice. In reality, the French army's performance during the Revolutionary War left little room for British optimism, and volunteer militiamen may well have performed poorly had an invasion actually taken place. Other prints, including *AN ACCURATE REPRESENTATION of the FLOATING MACHINE Invented by the FRENCH for INVADING ENGLAND* seem to satirize the more ludicrous invasion fantasies of the French, including windmill-propelled ships (cat. no. 154). However, we cannot always be sure of the artist's intent, as contemporaries were fixated with the potential of new technologies such as hot-air balloons. This is clearly shown in the French print *Divers projets sur la descente en Angleterre* which shows Britain being invaded by a conventional navy, tunnelling and an aerial armada. During the Napoleonic War, the British Foreign Office also received proposals that balloons be used for military communications, displaying French royalist images or even dropping propaganda leaflets over France. Other images followed the example of Gillray's *Fighting for the DUNGHILL – or – Jack Tar settling BUONAPARTE*, which dates from 1798 and suggests that the triumph of the common British sailor would leave Britain literally on top of the world, by celebrating the role of ordinary Britons in resisting the French (cat. no. 218). The same message was reiterated in 1803 in Gillray's macabre and disturbingly ambiguous *Buonaparté, 48 Hours after landing*, in which a British yokel is shown holding Napoleon's freshly severed head aloft on a pitchfork. It equated Napoleon with an outlaw and implied, somewhat improbably, that Napoleon might be defeated by stout-hearted English militiamen. Yet it also reveals anxieties about the British populace, especially fears that it might behave like a French Revolutionary mob, dispatching 'popular justice' and parading victims' heads upon spikes.

Anti-Napoleonic and patriotic themes were reinforced in popular broadside songs and ballads, and explored at greater length in pamphlet publications. After 1804, political events added new dimensions to the mythology of British, continental and émigré propagandists and the anti-Napoleonic Black Legend. The invasion of the Iberian peninsula, Napoleon's imprisonment of the Pope and the summoning of a Jewish Sanhedrin in 1807, fed increasing denunciations of his impiety, especially in Spain. Continuous bloody warfare led to him being portrayed as a voracious and bloodthirsty Corsican Ogre. After his divorce from Josephine, anti-Napoleonic satirists ceased to suggest

that the Emperor was sexually impotent. Instead, following the acquisition of a young Austrian princess, Marie-Louise, as his second wife in 1809, as part of the spoils of victory, they began accusing him of ravishment and other sexual crimes. It is no coincidence that around 1810, Lewis Goldsmith, 'Colonel Stewarton' (the *nom de plume* of an unknown anti-Napoleonic propagandist) and Jean-Baptiste Couchery began to publish absurd apocryphal stories of the sexual proclivities of the Emperor and his family.

There is little doubt that the tidal wave of anti-Napoleonic ephemera, pamphlet literature, ballads and cartoons published in 1803–4 reached almost the entire British populace and had an enduring impact. It succeeded in transforming the crusade against revolution into a war against France's supposedly insatiable tyrant and implanted images of Napoleon that remained remarkably enduring. Nineteenth-century Britons tended to view Jacobinism in the same way that their twentieth-century counterparts viewed Bolshevism, and they regarded Napoleon with the same universal horror that would later be reserved – with much greater justification – for Hitler. More than three decades after Waterloo, while en route for India, the statesman and historian Lord Macaulay was wryly amused to encounter an extreme manifestation of British attitudes in a fellow passenger who demonstrated – apparently in all seriousness – that if certain numerical values were ascribed to the letters of Napoleon's name, they would total 666, thereby establishing that Napoleon was the biblical beast of Revelation.

The anti-Napoleonic Black Legend served the immediate propaganda needs of the British and their allies, but proved counter-productive in the long term. After the restoration of the Bourbons in France in 1814–15, a domestic French liberal critique of Napoleonic despotism was drowned out rapidly by a combination of monstrous Black Legend images and vigorous pro-Napoleonic propaganda. Thus, despite the hardships of a dozen years of warfare, costly military defeat, occupation and reparations, anti-Napoleonic feeling never took off in France and lacked a patriotic appeal. Over time, the memory of the imperial regime was transformed: the costs and military defeats were forgotten, the victories and martyrdoms romanticized. Thus, although Napoleon was twice forced to abdicate after leading his country to disastrous defeat, by 1848 the Bonaparte name was powerful enough to ensure his nephew Louis-Napoleon victory by an overwhelming margin in the Second Republic's presidential election. French popular Bonapartism remained very much alive.

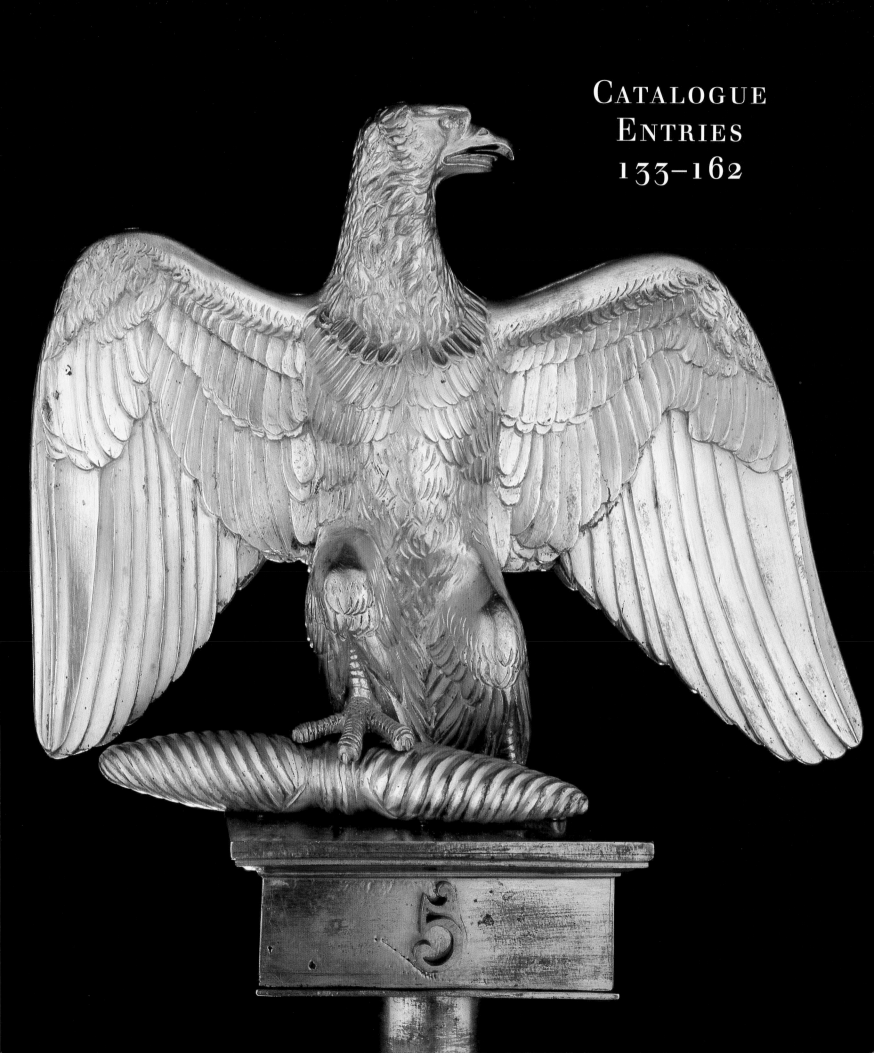

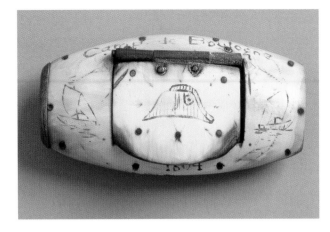

133.   Tobacco box, 1804
Unknown sailor
Bone
Inscription
Musée de la Marine, Paris; 7 SO 220; 490A

This simply made tobacco box was carved from bone and
decorated by one of Napoleon's men gathered at the
Boulogne camp. Between 1803 and 1805, more than
100,000 of the Grand Army assembled here in preparation
for an invasion of England. The hinged lid of the box is
crudely engraved with a picture of Napoleon's hat and the
top is decorated with small sailing boats and the words
'*Camp de Boulogne*'. The other side has an initial '*N*' beneath
a coronet and a scurrilous anti-British slogan '*Merde pour les
Goddems*'.   RP

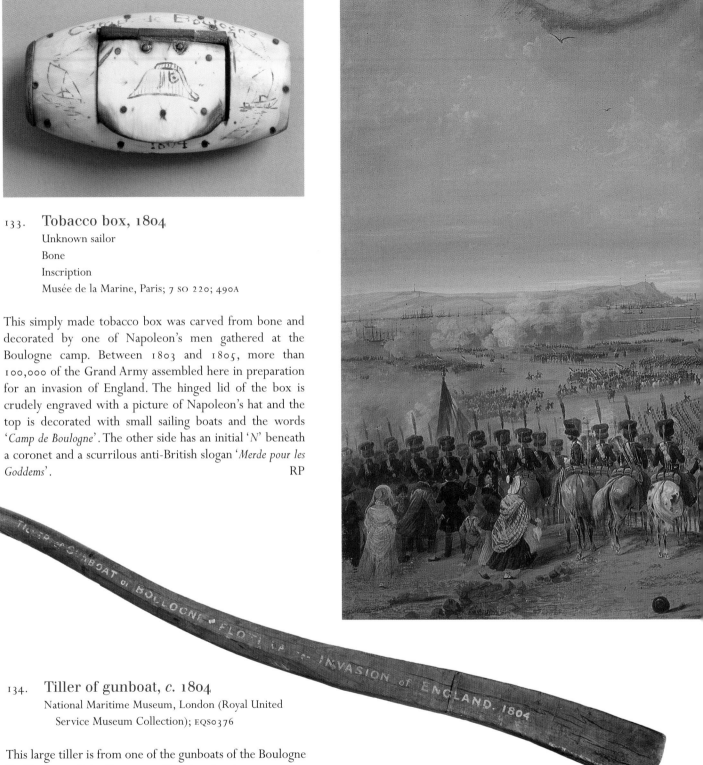

134.   Tiller of gunboat, *c.* 1804
National Maritime Museum, London (Royal United
Service Museum Collection); EQS0376

This large tiller is from one of the gunboats of the Boulogne
flotilla, part of the fleet assembled in 1804 in preparation
for Bonaparte's proposed invasion of England. Shallow-
draught landing craft were specially built and various types
of vessels prepared to convey large numbers of troops,
horses and equipment across the Channel.   RP

135. *Review at Boulogne, c.* 1830–40
Anonymous
Distemper on canvas
1170 x 2100mm
Museo Napoleonico, Rome; MN 1236

Originally planned for 5 August 1804, the ceremony at the Boulogne camp at which the first Légion d'honneur medals were to be distributed was rescheduled for the 16th to coincide (more or less) with Napoleon's birthday (and the day of St Napoleon) of the day before. In a large meadow which formed a natural amphitheatre, more than 80,000 soldiers were arranged in 'rays' around the 'sun' of the new emperor's throne (the perspectival centre of the painting here). Napoleon distributed the newly created *aigles* to military men and civilians alike, thus bringing back to France the idea of state honours, a concept banned by the Revolutionary government in 1792 because it was redolent of *ancien régime* inequality. The *Moniteur* newspaper of *5 fructidor an XII* (23 August 1804) noted that adverse winds unfortunately made it impossible for British ships off the coast to view (and be impressed by) the size and quality of this imposing force. Today the famous Boulogne column, upon which Napoleon stands with his back to England, and a smaller stone monument set on the exact spot where his throne stood, commemorate what was effectively the beginning of the Légion d'honneur.   PH

136. **One-gun caique, 1801–5**
Attributed to the workshop of the Arsenal
Scale 1: 30/32
Musée de la Marine, Paris; 17 MG 29

A contemporary model of a caique (above), representing the small to medium-sized vessels built for the proposed invasion of England in 1803. Built in lengths of up to 60 feet (18m), they were capable of carrying a variety of guns. This model shows provisions for a single 24-pound cannon mounted on slides in the stern, as well as smaller guns mounted on stanchions. It is rigged with two masts carrying standing lug sails, and the caique could also be rowed if becalmed or working in shallow waters. These vessels were capable of carrying up to 100 soldiers although their range was limited since there was no space for provisions and little protection against the elements. The model shows a grapnel anchor rigged over the port bow. This type of anchor was carried due to the lack of onboard space but also because it could be lifted and managed by the crew to secure the boat when landing on a shallow beach.   SS

137. **Cannoniere-Brick of the Boulogne flotilla of 1803**
Achille Beaugrand, 1806, signed on the model
Made in the models studio of the Arsenal, nineteenth century, Paris
Scale 1:48
Musée de la Marine, Paris; 17 MG 22

A contemporary model depicting one of the many designs, ordered and built for Napoleon's proposed invasion of England in 1803. Rigged as a brig, that is a two-masted vessel with square sails, the vessels were up to 110 feet (33.5m) in length and capable of carrying thirty to forty sailors and 120 soldiers. In terms of armament, the flat and wide hull was designed to support up to twelve 24-pounder guns as well as smaller guns mounted on stanchions on the gunwale. In reality, these rather lightly built vessels were not capable of carrying a full complement of heavy guns, especially in the rough weather that can be encountered in the English Channel. Although the primary propulsion was sail, they could also be rowed and this model shows how the oars were stowed in crutches at the stern when they were not in use.   SS

138. Letter to Citizen Couïn from
L. Doguereau, Boulogne, *14 nivôse
an XII* (6 January 1804)

Ink on paper

Jean-Louis de Talancé, private collection

In this letter to Couïn, a colonel of the horse artillery, L. Doguereau outlines the importance of the 400–500 boats that had been prepared to ship some 40,000 men across the Channel. He expresses his eagerness for the invasion to proceed, so that the French troops might see the land that they all apparently wished to possess, and notes that only another 200 boats and a fine day are needed before they can depart to take the apparently unsuspecting English by surprise.

Napoleon had actually hoped to assemble and transport some 150,000 troops across the Channel to invade Britain by means of a swift attack. His Army of England had been undergoing intense training in a string of camps along the Channel coast since 1803, participating in a gruelling round of drills and large-scale manoeuvres. However, for the plan to work, it was estimated that at least 2000 boats were needed to convey the troops. The number of boats and men available at any one time was often exaggerated to him: in October 1803 Admiral Decrès, Minister of Marine, reported that more than 1000 vessels were ready. This can be considered in contrast to the figures apparently reported by Doguereau from Boulogne in early 1804.　　CLW

LITERATURE: Elting, *Swords around a Throne*; Frank
　　McLynn, *Napoleon: A Biography* (London, 1998); Alan
　　Schom, *Trafalgar: Countdown to Battle* (London, 1990).

139. *Plan Général du Port de Boulogne /*
General plan of the Port of Boulogne

J-P. Salles, *floréal an XII* (April–May 1804)

Ink, wash and gouache on paper

940 x 1110mm

Musée de la Marine, Paris; 9 NA 14

Napoleon's English invasion plans envisaged a massive amphibious assault from ports between Flushing (Vlissingen) in the Netherlands and Étaples. In practice Boulogne, then an undeveloped minor port on the shallow River Liane, became the principal centre for his strategy. From May 1803 work began on new quays, defences and the great semicircular basin south of the river (top) for a large part of the 'National Flotilla' of invasion barges that were built in many ports at the same time. Everywhere the project massively overran on time and costs. Work at Boulogne was also slowed by British bombardment but by the summer of 1804 the port was impregnable in the centre 3-km (1.8-mile) strip of coastline defended by forts and batteries, mounting 180 fixed guns and more mobile artillery. This plan, by a naval gunner, shows the new port and the dispositions proposed to the Minister of Marine, Admiral Decrès, for 1300 invasion craft of all sizes carrying 66,000 men to leave Boulogne on a single tide – though it could not actually be done in less than four.　　PvdM

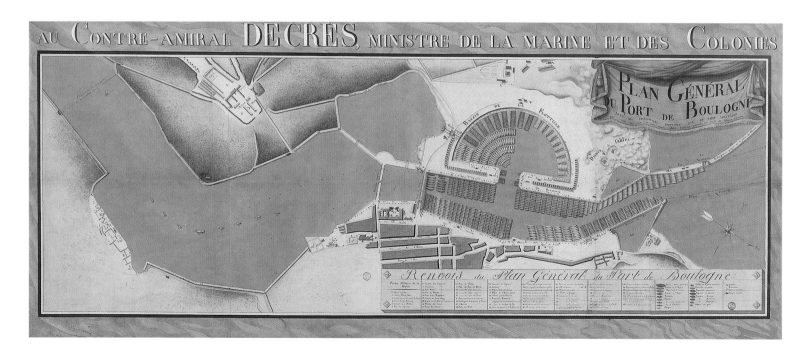

140. **Model of a gunboat, launched *c.* 1804**
Unknown, 1804
Scale 1:32 approx.
National Maritime Museum, London; SLR0648

Gunboats were small shallow-draught vessels capable of carrying a large gun that could be fired over the bow or stern. The gun was aimed by the steering of the vessel itself. Although the nationality of this model is not certain, the shape and layout of the hull suggest that it is one of several proposed designs for Napoleon's invasion flotilla, which he started assembling at the northern French channel ports in 1803. By 1804, part of this force was based at Boulogne and consisted of 160,000 men, 10,000 horses and a flotilla of 1300 vessels of various sizes to carry men across the Channel. This model illustrates a boat measuring 56 feet (17m) in length by 16 feet (4.8m) in the beam. It could carry the rudder at either end and thus be rowed in either direction. Internally, the long slide running from bow to stern is employed for working the gun at either end of the boat. When the gun was not in use, the centre portion of the slide was removed, allowing it to be stowed on the bottom boards. Together with the shot racked along the keel, it then acted as ballast and improved stability. The lockers under the thwarts were used for keeping the cartridges and provisions dry, while the weapons of the soldiers were stored around the inside of the gunwale under canvas covers.   SS

141. **Cross of the Légion d'honneur (1804), axe of the Légion d'honneur (1801) and certificate of the Légion d'honneur (25 September 1801)**
Silver and enamel; ink on paper
Musée National de la Légion d'Honneur et des Ordres
de Chevalerie, Paris; inv. 03122, 03121 and 3123

As earlier systems of reward had been abolished during the course of the Revolution, a system of 'arms of honour' was re-established in 1799 to reward soldiers for acts of

particular bravery or distinction. From May 1802, receiving these arms entitled recipients to become members of the newly created Légion d'honneur, a form of honour which was open to all citizens who had served the state, not just military personnel. The first medals were awarded in 1804: a silver star for *legionnaires* and a gold star for other ranks.

Shortly after the army's honours system was reintroduced, the navy was given its own award, which took the form of a miniature boarding axe draped in a standard. Only about fifty of these were given out, and the *hache d'abordage d'honneur* is thus relatively rare; it was incorporated into the new Légion d'honneur in 1804.   CLW

LITERATURE: Humbert and Ponsonnet, eds, *Napoléon et la mer*; Ellis, *Napoleon*; 'History of the Légion d'Honneur' www.legiondhonneur.fr/shared/us/musee/fmusee.html.

142. Imperial eagle of the 5th Infantry Regiment, *c.* 1804
Pierre-Philippe Thomire after Antoine-Denis Chaudet
Gilt bronze
Musée de l'Armée, Paris; Bd 41

After the proclamation of the Empire, Napoleon adopted the eagle with outstretched wings as a new national symbol, following the example of the ancient Roman Empire. From 27 July 1804 these gilt-bronze eagles, surmounting the colour-staffs of his regiments, were personally presented to them by the Emperor. PvdM

143. *Londres et les Anglais*, 1804
J. L. Ferri de St-Constant [Count Giovanni L. Ferri di San Costante]
Printed books
Pierre-Jean Chalençon, private collection

It is tempting to think that Napoleon ordered these four volumes of *Londres et les Anglais*, published in Paris, 1804, shortly before his attempt to invade Britain in 1805. However, although they certainly were part of his private library, their date of acquisition is uncertain. The work would have provided him with a comprehensive picture of England and its inhabitants, which the author attempted to do impartially, 'without hatred and without flattery'. In the first volume the focus is on London: its streets, houses,

palaces, taverns and other attractions are described in great detail – often with historical anecdotes. The characteristics of its inhabitants are also amply considered. The dominant attribute of the English of the time was apparently national pride. Their other traits included generosity, sincerity, reserve, a commercial spirit, and a hatred for foreigners. In the second volume the English education system is discussed and considered far from the perfection commonly supposed. The third volume looks at the arts, often neglected by travellers to the country – probably due to the fact that, as the editor states, the English were thought rarely to have enough talent to produce great works, although their wealth meant that they could often buy them. The fourth volume considers religion, the law and politics. CLW

144. Pocket-watch dial depicting French invasion, made *c.* 1803
Unknown maker
Silver case
Inscribed: *Descente en Angleterre*
National Maritime Museum, London (Walter Collection); JEW0265

The lower half of this Swiss-made pocket-watch dial is painted with a scene anticipating the French fleet invading Britain. At the centre of the dial is a small aperture which has a mock automaton of one of the fleet's ships against a white background. The watch has been crudely altered since it was first made. The watch mechanism is not the original one, and the automaton ship is cut from a late nineteenth-century watch dial. DR

145. **Medal commemorating the camp at Boulogne, and the planned invasion of England, 1804**

Dominique-Vivant Denon (1747–1825),
  Romain-Vincent Jeuffroy (1749–1826) and Louis
  Jaley (1763–1838)
Signed
Bronze
41mm diam.
National Maritime Museum, London; MEC0830

Obverse: the Emperor Napoleon I seated on a throne with two attendants standing behind him, handing a medal to a soldier in uniform, with three others, one bearing a staff with the Napoleonic eagle and wreath. Legend: 'HONNEUR LÉGIONAIRE AUX BRAVES DE L'ARMÉE' (Honour of the legion to the brave men of the army). Exergue: 'A BOULOGNE LE XXVIII THERM. AN XII XVI AOUT MDCCCIV'. Signature: 'DENON. D. JEUFFROY F'. Reverse: plan of the camp with numbers, inscription below. Inscription: 'SERMENT. DE L'ARMEE. D'ANGLETERRE A L'EMPEREUR' (The oath of the army for England to the Emperor Napoleon). Below, a list of the positions of cavalry, infantry, flags, legionnaires, officers, etc., according to the numbers on the plan. 'No.1. CAVALLERIE. 2 . INFANTERIES .3 GÉNÉREAUX . 4 DRAPEAUX . 5 LÉGIONNAIRES . 6 . GARDE DE L'EMPEREUR 7 .MUSICIENS . ET . TBOURS .8 .ET .MOR .DS CS 9 .ET . MOR .GAL 10 .LE TRONE'. Signature: 'JALEY F'. A medallic history was planned to illustrate the victories of Napoleon similar to the one previously produced for Louis XIV. In the event, the official series of medals was never struck but Dominique-Vivant Denon, Director of Museums and of the mint until

1815, produced a semi-official version. Denon, an archaeologist and artist who had taken part in the expedition to Egypt, encouraged a style that was strictly based on classical prototypes. This was proved eminently suitable for medal design.   BT

LITERATURE: Bramsen, *Médailler Napoléon le Grand*, I, 318.

146. *Physical Aid – or – Britannia recover'd from a Trance; – also, the Patriotic Courage of Sherry Andrew, & a peep thro' the Fog*

James Gillray, published 14 March 1803 by
  H. Humphrey
Hand-coloured etching
310 x 428mm
National Maritime Museum, London; PAF3967

With the rapid disintegration of the Peace of Amiens in the face of Napoleonic military build-up in the spring of 1803, the King suggested to Parliament the adoption of additional defences. This was debated on 9 March, when the advocates of peace, led by Addington, Fox and Sheridan, rejected such plans as unnecessary and denounced any move towards the resumption of war. This anti-war stance is the subject of Gillray's biting satire. Set on a cliff-top looking out to sea, a recumbent and dishevelled Britannia, having just awoken to the danger, cries out for assistance. She is supported by Addington and Hawkesbury, who offer her only platitudes. The scene is enveloped in thick, black fog, and in the background, in the midst of it, Fox, holding his hat before his eyes, declares he 'can't see any thing of the Buggabo's!'. Beyond the fog, however, the French fleet is visible, led by Napoleon (who is shown without a torso, that is, a 'Nobody'). It descends in droves upon the English coast. At the centre of the composition is a brutal lampoon of Sheridan, represented as a grotesque Harlequin holding a

Physical Aid .– or – Britannia recover'd from a Trance ; – also .the Patriotic Courage of Sherry Andrew ,& a peep thro' the Fog .–

club inscribed 'Dramatic Loyalty' and a shield with the image of Medusa, thus suggesting him, mockingly, as a Harlequin version of Perseus rescuing Andromeda. Ridiculous in his mock-heroic posture of defence of Britannia's honour, his Harlequin costume is a reference to Sheridan's career in the theatre, but also suggests that his and his colleagues' parliamentary performance is no better than a farce. GQ

147. A new MACHINE (or RAFT) to cover (or protect) the Landing of the FRENCH on their intended INVASION OF ENGLAND. Engraved after an Original Drawing made by a FRENCH PRISONER of WAR

Anonymous, British, eighteenth century, published
    29 January 1798 by William Hinton
Hand-coloured etching
269 x 392mm
National Maritime Museum, London; PAH7426

This is another variation on the supposed raft being built by the French for the invasion of Britain in early 1798. Unlike other prints produced during this wave of paranoia in London, which represent the vessel as an excessively fantastic contraption more appropriate to the tales of Baron Münchausen, this print pares it down to a severe geometric symmetry to assert its claim to being based in fact. Indeed, a greater air of authority is lent by the claim that the engraving is made after an original drawing by a

French prisoner of war, and by the wealth of statistical detail in the caption. The machine is described as:

> Flat; 2,100 Feet long, and 1,500 Feet broad; has 500 Cannon round it, 36 and 48 Pounders; at each end is two Wind Mills, which turns Wheels in the Water at every point of the Wind to Navigate; in the middle is a Fort enclosing Mortars, Perriers, &c. It carries 60,000 Men, Cavalry, Infantry, and Artillery.

Nonetheless, this does not disguise the unseaworthiness of the 'new machine', and neither is there any firm evidence that such a vessel was being constructed on the north French coast at this time. GQ

148. A Correct Plan and Elevation of the FAMOUS FRENCH RAFT, constructed on purpose for the Invasion of England and intended to carry 30,000 Men, Ammunition, Stores &c. &c.

Anonymous, British, eighteenth century
Hand-coloured etching
376 x 255mm
National Maritime Museum, London; PAD4060

Early in 1798 there were reports of a planned French invasion of the southern English coast, with the build-up of troops in the northern French ports. On the French side there was a belief that their invading army would be broadly welcomed by the majority of ordinary British people. By contrast, across the Channel fears of an invasion induced the

A new MACHINE (or RAFT) to cover (or protect) the Landing of the FRENCH on their intended
INVASION OF ENGLAND.
Engraved after an Original Drawing made by a FRENCH PRISONER of WAR.
This Machine is flat; 2,100 Feet long, and 1,500 Feet broad; has 500 Cannon round it, 36 and 48 pounders; at each end is two Wind Mills, which turns Wheels in the Water at every point of the Wind to Navigate; in the middle is a Fort enclosing Mortars, Perriers, &c. It carries 60,000 Men, Cavalry, Infantry, and Artillery.
London: Published by Wm. HINTON, Engraver and Printer, West Harding Street, Fetter Lane; Jan. 29, 1798.
PRICE ONE SHILLING.

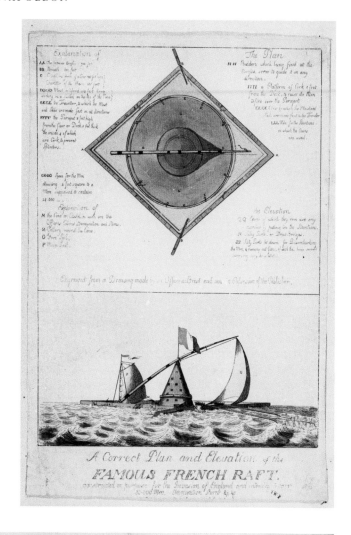

A Correct Plan and Elevation of the
FAMOUS FRENCH RAFT.

promulgation of a fable about an enormous raft that the French were supposedly constructing in order to transport huge numbers of French soldiers to England. Several prints, of which this is an example, were produced claiming to be based on eyewitness accounts or other authentic information. They vary in the raft's reported carrying capacity, most claiming that 60,000 troops could be transported. This print, which shows the raft as the impossible product of severe rational geometry, combined with the fantasies of Baron Münchausen and Noah's Ark, claims just 30,000 capacity. It is difficult to know how seriously prints such as this were intended to be taken. While there was genuinely founded fear of invasion, there was also widespread ridicule of the idea of a raft, including a theatrical afterpiece on the subject. J. C. Cross's *The Raft, or both Sides of the Water* had its first performance at Covent Garden on 31 March 1798, with the predictable denouement of the raft being blown up.

GQ

149. *Consequences of a Successful French Invasion; No. 1 – Plate 2nd. – We explain de Rights of Man to de Noblesse. – Scene. The House of Lords*

James Gillray, published 1 March 1798
Coloured etching
361 x 401mm
National Maritime Museum, London; PAG8509

The second of four prints executed by Gillray of a series of twenty proposed by the Scot Sir John Dalrymple. In response to the invasion scare of early 1798, Sir John approached Gillray to produce a series of loyalist, anti-Jacobin prints that 'might rouse all the People to an active Union against that Invasion; at a Time when above five Millions of Vultures, with Beaks and Claws, hover over them; and when the Indolence and Divisions of the people themselves are more alarming than all foreign Enemies'.

When hoped-for government funds to support the project were not forthcoming, it was abandoned with just four plates completed. Here, French troops are shown occupying the heart of the British constitution, the House of Lords, which is being looted and defiled. A guillotine presides on the throne and the visual emblem of Britain's maritime identity, the Armada tapestries, are slashed and burned at the instruction of the French admiral, who, as the caption explains, says, 'Me not like de Omen; destroy it'.

GQ

150. *The COFFIN EXPEDITION or BONEY's Invincible Armada Half Seas Over*

[Williams], published 6 January 1804 by S. W. Fores

Hand-coloured etching

240 x 353mm

National Maritime Museum, London; PAD4783

One of many prints published in the months after the renewal of war in May 1803 dealing with the threatened Napoleonic invasion of Britain. Like Gillray's *Destruction of the French Gun-Boats* (cat. no. 158), published just over a month earlier, it satirizes the impracticability of an invasion, presenting it as a doom-laden venture that will inevitably send thousands of Frenchmen to their certain deaths. The print takes this idea to bizarre and macabre lengths, by transforming the French gunboats into floating coffins manned by crews wearing shrouds and *bonnets rouges*. Some are already drowning in the water. One utters the opinion that Napoleon has deliberately launched the expedition 'on purpose for our Funeral', repeating the much-vaunted anti-Napoleonic black propaganda about Napoleon's supposed treachery and duplicity towards his own troops.   GQ

151. *THE UPSHOT OF THE INVASION, or BONY in a fair way for Davey's Locker*, 1804

Anonymous, British, nineteenth century

Hand-coloured aquatint

195 x 234mm

National Maritime Museum, London; PAD4797

A crudely executed allegory of the Anglo-French conflict and the feared French invasion of Britain, representing them simply as a single naval engagement between the respective ships of state. To the right, the French ship, the *Bonaparte*, its tricolour shot through and drooping over the stern, is fired upon and boarded by British sailors. In contrast, the unscathed British vessel to the left has as its figurehead the sea god Neptune carrying his trident, signifying dominion of the seas. Meanwhile, Napoleon at the centre falls into the water, looking back angrily over his shoulder at the British vessel. Attacked by British sailors, he is grabbed round the leg by a sea monster, pulling him to the 'Davey's Locker' of the title. This print served as the frontispiece to *The Anti-Gallican*, a collection of 'papers, tracts, speeches poems and songs . . . published on the threatened Invasion'.   GQ

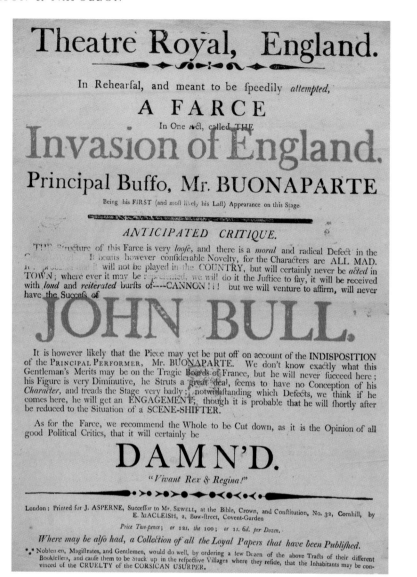

152. *Theatre Royal England. In rehearsal,*
and meant to be speedily attempted
a farce in one act, called The Invasion
of England. Principal Buffo,
Mr. Buonaparte

James Asperne, London, c. 1803

Propaganda poster

570 x 405mm

National Maritime Museum, London; PBF5077

This example of an anti-French propaganda poster was designed as a parody of a playbill. In 1803 the threat of invasion by Napoleon's army overshadowed England; this poster was produced as satirical propaganda to belittle the threat as mere farce. These popular propaganda posters would have been sold in their hundreds. They were printed by Elizabeth Macleish of Covent Garden (printer, 1799–1823), for James Asperne (1727–1820), a bookseller at the Bible, Crown and Constitution, No. 32 Crownhill, London.   HP

153. *Plain answers to plain questions in a*
dialogue between John Bull and
Bonaparte, met half seas over between
Dover and Calais

Published by J. Hatchard, London, 1803

Broadsheet

552 x 444mm

Bodleian Library, Oxford (John Johnson Collection);
French Wars and Revolution

This propaganda broadsheet in the form of a dialogue incorporates most major themes of Britain's anti-Napoleonic publicists. Napoleon admits that he not only allowed but actively encouraged his troops to 'murder in cold blood Thousands of poor Men, and ravish Thousands of poor Women' in order to spread terror. As evidence, he cites his callous massacre of prisoners and poisoning of his own sick troops at Jaffa – atrocity stories that first surfaced in Colonel Robert Wilson's *History of the British Expedition to Egypt* (London, 1802). He also confesses that he is an atheist who makes use of religion to appease local populations wherever he goes. He detests Britain's press liberty, because 'it makes me odious amongst my own subjects, and in all Europe'. Finally, Napoleon admits that his main allies in invading Britain are likely to be 'foggy weather', 'long nights', indiscipline among Britain's forces and disunion among her people. The publisher, J. Hatchard, priced the broadsheet at sixpence a dozen in order that gentlemen might buy them and distribute them among the lower orders.   SB

AN ACCURATE REPRESENTATION of the FLOATING MACHINE Invented by the FRENCH for INVADING ENGLAND. and Acts on the principals of both Wind & Water Mills. carries 60=000 Men & 600 Cannon.

Etch'd & pub'd by Dighton Char.g Cro/s. from a Drawing by Monsieur Freville. just arriv'd.

154. *AN ACCURATE REPRESENTATION of the FLOATING MACHINE Invented by the FRENCH for INVADING ENGLAND. and Acts on the principals of both Wind & Water Mills. carries 60,000 Men & 600 Cannon,* 1798

[?Robert] Dighton (1751–1814)

Hand-coloured etching

162 x 225mm

National Maritime Museum, London; PAH7433

Another print responding to the invasion scare of early 1798 and the rumours of an enormous raft that the French were supposedly constructing on the Channel coast in order to land vast numbers of troops. Here it is claimed that the vessel could carry 60,000 troops, though it is difficult to see how it could be believed that such a bizarre, Heath Robinson contraption as this could ever put to sea. Combining wind and watermills, with an enormous

'Gothic', Bastille-like tower and castle in the centre, it seems to recall contemporary fantasies about the appearance of the Ark. GQ

155. *Let Englishmen keep a watchful eye upon French spies*

Broadsheet, 1803

232 x 287mm

Bodleian Library, Oxford (John Johnson Collection);
    French Wars and Revolution

Reminiscent of twentieth-century propaganda posters and leaflets, such as the 'Walls have Ears' campaign, this broadsheet seeks to mobilize the population by showing that everyone has a role in the war effort. The fear of French spies reflects anxieties inspired by the activities of British

Let ENGLISHMEN

keep a watchful Eye upon

FRENCH SPIES,

who are employed to pull down or deface

all Loyal and Patriotic Papers.

Nichols and Son, Printers, Red Lion Passage, Fleet Street.

156. *A Correct VIEW of the FRENCH FLAT-BOTTOM BOATS, intended to convey their TROOPS, for the INVASION of ENGLAND, as seen afloat in Charante Bay in August 1803*

Anonymous, British, published 17 August 1803 by
    John Fairburn

Hand-coloured etching

259 x 403mm

National Maritime Museum, London; PAH7437

radicals in the 1790s, the recent conspiracy trial of Colonel Edward Marcus Despard, who was executed on 21 February 1803, and the continued presence, despite the Napoleonic amnesty, of several thousand French émigrés on British soil.

SB

This print, published only a few months after the resumption of war between Britain and France, and in response to a very serious invasion fear in Britain, recapitulates similar images produced during the invasion scare of 1798. Unlike the earlier prints, however, with their monstrous and bizarre 'rafts' for transporting huge numbers of troops, this shows much more feasible vessels and appears to be based on much better founded information. The caption claims that they could carry 500 men each. Showing the boats in both bow view and port profile, the print follows the

A Correct VIEW of the FRENCH FLAT-BOTTOM BOATS, intended to convey their TROOPS, for the INVASION of ENGLAND, as seen afloat in Charante Bay; in August 1803.___ Those flat-bottom Boats are about 120 feet long, and 40 broad, and will carry 500 Men each, they have on board 4 small Boats, calculated to carry out, or weigh, a kedge-anchor, with which they can heave the vessel a-head, on light, or contrary winds, when they are near the shore.

References {
1.1 A Draw-bridge for embarking and landing the Troops.
2.2. The Lee Boards.
} {
3.3. Two Guns, long 18 Pounders
4.4.4. Three Gunstres, for hea-ving the vessel a-head &c.
} Publish'd Aug 17 1803, by John Fairburn, 146 Minories, London. {
5.5. Boats, carrying out an Anchor.
6. A head view of one of the flat-bottom boats with a flying top-sail set.
} {
7.7. Eighteen Sweeps, on each side
8. The Draw-bridge.
9. A flat bottom boat embarking Troops.
}

visual conventions for documentary accuracy. However, the decorative treatment of the waves and the use of colour also give it the feel of a satirical print. If the caption is reliable in claiming that the boats were seen in August 1803, its publication on 17 August demonstrates a remarkably rapid response in broadcasting this information.   GQ

157. *The Storm rising; – or – the Republican FLOTILLA in danger*

James Gillray, published 1 February 1798 by
   H. Humphrey
Hand-coloured etching
279 x 667mm
National Maritime Museum, London; PAF3949

This is another print responding to the French invasion threat of early 1798 and to the reports of the construction of an enormous raft to carry Revolutionary troops across the Channel. Here the raft is being winched towards shore by the Whig Opposition 'collaborators' Fox, Sheridan, Tierney and Bedford. At the top right, however, Pitt – transformed into a god-like elemental fury – whips up the waves into a storm to swamp the vessel. Each gust of wind from his mouth bears the name of a recent naval hero. A contemporary German critic, writing of Gillray's series of

prints on the invasion theme, thought this the best of the lot, showing:

> the approach of what is supposed to be a large raft, containing windmills, castles and all the murderous instruments with which the French are threatening the English. On the shore we see a capstan or ship's winch with a rope, which is being turned by fat Fox (looking for all the world like a thresher) . . . A rope leads from the capstan through the water to the ship, hauling it in. The fat-cheeked winds, whose gusts bear the names of the great saviours of the nation . . . are trying as hard as they can to blow the terrifying machine away. I cannot begin to describe the impression which this characteristic print makes on all who see it.

Gillray also appears to be making reference to the increasing vogue for narratives and images of shipwrecks and nautical disasters, which assumed greater significance at this period as a metaphor for the crisis besetting the maritime nation. However, here the terms of the metaphor are inverted: the wreck of this particular vessel does not signify national disaster but deliverance, and the actions of the 'rescuers' on the cliff-top are not heroic but treacherous.

A very similar print was issued by Gillray's rival satirist Isaac Cruikshank just a few days earlier on 28 January.   GQ

The Storm rising : __ or __ the Republican FLOTILLA in danger .

Destruction of the French Gun-Boats — or — Little Boney & his Friend Talley in high Glee.

158. *Destruction of the French Gun-Boats –
or – Little Boney & his Friend Talley in
high Glee*
[James Gillray], published 22 November 1803 by
    H. Humphrey
Hand-coloured aquatint
249 x 370mm
National Maritime Museum, London; PAF4005

In this extravagant satire, Gillray derides Napoleonic plans
for a French invasion of England, suggesting that such a
scheme was instead conceived by a devious Napoleon as a
deliberate means of ridding himself of difficult, oppositional
elements in the army and navy, by sending them to certain
death. Set on the northern French coast, with Dover Castle
visible across the Channel, Bonaparte is seated like a puppet
on Talleyrand's shoulder. He peers through a rolled-up
document, inscribed 'Talleyrand's plan for INVADING
Great Britain', at the French gunboats being destroyed and
sunk by British cannon. Gillray shows Napoleon overjoyed
at this sight, exclaiming 'my good fortune never leaves me!
– I shall now get rid of a hundred-Thousand French Cut
Throats whom I was so afraid of! . . . Bravo, Johnny! –
pepper 'em, Johnny!'.   GQ

159. *The KING of BROBDINGNAG and
GULLIVER. (Plate 2d.) – Scene –
"Gulliver manoeuvring with his little
Boat in the Cistern" – vide, Swift's
Gulliver*
James Gillray, published 10 February 1804 by
    H. Humphrey
Hand-coloured etching
352 x 465mm
British Museum, London; 1861-10-12-46

On 26 June 1803 Gillray published a celebrated print, *The
KING of BROBDINGNAG and GULLIVER*, showing a minute
Napoleon, as Gulliver, in the palm of George III's hand,
being subjected to a searching scrutiny by the latter. This
print, its sequel, is an attempt to capitalize further on its
success. Both images were based on an idea from an
amateur, in this case Lieutenant-Colonel Braddyll. It refers
to a passage in Swift's *Gulliver's Travels*, in which Gulliver,
in the land of the giants of Brobdingnag, tells of rowing
and sailing for the entertainment of the king and queen,
which, however, only provokes their derision and laughter.
Here Gillray instead shows George III and Queen Charlotte
contemplating Napoleon-as-Gulliver with serious study,

while alongside the princesses and Beefeaters look on and laugh. It is a simple but clever mechanism to mock Bonaparte's maritime capability in the wake of renewed hostilities after the collapse of the Peace of Amiens.   GQ

The KING of BROBDINGNAG and GULLIVER. [Plate 2.] _Scene. Gulliver manœuvring with his little Boat in the Cistern._

160.   *FRENCH INVASION – or – BUONAPARTÉ Landing in Great-Britain*

James Gillray, published 10 June 1803 by H. Humphrey

Hand-coloured etching

293 x 682mm

National Maritime Museum, London; PAH7338

This is the first of a series of invasion prints by Gillray following the resumption of war between Britain and France in May 1803. In typical 'anti-gallican' style, it burlesques the attempt of the French to land on British shores, showing an orderly and upright British gun squadron on a cliff-top repelling the rabble of French troops, who are fleeing in disarray. In the centre of these is Napoleon on his white charger, looking over his shoulder in fright and flinging away his sabre. It is an exaggerated ridicule of the French army, which the contemporary German journal *London und Paris* compared to equally hyperbolic and hysterical French caricatures of the English. The German critic made a parallel between the military conflict and that between French and British engravers:

> As we write, the battle being waged between the caricaturists and engravers in London and Paris, with

their witty, highly explosive missiles, has become as bitter and hateful as the real fight between the two nations: a war which is fought with a thousand menacing, fire-spitting cannons.

This suggests the degree to which satires such as Gillray's were perceived as an important part of the propaganda war. The spate of prints of the second half of 1803 that dealt with the threatened invasion was accompanied by numerous broadsides and other published propaganda designed to encourage patriotic sentiment and, more practically, the recruitment of volunteers.   GQ

FRENCH INVASION _or_ BUONAPARTÉ Landing in Great-Britain

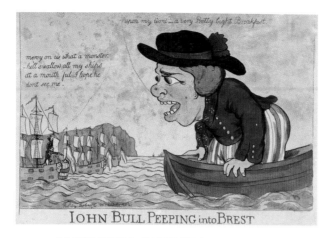

IOHN BULL PEEPING into BREST

161. *JOHN BULL PEEPING into Brest*
George Woodward (?), published [June] 1803 by
 Roberts
Hand-coloured etching
243 x 350mm
National Maritime Museum, London; PAF3950

A simply executed image extolling the might of British sea power over that of the French, with reference to the British blockade of Brest in 1803 by a squadron under Admiral Cornwallis. A gigantic figure of John Bull, dressed as Jack Tar, leans out of a boat off the French coast, eyeing the French ships at anchor in Brest harbour. He savours them

as 'a very Pretty light Breakfast'. In contrast, a diminutive Napoleon at the stern of one of the vessels utters the forlorn hope that 'he don't see me'. Gillray's 1798 print *JOHN BULL taking a Luncheon* had earlier portrayed John Bull, the icon of English national character, as the enthusiastic devourer of French ships, and it may be that the draughtsman of this print is consciously recapitulating that image.   GQ

162. Hat worn by Napoleon, *c.* 1805
Poupard, France
Felt
Pierre-Jean Chalençon, private collection

Napoleon's hat is of a summer-weight felt and dates to around 1805. It is possible that he could have worn it in August 1805, when he arrived at Boulogne to prepare for the launch of the invasion of England. Although 1200 boats were at Boulogne and an additional 1100 at nearby ports, they were undermanned and morale was extremely low. Further, the French fleet, under Villeneuve had retreated to Cadiz, prompting Napoleon to exclaim, 'What a Navy! What sacrifices all for nothing! All hope is gone! . . . It is all over.'   AM

The Royal Navy in 1803

N. A. M. RODGER

WHEN THE PEACE OF AMIENS ended the French Revolutionary War early in 1802, the Royal Navy was larger and in most respects more successful than ever before. It had more than 130,000 officers and men (compared to 105,000 at the end of the American War of Independence in 1782), and a fleet including 111 ships of the line in seagoing condition. Its recent decisive victories at Camperdown (over the Dutch), St Vincent (over the Spaniards), the Nile (over the French) and Copenhagen (over the Danes) had established an unchallenged practical and psychological supremacy over France and all her allies or potential allies. Nevertheless this success had been hard-won. In the early years of the war the French navy had performed unexpectedly well, notably at the Battle of the Glorious First of June, and the conquests of the French army had forced the British to evacuate the Mediterranean for eighteen months. Political weaknesses in the Cabinet and the Admiralty and disagreement and disloyalty among British admirals had significantly weakened the war effort at sea. The British campaigns in the West Indies had effectively destroyed the British army's only expeditionary force, and the Navy was partly to blame for the failure to complete a swift conquest of the French islands before tropical diseases could take hold. Above all the great mutinies of 1797 had paralyzed the main fleet and raised the spectre of Jacobin revolution in Britain. Authority had been re-established, at least on the surface, but there was a series of lesser, though by no means trivial, mutinies in the following years. Nobody, in the Navy or outside, was now sure how far its discipline could be relied on. This was a major reason why many senior officers welcomed the Peace of Amiens.

Junior officers' feelings were different. The Royal Navy was a unique career for boys and men from the wide area of British society which possessed, or claimed, or aspired to the status of a gentleman. It was highly honourable, it demanded very little

The Delegates in Council or Beggars on Horseback,
by Isaac Cruikshank (cat. no. 33).

money or influence (though influence never came amiss) and it offered young men of courage, skill and luck a rapid rise to fame and honour. Moreover, as Admiral Vernon had put it half a century before, the Navy's laurels came 'handsomely tipped with gold'. The captors of an enemy warship or merchantman were entitled to sell her for their own profit, and the profit was shared very unequally, the captain alone taking a quarter, and the commander-in-chief an eighth. Those who reached captain's rank, therefore, had a fair chance of making a fortune, sometimes a very large one. All this was possible only in wartime, however.

In peace there was no prize money and only a small seagoing Navy. All but a few of the ships went into reserve, the officers went on to half-pay, and the men were paid off to seek their livelihood elsewhere. For the young officer with nothing to live on but his pay, and no prospects in life but what his naval service might win him, peace was a disaster. Employment and promotion almost stopped, few young men joined to become officers and many left. As a result the supply of junior officers, fit and ready to serve, fell steadily in peacetime years, and there was always a shortage at the outbreak of war. Eighteenth-century naval careers were governed by the alternation of peace and war. The best recipe for a successful career was to be born at the right moment, to be just the right age to profit from the promotion boom which always followed the outbreak of a war. Nelson himself is a good example: born in 1758 and a lieutenant aged eighteen in 1777, perfectly placed to profit from the professional opportunities of the American War of Independence which advanced him to captain in twenty-six months. Wartime promotion rates always exceeded the long-term requirement, so that by the end of a war there were usually too many officers. Peace offered them nothing but a long wait on the overcrowded half-pay list, and perhaps a minimum prospect of resuming their naval careers in middle age.

The peace therefore brought gloom to many wardrooms, and

even more midshipmen's berths. On the lower deck, however, peace brought release from the unvarying round of naval service, the chance to relax ashore and the hope of higher earnings in merchant ships. In hard reality professional seamen could not be sure in peacetime of earning more than in the Navy, at least on the new 1797 wage scale, nor could they be sure of continuous employment, but the prospect of release was unquestionably popular among men many of whom had been pressed into service, and there were mutinies in some ships which were ordered to the West Indies rather than home to pay off. For the landsmen of the ship's companies, unskilled and poor men who had in most cases doubtless volunteered for the regular wage and good food which they could not expect at home, demobilization must have aroused more mixed feelings.

Whatever their feelings, the men of the Royal Navy were paid off in 1802. Though the demobilization was not quite complete in 1803, there were only about 50,000 men still in service. It was not until 1808 that the Navy regained its manpower strength of 1801. The whole exhausting, inefficient and painful process of raising men which made the mobilization of all eighteenth-century fleets so slow had to be gone through again. The fleet which faced the threat of invasion in 1803 and 1804 was still well

Captain Horatio Nelson, by John Francis Rigaud (cat. no. 69).

below its former strength. Nor was this its only weakness. The peace was popular among the British political nation at large but informed observers were well aware that it was a gamble on Bonaparte's good intentions. Lord St Vincent, First Lord of the Admiralty in the Addington government, was one of the few ministers to take it at face value and to plan on the assumption of many years of solid peace. Not only did he pay off the ships of the Navy as fast as he could, but he seized the opportunity to mount a wholesale assault on the machinery of naval administration, which he regarded as an enemy to be crushed. British naval supremacy had been built on almost 300 years of steady investment in the industrial and technical infrastructure of sea power; in the dry docks and dockyards, the victualling yards and gun wharves, in the tens of thousands of skilled men who worked in them, and the vast national and international network of contractors who supplied them with every sort of raw material and manufactured goods.

Naval warfare has always been the war above all of capital and technology, and British supremacy at sea depended on the range and depth of skills and resources which sustained the Navy ashore. St Vincent understood none of this. On almost no evidence, he had convinced himself that 'the civil branch of the Navy is rotten to the very core',[1] that little or no work was done in the dockyards, and that all contractors were dishonest. 'A Patriot-Conqueror and a Statesman-Reformer',[2] as he modestly described himself, was needed to root out the evil. He talked wildly of hanging senior officials out of hand, and when he found that that was impossible he tried to trick them into indiscretions which would allow him to dismiss them. Spies were installed in every office and dock-yard to report to the First Lord in person. Trust immediately broke down, and much of the higher reaches of naval administration were paralyzed. In the dockyards St Vincent caused uproar, dismissed about a fifth of the workers, including many of the most experienced men, and stopped the recruitment of all apprentices. He treated the timber contractors so badly that they refused to deal further with the Navy, and he can-celled all shipbuilding in private yards, on which the Navy had long depended to keep up its numbers in wartime.

When the war restarted in 1803, British naval administration was in crisis. 'We made use of the peace, not to recruit our Navy, but to be the cause of its ruin,' Nelson commented. The storehouses were empty and the dockyards' capacity to fit out and maintain the fleet had been crippled. At the time of Trafalgar, two-fifths of the ships of the line were out of commission, and only eighty-three were available for sea service. Of these eighteen were fit only for home waters, and none of the remainder had more than five years' estimated life left. The material margin of British naval supremacy, not large in 1800, had been reversed by the time the Spanish declaration of war in December 1804 gave Napoleon a fleet of 102 ships of the line. Everything now depended on the ability of British officers and men to keep their worn-out ships at sea long enough to defeat the enemy – and on the enemy to offer them an opportunity of victory.

France had the strategic initiative and without allies Britain necessarily stood on the defensive. There were two points at which it was both possible and essential to block Bonaparte's expansion: the English Channel and the central Mediterranean narrows. In May 1803 a French army marched to southern Italy, threatening Sicily, Greece and Egypt. Beyond them lay the East – and the other route to the East was potentially in French hands already, since at the peace Britain had returned the Cape of Good Hope to France's Dutch satellite the Batavian Republic. To prevent French advance into the Levant and beyond, it was necessary to hold Malta and keep a fleet in the western Mediterranean basin; but Malta itself was too far from Toulon to be useful as a base for a blockade, and to feed Malta it was necessary to draw on both Sicily and North Africa. The Mediterranean Fleet, and Nelson its commander-in-chief, therefore had to combine both an offensive watch on the French fleet in Toulon and the defensive care of Sicily and Malta. The British dockyards were far away and their stores were empty anyway, but St Vincent airily assured Nelson that he would not need them: 'I have no idea under the vigour of your character that there will be an imaginary difficulty; real ones cannot exist. In short, cordage may be manufactured at sea; caulking and every other refitment, which in England requires dock yard inspection, your Lordship knows is much better performed by the artificers of the squadron; and barring accidents by shot, there is nothing that cannot be provided for.'[3] Toulon was impossible to blockade closely, as frequent winter gales blew squadrons offshore, and from the hills behind the port it was easy to tell where or whether the enemy was on station. Nelson insisted that he was not attempting a blockade, only watching the port from a distance with the intention of intercepting when the enemy should sail – but 'I am distressed for frigates, which are the eyes of a fleet', as he wrote, and watching the enemy from a distance was chancy even with many scouts.[4] Nelson based his squadron on the remote anchorage known to the British as Agincourt Sound in the Maddalena Islands. From there he kept an unbroken watch on Toulon for almost two years, continually at sea, keeping his men in good health and spirits, scrimping naval stores and patching his old ships.

In home waters the strategic situation of the two sides remained broadly as it had been in the latter years of the French Revolutionary War. The invasion threat was much graver than before, because backed by a bigger army and a more formidable general, but it was very similar in nature to that which the Royal Navy had faced in the 1790s and often before. Britain's strategic response, slowly developed over a century of experience, was based on an essential fact of geography: the prevailing winds over the British Isles for most of the year are from the west and south-west. France had no naval base in the Channel or the North Sea, and an invasion from Boulogne or any other French Channel port would have to cross without cover unless a fleet from Brest or elsewhere came up the Channel to protect it. Experience had shown the British that if the main fleet were kept in the Western Approaches, to windward of the mouth of the Channel, it was positioned to watch all the French Atlantic bases, to intercept any enemy fleet attempting to enter the Channel and at the same time to disrupt enemy trade and cover British convoys outward and homeward. None of this was easy: it required excellent intelligence, a large force of frigates to report the enemy's movements, highly seaworthy ships with an administrative system capable of keeping them supplied for long periods at sea and a considerable

Bilston-ware patch box commemorating the Peace of Amiens (cat. no. 124).

measure of luck to intercept enemy squadrons in an area of about 150,000 square miles stretching from Ireland to Spain. With a French invasion attempt imminent, and the main enemy fleet conveniently – but also dangerously – close in Brest, the British main fleet took up in 1803 the close blockade of Brest which it had developed in the closing years of the previous war. The object was not so much to keep the enemy fleet in port as to make it impossible for it to sail without fighting. This required the ships of the Channel Fleet to spend long periods close in with one of the most dangerous coasts in the world. In October 1803 Collingwood was commanding the Inshore Squadron, 'a station of great anxiety and required a constant care and look out, that I have often been a week without having my clothes off, and sometimes up on deck the whole night'.[5]

It was only possible because of the very high level of professional skill which the British had developed in ten years of almost continuous warfare. One of the Royal Navy's greatest strengths was its emphasis on practical seamanship. Future officers went to sea as boys, typically between twelve and fourteen, and learnt their profession working with the seamen, often aloft. Nineteen, one mother was told, 'is more than six years too old to begin a sea life'. By their late teens, these boys were already finished seamen, ready to take on the responsibilities of junior officers. The best of them were captains in their early twenties, combining the quickness and stamina of youth with the maturity of long experience. In the ships' companies good seamen were always scarce in wartime, especially the essential topmen who worked aloft, but it was possible to dilute the skilled men with a large admixture of ordinary seamen and landsmen. Most of the work in a warship consisted of pulling and hauling the falls of the running rigging on deck and hauling on the gun tackles to run out the guns in action. It called for organization and teamwork rather than a high degree of individual skill. Ships which spent many months and even years at sea could be worked up to a high level of efficiency even if professional seamen were a minority aboard. This was perhaps the single most important British advantage in war. Long periods at sea wore out ships and men, and the wear and tear of the ships was a desperate burden on dockyards which St Vincent had crippled, but the more the enemy was kept in port and the British kept the sea, the greater grew the disparity in skill between them.

The difference was as much a matter of morale as of actual ability. Accustomed to facing the dangers of the seas and conscious of their professional superiority, British officers and men went into action when the opportunity offered with a confident determination which was both the effect and the cause of numerous victories. However brave French and Spanish officers were, they could not but be aware of the huge disparity in professional ability between the two sides. British gunnery tactics were an expression of this difference. Nelson and most (though not all) of his contemporaries believed in closing the enemy as quickly as possible, holding fire until the last possible moment and then delivering a devastating volume of rapid fire at very close range. This tactic called for very high discipline, for officers and men had to accept being shot at for some time before they opened fire themselves, but it was brutally decisive. French naval doctrine, by contrast, taught that the heavy guns should be abandoned as quickly as possible for small arms and boarding. Even officers like Captain Lucas of the *Redoutable* (the ship which fought the *Victory* at Trafalgar and killed Nelson), who had his men highly trained and could have selected other tactics had he wished to, chose to renounce the most decisive weapon available. The result at Trafalgar was that the allied fleet suffered about ten times the casualties of the British, though the British fleet was substantially outnumbered, and only about half its ships were heavily engaged.

Behind this remarkable record of professional dominance lies the untold and largely unnoticed story of the social reconstruction of the Navy after the great mutinies of 1797. The mutinies administered a profound shock to the Navy, the government and the country. In the short term the government reacted by conceding the mutineers' main demands, in particular for higher pay, but this went only a short way to solve the officers' problem. Any system of rule by the few over the many (where the few have no monopoly of weapons) must ultimately rest on consent, and after 1797 everyone knew that the men's consent was precarious. Ships' companies themselves were confused and excited. Officers were frightened. The weaker captains lost their nerve and the tougher ones reacted with severity to the slightest sign of trouble. By 1803, however, the climate of opinion was more relaxed and confident. The peace itself, by giving so many officers and men the chance to escape naval service for a while, must have relieved tension. The lapse of time, the failure of the great mutinies to lead to any general revolution, helped to re-establish the self-confidence of both officers and men. It was customary now for officers to devote much thought to discipline and social relations, subjects which had before been taken for granted. Professional opinion, and increasingly Admiralty regulation, demanded higher standards of conduct. Captains were expected to take pains to look after their men's welfare. This was not new in itself – good captains had always done so – but the seriousness with which the subject was now treated, the pressure of service opinion enforcing higher standards, was new. The professional press was full of writings on discipline, ships' internal organization and related subjects which had hitherto attracted relatively little attention. It is scarcely going too far to describe this as a social revolution, which would not have happened without the great mutinies, and which was necessary to support the acute strains of the Napoleonic War, with ships spending long months and even years of boredom and danger on blockading stations.

It was intensely frustrating for the Royal Navy that the enemy offered so few opportunities for battle. When the war restarted in 1803 it was more than frustrating, for the mortal threat of invasion and the precarious material condition of the British fleet made a decisive victory more urgent than ever. However confident British naval officers were in their professional superiority, the reputation of the British army was miserably low, and no one underestimated the threat which Napoleon and the French army presented. In the longer term, moreover, a French empire that was master of the shipyards and resources of all Europe might easily outbuild Britain and create a fleet of overwhelming strength. To put an end to the risk of invasion, and to regain Britain's numerical margin of strength, it was essential to fight and win a great battle. What no one could have foreseen was that Napoleon would offer the British their chance in 1805, not in the course of mounting his invasion, but in support of a subsidiary, not to say trivial, military operation in southern Italy.

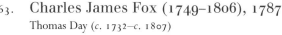

163. Charles James Fox (1749–1806), 1787

Thomas Day (c. 1732–c. 1807)
Watercolour and bodycolour on ivory
67 x 51mm
Signed with initials and dated 1787
National Portrait Gallery, London; NPG 6292

From 1782 to 1806 Fox was leader of the Whig Opposition against successive Tory governments led by William Pitt. A close friend of the Prince of Wales, he was a gifted orator and championed personal liberty, domestic reform and the political aspirations of the French Revolution.   RQ

164. George III (reigned 1760–1820), 1809 or before

Unknown artist, signed *GJ* (?) in monogram
Watercolour and bodycolour on ivory
30 x 19mm
Locket case engraved verso: *George 3 / was born 4. June 1738. / ascended the British Throne / 25 Octr. 1760 / The / Grand National Jubilee / celebrated 25 Octr. 1809*
National Portrait Gallery, London; NPG 6288

Nelson first met George III in June 1783 when, as a junior captain, he was presented at court by his patron, Lord Hood. From Nelson's writings it is clear that he saw his service in the Royal Navy as a personal service to the King, and it was from the King that he received the insignia of the Order of the Bath at St James's Palace in September 1797. The King later strongly disapproved of aspects of Nelson's conduct at Naples, and his liaison with Lady Hamilton, whom he refused to receive at court. Although he snubbed Nelson after his return from the Mediterranean in 1800, the King remained appreciative of Nelson's abilities and was shocked when he received the news of Trafalgar and Nelson's death early on 7 November 1805.   RQ

165. Medallion of William Pitt the Younger, 1809

Peter Rouw (1770–1852)
London
Wax, 102mm diam.
National Portrait Gallery, London; NPG 1747

This wax medallion of the statesman and Prime Minister William Pitt the Younger (1759–1806) was modelled by Peter Rouw, who in 1807 was appointed 'Sculptor, Modeller of

gems to HRH the Prince of Wales'. Between 1787 and 1833 he exhibited twenty-two portraits in wax at the Royal Academy, and twice modelled Pitt, in 1808 and 1809.

Pitt had become Chancellor of the Exchequer in 1782 at the age of twenty-three; eighteen months later, as First Lord of the Treasury, he took over the leadership of a powerful and long-lasting government. The victory at the Nile helped Pitt form a strong European coalition against France. Having resigned in 1801, he was recalled to office in May 1804, after war with France had broken out again following the short-lived Peace of Amiens. He lived to see victory at Trafalgar but his health was failing. He died in January 1806, soon after hearing news of Napoleon's success at Austerlitz the previous December.   RP

LITERATURE: Pyke, *A Biographical Dictionary of Wax Modellers.*

166. Model of Murray's shutter telegraph hut, c. 1795

Wood
National Maritime Museum, London (Admiralty Collection); MDL0020

The first English shutter telegraph system was designed by the Revd Lord George Murray in 1795 as a means of communicating vital information between the south coast and London. Mr George Roebuck, a civilian surveyor, was contracted to select sites and erect the stations. Before the end of 1796 there were lines in working order linking London with Deal, Sheerness and Portsmouth. A chain of relay stations along the route, within visual distance of each other, passed on signals to the next station down the line. When the message reached Whitehall, a shutter apparatus on the roof of the old Admiralty building provided the final telegraph station. This rapid and efficient system was a marked improvement on traditional methods of sending news by messenger on horseback, although it could not be used at night or in bad weather. An earlier French version of the mechanical telegraph, invented by Claude Chappe, who had coined the term 'télégraphe', had been in use since 1793.

The model exhibited here is Murray's own original explanation of his invention. The apparatus on top of the building consisted of six octagonal shutters arranged in two frames. By pulling on ropes to open and shut these in various combinations, the operators could form sixty-three different signals. Words could be spelled out, but were sometimes contracted. The stations were in the charge of four officials, consisting of a naval officer (usually a lieutenant) and three men to assist him in receiving the messages and transmitting them to other stations. The operators became very skilful, and in favourable conditions an average message could be passed between Portsmouth and London in about fifteen minutes. The shutter telegraph line to Portsmouth was used until 1816, after which it was replaced by a more flexible semaphore system, which used a machine with pivoted arms.   RP

LITERATURE: Wilson, G., *The Old Telegraphs*, pp. 11-17; Holmes, T. W., *The Semaphore*, pp. 30-34.

167. The Blockade of Boulogne, October 1804

E. D. Lewis

Watercolour

622 x 760mm

National Maritime Museum, London; PAI6989

After the war between Britain and France resumed in 1803, the French built up a huge invasion fleet, mainly based at Boulogne. Though the British were confident that they could defeat any French invasion, they needed to be constantly vigilant. In the foreground of this watercolour is the main British squadron with a two-decker flagship in the centre and frigates and sloops around it. Behind them is a line of smaller British sloops and brigs. Behind that, to the left, a Dutch merchant ship is about to be intercepted.

LXXXVII — 11

Some of the French invasion craft are in a line close to the shore, behind an invisible sandbank. The town and harbour of Boulogne are behind, also filled with invasion craft, and there are fortifications on the hills. The print shows the intense naval effort needed to prevent a French invasion force getting out.   BL

168. The 'Shipwreck' sketchbook, *c.* 1805–6
Joseph Mallord William Turner (1775–1851)
118 x 185mm
Provenance: bequeathed by the artist, 1856
Tate, London; D05386 (Finberg no. LXXXVII.11)

Turner was deeply aware of the maritime dimension of British life – from the hardships of fishermen to the Navy's role as the nation's prime defence (though, curiously, he showed little interest in major wealth-creating aspects like East India shipping). Much of his early oil work, in particular, was marine, including his first exhibited painting at the Royal Academy in 1796. *The Shipwreck*, which followed in 1805,

and for which the open page here is one of the sketches, was also his first oil painting to be engraved, in 1806. With its combination of horror and the bravery of attempted rescue (from the vessel on the right in the sketch, plus others in the finished oil) it was one of several that offer the perils of the sea as a metaphor for the dangers facing Britain, as Napoleon's armies engulfed the rest of Europe. It may also have been prompted by a highly successful 1804 reissue of William Falconer's epic poem *The Shipwreck*, illustrated by the marine painter Nicholas Pocock.   PvdM

169. *Boats beside a man-of-war, c.* 1796
Joseph Mallord William Turner (1775–1851)
Gouache and watercolour on paper
359 x 592mm
Provenance: bequeathed by the artist, 1856
Tate, London; D00902 (Finberg no. XXXIII.e)

This study, made when Turner was about twenty-one, shows small craft tending on a frigate or smaller ship with a

single gun-deck. The muted colour and motion of the sea evocatively suggest poor 'Channel weather', in which the solidity of the anchored ship contrasts with the movement of the frailer boats alongside. Turner returned to this contrast of small service vessels and even larger warships in 1818 in his famous watercolour *A first-rate taking in stores* (Cecil Higgins Art Gallery, Bedford). Such drawings, as much as his major paintings, show his awareness of the complexities and hardships of seafaring, on which Britain's wealth and defence by the Navy's 'wooden walls' were based. PvdM

complement of boats, from the large launch to the smaller jolly boat mounted on davits rigged over the stern. It has copper sheathing below the waterline, as introduced by the Navy in the 1780s. The purpose of this sheathing was twofold: to prevent barnacle and weed growth that would reduce a ship's speed, and to prevent damage to the timbers by the *teredo navalis*, a marine boring mollusc. SS

170. Model of a 36-gun frigate, launched *c.* 1805

Unknown, *c.* 1805
Scale 1:48
National Maritime Museum, London; SLR0346

By the end of the eighteenth century, these heavily armed frigates were used in a variety of roles: fleet reconnaissance, patrolling the sea-lanes and as escorts for convoys of merchant ships. Built in large numbers by private as well as the royal dockyards, frigates took part in virtually every major action during the Napoleonic War.

This contemporary model is fully rigged with sails, thought to be original. The hull has solid bulwarks on the upper decks and an enclosed waist, both of which offered greater protection to a crew under fire. It has a full

171. Boardroom of the Admiralty

After Augustus Charles Pugin and Thomas Rowlandson;
published by Rudolph Ackermann, 1 January 1808

Hand-coloured aquatint

195 x 255mm

National Maritime Museum, London; PAD1358

This is plate 3 from Ackermann's *Microcosm of London* (1808–11), in which Rowlandson supplied the figures for Pugin's settings. The *Microcosm* states that 'the . . . print is a correct interior view of THE BOARD ROOM OF THE ADMIRALTY, with its appropriate decorations of globes, books, maps, &c. The lords commissioners are represented as sitting at the table, and may be naturally supposed engaged in some business . . . of more real importance to this country, than any other subject [and] also a matter of infinite importance to all Europe.' Although a little changed the boardroom still exists in the old Admiralty, in Whitehall.   PvdM

172. *Disposition of His Majestys Ship the Bedford, Lower Deck, c.* 1790

Pen and coloured inks on paper

National Maritime Museum, London (Admiralty Ship Plans Collection); ZAZ6793

Space was limited on warships and the first lieutenant had carefully to allocate the space below deck. Samuel Leech remembered in his autobiography, *Thirty Years from Home, or A Voice from the Main Deck*:

> Every hammock has its appropriate place. Below, the beams are all marked; each hammock is marked with a corresponding number, and in the darkest night, a sailor will go unhesitatingly to his hammock. . . . Each man is provided with two, so that while he is scrubbing and cleaning one, he may have another to use. Nothing but such precautions could enable so many men to live in so small a space.

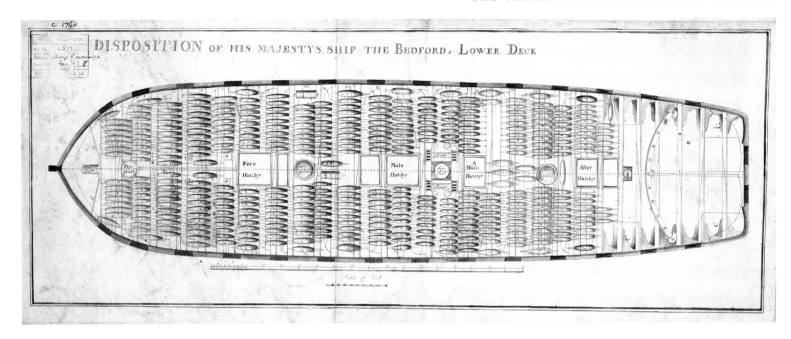

Regulations stipulated a personal space of 14 inches (35.5cm) for each hammock, or 28 inches (71cm) for a petty officer who would have slept near the sides of the ship. At sea this space was doubled because one watch was always on duty. The plan of the lower deck of *Bedford* (1775) illustrates the cramped conditions. It shows that each hammock and row had a number allocated to it and the two colours are thought to represent the sailors (blue) and the marines (red).

The reverse of the plan has a table entitled 'Birthing List for the Hammocks', illustrating the careful coordination required. It reveals the relevant information a lieutenant might record about a sailor: his station, allocated hammock number, on which side of the ship he slept, and his name.

The hammocks (pieces of canvas 6 feet long and 3 feet wide – 1.8 x 0.9m) were the property of the government and thus only loaned to the sailor. He had to provide his own bedding, purchasing it from the purser or bringing it onboard. When not in use hammocks were lashed into a sausage shape and stowed in the netting troughs that lined the sides of the quarter-deck and forecastle. In battle, they acted as protection for the men against small-arms fire and splinters, and might be used as a form of lifebuoy for seamen who fell overboard. JM

LITERATURE: Lavery, *Nelson's Navy*; Leech, *Thirty Years from Home*.

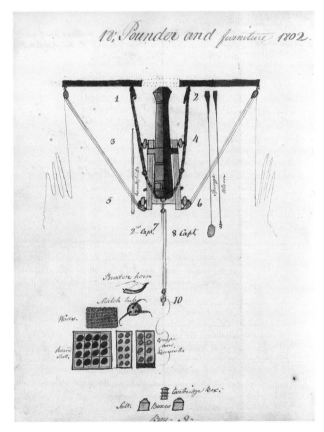

173. A gun crew, 1802
John Skinner
Ink on paper
National Maritime Museum, London; JOD/45

Captain Edward Riou issued detailed instructions to his crew when he took command of the frigate *Amazon* in 1799. He was killed under Nelson at the Battle of Copenhagen in

1801, but his orders continued in use for some time. Midshipman John Skinner made this copy in 1802.

This page shows the positions of the crew of a gun in action and also their implements such as sponges and rammers. The men, shown here by numbers 1 to 6, would haul on the gun tackles to run the gun out through the gun port. The gun captain, number 8, stands beside the train tackle which holds the gun in position while it is being loaded. Behind him are different types of ammunition, such as grape and round shot, and a cartridge containing powder, looked after by a boy. BL

174. *Invade us boys!*

> JN? [John Nixon?], published 6 October 1803 by
>   William Hodgson
> Hand-coloured etching
> 312 x 250mm
> National Maritime Museum, London; PAF3881

A typically rousing loyalist print centring on the virtues and heroism of the British tar. Many similar prints were produced at this time, soon after the recommencement of hostilities with France and in the face of another invasion scare. This image is an adaptation of a long-standing iconography of the sailor ashore, free from the confines and disciplinary routine of the ship and ready to revel. Here, however, his energies are directed not to debauchery, as was

the stereotypical image of the lower-deck sailor, but to defending British shores against the French. Thus on his hatband he sports the motto 'Nelson for ever', which also points to the supposed popularity of Nelson among the lower deck, and the verse caption resembles the numerous popular songs and ballads by Charles Dibdin and others on similar themes that were being performed nightly at the London theatres. This image of the tar is a far cry from the mutinous figure that had shaken the nation only five years earlier in the mutinies at Spithead and the Nore, and he himself probably owes something to the theatrical incarnation of the tar at this time: his given name in the verse, 'Ben Block', is typical of the figures that populated so many comedies and afterpieces of the period. GQ

175. Letter signed by Nelson to the Commissioners for Victualling His Majesty's Navy

> Ink on paper
> Lloyd's of London; Nelson Collection, L369

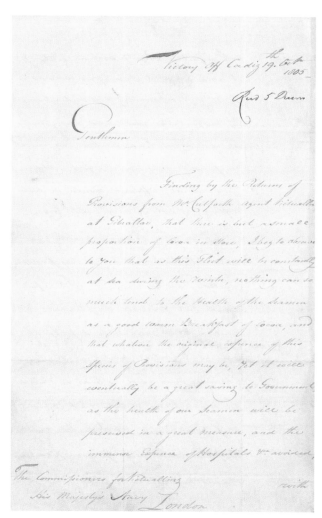

Like many senior officers of his day, Nelson was concerned about his seamen's health. In 1803–4, more than 200,000 men were impressed into the Navy; although some were later released, the vast majority remained and had to be provisioned. The Board frequently supplied what appeared to be unsuitable substitutes for usual rations: Nelson had already complained about being sent rice instead of cheese, which was unpopular with the men. In this letter, Nelson is requesting supplies of cocoa and recommending its use as a breakfast drink. Throughout the Navy drunkenness was a common problem, despite the heavy floggings meted out to seamen found drunk on duty. Nelson was particularly concerned to eliminate it if possible. To this end, he ordered that good quality wine should be available instead of strong spirits and made every effort to ensure that the men did not smuggle illegal liquor on board. His request for cocoa addresses the two issues of health and drunkenness, as it would be both nourishing and non-alcoholic. It would probably also make a welcome change from what was often the standard breakfast drink: 'coffee' made from burnt breadcrumbs boiled in water.   DK

176. Naval medicine chest, c. 1801
Mahogany
National Maritime Museum, London; TOA0130

This medicine chest was owned by Sir Benjamin Outram KCB (1774–1856), Surgeon RN, and is said by his descendants to have been used at the Battle of Copenhagen (1801). The medicine chest is fitted with a lock and carrying handle, and opens to reveal drawers and compartments containing scales, bottles for drugs, pestle and mortar, and other medical equipment.

Outram joined the naval medical service in 1794 and was promoted to surgeon in 1796, serving in *Harpy*, *Nymphe* and *Boadicea*. He was surgeon of the *Superb* in the victory over the French and Spanish fleets off Cadiz of 12 July 1801, and was later surgeon to the *Royal Sovereign* yacht. He was the author of a pamphlet, *Suggestions to Naval Surgeons previous to, during and after a Battle*, and became Inspector of Hospitals and Fleets in 1841. The Museum also acquired his naval uniform with the medicine chest.   RP

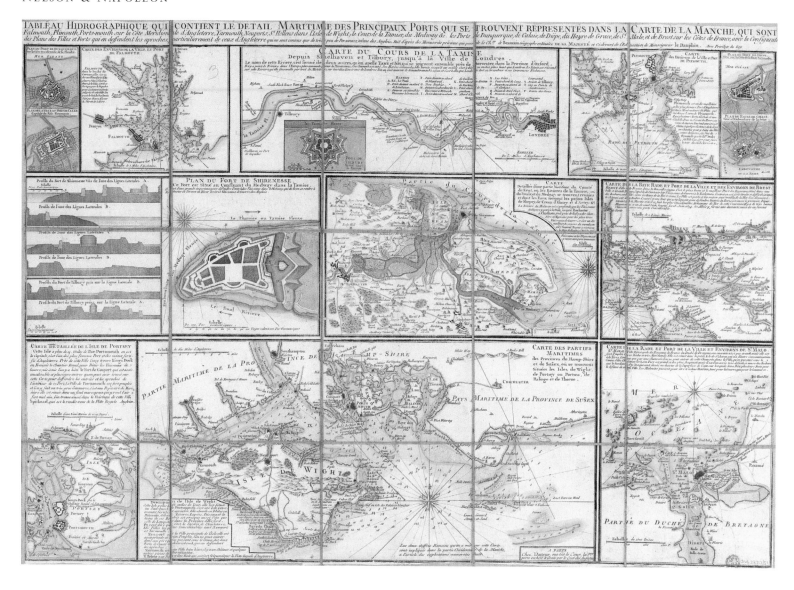

177. *Tableau hidrographique qui contiènt le detail maritime des principaux ports qui se trouvent representés dans la carte de la Manche* / Hydrographic table containing the maritime details of the principal ports represented in the chart of the English Channel

Anonymous

Hand-coloured engraving, after Jean de Beaurain,

  c. 1780

510 x 730mm

National Maritime Museum, London; DUC223:2/51

Fear of a French assault on the south coast of England was neither new nor irrational. The French maintained a body of intelligence about English coastal fortification and potential landing places. This pre-Revolutionary map, printed at Paris, was probably drawn during the American War of Independence, when, between 1778 and 1783, France sided with the American rebels and was at war with Britain. While British ships and forces were deployed on the other side of the Atlantic, the English Channel coast and the Thames and Medway might have been vulnerable to French attack.

The source information is credited to Jean de Beaurain (1696–1771), Geographer to the King of France. Beaurain produced a series of maps during the previous war between France and Britain – the Seven Years War (1755–63).   GH

178. **Mortella tower**
Ink and watercolour by 'CFD'
371 x 243mm
National Maritime Museum, London; PAD1621

This ancient tower on Mortella Point guarded the anchorage in San Fiorenzo Bay (now St Florent), northern Corsica. It had two 18-pounder guns on top and made the bay impossible for the British to use in their invasion of February 1794. When two British warships attacked it from the sea it returned red-hot shot that started a fire in one of them. It was only captured after British shore guns used hot shot that set fire to 'bass-junk' (brushwood used as protection) on the parapet and 'smoked out' the French defenders. The British later blew up the tower – though part survives – but were so impressed that from 1805 they based their own 'Martello tower' coastal defences against Napoleon on it. They corrupted the Italian name *mortella* (myrtle) into 'martello' (which, coincidentally, is Italian for hammer) from the start. This name was spread by a print of the tower for which this is one of three anonymous drawings used.　　PvdM

MORTELLA TOWER. *Corsica.*

A *Middle Story*
B *Second Story*
C *Entering door*
D *Powder room*
E *Kitchen*
F *Embrasures for 2 Guns*
G *Cistern*
H *spout for emptying the Cistern.*

179. **Prize medal, Corps of River Fencibles of the City of London, 1804**
Silver
57mm diam.
National Maritime Museum, London; MED0240

Engraved prize medal. Obverse: within a border of palm leaves, separated by four roses at the cardinal points of the compass, a female figure of London standing, robed, her left hand resting on an anchor, her right holding a wreath. Inscription: 'L.L.V. River Fencibles'. Reverse inscribed: 'From Commodore Lucas awarded to AMOS PEVERIL 16 May. 1804. for MERIT'. Cast with an ornamental loop. The River Fencibles were officially established in 1803, and by 1804 had uniformed commissioned officers. Members of the London Corps in small boats escorted the barge carrying the body of Nelson along the Thames during his state funeral in 1806. The force was disbanded in 1813.　　BT

180. **Prize medal, Corps of River Fencibles of the City of London, 1800**
Gilt copper
74mm diam.
National Maritime Museum, London; MED0237

Medal made as an engraved plate, presented to Matthias Prime Lucas (*c.* 1762–1848), Commodore of the City of London River Fencibles, by General Francis Augustus Elliott, 2nd Baron Heathfield (1750–1813). Obverse: a female figure of London robed, her left hand resting on an anchor, her right holding a wreath, standing before a boat, a

Corps. He became a prosperous citizen and was elected Lord Mayor of London in 1827. BT

LITERATURE: Lapthorne, 'The City of London River Fencibles', *Coast and Country*, 8, pp. 8–11.

ribbon behind inscribed: 'GOD SAVE THE KING', 'THE RIVER FENCIBLES'. Exergue: 'LOYAL LONDON VOLS'. Reverse inscribed: 'PRESENTED BY MAJOR GENERAL LORD HEATH-FIELD TO COMMODORE LUCAS As a mark of appreciation of his SKILL in defeating the invading FLOTILLA & taking 86 Prisoners at the SHAM Fight July. 1800'. Thames watermen and other groups of river tradesmen voluntarily formed associations of River Fencibles in 1798, the same year that the Corps of Sea Fencibles was established as a coastal home guard. Lucas had been apprenticed to his father as a lighter-man and took an active role in raising the City of London

181. The presentation of colours to the Bank of England Volunteers at Lord's Cricket Ground, 2 September 1799

Thomas Stothard (1755–1834)
Oil on canvas
875 x 1200mm
The Bank of England

The earl [of Egremont] made sure that his own uniform was finer still [than his men's] . . . Then, like scores of other volunteer commanders throughout the land, he rushed off to have his portrait painted.

Mrs Thornton, wife of Samuel Thornton MP, Governor of the Bank of England, presents colours to its volunteer militia company. The raising of such home-defence corps and

their coastal equivalents, the Sea Fencibles, was a notable feature of the French Wars. Militia were first raised under an Act of 1757, strengthened by a Supplementary Militia Act of 1796, the Defence of the Realm Act of 1798 and the Military Service Bill (Levy en masse Act), 1803. Local gentry usually took the lead and constituted themselves the officers but companies could also have an institutional basis. The government remained ambivalent about having an armed citizenry, especially of the 'lower orders', but the self-funding nature of the corps limited membership to those who could afford it or their employees. Nelson was briefly involved in this area when in charge of naval defence of the south coast, just before the Copenhagen campaign in 1801.

This painting was commissioned by Joshua Pitt, the Volunteers' Deputy Quarter Master. Subscriptions from members were intended to pay for it, but the overall cost of just under £142 was too high and the Bank discharged the debt in June 1800. Stothard charged 80 guineas (£84) and 'Mr. Pym' – possibly the miniaturist B. Pym – was paid 20 guineas (£21) for doing individual portraits of those shown.

PvdM

LITERATURE: Linda Colley, *Britons: Forging the Nation, 1707–1837* (London, 1992), p. 288.

182. Shoulder-belt plate, Writtle Loyal Volunteers, *c.* 1804

Gilt metal

National Army Museum, London; 6309-265-5

A rectangular shoulder-belt plate with an engraved design, formerly in the Royal United Service Museum Collection (RUSI 9258). Superimposed upon an eight-pointed star, a garter with the inscription 'WRITTLE LOYAL VOLUN-TEERS'. Within the garter, the arms of Essex – three sea axes fessewise – with points to the sinister and cutting edges upwards. (Writtle is now a suburb of Chelmsford.) A royal crown is placed above the garter.

BT

183. Shooting medal, Westminster Volunteers, 1805

Thomas Phipps and Edward Robinson[?]

Silver-gilt

61mm diam.

1805–6 (London hallmark)

National Army Museum, London; 1975-12-3

Obverse: the repoussé design is within a raised fluted rim. In the centre are the chained portcullis of Westminster, within a wreath of shamrock, roses and thistles and a trophy of arms, a royal crown above. Reverse: on a convex surface within a raised rim is the engraved inscription: 'Presented by LIEUT. SENIOR of the 4th. Battalion Company, R.W R.V. to Mr John Manson, being the best Shot 26th Augt. 1805'. The hallmark and maker's initials TP EJR are in a four-leaved cartouche. The medal has a fixed and loose ring suspender.

BT

184. Shooting medal, Prince of Wales's Loyal Volunteers, Middlesex, 1804

Gilt metal

52mm diam.

National Army Museum, London; 1975-07-29

The design is engraved on an unpolished surface within a raised threaded rim. Obverse: the star of the Order of the Garter without its motto, encircled by a garter inscribed:

'PRINCE OF WALES'S LOYAL VOLUNTEERS', the whole on a trophy of arms composed of colours, spontoons, swords and muskets. Above all the Prince of Wales's plume, coronet and motto 'ICH DIEN'. Reverse: inscription 'PRESENTED by Captn. Blagrave Lervis OF THE Third Company for the best Shot at a TARGET on the 2nd. Day of May 1804'.

The regiment was raised in 1797 as the St Martin's-in-the-Fields Volunteers. It was disbanded in 1802 and re-raised in 1803 as the Prince of Wales's Loyal Volunteers. Thomas Ward Blagrave became captain in the regiment on 8 September 1803.   BT

185. British coatee, 1803–8
Wool, silk
National Army Museum, London; 1997-06-22

As Napoleon's plans to invade Britain appeared more certain, the British government introduced the Defence Act in order to establish a reserve army. On 18 July 1803 further legislation was passed to augment the Defence Act, which served to put all men between the ages of seventeen and fifty-five in local militia. They were to drill one day a week and undergo between '14 and 20 continuous days' training before the end of one year'. This coatee is from one such militia, the Tetbury Loyal Volunteers of Gloucestershire. It belonged to a regimental officer, probably Quartermaster John Scott who is named on the 1805 *Militia List*, and dates from 1803 to 1808, a time when the fear of French invasion was at its highest.   AM

186. Recruitment poster
W. & A. Lee, of Lewes, Sussex, *c.* 1797
Paper
National Maritime Museum, London; PBB7084

Volunteers . . . let us, who are Englishmen, protect and defend our good King and country against the attempts of all Republicans and Levellers, and against the designs of our natural enemies. . . . Royal tars of old England, if you love your country, and your liberty . . . repair . . . to Lieut W J Stephens at his rendezvous, Shoreham.

The Admiralty in the eighteenth century had problems finding men willing to join the Navy. Press-gangs were used and recruitment posters nailed up all over the country where seamen congregated. Prize money and plenty of grog were promised as incentives. However, this example, printed not long after the mutinies at Spithead and the Nore, appeals to patriotism.   LV

187. **Tarleton helmet from the Tenby Loyal Volunteers, 1798**

Britain

Leather, silver and feathers

John Goldstein, private collection

On 22 February 1797, a small untrained French force, predominately made up of former prisoners under the command of Colonel William Tate, a septuagenarian from South Carolina, landed at Fishguard. After a looting spree of two days, they surrendered to local militia led by Lord Cawdor. Although unsuccessful, the landing of French troops on British soil caused widespread panic. As a result of this and the increasing threat of a large-scale French invasion, local militia, such as the Tenby Loyal Volunteers, were formed.

AM

188.   £1 note, 1797
Bank of England

from 2 March 1797 (it issued £2 notes at the same time). The Bank was authorized to stop payment on its notes during what became known as the Restriction Period: this lasted until 1821. This simply printed note has been filled in with the name of the payee and signed by Abraham Newland, Chief Cashier 1778–1807 (the £1 notes were nicknamed 'Newlands').   BT

LITERATURE: Duggleby, *English Paper Money*, p. 32.

The invasion scare of February 1797 caused people to exchange their paper money for gold coins which would be more likely to retain their value during an emergency and the possible collapse of central government. The guinea and half-guinea were swiftly driven out of circulation. This is an example of the £1 note that the Bank issued to replace them

189.   Spanish coins countermarked with the head of George III, 1797
Silver
38mm diam.
Bank of England

In an attempt to fill the currency gap left by the run on gold, the Bank of England countermarked foreign silver coins they were holding for their bullion value. Most of these were eight-reale pieces bearing a profile of Charles IV of Spain. The head of George III was stamped on the neck of the portrait – 'The Bank to make their Dollars pass Stamp'd

the head of a fool on the neck of an ass'. On one coin the Spanish monarch has been provided with a speech bubble reading 'On the 27th of Feby 1797 the BANK of ENGLAND stopp'd Payment of CASH'. Silver coins at this time (particularly Spanish dollars) were sometimes smoothed and re-engraved with a personal or political image or inscription. This one is a protest against the Restriction Period.   BT

LITERATURE: W. Marston Acres, *The Bank of England from Within, 1694–1900* (London, 1931).

190. *An Elevated View of The New Docks
       & Warehouses now constructing on the
       Isle of Dogs near Limehouse for the
       reception & accommodation of
       shipping in the West India Trade . . .*
       Drawn, engraved and published 15 October 1802 by
           William Daniell
       Aquatint and etching with hand-colouring
       462 x 800mm
       National Maritime Museum, London; PAI 7124

Daniel's print demonstrates the importance of the West India trade and the wealth of the London merchants who traded in the West Indies. Their subscriptions paid for the construction of the docks which were completed only a few years before the decline in the Caribbean trade, although London saw a generally massive expansion of its artificial dock capacity from the 1790s onward – a testament to the growing importance of British overseas trade both through-out and beyond the French War period.   RQ

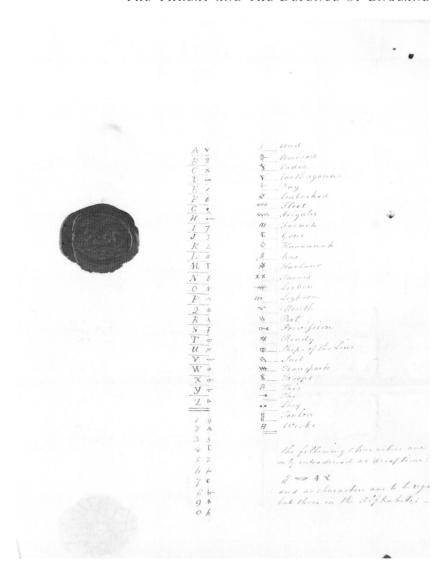

191. Letter from Robert Wilks to
      Sir Evan Nepean, 29 February 1797
      Ink on paper
      Lloyd's of London; Nelson Collection, L240

Accurate information, securely communicated, has always been an essential component of military operations. This letter illustrates clearly the methods the British used to convey intelligence reports on the eve of the Battle of St Vincent. Wilks is sending to Nepean, the Secretary of the Admiralty, a seal and secret code to be used by the officers of selected ships and the commander of the Mediterranean Fleet. The code comprises symbols for the letters of the alphabet and additional symbols for commonly used words such as 'port' and 'fleet'.   DK

192. **Brass-barrelled pistol designed in 1796 for Vice-Admiral Philippe d'Auvergne, Prince of Bouillon**

Henry Nock (1760–1810) and Durs Egg (1748–1831)

Brass, walnut

Inscribed: H Nock

National Maritime Museum,
   London; AAA2439

Born in Jersey in 1754, Philippe d'Auvergne entered the Royal Navy at the age of sixteen and, with Nelson, was a midshipman on Captain Phipps's North-East Passage expedition to Spitsbergen in 1773. While stationed in the Channel Islands during the Napoleonic War, he ran a secret service network passing information from French royalists to the British government. He also formed a military corps from French royalist refugees who had fled to Jersey. It is believed that 200 pairs of these pistols were made for them at 48 shillings a pair. LV

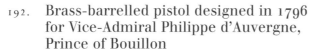

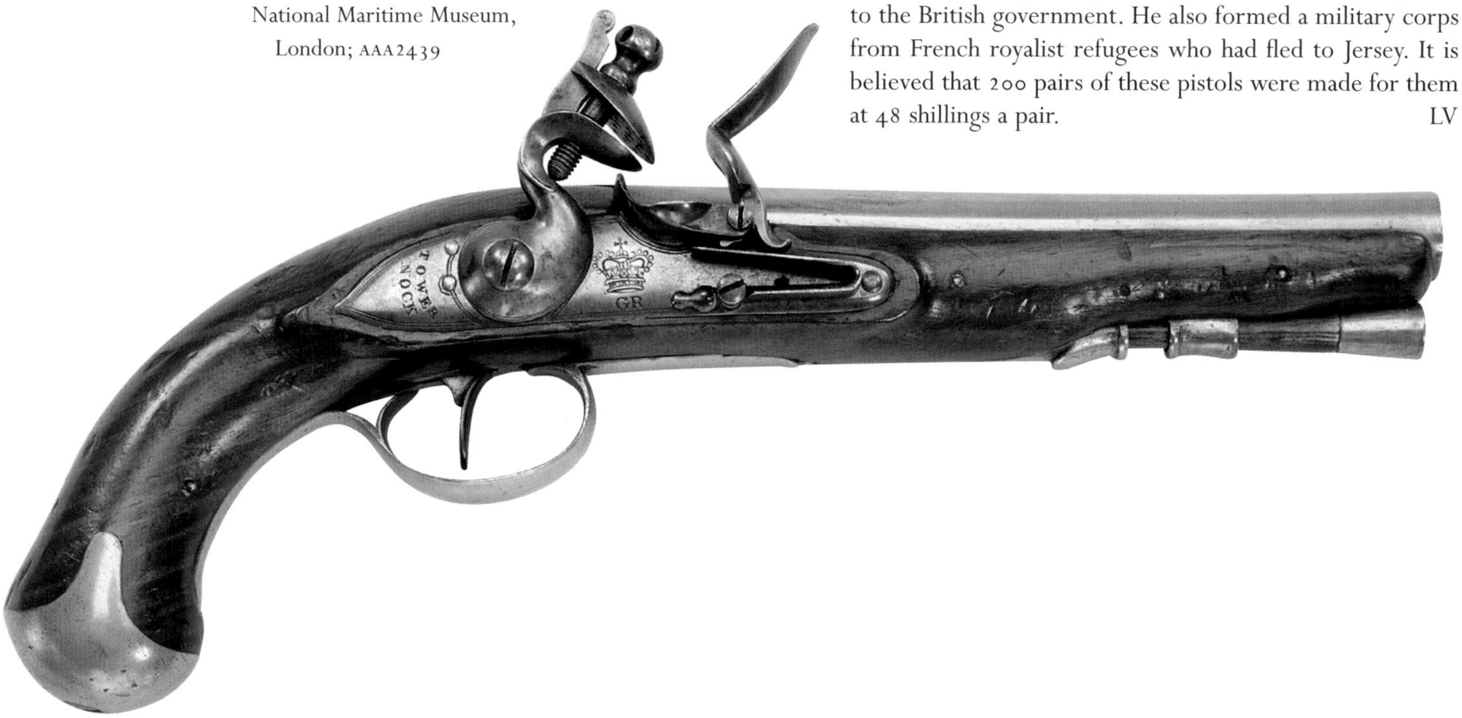

THE THREAT:
THE 1805 CAMPAIGN

The Impact of Nelson and Naval Warfare on Women in Britain, 1795–1805

MARGARETTE LINCOLN

NELSON'S AFFAIR with Emma Hamilton and his separation from his wife, Frances, are common knowledge. To some, it counts as one of the world's greatest love stories, on a par with Antony and Cleopatra, or even Dido and Aeneas – a parallel that was satirically drawn at the time (see p. 178). But what about Nelson's wider effect on women in society? How did women celebrate his achievements? What was the wider impact of naval warfare on women in society? Could they use their public support for naval heroes to articulate their own concerns, or was their social position so constrained that they were bound to follow a conventional path?

At the time of Nelson's victories, it was difficult for women to command influence in public life, although they were highly visible in the literary landscape. Women were the pre-eminent novelists, considerable numbers published poetry at a time when it received avid public attention, and some women writers were highly regarded. But male critics often read women's writing in the light of assumptions about gender, which questioned any claim women might have to an authoritative public voice. Some women protested. Why were women written out of history, they asked? And why were their literary achievements so often dismissed? Recent scholarship has shown that it would be wrong to think that women of the period were entirely relegated to the domestic sphere, but public life was overwhelmingly male-dominated. Men naturally dominated in the military arena – and in wartime their actions were well publicized. They also dominated in politics, religion, science, the arts and in medicine.

At the same time it was usual to credit women with being the moral touchstone of society. Social commentators warned that men degenerated when excluded from the polite influence of women; the beneficial influence of women on society was even preached from the pulpit. Obviously this served to control female ambition and direct women into narrow paths of righteousness where their desires would be less troublesome. Some did their best to turn the moral influence assigned them to advantage. The writer Hannah More, for example, claimed that women were uniquely equipped to regulate the moral temperament of the nation *because* they were excluded from the formal network of political power and were untainted by it. In the 1790s, her *Cheap Repository Tracts*, aimed at the lower orders, were often credited with averting a French-style revolution in Britain. Many women, striving to express moral authority in print, safely chose to praise naval achievements and elevated the status of naval heroes. Wartime offered women opportunities to voice their patriotism and gain more of a public role by, for example, presenting banners to volunteer regiments and contributing subscriptions. But, ironically, propagandist discourse also worked to subject women further to prescribed roles. On the one hand it positioned them as vulnerable and dependent, likely to be raped and slaughtered by an invading force unless protected. On the other, it encouraged them to be strong-minded and breed sons who would practise arms, defend their country and perhaps die a violent death.

As the poems of many women writers of the time remind us, war had a horribly dislocating effect on society and on domestic life: it caused separation, grief and economic hardship for women left at home. According to estimates, by 1803 over one in five of the British population capable of bearing arms were engaged in military service. By 1805 around 120,000 men were serving in the Royal Navy alone, while philanthropic initiatives such as Lloyd's Patriotic Fund provided merely an erratic means of relieving their families.

MALE AUTHORS also wrote about the devastating social effects of war, helping to produce materials that reached all levels of society. But women's writings dwell more consistently on the emotional damage war causes, and strongly testify to a contemporary anti-war movement – though such sentiments were smothered during invasion scares. Women's poems often describe separated lovers, women dying of grief, or mothers struggling to bring up their children alone. Amelia Opie pointedly chose not to celebrate Nelson's victory at the Nile in her poem, 'The Orphan Boy's Tale'. Instead, she described how the boy is forced to beg after his father is killed and his mother dies from grief.

> Poor foolish child! how pleased was I,
> When news of Nelson's victory came,
> Along the crowded streets to fly
> And see the lighted windows flame!
> To force me home my mother sought;
> She could not bear to see my joy;
> For with my father's life 'twas bought,
> And made me a poor Orphan Boy.[1]

Helen Maria Williams, an enthusiastic republican, also refused to echo the general praise of Nelson's achievements. In her *Sketches of the State of Manners and Opinions in the French Republic, towards the Close of the Eighteenth Century* (1801), she criticized Nelson's support for the 1799 counter-revolution in Naples, claiming that passion for Emma had clouded his judgement. In an age of martial conflict and political repression, women writers may have been more sensitive to the abuse of power since they were rarely empowered themselves.

A favourite image in poetry of the time is that of the madwoman, drawn to the shore where she last saw her lover or husband. In one such poem titled 'The Maniac', in *Poems. By a Lady* (1798), the author denounces the kind of male ambition that welcomed the outbreak of hostilities. Blinded by a desire for glory, the men in her poem willingly invoke 'the power of war'. As they depart for battle in the name of honour, the Muse turns to the domestic scene and contemplates the pain of widows, virgins and orphans. Contemporary women poets excelled in elegiac lyrics, and the conditions of war lent themselves to fashionable poems of sensibility. Their work expresses a sense of impotence in the face of terrible events which ordinary people, especially women, could do little to control.

As the war against Napoleon dragged on, anti-French feeling prevailed in the face of invasion threats, particularly during 1803, and society became more militaristic. Women poets increasingly focused on themes of exclusion and alienation. In this respect, they set a trend – but pointed criticism of the war was dangerous. When Anna Barbauld mentioned Trafalgar in her satire, 'Eighteen Hundred and Eleven', she was bold enough to denounce the prolonged war and predict national disaster. The poem, published in 1812, evoked broad public criticism. Male critics thought it subversive, because it was topical, and because

Barbauld had dared to make a political comment. As the poem was nevertheless well written, they chiefly attacked her as a woman writer. The opinionated John Wilson Croker, reviewing for a Tory magazine, famously called Barbauld an interfering spinster (though she was in fact a widow) and implied that she would be well advised to return to her knitting and leave the public arena to men. Clearly women writers were not expected to comment on political events, though their lives might be directly affected.

It is no surprise, in this context, that many women addressed their poems to 'Hope'. Often the solitary female speaker in such poems invokes Hope while standing on a cliff or looking out to sea, since this female representation had long been associated with waiting for the return of seamen. The theme is reflected in jewellery and commemorative ware of the time. Items as varied as lockets, pendants, rings and earthenware jugs were all decorated with the figure of Hope in classical dress with a departing warship in the background, or else pointing out to sea with an anchor in the background. This figure therefore came to stand for a common female condition, and women came to be positioned as somehow adapted to the state of anxious waiting. Yet while some women took solace from depictions of this figure – certainly some jewellery items featuring Hope were worn as love tokens – others were resentful. Lady Charlotte Campbell, whose 'Ode to Evening' contained a typical address to Hope from a cliff top, also wrote a poem 'On Suspence' describing how this condition blighted hope and embittered life.

Another figure, Britannia, was used like that of Hope to suggest appropriate female responses to war and to male heroic achievement. By the eighteenth century Britannia had become a strong cultural signifier of British national identity. In wartime this martial, female icon is sometimes shown urging her sons to battle and at others mourning those who have fallen. Her armour is at once warlike and, given women's general inability to figure in the military arena, informed by notions of female restraint and repression. Though the meaning invested in Britannia could be contested, it allowed the articulation of processes and impulses within society otherwise difficult to describe. When Britannia is depicted sending her sons to war, this can be read as a wholly patriotic act since, as a female figure, Britannia is excluded from the corrupting forces of public life. The onlooker is encouraged to accept that the action of sending young men to war stems from moral impulse rather than political self-interest or callousness, which reflects well on the representation of the conflict itself. Yet we know from women's writing of the period that in wartime the conflicting imperatives of patriotism and maternal love caused them great pain.

Some women consciously identified with the iconographical figure of Britannia, or at least found that the association enhanced their status. Emma Hamilton, for example, famously posed as Britannia in one of her 'attitudes'. The dynamic and martial figure suggested a female public role that was denied to women in fact. Britannia was also employed when national grief needed to be represented, and often figured on tombstones and memorials to fallen officers. On Nelson's death, creamware and earthenware items were produced showing Britannia grieving over his ashes. Prints were issued on the same subject: a drawing by Thomas Baxter, engraved by A. R. Burt and published on 5 December 1805, actually depicts Emma as Britannia crowning a bust of Nelson (cat. no. 302). Given the notoriety of Emma's affair with Nelson and the conventional use of Britannia as an icon of national spirit, this solemn print indicates the degree to which individuals were able to identify with symbolic figures. Yet the message could be subverted: the market had become so saturated with hagiographic depictions of Nelson's death that James Gillray detected a niche market for a satirical version of the well-worn theme. He produced a mischievous print showing a saintly Nelson collapsing into the arms of an ample Britannia – bearing a marked resemblance to Emma. Support for Nelson was not universal: in some social circles his domestic situation was frowned upon. Gillray saw that Nelson's relationship with Emma could be used to qualify his fame.

In their leisure hours women replicated the image of Britannia. After Nelson's death, some embroidered Britannia, limp with grief, in silk pictures commemorating the hero. Such individually worked pieces were not simply the stuff of private meaning: in this medium, Britannia, as a cultural signifier, became overlaid with messages relating to class and social status. Fine embroidery had been attacked in the 1790s as a frivolous upper-class pastime of women neglectful of their family or parish duties. Only the rich had the leisure and resources to attempt

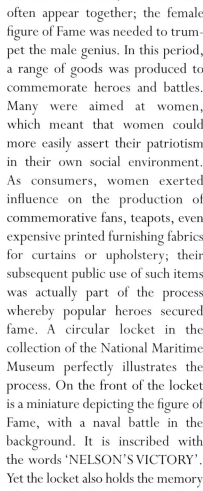

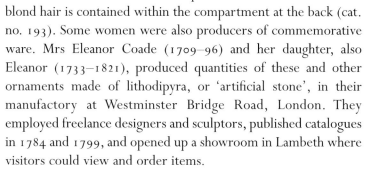

The Death of Admiral Lord Nelson – in the moment of Victory, by James Gillray (cat. no. 308).

decorative needlework in such fine materials; lower-class women were burdened with functional needlework. Presumably, a silk picture mourning the death of a national hero was less likely to attract criticism.

The figure of Britannia was commonly linked to that of another female icon, Fame. The two often appear together; the female figure of Fame was needed to trumpet the male genius. In this period, a range of goods was produced to commemorate heroes and battles. Many were aimed at women, which meant that women could more easily assert their patriotism in their own social environment. As consumers, women exerted influence on the production of commemorative fans, teapots, even expensive printed furnishing fabrics for curtains or upholstery; their subsequent public use of such items was actually part of the process whereby popular heroes secured fame. A circular locket in the collection of the National Maritime Museum perfectly illustrates the process. On the front of the locket is a miniature depicting the figure of Fame, with a naval battle in the background. It is inscribed with the words 'NELSON'S VICTORY'. Yet the locket also holds the memory of a particular loved one: a lock of blond hair is contained within the compartment at the back (cat. no. 193). Some women were also producers of commemorative ware. Mrs Eleanor Coade (1709–96) and her daughter, also Eleanor (1733–1821), produced quantities of these and other ornaments made of lithodipyra, or 'artificial stone', in their manufactory at Westminster Bridge Road, London. They employed freelance designers and sculptors, published catalogues in 1784 and 1799, and opened up a showroom in Lambeth where visitors could view and order items.

Fame was something that few women openly pursued for themselves. Felicia Hemans, the best-selling poet of the nineteenth century, remarked on 'the nothingness of fame, at least to a woman'.[2] The iconography of Fame ironically called for female self-effacement: given that women's social influence partly depended on their moral probity, fame – which could so easily descend into notoriety – was a double-edged sword. Typically, Frances Nelson, as a rejected wife, took care to live 'more circumspect and cautious than any young miss of 16'.[3] In contrast, Emma Hamilton mismanaged her fame: widowed, she continued to present a target for dubious jokes and innuendo. Lady Anne Hamilton (no relation), addressing Emma in her poem about society, confirms that Nelson's love affair remained controversial even after his death:

> Scandal may still reproach the
>   hero's name,
> Who left his wedded love for
>   thee and shame;
> Or modern virtue may deride
>   the charge,
> And hold a heart, when
>   profligate, is large;
> In vain they palliate, needlessly
>   they blame,
> Such deeds, bright fair, must
>   fix a deathless fame.[4]

Lady Anne Hamilton appears to take pleasure in Emma's decline after Nelson's death, implying that her fame is exactly the kind one would not wish to endure. A female author would have found it difficult to write otherwise: only by preserving a disinterested viewpoint could she aspire to moral authority. It is interesting to note that women of character had commercial value when it came to promoting naval heroes. In June 1799, as Frances Nelson waited for her husband to return home after the Battle of the Nile, the engraver William Barnard published a print of Abbott's portrait of Nelson and dedicated it to her, presumably to bolster sales. Ironically, it underlined the marital tie publicly just as Nelson's name was being linked with Emma's.

Women were encouraged to demonstrate patriotism by wearing fashions linked to Nelson's name. Nelson's victory at the Nile had a huge impact on male and female fashions in this country and abroad. As his fame increased, many women courted the publicity that an association with Nelson would bring. The wealthy could get their name in the papers by ostentatiously presenting well-chosen gifts: on 4 February 1801 *The Times*

Trafalgar furnishing fabric, 1806–7, by John Bury.
Victoria and Albert Museum, London; T98-1959.

reported that the Countess of Spencer had given him 'a gold fork with four prongs' one of which could be used as a knife so that he could eat with one hand. Some women eventually seem to have attracted criticism for exploiting naval heroes at themed social gatherings. Yet Nelsonic fashions continued after his death: *La Belle Assemblée, or Bell's Court and Fashionable Magazine*, which included fashion plates in each monthly edition, illustrated a 'Trafalgar dress' in February 1806. It was made of white satin, trimmed with gold, silver or lace, and accompanied by a feathered turban with 'Nelson' emblazoned across the front. The March issue carried details of a Bronte hat and Bronte muff and tippet 'worn only by the higher order of fashionables'. Artefacts with a naval theme made by or for women notably associate sentiment with seamen and naval heroes. It was important that officers were reputed to be just and benevolent, and Nelson's reputation as a kind commander, much loved by his men, was carefully burnished. Prevailing opinion held that a civilized man was marked by his capacity for sympathetic feeling – an emotion that ran against the country's need for battle-hardened warriors. Therefore, as both producers and consumers women often performed an important social function in countering anxiety that years of warfare were turning male Britons into fighting automatons.

This theme is evident in women's needlework commemorating Nelson. Samplers survive, worked in cross-stitch, marking Nelson's achievements, as do elaborate silk mourning pictures in his memory.[5] As suggested earlier, needlework was a subject of debate in this period: it was both integral to a girl's education and arguably an instrument of social control that kept girls and women sedentary for hours. Mary Lamb claimed, in her essay for the *British Lady's Magazine* in 1815, that needlework for upper- and middle-class women was a form of 'self-imposed slavery'. Yet women could still use needlework to express their own identity and in such works their references to Nelson contain a personal message. Emma Hamilton is credited with the production of a silk needlework picture based on an illustration to Laurence Sterne's *A Sentimental Journey*. The illustration depicted Maria, mentally unhinged by the desertion of her lover, with Yorick, Sterne's sentimental, first-person narrator. Emma adapted the scene to represent herself and Nelson walking. In the background is a distant prospect of the home they briefly shared, Merton Place. Maria and Yorick seem to have been a popular subject for silk pictures as other versions survive. In Sterne's novel, Yorick, seeking a meeting with Maria, exclaimed, 'I am never so perfectly conscious of the existence of a soul within me, as when I am entangled in [melancholy adventures]'.[6] On one level, the two figures, weeping copious tears into a shared, damp handkerchief represent perfect sympathy between human beings and serve as a token of immortality. Yet Sterne mischievously eroticized the episode. Maria, for example, innocently offers to dry the wet handkerchief in her bosom, and doubtless this sexual charge added to the scene's popularity. Emma's silk needlework throws light on how the couple perceived their relationship and also on Nelson's description of her as his 'guardian angel'.

Other forms of needlework alluding to Nelson have a political and a personal resonance. The Museum has an anti-slavery wool-work sampler that shows, in profile, a manacled black slave kneeling in a position of supplication. The anti-slavery movement had used this figure from the 1780s, often encircled with the words 'Am I not a man and a brother?' This proved an effective image that rapidly became part of the abolitionist iconography. But in this enigmatic sampler, the words 'Nelson's Moniment' [sic] are sewn instead over the head of the slave. The woman who created this work was not illiterate – 'moniment' is an obsolete form of 'monument – and the striking conjunction of image and caption merits discussion. This is an

Emma's embroidered adaptation of a scene from Sterne showing herself and Nelson at Merton (cat. no. 207).

Woolwork sampler, *c.* 1820.
National Maritime Museum, London; ZBA2840.

example of Berlin work which became popular in the 1820s when there was renewed agitation to abolish slavery in the colonies (Britain had abolished the trade in enslaved peoples in 1807). Monuments to Nelson were still a topic for discussion and by this time there was a tendency to use him as an example to future generations – as in John Flaxman's monument to Nelson, installed in St Paul's in 1818. Many cities had erected monuments to him with local funding but a national monument in London had still not won backing. It is not surprising, then, that in this climate a needle-woman should consider creating her own 'monument' to Nelson. But what was the topical basis for the connection she made between Nelson and slavery?

Nelson, in command of the Mediterranean Fleet, had been strongly associated with the defence of Britain's sugar islands against the French. In August 1805, the West India Merchants had fulsomely and publicly thanked him for his efforts. When grief at Nelson's death was at its height, in November, the *European Magazine* happened to print the resolution passed by the Committee of West India Merchants the previous August, offering Nelson their 'unfeigned thanks' for saving the sugar islands. It also printed Nelson's grateful letter of acknowledgement in return. Nelson's support for the plantation interest was not in doubt. It is therefore possible to read this sewn picture as a satirical commentary, albeit one that is highly individual, on Nelson's role in safeguarding Britain's West Indian interest, and also as a reflection on the establishment's continuing efforts to honour his memory.

Since women had few means of public expression open to them, it is interesting to see how a medium almost wholly restricted to female employment has been utilized to convey a

Dido, in Despair! James Gillray, published 6 February 1801 by H. Humphrey. National Maritime Museum, London; PAF3874.

complex message. Many women empathized with the African cause and played a prominent role in the abolitionist movement, seeing parallels with their own marginalization within society and empathizing particularly with female slaves. Society then was no more homogeneous than society today and this richly coded picture reminds us that, while Nelson was widely admired, in war-weary Britain opinion of him was not unmixed.

While the material culture of the time yields evidence of a female response to Nelson's victories at a number of social levels, a regional female response is harder to recover. By 1800 there were more than seventy provincial newspapers produced each week but they perhaps reached in excess of only 8 per cent of the population outside London, and remote areas still received the news by haphazard means. News of Nelson's victories may have travelled across the country fairly quickly but the details would have been more difficult to learn in the countryside, and this affected the way in which individuals responded to the news. On Christmas Day 1805, Dorothy Wordsworth wrote to Lady Beaumont:

> I was exceedingly interested with your Extract from the Newspaper concerning Lord Nelson's last moments – how very affecting the noble Creature's thoughts of his early pleasures, and the happy Fair-day at home. My Brother was at Park house when I received it – he had seen the same

account at Penrith; but it was not in the *Courier*, the paper we have at Grasmere, therefore your kind attention was a great gain to me.

Dorothy sentimentalizes Nelson's memory, working on the few details available to her. In November, hearing of his death, she had told Lady Beaumont, 'I believe that every truly *brave* Man, in the highest sense of the word, is, as you describe Lord Nelson to have been, tender and humane in all the daily acts of life.'[7] Here again we see an impulse to endow all naval heroes with tenderness as well as bravery rather than focus on the reality of war. Her brother noted more prosaically that Nelson could not have died at a more opportune moment since, had he survived, he would only have lingered on, in ill health.

Women at the lower levels of society have left scant testimony to the impact of naval warfare on their lives, but this discussion indicates the pervasiveness of that impact and the social importance of the women's responses to it. Few women had the means of openly voicing political opinions: prevailing rhetoric and expectations of female activity channelled their responses into conventional paths. But these turbulent times nevertheless permitted women to set cautious precedents for taking greater part in public life, and some women writers discovered that naval conflict and naval heroes afforded particular opportunities for public statement that conveyed more than unalloyed patriotism.

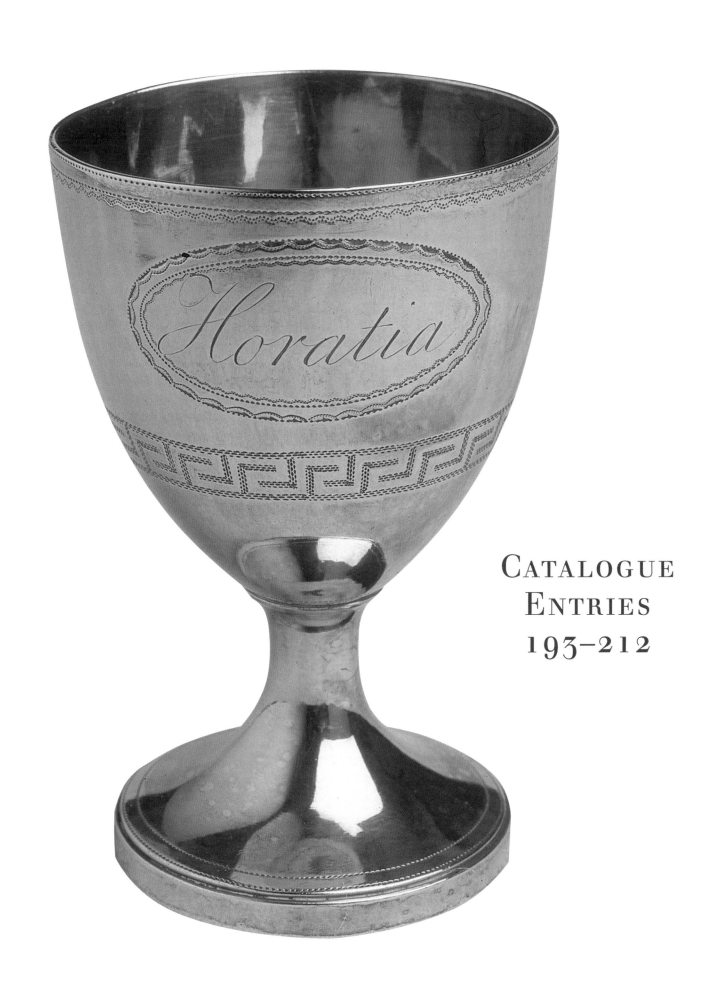

CATALOGUE
ENTRIES
193–212

193. Locket depicting Fame and naval battle, 1798–1806

Glass, gold alloy and human hair

National Maritime Museum, London (Sutcliffe-Smith Collection); JEW0196

Circular locket, in a glazed, gilt-metal setting with a suspension ring. On the front of the locket is a miniature painted on ivory. It depicts a figure representing Fame – recognizable by her attributes of wings and trumpet – standing on the shore with a naval battle in the background. 'NELSON'S VICTORY' is inscribed on a rock. A compartment at the back of the locket contains a lock of blond hair.　BT

194. Locket depicting Hope and a departing warship, *c.* 1800

Gilt metal, silver and glass

National Maritime Museum, London (Sutcliffe-Smith Collection); JEW0206

Circular locket, in a glazed, gilt-metal setting with a suspension ring on a hinge. On the front is a miniature, painted on ivory. It depicts a figure representing Hope with a departing warship in the background. There is an empty compartment at the back (presumably for hair), which is lined with silver foil. In the classical tradition, virtues or other abstract qualities were represented by female figures identified by the attributes they held.　BT

195. Locket depicting Hope and a departing warship, *c.* 1790

Gilt metal, silver and glass

National Maritime Museum, London (Sutcliffe-Smith Collection); JEW0211

Oval locket, with a glazed, gilt-metal setting, surrounded by a wreath of silver thistles. A bolt ring is attached for suspension. In the front of the locket is a miniature, painted on ivory, depicting the figure of Hope with a departing warship in the background. There is an empty compartment at the back.　BT

196. Pendant with Hope leaning on an anchor, early nineteenth century

Nacre, 47mm diam.

National Maritime Museum, London; JEW0148

Disc-shaped, mother-of-pearl pendant pierced for suspension. The front is engraved with a female figure representing Hope leaning on an anchor and a departing warship in the background. The back of the pendant is decorated with two overlapping hearts and bears the inscription 'Though Far Apart near an [*sic*] Heart HMJ'. The back of the pendant is also decorated around the edges with a pique-point design. The exchange of gifts was a significant part of eighteenth-century courtship.　BT

197. Gold ring, *c.* 1805

Gold, glass and ivory

National Maritime Museum, London (Walter Collection); JEW0186

Gold ring with a marquise (almond-shaped) bezel set with a glazed miniature painted on ivory. The miniature depicts a woman wearing classical dress who is pointing to a departing warship.　BT

198. Locket depicting Hope and a departing warship, late eighteenth century

Glass, gilt metal and silk

National Maritime Museum, London (Sutcliffe-Smith Collection); JEW0207

Circular locket, contained within a glazed, gilt-metal setting, with a suspension ring. The glass on the front of the locket is decorated with a border of *verre églomisé*. This

covers a miniature painting depicting a figure representing Hope; a departing warship is shown in the background. There is an empty compartment at the back of the locket, lined with pink satin; this would have been intended to hold a lock of hair or other memento.   BT

199. *The Maiden's Lamentations for the loss of her Sailor, c. 1803*
Mantz Finsbury (author) and John Pitts (printer)
Printed broadsheet
255 x 90mm
National Maritime Museum, London; p.204.60

Broadsheet ballads were sold on the streets to the general public. In the nineteenth century, the Seven Dials area of London (near St Martin's Lane) was renowned for the production of these publications. John Pitts, printer and stationer, produced and sold this typical lament illuminating the plight of women whose loved ones were at sea: 'Ye Neptune gods be kind to me, / And send him safely here, / On his dear breast my head shall rest, / He's my jolly sailor dear.' Pitts was based in Great St Andrew Street, Seven Dials, from 1802 to 1824.   HP

200. Merton Place, 1802 or later
Thomas Baxter (1782–1821)
Watercolour, graphite, pen and ink
130 x 208mm, 130 x 207mm (two sheets)
Inscribed on mount: *House (two sides) and grounds.*
   The little railings . . . may be/those wh Nelson wrote
   should be to prevent Horatia tumbling . . .
National Maritime Museum, London; WAL/49 (album)

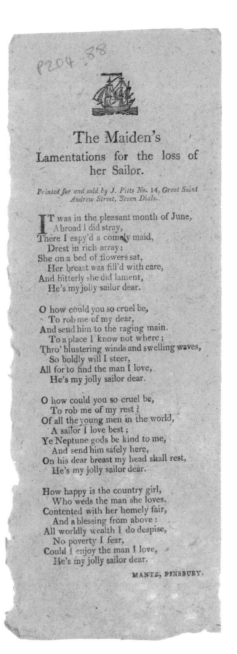

Nelson purchased Merton Place in 1801 for himself, Emma and Sir William Hamilton. He and Lady Nelson were now living apart, their marriage a mere formality. Nelson actually lived at Merton for only two brief periods – from 1801 until Sir William's death in 1803 and then again for a few short weeks before Trafalgar. After Sir William's death Horatia, Nelson and Emma's daughter, joined the household. When Nelson left Merton for the last time he wrote, 'Friday night at half past Ten drove from dear dear Merton, where I left all which I hold dear in this world, to go to serve my King and Country'.

Baxter met Nelson and the Hamiltons during their tour of the west of England and made visits to Merton between 1802 and 1805. The album of drawings by him provides a vivid impression of the house and grounds and of family life there. Baxter was a porcelain painter at Worcester and Swansea and also exhibited enamels at the Royal Academy, including one of Sir William Hamilton in 1805.   RQ

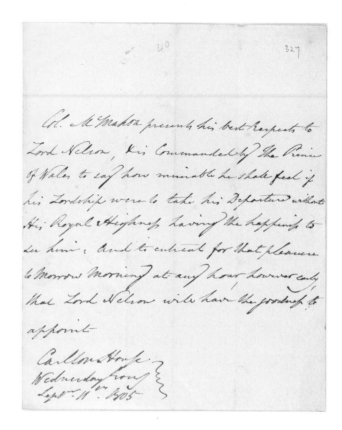

201. Pair of fede rings, c. 1805
Gold
National Maritime Museum, London (Nelson-Ward
    Collection); JEW0168
Royal Naval Museum, Portsmouth; 57/XX

Gold fede, or betrothal, rings; the bezels are made in the form of two clasped hands. This pair was exchanged by Nelson and Emma Hamilton. They took communion together before Nelson's last departure and probably exchanged rings at this time. They were enacting the more informal kind of betrothal that preceded the 'Act for the Better Preventing of Clandestine Marriages' of 1753. These unofficial ceremonies might include the exchange of vows. Both rings were passed down through the family of their daughter, Horatia Nelson-Ward. Nelson was wearing his ring (above left) at the time of his death.   BT

202. Letter from Colonel Mahon to Nelson, 11 September 1805
Ink on paper
Lloyd's of London (Nelson Collection); L327

Nelson arrived back in Portsmouth on 18 August 1805, after more than two years at sea. Despite his fears that the public would blame him for failing to stop the French, he received a hero's welcome and was mobbed and fêted everywhere he went. His brief period ashore was spent partly at Merton with Emma Hamilton and partly in London, where his opinions on the progress of the war against Napoleon were much in demand.

This letter shows how much he was valued at the highest levels. The Prince of Wales says that he will be 'disappointed' if he cannot meet with Nelson before his departure and is willing to see him 'at any hour, however early, that Lord Nelson will have the goodness to appoint'.
                                                    DK

203. **Emma Hamilton's
writing box**

Wood

National Maritime Museum, London; REL0071

204. **Letter from Nelson
to Emma Hamilton, 16 March 1805**

Ink on paper

Provenance: purchased from Earl Nelson in 1947

National Maritime Museum, London; TRA/13

Written during Nelson's long period of command in the Mediterranean, this letter to Emma clearly displays how the separation from the 'wife of his heart' was preying on his mind: the couple had not seen each other since May 1803. Nelson writes of his desire to 'embrace the substantial part' of her, but he would have to chase the French fleet across the Atlantic and back before being able to return to 'Paradise Merton'. This was the house the couple had purchased in Surrey, with Sir William Hamilton, when their living arrangements had scandalized society. Nelson's letter contains what appears to be a prophetic statement (possibly preparing Emma for the worst) that he will come home for only a short time, before returning to sea; he returned to Emma for barely a month, in August, before being recalled to face Villeneuve's fleet. AD

205. **Letter from Emma Hamilton to
John Scott, 14 September 1805**

Ink on paper

Clive Richards Collection; CRC/91

This note was written by Emma Hamilton to Nelson's secretary John Scott on the day after he left Merton to travel to Portsmouth to rejoin the *Victory*. It vividly conjures up the distress that he had left behind him:

> Cou'd you see us all My dear Mr Scott the party how wretched we are you wou'd pitty us. He went last night & by this time I hope he is on board safe and off, for after he leaves me my anxiety is that he shou'd be wherever he ought. All these 3 short weeks of happiness seems like a dream – in short I am all most disturbed. Write me a line to say he is safe. Poor little Horatia cryed at breakfast for god papa, but I Cannot describe to you – you Can imagine all our wretchedness. Take care of him God send him victory & safe home again & <u>for the good of the Nation</u> moored at the Admiralty, where he tells me if he ever is you are to be his Secretary – as to all ministers & their business I have a Contempt for them seeing this

Dear Glorious Man spoils me for all others. He wou'd do all the business of the nation whilst the others are snoring. God bless you ever your affectionate friend E Hamilton.

CSW

206. **Letter from Emma Hamilton
to Nelson, 8 October 1805**

Ink on paper

Clive Richards Collection; CRC/92

This is one of very few letters from Emma Hamilton to Nelson to have survived. He usually destroyed her letters to prevent them from falling into the wrong hands. However, this letter did not reach the *Victory* until after Trafalgar and was returned to Emma by Captain Hardy, when he handed over her lover's possessions.

It is a chatty letter, from Canterbury, where Emma was staying with Nelson's elder brother, the Revd William Nelson. She gives him news of their daughter Horatia:

> You will be even fonder of her when you return. She says 'I love my dear godpapa but Mrs Gibson [her nurse] told me how he killed all the people and I was afraid.' Dearest angel she is. O Nelson how I love her but how I idolise you – the dearest husband of my heart you are all in this world to your Emma. May God send you victory and home to your Emma, Horatia and paradise Merton for when you are there it will be paradise.

CSW

207. Needlework picture
Silk embroidery
National Maritime Museum, London (Nelson-Ward
    Collection); TXT0056
See page 177

Tradition has it that this needlework picture was worked by
Emma Hamilton and depicts Nelson walking with Emma
and their dog Nileus at Merton. The picture is worked in
coloured silks on a silk taffeta ground, with the faces and
hands painted in watercolour. This was a common 1790s
technique for such pictures, which were bought ready
drawn to be completed by women at home. Two other
versions from different sources are in the collection, also
said to represent Nelson and Emma.

The scene is based on an illustration for Laurence
Sterne's *A Sentimental Journey* (1768), showing the characters Maria and Yorick. Sterne describes Maria:

> She was dressed in white, and much as my friend
> described her, except that her hair hung loose which
> before was twisted within a silk net. She had super-
> added, likewise, to her jacket, a pale green ribbon,
> which fell across her shoulders to the waist, at the
> end of which hung her pipe – Her goat had been as
> faithless as her lover; and she had got a little dog in
> lieu of him, which she had kept tied by a string to
> her girdle. . . . Maria put her arm within mine, and
> lengthening the string, to let the dog follow – in that
> order we entered Moulines.

The 1794 edition published by John Creswick has an
engraving by W. Bromley after M. Archer, which is close
enough in dress, gestures and other details to have been
the source of the silk embroideries, although the building
on the right side is absent. The costumes shown in the
embroidery date from the 1780s.   RP

208. Horatia's dessert knife
Silver-gilt, ivory
National Maritime Museum, London; PLT0750

Nelson also purchased from John Salter the silver-gilt
dessert knife with ivory handle which is displayed with the
cup. The blade is inscribed 'To my much loved Horatia 21
August 1805. Nelson & Bronte'. The knife was given to the
National Maritime Museum in 1939 by Horatia's grandson,
the Revd Hugh Nelson-Ward.   RP

209. Horatia's christening cup, 1805
Silver-gilt
Royal Naval Museum, Portsmouth (Suckling Ward
    Collection); 57/60

Nelson purchased this cup for his daughter Horatia at
Salter's, a silversmith in the Strand, London, on 30 August
1805. The engraved inscriptions were added later by Emma
Hamilton. According to a note by Emma (RNM 84/57),
'The Victor of Aboukir Copenhagen & Trafalgar &c &c &c
the glorious the great & good Nelson bought this for His
daughter Horatia Nelson August 30th 1805. She used it till
I thought it proper for her to lay it by as a sacred relic.' The
cup remained in Horatia's family until it was presented to
the Victory Museum in 1957 by Mrs Maurice Ward, wife of
one of Horatia's grandsons.

Horatia is shown holding the cup in a pencil sketch
painted at Merton in about 1807–8 by Thomas Baxter
(NMMWAL49).   CSW

[Facsimile of Nelson's handwritten letter, dated "Victory Octbr 19th 1805", beginning "My Dearest angel..."]

[Facsimile of second page of the letter, ending "...Dearest good Lady Hamilton. Be a good Girl mind what Miss Connor says to you. Receive My Dearest Horatia the affectionate Parental Blessing of Your Father Nelson Bronte"]

210. Nelson's last letter to Horatia

Ink on paper
National Maritime Museum, London; NWD/19

While at sea, Nelson frequently wrote to both Lady Hamilton and their daughter Horatia, and this letter was written just before the Battle of Trafalgar. It was usual, as many accounts testify, for sailors to write home before a battle in the hope that if they were killed their final thoughts and wishes would be conveyed to their families.

Horatia's birth and parentage were kept secret. She was brought up by a Mrs Gibson in London and rarely visited her parents, even while Nelson was at home at Merton before the Trafalgar campaign. Nelson's message, not mentioning the relationship between them, is all the more poignant for its instruction to the four-year-old Horatia to 'Give her [Lady Hamilton] a kiss for Me'.   DK

211. Necklace given to Horatia by Nelson

Gold
National Maritime Museum, London (Nelson-Ward
    Collection); JEW0369

A gift from Nelson to his daughter Horatia Nelson-Ward (1801–81) in answer to her letter saying that he had promised

her a dog. The chain is made of loops of gold strip joined by wire links with a ring at either end of the chain for a ribbon tie. At the centre there is a gold silhouette of a dog within an oval frame. Nelson wrote to Horatia from *Victory* on 14 January 1804:

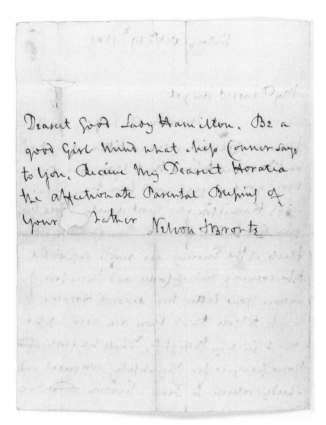

As I am sure that for the world you would not tell a story, it must have slipped my memory that I promised you a watch. Therefore I have sent to Naples to get one and I will send it home as soon as it arrives. The dog I never could have promised as we have no dogs on board ship; only I beg my dear Horatia to be obedient and you will ever be sure of the affection of Nelson & Bronte.

BT

LITERATURE: Loan exhibition of Nelson relics exhibited at Spink & Son, King Street, St James's (London, 1928), catalogue item 51.

212.	## Nelson profile plaque, 1805
Catherine Andras, London
Wax
Incised below the shoulder: *C Andras 1805*
National Maritime Museum, London (Girdlestone
    Collection); OBJ0575

This pink wax relief plaque depicts Nelson in profile wearing vice-admiral's full dress uniform with the Order of the Bath and a naval gold medal. It was modelled by Catherine Andras (1775–1860), Modeller in Wax to Queen Charlotte. Andras had already received a prize for her 1801 wax model of Nelson and in 1805 he sat to her for another portrait. It was a great success and casts of this relief were produced for sale between 1805 and 1812. This is one of the early examples. She was subsequently commissioned by the Dean and Chapter of Westminster Abbey to model a full-size wax effigy of Nelson.

Lady Hamilton was particularly impressed by the accuracy of the small relief plaque:

> She shewed me the inclosed wax profile which she declares is the most striking likeness that has been taken, and much more so than our little drawing or print by Mr Da Costa. On asking Lady H in what features the model so closely resembled Lord Nelson as she had declared, she said, in the direction and form of the nose, mouth and chin, that the general carriage of the body was exactly his, and that altogether the likeness was so great it was impossible for anybody who had known him to doubt about or mistake it.
>
> RP

LITERATURE: Walker, *The Nelson Portraits*, pp. 150, 260; Pyke, *A Biographical Dictionary of Wax Modellers*, pp. 5–6.

TRAFALGAR

Trafalgar

COLIN WHITE

O N 19 JANUARY 1805, the British Mediterranean Fleet, under the command of Vice-Admiral Lord Nelson was at anchor in Agincourt Sound, a superb natural harbour among the islands of Maddalena, Caprera and San Stefano. It was a wild day, with gales from the north-west, but within the shelter of the Sound the British crews were busy replenishing their water, and taking on stores from the shore and from transport ships sent from Malta. Despite the hard work of manhandling the heavy barrels, it was a welcome respite from the monotony of their patrols off the French naval base at Toulon.

Suddenly, two British frigates appeared from the north-west and, as they came closer, they were seen to be flying the signal 'Enemy is at sea'. The French fleet, which they had been watching for so long, had at last emerged from harbour. At 3 p.m. the frigates anchored close to the flagship *Victory* and, by 4.30 p.m., the entire fleet of eleven battleships – two of them three-deckers – was under sail, moving in a single column down the narrow channel that led out of the eastern side of the anchorage, each ship steering by the stern lanterns of her next ahead in the fast-failing light.

It was a remarkable feat of seamanship, a vivid demonstration of how much Nelson had achieved during his twenty months as commander-in-chief in the Mediterranean and a tribute to his abilities as a fleet administrator. When the crisis came his ships were ready for immediate action: equipped and stored for a long voyage and with their crews healthy and fit. After their long months at sea, his captains and crews were so highly trained and experienced that he was able to lead them confidently through a narrow and hazardous channel in the gathering gloom. Moreover, he was sure he knew exactly where the French were going and believed that, by taking the easterly route, he would place his fleet in an ideal position to ambush them. As he wrote that evening to his second in command, Sir Richard Bickerton: 'I am a little anxious naturally but no man has more real cause to be happy. I hope tomorrow we shall get hold of them, and the result I ought not to doubt. You will be a peer as sure as my name is Nelson.'[1]

Nelson was working on the assumption, based on consistent intelligence received over many months, that the French fleet (which was known to have troops on board) was heading to attack Britain's ally, the Kingdom of Naples and Sicily – either at Naples itself, or somewhere in Sicily. That may well have been the French aim months before when the intelligence was gathered but, by January 1805, it was no longer the case. For the ships under Vice-Admiral Pierre Villeneuve were now operating as part of a major fleet deployment devised by the Emperor Napoleon in support of his ambitious plans to invade Britain.

NAPOLEON'S PLAN

W HEN WAR between France and Britain restarted in 1803, following the brief Peace of Amiens, Napoleon began concentrating an army around Boulogne and Calais in north-eastern France and building a large flotilla of specially designed boats to carry the troops across the Channel. The British responded by organizing a three-tiered defence. First, there was the Channel Fleet, under Admiral William Cornwallis, cruising off Brest, holding down the main French battle fleet under Admiral Ganteaume. Then there were squadrons of smaller vessels, stationed in the Channel itself under Admiral Lord Keith, and operating right on the French coast, ready to harry the invasion forces as they emerged from port. Finally there was a system of land defences involving specially constructed fortifications and a large force of militia and volunteers.

Clearly, the French invasion flotilla could not hope to reach Britain unless it was protected by a large fleet. To achieve this, Napoleon devised a strategy to draw the British away from their usual blockading stations and enable him to concentrate a significant force of ships in the Channel. He ordered his admirals at Brest, Rochefort and Toulon to emerge from port and rendezvous in the West Indies, where they were to attack the rich British islands and the merchant ships that operated from them, thus forcing the British to divert warships for their defence. They were then to return swiftly to the mouth of the Channel in a concentrated force large enough to sweep aside the remaining British defenders and finally to move into a position that would enable them to cover the invasion flotilla as it made its crossing.

It was essentially a soldier's plan, devised by a man gifted at synchronizing exactly the movements of individual groups of his forces so as to bring them to a given destination as a unified body,

The Victory *and the Mediterranean Fleet off Stromboli, c.* 1810, watercolour by Nicholas Pocock.
National Maritime Museum, London; PAF5885.

but who had little understanding of the uncertainty that winds and weather brought to naval planning. It was also the brainchild of a native of the Mediterranean with little understanding of tides. Napoleon assumed that the embarkation of his troops could proceed smoothly and continuously as soon as he gave the order: he did not appreciate that in the Channel there would be long periods when his transport barges would be beached and useless. As a result, his exhortations to his admirals (whom he clearly regarded as faint-hearted obstructionists) were peppered with impractical claims: 'The English do not know what awaits them! If we are masters of the Channel for twelve hours England is finished!' ²

However impractical the plan might have been, it did result in a major series of fleet movements in the summer of 1805. Arguably, these gave the British government far more cause for

concern than all the warlike preparations on the other side of the Channel.

When Villeneuve left Toulon on 18 January 1805, his voyage was part of this wider plan. His colleague, Rear-Admiral Missiessy, had already left Rochefort on the French Biscay coast on the 11th and headed, as ordered, for the West Indies. However, while Nelson was sailing headlong for the southern end of Sardinia, confident that he was placing his ships in the path of the approaching enemy, the French found themselves battling with a westerly gale. Their ships were so badly damaged that Villeneuve decided the only safe course was to put back into Toulon for repairs. He arrived there on the 21st, after less than three days at sea.

When the French failed to appear, Nelson decided they had slipped past him and, finding from his scouting frigates that they had not gone to Naples or Sicily, decided that they must be bound for Egypt and rushed there with his fleet: 'You will believe my anxiety. I shall die if I do not meet them of a brain fever,' he told one of his captains. After such a long detour, he did not regain his station until the end of February and it was only then that he learned what had happened to the French. 'Buonaparte himself cannot be more disappointed and grieved at the return of the French fleet crippled into Toulon,' he told the First Lord of the Admiralty, adding contemptuously, 'These gentlemen are not used to a Gulph of Lyons gale which we have buffeted for 21 months and not carried away a spar.' He had judged Napoleon's reaction exactly right. 'What is to be done', wrote the irate Emperor, 'with admirals who allow their spirits to sink and determine to hasten home at the first damage they receive?'

THE NAVAL CAMPAIGN: APRIL–JULY 1805

TWO MONTHS LATER, on 30 March, Villeneuve made a second attempt. This time, however, Nelson had set a trap for his opponent. First, he appeared with his fleet near Barcelona and deliberately allowed it to be seen; then he hastened across to Pulla on the south coast of Sardinia, expecting that Villeneuve would head directly south from Toulon in order to keep away from his last reported position, and so fall into his arms. The plan nearly worked: at first, Villeneuve steered the course Nelson had hoped but, by a lucky chance, he then fell in with a neutral ship that reported where Nelson really was. Veering off to the west, he escaped a battle and got clean away out of the Mediterranean, sailing first to Carthagena and then to Cadiz to collect Spanish ships that were stationed there, before beginning the long Atlantic crossing.

Villeneuve arrived in the West Indies in mid-May, expecting to rendezvous with his colleagues. But, already, Napoleon's plan had begun to unravel. Missiessy, having waited for nearly three months, had sailed for home. Moreover, the Brest fleet was unable to leave port because of the tight blockade imposed by Cornwallis's Channel Fleet. Finally, as the French intentions became clear, the British squadrons responded by falling back northwards on the Channel Fleet. As a result, by early June 1805, far from being dispersed as Napoleon had intended, a large proportion of the Royal Navy's battleships were concentrated in the mouth of the Channel.

Nelson, however, was not with them. Having first searched for Villeneuve in the Mediterranean, he eventually passed through the Strait of Gibraltar in early May. Establishing that the Combined French and Spanish Fleet, now numbering seventeen battleships, had sailed for the West Indies, he resolved to go after them with his ten battleships. He made a quick passage and arrived at Barbados on 4 June, thinking, for the second time in three months, that he was on the eve of a battle. As he wrote to Emma Hamilton, 'My own dearest beloved Emma, Your own Nelson's pride and delight, I find myself within six days of the Enemy and I have every reason to hope that the 6th of June will immortalize your own Nelson, your fond Nelson.'

However, once again Villeneuve managed to elude him. Nelson received false intelligence that the French had gone to Trinidad whereas, in fact, Villeneuve was miles to the north, in Martinique. Hearing that his opponent had arrived, he abandoned his plans for further operations in the West Indies and started the voyage home on 10 June. Nelson learned of this two days later and set sail himself, sending the fast brig *Curieux* ahead to warn the Admiralty of Villeneuve's movements. On the 19th, she sighted the Combined Fleet briefly and so was able to carry accurate information about their course, which appeared to be heading for northern Spain, rather than the Mediterranean or the Channel.

This news reached the First Lord of the Admiralty, Lord Barham, in Whitehall on 8 July and he immediately ordered Cornwallis to send a detachment from the Channel Fleet under Vice-Admiral Sir Robert Calder off Ferrol to intercept the approaching enemy. So it was that when Villeneuve eventually arrived off Cape Finisterre on 22 July, he found a British fleet waiting for him in the mist. In the ensuing battle he lost two Spanish ships but was able to escape, first into Vigo and then into Ferrol, where he collected more Spanish reinforcements, bringing his force to twenty-nine battleships. Pleased with his achievement, Calder wrote to Barham to hint about the sort of honours that he hoped to be given. But his satisfaction was not shared at home: he was so severely criticized for not achieving a greater victory that he demanded a court martial, expecting to be able to clear his name. In fact he was severely reprimanded for not renewing the action and never served at sea again.

With hindsight, we can see that Calder's action – which caused such disappointment at the time and is scarcely known today – was one of the turning points of the 1805 campaign. Villeneuve had clearly been unnerved by the way that his every move had been countered by the British and so, when he emerged again in early August, he did not sail northwards, as Napoleon intended, to join Ganteaume off Brest. Instead, he went south and took refuge in Cadiz. By then Napoleon had learned that Austria had begun to mobilize and was concerned that he might be faced with a war on two fronts. So, when the

The aftermath of Sir Robert Calder's action off Cape Finisterre, 23 July 1805, by William Anderson (cat. no. 234).

news of the retreat of his fleet arrived, he first flew into a rage – 'What a navy! What an admiral!' – and then used it as an excuse to return, with evident relief, to the sort of warfare he understood best. Turning his army around he struck at Austria while she was still preparing, in a brilliant feat of planning and speedy manoeuvre.

NELSON AT HOME:
AUGUST–SEPTEMBER 1805

BY THE END OF August 1805 the immediate threat of invasion was over, although that was not yet apparent in Britain. Nelson took his fleet to join with Cornwallis off Brest and then returned home in the *Victory* for a long overdue spell of leave. More than two years had elapsed since he had last set foot on dry land. Now he was looking forward to some rest with Emma Hamilton, and their five-year-old daughter Horatia, in the house they shared in Merton, then a village to the south-west of London.

Instead, he found himself at the centre of affairs – the personification of Britain's resistance to the French. Everyone from Prime Minister William Pitt down wanted to consult him and he was often called to London for meetings and briefings. It was regarded as a matter of course that he would quickly return to sea to finish off the naval campaign. He was conscious of the precariousness of his sudden popularity, remarking to Captain Richard Keats, one of his close professional colleagues, 'I am now set up for a *Conjurer* and God knows they will very soon find out I am far from being one. . . . if I make one wrong guess the charm will be broken.'

Keats was also treated to a preview of the tactics that Nelson planned to use in the battle everyone believed was imminent. As they walked together in the grounds at Merton, Nelson explained how he would form his fleet into three divisions, and then concentrate one of them on a part of the enemy line, crushing it with superior gunfire. In the meantime, the other two divisions would prevent the remaining enemy ships from coming to the aid of their comrades. This, he hoped, would bring

Nelson's battle plan for Trafalgar, 1805,
sketched on a torn scrap of paper with various
'memo' notes to himself on the other side
(cat. no. 235).

'a pell-mell battle', a close-quarters action, in which the superior gunnery and ship-handling of his crews would have maximum advantage.

Keats's account of their conversation was recorded many years after the event but the accuracy of his memory has recently been demonstrated by the discovery in the archive of the National Maritime Museum of a rough sketch, drawn by Nelson at about this time, and showing very much the same tactics that Keats remembered (cat. no. 235).[3]

In between these official meetings, Nelson found time for his private affairs. In shopping expeditions to London, he bought a new uniform hat at Locks in St James's, together with a delightful silver-gilt cup for Horatia, at Salter's in the Strand (cat. no. 209). Before he left Merton, he went with Emma to the local parish church, where they took private communion and then exchanged rings in a quasi-marriage service. Both the rings have survived (cat. no. 201).

He left Merton for Portsmouth late at night on 13 September. Afterwards, Emma tried to comfort herself by claiming that she had bravely urged him to go back to sea but the couple's friend Lord Minto remembered her in floods of tears at

their last dinner together. A recently discovered letter from Emma to Nelson's secretary, John Scott, written on the morning of the 14th, gives a poignant picture of the distress the admiral left behind him: 'Cou'd you see us all My dear Mr Scott the party how wretched we are you wou'd pitty us. He went last night & by this time I hope he is on board safe. . . . Poor little Horatia cryed at breakfast for god papa' (cat. no. 205).[4]

PREPARING FOR BATTLE: SEPTEMBER–OCTOBER 1805

NELSON ARRIVED off Cadiz in the *Victory* on 28 September. Only a handful of the captains in the hastily assembled fleet had served with him before and so he had to build his team swiftly. The next day, his forty-seventh birthday, he held a dinner party, and another the following day, at which he explained to his captains his plans for defeating the enemy. He then committed his thoughts to writing in a memorandum, a copy of which was sent to every captain. With his characteristic gift for the telling phrase, he dubbed the plan, 'the Nelson Touch' (cat. no. 236).

A persistent Trafalgar myth is that this plan was completely new and the product of Nelson's personal tactical genius. In fact, none of the individual elements, as outlined to Keats and illustrated in Nelson's sketch – attack in divisions, concentration on one part of the enemy line, a 'pell-mell', close-quarters action – was particularly new or revolutionary. Nelson was building on years of tactical experiment in the Royal Navy. Indeed Villeneuve, who had fought Nelson before at the Battle of the Nile in August 1798, predicted with extraordinary accuracy what the British tactics would be: 'The enemy will not trouble to form line parallel with ours and fight it out gun to gun,' he told his captains. 'He will try to double our rear, cut through our line and bring against the ships thus isolated groups of his own to surround and capture them.' But he was unable to offer any counter to such tactics, contenting himself with the exhortation 'Captains must rely upon their courage and love of glory rather than on the signals of the admiral.'

The two distinctive aspects to Nelson's plan were, first, the way in which he discussed it well in advance, and in detail, with his subordinates. Second, he was prepared to delegate responsibility – not just to the second in command, his old friend Vice-Admiral Cuthbert Collingwood, but also to individual captains. 'In case signals can neither be seen or perfectly understood,' he wrote, 'no captain can do very wrong if he places his ship alongside that of an enemy'. No wonder some of the captains gathered round his table wept with excitement.

The Combined Franco-Spanish Fleet emerged from Cadiz on 19 October 1805, heading south. Napoleon had now ordered Villeneuve to start a new campaign, this time against Naples. The aim was to force the Austrians to divert troops to Italy in support of their allies, thus weakening themselves in the main theatre of the newly emerging campaign in central Europe.

Nelson was determined that the enemy would not elude him a third time. Keeping the main body of his fleet out of sight of the watchers on land, he remained in touch with the allied fleet's movements by means of a chain of frigates and fast battleships, with whom he communicated easily using the recently developed telegraphic signalling system of Sir Home Riggs Popham.

THE BATTLE OF TRAFALGAR:
21 OCTOBER 1805

THE TWO FLEETS sighted each other at about 6 a.m. on 21 October: as John Brown, a sailor in the *Victory* remembered, 'At daylight the French and Spanish fleets was like a great wood on our lee bow which cheered the hearts of every British tar in the *Victory* like lions anxious to be at it.'[5] However, the wind was light and so the first shots were not fired until midday. As there were not sufficient British ships to make up the three divisions Nelson had envisaged, the attack was made in two. One, led by Collingwood in the *Royal Sovereign*, headed for the rear of the allied line; meanwhile Nelson in the *Victory* aimed his division at their van, thus preventing them from turning to help their comrades. Scarcely any operational signals were required – a tribute to the thoroughness of Nelson's pre-battle briefings. Indeed, when the flags were hoisted with his famous message of encouragement, 'England expects that every man will do his duty', Collingwood's first reaction on seeing the flags breaking out in the *Victory* was to remark crossly that he wished Nelson would stop signalling as they all knew what they had to do. But Nelson had caught the almost festive mood in which most of his men were facing the battle. Midshipman W. S. Badcock of the *Neptune* later recalled, 'One would have thought that the people were preparing for a Festival rather than a combat; the bands playing. . . . the crews stationed on the forecastles of the various ships cheering the ship ahead of them.'

Collingwood was first into action, firing a broadside into one of the Spanish flagships, the *Santa Ana*, as he passed under her stern at about 12.20 p.m. He was followed by the ships of his division, which approached in a slanting 'line of bearing', spreading the force of the impact and enveloping the allied rear. Meanwhile Nelson was still heading for the allied van, keeping them guessing until, almost at the last moment, he altered course and smashed through the centre, directly astern of Villeneuve's flagship, the *Bucentaure*.

As the *Victory* moved on she became entangled with the *Redoutable*, under Captain Jean Lucas, and the two ships drifted away, locked in a deadly close-quarters struggle. This created a large gap in the allied line through which the ships of Nelson's division poured, splitting the enemy fleet in two.

Thereafter the battle developed into a ferocious pounding match. Royal Marine Lieutenant Lewis Rotely in the *Victory* remembered the noise: 'There was the fire from above, the fire from below, besides the fire from the deck I was upon, the guns recoiling with violence, reports louder than thunder, the decks heaving and the sides straining. I fancied myself in the infernal regions where every man appeared a devil.' The French and Spanish ships fought with great bravery: as Lucas of the *Redoutable* remembered, 'In the midst of all this carnage and devastation my splendid fellows kept on cheering, "*Vive l'Empereur! We are not taken yet! Is the Captain still alive?*" However the allies were isolated and leaderless, while the British were working to a single preconcerted plan, and were better trained in delivering

The Battle of Trafalgar, 21 October 1805; beginning of the action, by Nicholas Pocock (cat. no. 252).

rapid, accurate gunnery. Collingwood's ships gradually subdued the allied rear, while Nelson's division first captured most of their centre and then fought off a belated counterattack by the van under Rear-Admiral Dumanoir. When the battle finally ended at about 4.30 p.m., seventeen allied ships had been captured and another was a blazing wreck. Four ships escaped with Dumanoir but were captured a few weeks later at the Battle of Cape Ortegal (4 November 1805). Only eleven managed to struggle back into Cadiz, under the command of the Spanish senior admiral, Don Frederico Gravina y Napoli, who was himself badly wounded.

For the British, triumph at this extraordinary result was overshadowed by the news that Nelson was dead. Struck down on his quarter-deck by a French musket ball at about 1.15 p.m. he was carried down to the *Victory*'s cockpit. Popular myth has always maintained that he was wearing his gold-encrusted full dress uniform, hung about with stars and medals, and so an idea has arisen that he deliberately courted death – or at any rate deserved it because of his vanity. The coat he was wearing still exists. Having been purchased for the nation by Prince Albert in 1845, it has always formed the iconic centrepiece of the Nelson relics at Greenwich. We can see that what he actually had on was a threadbare, undress uniform with very little gold braid and only small, wire-and-sequin facsimiles of his stars (cat. no. 268).

The French musket ball that killed him has also survived. It was removed by the *Victory*'s surgeon, William Beatty, during the autopsy and preserved in a locket, which Beatty presented to his patron, and Nelson's former friend, the Duke of Clarence, later King William IV (cat. no. 270).

Although in agony, Nelson clung to life long enough to hear that had won the decisive victory for which he had planned so carefully and, having famously asked Captain Thomas Hardy for a kiss, he died at about 4.30 p.m. Captain Henry Blackwood, who arrived on board the *Victory* just too late to make his own farewell, told his wife, 'so entirely am I depressed with the private loss I have had that really the Victory and all the prize money I hope to get appear quite lost by the chasm made by Lord Nelson's death'.[6]

The British triumph was further dissipated by a storm that blew up after the battle, forcing them to scuttle most of their hard-won prizes. A daring sortie from Cadiz on 23 October by some of the survivors of the allied fleet under Commodore Cosmao-Kerjulien succeeded in wresting two of the prizes from their British captors, but the allies lost a further three ships in the process. Villeneuve later ruefully summed up the battle and its aftermath in his report: 'So much courage and devotion deserved a better fate but the moment has not yet come for France to celebrate her successes on the sea as she has been able to on the Continent.'

REWARDS AND REFLECTIONS

NEWS OF TRAFALGAR reached London about a fortnight after the battle in the early hours of 6 November, carried home in the schooner *Pickle* by Lieutenant John Lapenotiere.

Public rejoicing at the victory was muted by sorrow for the death of Nelson. Collingwood was made a baron, all the captains received the King's Naval Gold Medal and a special grant was made by the government to all those who had taken part to compensate them for the prize money they had lost when their captures sank in the storm. The Patriotic Fund at Lloyd's presented all the captains with handsome silver vases or ceremonial swords, according to their individual tastes, and granted pensions to the wounded and the widows of those killed in action. And Nelson's body was brought home to Britain and buried in St Paul's Cathedral with the elaborate ceremonial of a full state funeral.

In the short term, Trafalgar had little immediate effect on the course of the war. The day before, Napoleon had defeated the Austrians at Ulm and six weeks later he was to confirm his ascendancy over Europe with an even more decisive victory over the Austrian and Russians at Austerlitz (2 December 1805).

However, in the longer term, by establishing Britain as the dominant sea power Trafalgar laid the foundations of Napoleon's eventual defeat. Moreover, the psychological effect of the battle was immeasurable. It demonstrated that in 1805 the Royal Navy had superiority in training, professionalism and expertise in naval tactics that set it apart from any of its rivals. Above all, it gave the Navy an unmatched tradition of victory that is still potent, even 200 years later.

England expects every Man to do his duty.

LORD NELSON explaining to the Officers the PLAN of ATTACK previous to the BATTLE of TRAFALGAR

Adml. Lord Nelson	Capt. Bayntun		Capt. Grindall	Capt. Morris
Capt. T. M. Hardy	Capt. Codrington	NAMES of the GALLANT HEROES who Commanded on the 21st Octr. 1805.	Capt. Hargood	Capt. Mansfield
Mr. Scott Sec.y	Capt. J. Cooke			Capt. J. Pellew
Adml. Collingwood	Capt. Conn		Capt. G. Hope	Capt. Rutherford
Capt. Rotheram	Capt. H. Digby		Capt. E. Harvey	Capt. Redmill
Adml. Lord Northesk	Capt. Duff		Capt. King	Capt. Tyler
Capt. Bullen	Capt. Durham		Capt. Sir F. Laforey	Lieut. J. Pilford (acting)
Mr. Sir E.d Berry	Capt. Freemantle		Capt. Moorsom	Lieut. J. Stockham (a)

POSITION of the COMBINED FORCES of FRANCE & SPAIN,

at the commencement of the Action 21st. Octr. 1805. with LORD NELSON, Cape Trafalgar, bearing E.S.E. 4 Leagues.

Reference
English ___ Red
French ___ Blue
Spaniards ___ Yellow

Spartiate

Minotaur

Dreadnought

Orion

Defiance
Thunderer
Prince
Ajax
Entreprenant Cutter

Defence
Agamemnon
Phœbe

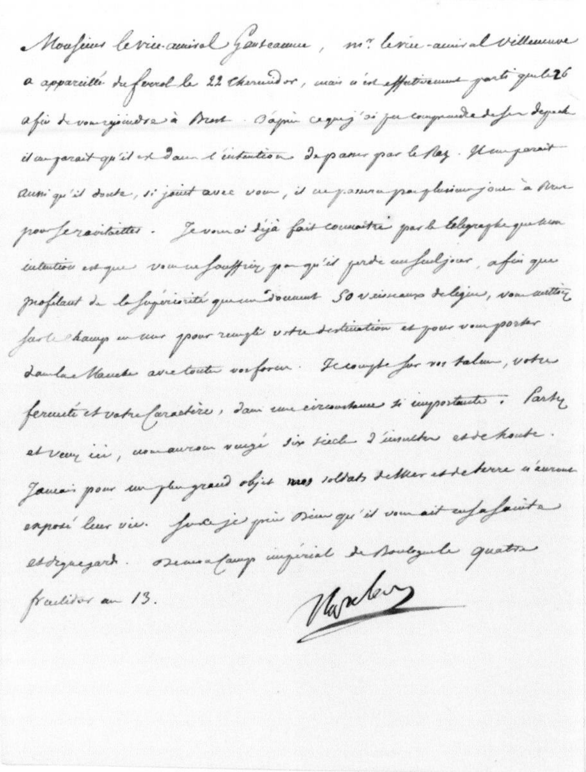

213. Letters signed by Napoleon to Admirals Villeneuve and Ganteaume, 22 August 1805 [4 *fructidor an XIII*]

Ink on paper

Zvi Meitar, private collection

On 22 August 1805 Napoleon dictated and signed these two letters 'From my Imperial Camp at Boulogne'. At this stage in the campaign he was still hoping that his two main fleets, under Vice-Admiral Pierre de Villeneuve and Vice-Admiral Honoré Ganteaume, would be able to unite and enter the Channel to cover his invasion fleet as it made its crossing to England.

The letter to Ganteaume tells him that Villeneuve is on his way north, and 'you must not allow him to lose a single day' but 'put to sea at once and arrive in the Channel. . . . Depart and come here, we will have avenged six centuries of insult and shame.'

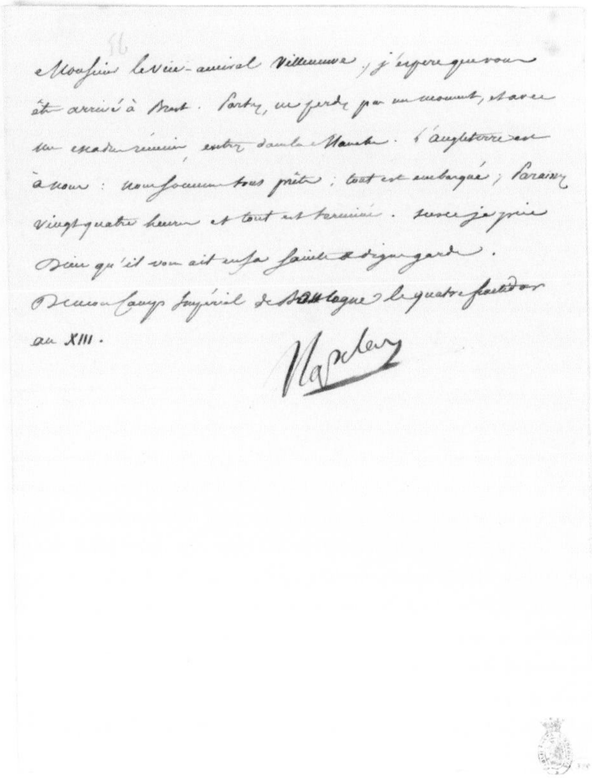

The letter to Villeneuve carries a similar message: 'I hope you have arrived at Brest. Depart, lose not a moment and with a united squadron enter the Channel. England is ours . . . . Appear for twenty-four hours and all is finished.' In fact, Villeneuve had already sailed south and arrived in Cadiz on 21 August, the day before these two letters were written. On 25 August, Napoleon abandoned his plans for the invasion of England, turned his army around and marched on Austria.

CSW

214. *The Plumb-Pudding in danger; – or – State Epicures taking un Petit Souper*

James Gillray, published 26 February 1805 by
    H. Humphrey

Hand-coloured engraving

276 x 381mm

British Museum, London; 1851-9-1-1164

A simple but devastating summation of the state of French and British imperial ambitions at the beginning of 1805. Pitt and Napoleon are represented as equals, dinner companions seated either side of the globe in the form of a giant, steaming plum pudding. They are literally carving up the world between them: while Napoleon voraciously hacks off Europe with his sword, Pitt, more genteel, plunges in his fork (significantly, in the form of a trident) and helps himself to 'OCEAN' (the Atlantic and West Indies). However, the logic of the image is inescapable, as the caption, quoting Shakespeare's *The Tempest*, makes clear: '"the great Globe itself, and all which it inherit", is too small to satisfy such insatiable appetites'. For the contemporary German critic writing in *London und Paris*, this logic was all too apparent, with the vision of Napoleon slicing off Europe having dreadful implications for his own country: 'The Briton will merely laugh at this caricature. But for us *Allemanen* or 'men of all the world', it's another matter altogether'. He quotes from Schiller's 1803 poem 'Am Antritt des neuen Jahrhunderts', which could stand as a literary counterpart to Gillray's image:

> Two mighty nations struggle, and contend
> For the sole possession of the world.
> And to devour the freedom of all peoples
> Is the trident brandished, lightning hurled.
>
> The Frenchman lays his brazen sword – like Brennus,
> Barbaric chieftain in the days of old –
> To weight the scales in place of justice, forcing
> Each country to yield up its store of gold.
>
> Like tentacles of greedy octopus
> The Briton's trading fleet is spread afar;
> And the whole kingdom of free Amphitrite,
> Is as his own house, under lock and bar.
>
> On to the south pole and its unseen stars,
> To coasts and islands in earth's farthest zone,
> Restless, unchecked, he still expands his power,
> Leaves undiscovered Paradise alone.

GQ

215. Presentation sword, 1804

R. Teed (1757–1816)
Gilt, gold and damascened steel
Inscribed: 'PRESENTED IN 1804 BY THE ASSEMBLY OF JAMAICA TO VICE ADML SIR J T DUCKWORTH IN REMBRANCE OF THE EFFECTUAL PROTECTION AFFORDED TO THE COMMERCE AND COASTS OF THE ISLAND BY HIS ABLE & DISINTERESTED DISTRIBUTION OF H M NAVAL FORCES UNDER HIS COMMAND & AS A TESTIMONY OF THE HIGH SENSE ENTERTAINED BY THE ASSEMBLY OF THE EMINENT SERVICES HE HAS THEREBY RENDERED TO THAT COUNTRY'
National Maritime Museum, London; WPN1120

These swords were presented by individuals and bodies such as the City of London and the Lloyd's Patriotic Fund to naval officers in recognition of acts of bravery or as a mark of respect. This example was presented by the Assembly of Jamaica to Admiral Sir John Duckworth who, as commander-in-chief at Jamaica, directed the operations which led to the defeat of the French army in San Domingo. The West Indies trade was important to Britain, and one of the Navy's roles was to defend it. This explains why Napoleon attacked British colonies there in 1805 when aiming to draw the British Navy away from the Channel.   LV

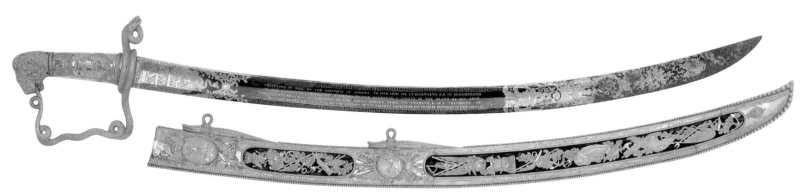

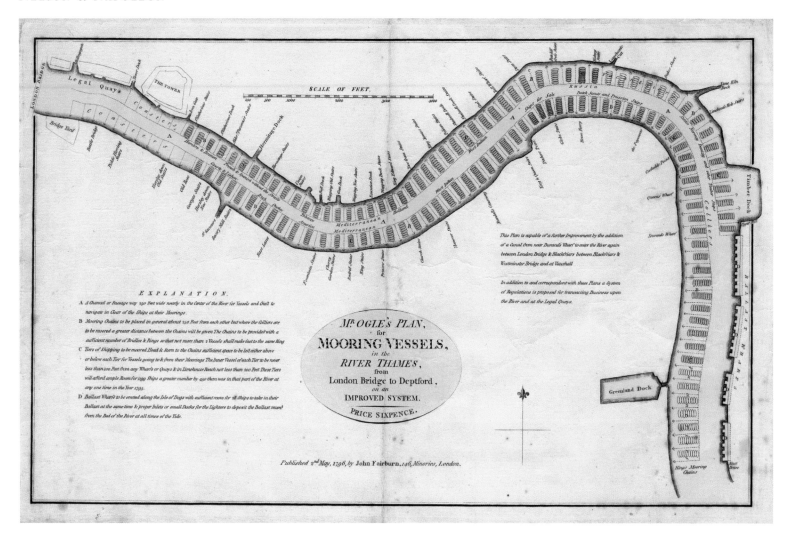

216. *Mr Ogle's plan, for mooring vessels, in the River Thames, from London Bridge to Deptford, on an improved system*

Engraved chart, published by John Fairburn, 1796

National Maritime Museum, London; G218:9/78

Ogle's plan illustrates the range and volume of trade to London. He attempts to deal with problems of overcrowding and consequent delays, caused by the doubling of London's seaborne trade since 1760. By 1796, more than 10,000 coasters and nearly 3500 foreign-going vessels were sailing up to London each year. Ships anchored in the river wherever they could find space, and had to be unloaded by thousands of lighters.

Ogle's plan was to accommodate the ships on tiers between mooring chains, grouping all shipping from different geographical areas on the basis that Baltic timber ships would need different shore facilities from, for example, American tobacco ships. Colliers were the most important element of the coastal trade; vessels trading with the West Indies and the Mediterranean predominated among

foreign-going ships. The East India ships were omitted from this scheme, as they moored downriver from Deptford.

In the event, this 'improved system' was not adopted but more ambitious West India Docks and Wapping Docks schemes began in 1799 and 1800.   GH

217. Model of *L'Éole*, French 74-gun ship, launched 1789

Unknown maker, *c.* 1789

Scale 1:60

National Maritime Museum, London; SLR0556

L'Éole was typical of the large 74s built by the French towards the end of the 1790s. Measuring 182 feet (55.5m) along the gun-deck by 48 feet (14.6m) in the beam, it had a displacement of 1900 tons and carried twenty-eight guns on the gun-deck and thirty on the upper deck. Under the overall command of Villaret-Joyeuse, *L'Éole* took part in the Battle of the Glorious First of June in 1794. In 1805–6, *L'Éole* was in Vice-Admiral Willaumez's squadron in the West

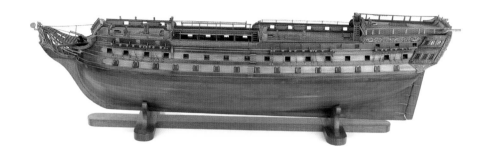

Indies. Under the command of Captain Louis Gilles, *L'Éole*, with the *Patriote*, made for the safety of the Chesapeake Bay during a storm. Arriving damaged and dismasted, they were blockaded there later by some British ships detached from the Halifax Station. *L'Éole* never left the bay and was eventually broken up.

The model itself illustrates the French style of craftsmanship where the use of the darker woods was preferred. Horn has been used along the mainwales while the overall decoration along the bulwarks and stern has been carved in boxwood. Typical design features of the French warship include the tall capstan on the foredeck, the curved drift rails on the bow behind the figurehead and the almost rounded shape of the taffrail and stern. SS

218. *Fighting for the DUNGHILL – or – Jack Tar settling BUONAPARTE*
James Gillray, published 20 November 1798 by
   John Miller
Hand-coloured etching
220 x 287mm
National Maritime Museum, London; PAD4792

This is the earliest of Gillray's portrayals of Bonaparte as the symbolic personification of France. Here he is caricatured in a manner deriving from earlier eighteenth-century lampoons against the French, particularly by Hogarth, in being shown semi-naked and emaciated. Gillray also plays upon Bonaparte's Corsican roots, notably in the Italian spelling of his name in the title. Seated atop a globe, he is being knocked down and has his nose bloodied by a stout British tar with the profile features of George III. It is a simple but effective piece of propaganda, casting France with the dark, benighted side of the globe, and Britain with the bringing of light. At the same time, the fusion of the King with Jack Tar is a brilliant means of suggesting a national unity between the upper and lower orders that was, at this time, far from being the case. GQ

219. *De la préponderance maritime et commerciale de la Grande Bretagne, ou des intérêts des nations relativement à l'Angleterre et à la France*
By M [onsieur] Monbrion, Paris, 1805
National Maritime Museum, London

As for you, proud English, the fate that overcame Tyre, Corinth, Palmyra, Venice, all victims of their greed and mercantile ambition, is a sad foretaste of your fatal destiny [p. 106].

Fighting for the DUNGHILL ___ or ___ Jack Tar settling BUONAPARTE.

This work, *On the maritime and commercial preponderance of Great Britain, or the interests of nations considered in relation to England and France*, is one of a number addressing the French problem of Britain's overwhelming maritime supremacy in a Napoleonic perspective, that 'creative Genius, who so gloriously governs the French Empire' (p. 120). The sceptical French purchaser of this copy noted inside the cover in 1806:

> This work is written skilfully enough by one of the clerks in the office of Lord Talleyrand [Napoleon's Foreign Minister] – his aim is to convince the European powers that France *alone* should possess all the maritime and commercial advantages, as much for their interests as their safety. The *shrewd* Reader will decide to what point Mons. Monbrion is right.

Monbrion was a prolific author and later edited a *Universal Dictionary of Commerce* (1838–41). PvdM

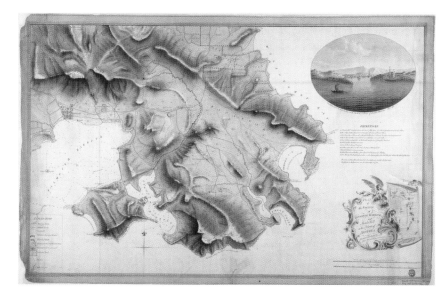

220. *Le réveil de George, Sept. 1803*
Anonymous
Engraving
210 x 310mm
Musée Carnavalet, Paris; G.27204/PC 31D

King George III is seated at a table, visibly taken aback as he sees the arrival of the French fleet. An allegorical figure of the naked Truth (with her mirror and diaphanous skirt) approaches him, allowing the reflection from the mirror of truth to enlighten him, while indicating to him the flag on the French ship which reads 'LIBERTÉ DES MERS' (Freedom of the oceans), a challenge to Britain's perceived monopoly on overseas trading. George treads underfoot the Peace of Amiens, the treaty that Britain and France had signed on 25 March 1802. This probably refers to Britain's refusal to hand back Malta to the Knights, which effectively broke the treaty.

Talleyrand had wanted an alliance with Britain but Napoleon thought it was too soon and was busy resuming the colonial policy of the *ancien régime* both in the West Indies and in India, where he aimed to recover French trading ports. In 1803 he annexed Piedmont and Elba and became President of the Italian Republic. The French kept control of Belgium and continued to occupy Holland. This expansionism posed a real threat to the British, as did French exclusion of British goods from ports wherever possible. In Britain, there was a serious fear that France would create a fleet which might even overpower the Royal Navy. On 18 May the British declared war. Napoleon had acknowledged in 1798 that he was outclassed in naval matters by the British but he now set out to disprove this. This print is a cautionary warning to George III not to underestimate the strength of the French fleet. HW

221. *Plan of the environs of English Harbour and Monks Hill in the Island of Antigua surveyed and drawn by John Brown, surveyor and draughtsman to the army in the West Indies 1782*
Ink and watercolour
560 x 870mm
National Maritime Museum, London; G245:15/5

English Harbour, Antigua, had been selected as a naval base because it was shielded from hurricanes by high land on all sides which could also be fortified against land attack. It had been developed during the eighteenth century to provide the Lesser Antilles with protection against French privateers and as a first defence from hostile fleets from Europe. The main British naval base at Jamaica was more than 1000 miles to the west and downwind in the predominant trade winds.

British naval bases in the West Indies became more important as the value of the West Indian trade to the British economy increased. GH

222. *A letter to the Members of Parliament who have presented petitions to the Honourable House of Commons, for the abolition of the slave-trade, by a West-India Merchant* (London, 1792)
Anonymous pamphlet
National Maritime Museum, London; 529.78:094

In March 1792, the House of Commons voted to abolish the slave trade before the bill was overturned by the Lords. In response to the abolition campaign, and to the impact of abolitionists like the black writer Olaudah Equiano, West

Indian planters and merchants mounted a spirited counter-attack. This 'letter', which is actually an eighty-four-page pamphlet, was part of that campaign. In it, the author (possibly the merchant and politician James Baillie) took shots at what he regarded as the follies of the abolitionists before turning his fire on the East India Company. He emphasized the importance of the West Indies (and of slavery) to Britain. He argued that 'there is not a Tradesman in Great Britain who does not directly, or indirectly, derive advantage from the African and West-India Trade' (p. 3). He also highlighted other reasons for maintaining the slave trade that ranged from the risk of rebellion in the Caribbean to the 'backwardness' of 'savage' Africans. However offensive and wrong-headed these attitudes now seem, they were not confined to planters and merchants. Nelson would certainly have agreed with the author's sentiments. Indeed, before 1807, there was a widely held belief that the West Indies represented vital economic and strategic interests for Britain. British naval stations were maintained at Jamaica and Antigua, there was fierce local Anglo-French rivalry and any threat was taken very seriously. When the French fleet under Villeneuve set sail for the Caribbean in 1805, the Royal Navy had to respond. DJH

sugar for sale to the public was further refined and sometimes sold as solid cones known as sugar loaves. Sugar nippers like these were used to break chunks from the sugar loaf. Their simple design suggests a wide availability among people in Britain. The growth of sugar consumption led to an increase in related goods, like tea services. The porcelain sugar bowl, from Nelson's collection, is an interesting example. The oak leaf, used as the pattern, was an important symbol of Britishness during the Napoleonic War. The oak represented maturity, the slow and steady growth of society (rather than revolution) and the protection provided by its branches. It was also important for the Royal Navy, as the wood used in ship construction.

DJH

223. **Sugar nippers,** *c.* 1800
Steel, English
National Maritime Museum, London (Michael Graham-Stewart Collection); ZBA2490

224. **Sugar bowl,** *c.* 1802
John Rose & Co., Porcelain by Coalport Porcelain Works, Shropshire, England
National Maritime Museum, London (Nelson-Ward Collection); AAA4553

Demand for sugar in Britain soared throughout the eighteenth century and it became a staple of British diets as a sweetener and a preservative. Sugar cane was grown in the West Indies and went through preliminary refining in the islands before being shipped to markets in Britain. Sugar was central to the wealth of the Caribbean islands. The Royal Navy played an important role in protecting the islands and in convoying the ships which brought the sugar to Britain. Once there,

225. **Letter from Napoleon to Admiral Ganteaume regarding operations against the English fleet, 15 March 1805**
Ink on paper
National Maritime Museum, London; COP/1C

This letter is dated in the new French Revolutionary calendar *24 ventose an XIII*. Appropriately for the 'wind month' of the Revolutionary calendar, Napoleon mentions the storms that the English fleet have had to endure over recent weeks. He believed that the English fleet would be worn out and incapable of fighting efficiently after the long months they had already spent at sea and was hopeful that the weather would help him to victory. He encourages Ganteaume to act with daring, assuring him that if he did so, he would be sure to be victorious (*Si vous ne manqué point d'audace, le succès est infaillible*). DK

226. Nelson's weather log
10 September–23 October 1803

Brown ink on paper

Four folios quarto, marbled paper covers, hand-sewn

National Maritime Museum, London; AGC/18/10

This is Nelson's private weather log kept during the early stages of the Mediterranean campaign and said to have been pinned up in his cabin during the voyage. The inner leaves are ruled in a standard fashion but the details are completed in Nelson's hand. As is usual, the log records the date, several barometer readings per day, with times for each, and brief notes on the weather. These are generally confined to the strength and direction of the wind. It would appear that the weather during this period was very variable, with winds up to gale force, but also sometimes 'good'.   DK

227. Draft letter from Nelson to
the Captain Pasha, June 1803

Ink on paper

National Maritime Museum, London; AGC/18/9

Written at the beginning of the campaign of 1803, this letter was intended to introduce Nelson as the new Commander-in-Chief of the Mediterranean Fleet and to establish friendly relations with the Sublime Porte. It shows Nelson's method of dealing with foreign correspondents and clearly indicates his feelings about Napoleon: 'The ruthless ambition of the Person who for the misfortune of Mankind still rules the Government of France' has forced Nelson out of retirement. He hopes that the Ottoman Empire will not be 'unjustly' invaded again – a reference to Napoleon's previous invasion of Egypt in 1798. However, Nelson continues, should the French attack, 'I am instructed to use every means to afford to the Sublime Porte and its subjects any assistance in my power.' On the reverse is a French translation, probably produced by the Revd Alexander John Scott, the *Victory*'s chaplain and Nelson's diplomatic secretary and interpreter from May 1803 until his death. Scott had worked with Nelson on the Baltic campaign and had demonstrated his flair for languages during the armistice negotiations after the Battle of Copenhagen.

DK

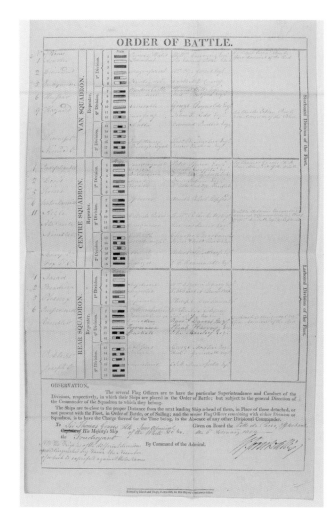

228. Cornwallis's order of battle,
6 February 1804

Ink and print on paper

On loan to the National Maritime Museum, London;

GNS/13

On the resumption of war in 1803, Admiral William Cornwallis arguably held the most important position for British security – command of the Channel Fleet. With rumours rife about Napoleon's preparations for invasion, it was Cornwallis's fleet that was charged with preventing the French landing troops. This order of battle, showing how the fleet would line up in any large engagement, was drawn up for Rear-Admiral Sir Thomas Graves, of the *Foudroyant*, who was the junior admiral in the central squadron. Many of the vessels here, including *Téméraire*, *Britannia* and *Mars*, would form part of the Mediterranean Fleet that fought at Trafalgar a year later. The daily reality of naval life for the Channel Fleet was far removed from the impression of battle given here. It spent much of the war involved in the dull, repetitive task of blockading the French Brest fleet in port. Unglamorous as this was, by preventing the French from massing their ships together and thus gaining control of the Channel, Cornwallis and his squadron made a huge contribution towards winning the war against Napoleon.

AD

229. *Dépêche Extraordinaire de la Flotte Anglaise (pour amiral Nelson)* / Extraordinary dispatch of an English fleet (for Admiral Nelson)

French, published summer 1805
Hand-coloured engraving
Musée Carnavalet, Paris; PC33a 6.27275

A fat courier here brings Nelson the news of ship losses. According to the official French government newspaper, the *Moniteur*, dated 11 April 1805, an 18-gun British cutter, *le Georges* (*sic*), was taken by three Spanish gun launches after a fight of one and half hours and brought to the port of Ceuta. A British 6-gun cutter, *Dove* (not the frigate *Love*), was taken by the Rochefort squadron on 5 August. PH

230. *Deliberation à l'anglaise* / Discussion, English-style

French, published 1805
Hand-coloured engraving
Musée Carnavalet, Paris; PC33a 6.27271

The scene is presumably Lloyd's Coffee House in London, here used as a symbol of British commercial might, the traditional bugbear of Revolutionary France. A pencil note on the engraving dates it to May 1805. Admiral Villeneuve had recently slipped through the British blockade en route for Martinique, although no one in Britain knew for certain where he was heading. At the same time, the French invasion army stood ready on the coasts of northern France and the Low Countries. The caricaturist here makes fun of this situation. Four speculators argue over a comic map which conflates two British phobias: attack in the North Sea and attack in the West Indies. Yet others scour the newspapers wondering (as the caption tells us) 'Where can the French fleet have gone? The papers will doubtless tell us'. To the left stands the produce of the colonies (tobacco and rum for the punch), which the British are about to lose. And the punning words on the counter say: '*Ici on fume*' (You may smoke here / Here they fume!). These traders are not only about to lose their investments but also their native land!

PH

Dépêche Extraordinaire de la Flotte Anglaise

DÉLIBÉRATION À L'ANGLAISE

231. Freedom of the Borough of Boston, 2 August 1805

Ink on parchment, applied wax seal
National Maritime Museum, London; TRA/8

Boston, Lincolnshire, a wealthy port in this period, awarded Nelson the freedom of the city after his great chase to the West Indies. Boston's Corporation was of the opinion that 'the Nation is indebted [to Nelson] for the Security of her West Indian Possessions'. The revenue from the West Indies

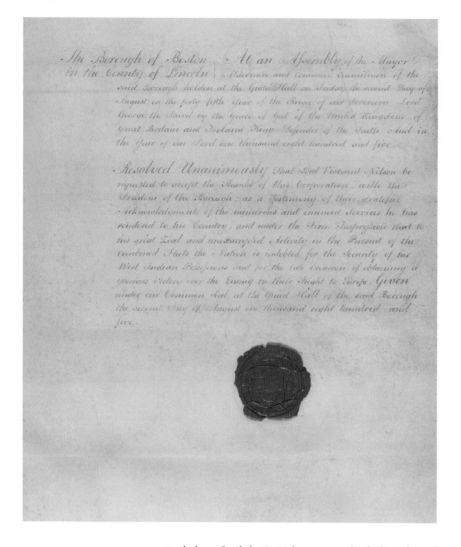

233. Rear-Admiral Sir Robert Calder, 1745–1815

Lemuel Francis Abbott (1760–1803)

Oil on canvas

760 x 635mm

National Maritime Museum, London (Greenwich
   Hospital Collection, bequeathed by Mrs Elizabeth
   Cooke, 1859); BHC2593

Probably the portrait exhibited at the Royal Academy in
1798, the year after the Battle of St Vincent at which Calder
was first captain to Sir John Jervis in the *Victory*. At the
Battle of the Glorious First of June (1794) he commanded
the *Theseus* and in the portrait he wears the First of June
medal. In July 1805 he tried to prevent Villeneuve reaching
Ferrol from the West Indies. In the resulting action he
did not press his advantage and the French fleet got
away. Calder was recalled, court-martialled and severely
reprimanded.   RQ

sugar trade benefited the British economy both directly and
indirectly. The loss of these islands would have meant ruin
for merchants and investors across the country, or at least a
considerable reduction in wealth.   DK

232. Memorandum, 4 June 1805

Ink on paper

National Maritime Museum, London; AGC/18/17(1)

This single sheet is a working memorandum of the instructions for embarking marines and artillery at Barbados. The
numbers are significant, the *Victory* taking 150 men and
sharing the six guns equally with the *Northumberland*. The
regiments involved in this embarkation are both British and
West Indian. The *Spartiate* was to take on board the medical
staff. The main purpose of this expedition, as with others to
the West Indies, was to protect British sugar interests in that
part of the world. Nelson and his fleet were acting as troop
carriers in an ongoing struggle for imperial dominance in
the area.   DK

234. Sir Robert Calder's action off Cape Finisterre, 23 July 1805: the aftermath

William Anderson (1757–1837)

Oil on canvas

775 x 1230mm

National Maritime Museum, London (Caird
   Collection); BHC0539

See page 192

Vice-Admiral Calder's squadron intercepted the Franco-Spanish fleet under Admiral Villeneuve off north-western Spain, as it returned from its diversionary voyage to the West Indies just before Trafalgar. At a time when Britain had become used to Nelsonic victories, Calder's failure to engage it decisively led to his formal censure and he was never given another command. This shows the day after the action, 24 July. British frigates have Calder's two prizes, the *Firme* and the *San Raphael*, under tow on the right and the damaged *Windsor Castle*, too, on the left. Calder's fleet is in formation in the centre and the departing enemy in the distance. Anderson was a Scottish-born shipwright, who became an accomplished marine painter in London after about 1787.

RQ

235. **Nelson's battle plan, *c.* 1805**

Ink on paper
One sheet
On loan to the National Maritime Museum, London; BRP/6/5
See page 193

This sketch, hastily made on the back of a scrap of paper, appears to outline Nelson's plan for the Battle of Trafalgar, showing the enemy line cut in two places. There are accounts of Nelson outlining his tactics for the next engagement with the French to visitors to his house – Captain Richard Keats, captain of the *Superb* during the chase of the French fleet, told of such a conversation taking place when he and Nelson walked in the grounds of Merton. This sketch could well have been drawn during one of these discussions to illustrate Nelson's plan. The sketch is on the reverse of a series of notes made by Nelson relating to the promotion and patronage of junior officers, among a bundle of papers from Nelson to his brother, William. The notes have helped to provide a rough date for the sketch.

AD

Literature: White, 'Nelson's 1805 Battle Plan', *Journal of Maritime Research*, May 2002, www.jmr.nmm.ac.uk.

236. **Nelson's 'Trafalgar' memorandum – the original draft, October 1805**

Ink on paper
British Library, London; Add. MS 37953

On 29 and 30 September 1805, Nelson held briefing sessions with his captains in the great cabin of *Victory* at which he explained his special battle plan – what he called 'the Nelson Touch'. Ten days later, he circulated a 'memorandum' in which he set out his ideas in more detail.

This is the original draft, in his own hand, with all his

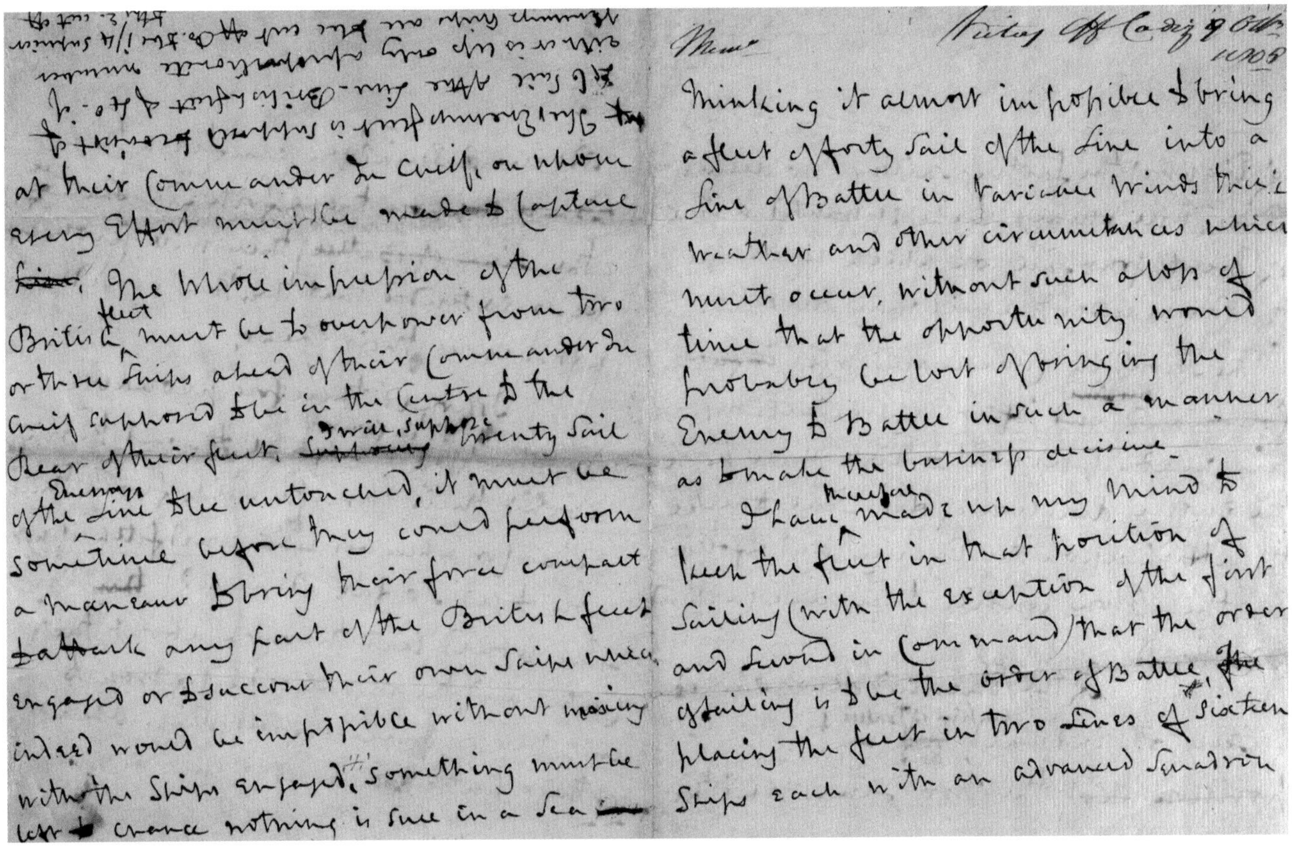

at their Commander in Chief, on whom
every Effort must be made to Capture
The whole impression of the
British fleet must be to overpower from two
or three Ships ahead of their Commander in
Chief supposed to be in the Centre to the
Rear of their fleet. I will suppose twenty Sail
of the Enemys Line to be untouched, it must be
sometime before they could perform
a manoeuvre to bring their force compact
to attack any part of the British fleet
engaged or to succour their own Ships which
indeed would be impossible without mixing
with the Ships engaged. Something must be
left to chance nothing is sure in a Sea

Memo. Victory off Cadiz 9 Octr 1805
Thinking it almost impossible to bring
a fleet of forty Sail of the Line into a
Line of Battle in variable Winds thick
weather and other circumstances which
must occur, without such a loss of
time that the opportunity would
probably be lost of bringing the
Enemy to Battle in such a manner
as to make the business decisive.
I have therefore made up my mind to
keep the fleet in that position of
Sailing (with the exception of the first
and second in Command) that the order
of Sailing is to be the order of Battle,
placing the fleet in two Lines of Sixteen
Ships each with an advanced Squadron

corrections and additions. From this document, Nelson's secretaries prepared the fair copies, which were circulated to all his captains.

The memorandum explains that Nelson intends to attack at once, without wasting time forming up his fleet. For this reason, 'the Order of Sailing is to be the Order of Battle'. It then shows how he intends to attack in three divisions – two to carry out the actual assault and one to hold down the vanguard of the enemy's fleet, thus preventing them from turning to assist their comrades.

Most importantly, the memorandum underlines that Nelson is not planning to control the battle himself. Instead, he proposes to delegate responsibility – both to his second in command, Vice-Admiral Collingwood, and to the individual captains of ships: 'In case signals can neither be seen or perfectly understood, no captain can do very wrong if he places his ship alongside that of an enemy.' This is the essence of 'the Nelson Touch'.　　　　　　　CSW

237. Codrington's copy of Nelson's Memorandum, 9 October 1805

Ink on paper

One sheet quarto

On loan to the National Maritime Museum, London, COD/5/9/2

Edward Codrington captained *Orion* at the Battle of Trafalgar. This is his copy of the secret memorandum issued by Nelson explaining how he planned to engage the French fleet. Nelson had earlier outlined these tactics to his captains over dinner on 29 and 30 September 1805 (cat. no. 236).　　　AD

238. Nelson's cabin armchair, *c.* 1800

Mahogany, leather and brass

National Maritime Museum, London (Trafalgar House Collection); AAA3400

This armchair with separate cushions was part of Nelson's cabin furniture in the *Victory*. The 3rd Earl Nelson claimed that it was Nelson's personal chair and the last he sat in before Trafalgar. On *Victory*'s return to England, Captain Hardy gave the chair to Isabella Thompson of Portsea, whose nephew bequeathed it to the 3rd Earl. Originally there was a black silk-covered pad on the right arm of the chair on which Nelson could rest the stump of his arm.

A memoir of the Revd Scott, Nelson's chaplain and secretary, published in 1842, describes how:

Day after day might be seen the admiral in his cabin, closely employed with his secretary over their interminable papers. They occupied two black leathern armchairs, into the roomy pockets of which, Scott, weary of translating, would occasionally stuff away a score or two of unopened private letters, found in prize ships.

The Greenwich chair has been extensively restored, but at Portsmouth there is a similar armchair from Nelson's cabin, which still has the pockets. There is also an upholstered bed-settee from Nelson's cabin in the collection at Greenwich.　　　　　　RP

239. Nelson's writing box, *c.* 1798

Wood, brass

National Maritime Museum, London; AAA3398

This brass-bound writing box bears a brass plaque on the lid inscribed, 'Part of L'ORIENT blown up at the Battle of the Nile 1st August 1798. In Lord Nelson's possession at the time of his death 21st October 1805'.

The loud explosion of the French flagship *L'Orient* during the Battle of the Nile evidently impressed itself on Nelson, and he kept a number of mementos made of her wood, including the top of her mainmast, a coffin and a snuff box made of her timber, as well as this writing desk.

The box, which has recessed brass handles and lock, opens to reveal a green baize-covered writing slope, a pen

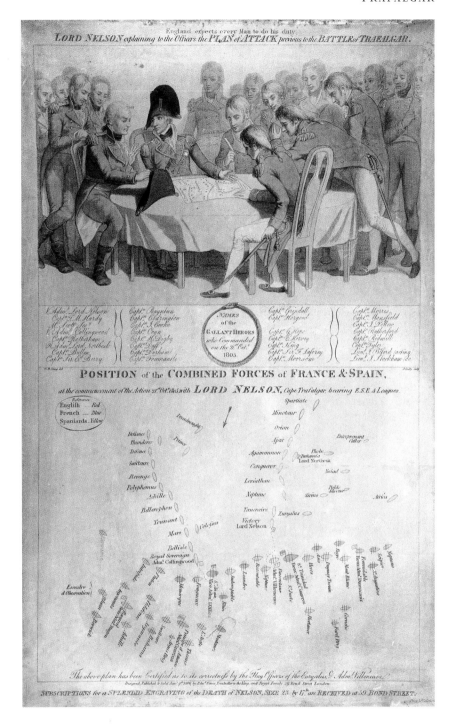

tray and compartments with glass ink bottles. There is an additional slim drawer in the base of the box. The writing box is similar in appearance to that in T. J. Barker's later painting of Nelson at prayer in his cabin before Trafalgar.

RP

240. Nelson's last prayer

Ink on paper

National Maritime Museum, London; JOD/14

Nelson maintained a simple Christian faith throughout his life. He is known to have encouraged the men under him in this, by ordering supplies of bibles and other devotional works for his ships. Partly because of his faith, he had no apparent fear of death but rather a fatalistic attitude towards the likelihood of dying at sea, and particularly during battle. He also had a great sense of patriotism and is said to have had a vision during an earlier period of illness, which made him determined to live and die a hero in the service of his country. His last prayer displays bravery and resignation: 'If it is His good providence to cut short my days upon Earth I bow with the greatest Submission . . . His will be done amen amen amen amen.' It was written with considerable care on the morning of Trafalgar, with his short last will, and he wrote two copies. One was returned to Lady Hamilton. The other, as his will, is preserved in The National Archives (Public Record Office). The version now held at the National Maritime Museum was used by Sir Nicholas Harris Nicolas when he came to write his 1845 volume of Nelson's letters, and he described it as an 'autograph or facsimile copy' of the will.

DK

241. *England expects every Man to do his duty / LORD NELSON explaining to the Officers the PLAN OF ATTACK previous to the BATTLE of TRAFALGAR*

James Godby, after William Marshall Craig, published
9 January 1806 by Edward Orme

Hand-coloured stipple engraving

434 x 808mm (plate)

National Maritime Museum, London; PAG9025

When I came to explain to them the Nelson touch, it was like an electric shock. Some shed tears, all approved – 'It was new, it was singular – it was simple'.

Nelson to Lady Hamilton

Edward Orme, 'Printseller to the King, and Royal Family', issued this print on the day of Nelson's funeral. It has subsequently become part of the Nelson myth as showing how he briefed his captains before Trafalgar and, by implication, on earlier occasions. There is no reason to think it accurately records the scene, which in fact took place in two separate dinner briefings off Cadiz (29-30 September). Getting everyone's name and face in was probably Orme's key commercial criterion in the combined design. The plan showing the start of the action is based on a drawing that was agreed as accurate by the captain of the *Bucentaure*, Admiral Villeneuve's flagship. This is also in the Museum collection.   PvdM

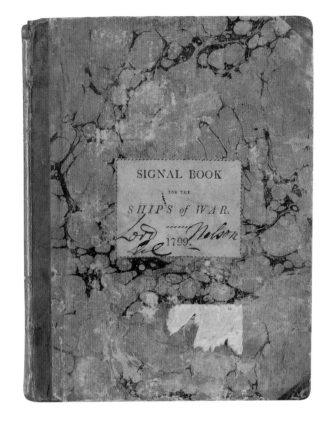

242. *Admiralty signal book, c.* 1805
Printed book
National Maritime Museum, London; SIG/B/76

This volume was the first Admiralty-issued signal book, outlining all the standard signals for use in the fleet. Previously, individual admirals had devised their own systems, which had caused confusion whenever ships changed fleet. The signal book was devised by Captain Gambier, senior naval member of the Board of Admiralty, and issued in 1799. It was felt that the volume did not encompass enough detail to allow the admiral to communicate his intentions to the fleet, and an unofficial, supplementary system devised by Home Popham, sprang into use alongside this version. The two would be combined in a volume produced in 1816, the *Book of Signals*.

This volume appears to have been printed between May 1805 and February 1806, and bears the signature 'Lord Nelson' on the front cover, and 'Exd TMH' (examined Thomas Masterman Hardy) on the frontispiece. It therefore seems likely that the volume was on board one of the ships at Trafalgar.   AD

LITERATURE: Tunstall, *Naval Warfare in the Age of Sail*, p. 251.

243. Telescope, *c.* 1800
English
Mahogany, brass, glass and silver
Inscribed: on silver plaque: *This telescope THEN IN THE POSSESSION of John Pasco Flag Lieutenant to Lord Nelson WAS ON THE Victory's poop AT THE BATTLE OF Trafalgar 21st October 1805*
National Maritime Museum, London (Royal United Service Museum Collection); NAV1649

John Pasco (1774–1853), as Nelson's flag-lieutenant on *Victory* at Trafalgar, was responsible for sending the famous signal 'England expects that every man will do his duty'. This telescope is typical of the type used for signalling at that date and the commemorative plaque has the signal flags around the border. It was passed down through the family and later presented by Commander Crawford Pasco to HRH Prince Alfred, Duke of Edinburgh (1844–1900), second son of Queen Victoria. The occasion was Prince Alfred's visit to the Australian colony of Victoria as a Royal Navy captain commanding *Galatea*, to which he was commissioned in 1867.

GC

244. Bar shot, eighteenth century

Iron

Provenance: on loan from HM The Queen

National Maritime Museum, London; KTP1079

Bar shot was designed to be fired at masts and rigging to disable ships. This example is from the Spanish ship *Santísima Trinidad*, flagship of Rear-Admiral Cisneros. At Trafalgar, she was dismasted during an engagement with the *Neptune* and sank after the battle. An officer on board the *Britannia* said that the *Santísima Trinidad* was the most beautiful ship he had seen with a 'rich display of sculpture, figures, ornaments and inscriptions'.

LV

245. Logbook of the *Victory*, 1805

Bound volume; ink on paper

The National Archives, London; ADM/52/3711

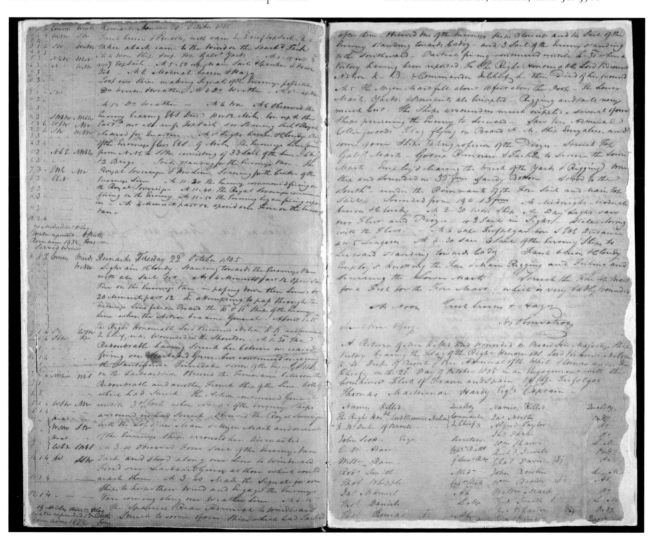

This log was written by the master, Thomas Atkinson, who had already seen action with Nelson at the Battles of the Nile and Copenhagen. *Victory* was the first ship to engage the enemy, attacking the *Bucentaure* and afterwards engaging the *Redoutable*. The engagement with the *Redoutable* was so close that the French were able to use grenades to devastating effect. It was a shot from this ship which fatally wounded Nelson about an hour into the battle at 1.15 p.m. *Victory*, much damaged, put into Gibraltar for repairs on 28 October and left on 3 November carrying Nelson's body back to England. DK

246. Model of *Victory*, 100-gun ship, launched 1765
Unknown maker, *c.* 1805
Scale 1:48
National Maritime Museum, London; SLR0513

This contemporary model illustrates the largest type of warship built during the eighteenth century; a first-rate with 100 guns mounted on three decks. *Victory* had a very active career, serving almost continuously as flagship of a number of distinguished naval officers. During the French Revolutionary and Napoleonic Wars, she was Hood's flagship at the capture of Toulon in 1793, Jervis's at the Battle of St Vincent in 1797, and Nelson's at Trafalgar in 1805. She is shown here after her 'great repair' of 1800–1803 when the open stern galleries were removed and closed in, and a new, simplified figurehead

fitted. She never had the solid bulwarks shown here but kept the more lightweight bulwarks (frames to house the hammocks in netting, which offered limited protection to the crew against small-arms fire). Otherwise the model shows *Victory* as she would have appeared at Trafalgar. SS

*247. Spanish naval ensign captured at Trafalgar
(Not on display)
Wool
9830 x 14402mm
National Maritime Museum, London (Greenwich Hospital Collection); AAA0567

This is from *San Ildefonso*, 74 guns, captured by the *Defence* at Trafalgar. It was hung in the crossing of St Paul's Cathedral during Nelson's funeral service on 9 January 1806 and was presented to the Royal Naval Museum by the Dean and Chapter of St Paul's in 1907. The design was in use from 1785 to 1931. The field is divided into three horizontal red/yellow/red stripes. On an applied patch in the central stripe is an oval containing the arms of Castile (a yellow castle on a red field) and Leon (a white field with a red lion rampant), a crown above. The arms appear to have been printed or stencilled. 'SAN ELDEFONSO' is inscribed on the hoist in ink. The flag is made of wool bunting made of twenty-one 405mm-wide breadths (16 inches), hand-sewn horizontally with overstitched seams. There is a narrower

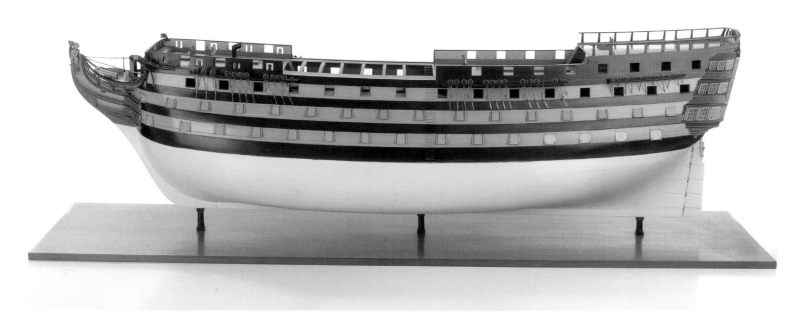

band of fabric at the top and bottom edge. There are some rectangular holes probably cut by souvenir hunters at the hoist end and neat patches indicating repairs made soon after the date of manufacture. The ensign has a linen hoist containing a rope. A very similar ensign, worn by *San Juan Nepumuceno* during the Battle of Trafalgar, is in the collections of the Museo de Ejército, Madrid.   BT

248. Model of *Entreprenante*, 8-gun cutter, launched 1798

W. Rodney Stone, midshipman, 1806
Scale 1:108 approx.
National Maritime Museum, London; SLR0654

Thought to have been built in France in 1798, the *Entreprenante* was taken as a prize in 1800 and added to the Royal Navy with the same name. Originally rigged as a cutter, she measured 67 feet in length by 21 feet 6 inches (20.4 x 6.5m) in the beam and had a displacement of 123 tons. *Entreprenante* was armed with twelve 8-pounder carronades and crewed by forty men. She was one of the two smallest vessels present at Trafalgar, the other being the schooner *Pickle*. Their role in the fleet was to act as dispatch boats, carrying written orders and messages to other ships, and to and from the Admiralty in the UK. Under the command of Robert B. Young at Trafalgar, the *Entreprenante* stood by to pick up survivors from the burning French ship *Achille*, which had been set on fire by the British *Prince* towards the end of the battle.

This model depicts her towards the end of her career rigged as a yawl, defined by the small mizzen mast mounted abaft the rudder position. The boats are shown rigged on davits and the armament has been reduced to two 6-pounder guns. From 1806 onwards, *Entreprenante* was stationed in the Channel and captured a number of small privateers before finally being broken up in 1812.   SS

249. Logbook of *Bellerophon*

Leather-bound volume; ink on paper
National Maritime Museum, London; ADM/L/B56

This log was written by the first lieutenant, William Cumby, who took command of the ship after Captain John Cooke was killed at Trafalgar. He was described as a 'merry, clever little fellow' and an 'excellent officer' but he was already thirty-three years old when he was appointed. His actions during the battle earned him promotion to captain.

The *Bellerophon,* often called 'Billy Ruffian' by the men of the lower deck, was a 74-gun, two-decker ship of the line built in 1786. She fought at two major earlier battles: the 'Glorious First of June' in 1794 and the Nile in 1798.

Cooke had determined to follow Nelson's plan and hold fire until he was passing through the enemy line. However, this resulted in so many casualties that he decided to open fire sooner to boost crew morale. The ship collided with the French *L'Aigle*, which had many sharpshooters positioned in the rigging, one of whom shot Cooke. Cumby then had to take charge and immediately ordered the men on the poop deck to go below to avoid further casualties. The French retaliated by throwing grenades through the gun ports, causing further casualties and starting a fire in the gunner's storeroom. The ship suffered heavy losses: more than 400 killed and injured in the first hour and a half of action.   DK

250. *Friedland*, 80-gun French two-decker, 1810

Unknown maker
Scale 1:48
Musée de la Marine, Paris; 17 MG 3

French warships of Nelson's period were renowned for their speed and sea-keeping qualities, whereas the British opted for a much stronger construction which enabled the fleet to remain at sea for longer periods of time. In 1786, the new administration of the French navy decided to embark upon a large building programme with the aim of further strengthening their ships of the line. Of the eighty ships ordered, twelve were built as two-deckers to the designs of Jacques-Noël Sané. Measuring 59.26m (194 feet) along the gun-deck, this class carried 36- and 24-pounder guns on two decks and had a complement of more than 900 men. In all, four of this class took part in the Battle of Trafalgar fighting alongside the more numerous 74s. This contemporary model was built in Paris to the original plans by Sané and represents the *Friedland*, which was built at Antwerp and launched in 1810.   SS

251. Model of ship of 74 guns, *c.* 1790

Unknown maker
Scale 1:48
National Maritime Museum, London; SLR0558

During the later eighteenth century, the 74-gun, two-decker ship of the line became the ideal in British sailing warship design, providing the optimum balance between armament and speed. Their design was heavily influenced by the French 74-gun *Invincible*, captured in 1747. It evolved over a period of sixty years to produce an effective fighting machine that made economic use of manpower and was able to sail well in most weather conditions for long periods of time. It had a gun-deck length of 168 feet (51m), able to carry an effective battery of 32-pounder guns. By 1803, there were eighty-seven of this class in the Navy, comprising over half of the line-of-battle fleet. At the Nile and Trafalgar, 74-gun ships far outnumbered all other classes on both sides.

This is a contemporary model and was probably built by a shipwright as there is a high level of detail. Unusually, it shows the ship 'as built' with a complete set of frames, each made from individual timbers correctly joined and scarfed. The hull planking below the wale (the large black band of planks just below the main gun-deck), has been laid 'anchor stock' fashion. This extravagant use of timber was only employed where additional strength was needed. The rather limited decoration has been carved from typical materials: bone and boxwood. A noticeable difference between the designs of British and French ships of the period is the shape of the stern: British stern galleries are more angular than the rounded 'horseshoe' shape of the French, as shown in the model of *L'Éole*.   SS

252. *The Battle of Trafalgar, 21 October 1805; beginning of the action*

Nicholas Pocock (1740–1821)
Oil on canvas
712 x 1016mm
National Maritime Museum, London; BHC0548
See page 195

The start of the action at about 12.30 p.m., seen in bird's-eye view from the north-east, the Spanish coast around Cape Trafalgar being out of sight to the left. The Franco-Spanish Combined Fleet is heading north for Cadiz in a single irregular line of battle, top left to bottom right. It is in the process of being broken at two points on either side of the centre by Nelson's two parallel lines of ships in 'order of sailing' – 'the Nelson Touch' – approaching diagonally from seaward, upper right. The British leeward division, led by Vice-Admiral Collingwood in the *Royal Sovereign*, is in the distance and was the first in action: Nelson in *Victory* is in the centre, at the head of the windward division and raking Admiral Villeneuve's flagship *Bucentaure* from astern as he breaks through the enemy line just ahead of its centre. The action quickly became general and continued for more than three hours, by which time seventeen enemy ships had surrendered and one, the *Achille*, had blown up.

The picture is one of a pair by Pocock, a former merchant sea captain and the leading specialist marine artist of the time: the other is of the shattered fleets at the close of the battle. They are from a series of six which Pocock did especially for engraving in Clarke and McArthur's two-volume *Life* of Nelson of 1809. This includes lengthy explanatory texts and a key identifying all the ships shown.   PvdM

253. French boarding axe, early nineteenth century

Steel, wood
Musée de la Marine, Paris; 33 AR 214

Axes or tomahawks were issued to the ship's company together with pikes and cutlasses. They were used for cutting the rigging of enemy ships but also as a back-up weapon when necessary. According to one report, Rear-Admiral Magon, in his flagship *Algeciras*, 'was struck down, as he was in the act of heading his men, a tomahawk in his hand, in an effort to repel a British boarding party from the *Tonnant*. He fell with the words on his lips, "*Sauvez, Sauvez, l'honneur du Pavillon*"' (Save, save the honour of the flag).   LV

254. French naval sword, 1800

Gilt metal, ebony and steel
National Maritime Museum, London; WPN1049

This pattern of sword was introduced into the French navy around 1800 and has a straight stirrup hilt in gilt metal, a fluted pommel and an ebony grip. The end of the quillon (the extended crosspiece of the hilt of a sword, usually straight but sometimes curved) is decorated with a lion's

head and the langets (the two small extensions of the guard on which there is often engraved a badge or motif) are embossed with a foul anchor. It is said to have been surrendered to Captain Thomas Fremantle when he was in command of the *Neptune* at Trafalgar by Captain J-J. Magendie of the *Bucentaure*. The *Bucentaure* was the flagship of Admiral Villeneuve whom Fremantle entertained on board the *Neptune* after the battle, writing to his wife, 'I found him a very pleasant and Gentlemanlike man, the poor man was very low!'   LV

255. Spanish naval officer's fighting sword, 1797

Gilt brass, wood and steel
Inscribed on blade: obverse: Rl Fr D TOLo (Real
Fabrica De Toledo); reverse: cutler's mark, A N O
1797
Private collection

This sword was surrendered to Admiral Collingwood after the capture of the *Santa Ana* during the Battle of Trafalgar. For some time Collingwood was under the impression that it belonged to the wounded Vice-Admiral de Alava, whom he, therefore, considered a prisoner of war. But following the escape of the *Santa Ana* to Cadiz, de Alava wrote to Collingwood on 23 December 1805:

> In consequence, however, of your Excellency's assertion, the moment I found myself capable of resuming the subject, I enquired of that officer, Don Francisco Riquelme, and was informed that the sword presented by him on board the *Royal Sovereign* was his own . . . I must add that the sabre which I used in battle, and the swords which I generally wear, are still in my possession'.

LV

256. Spanish dress sword, *c.* 1800–5

Steel, leather
Nelson Museum, Monmouth; sword no. 384

This sword has a steel hilt with an Adam pommel and heavily embossed decoration on the grip. It is believed to have been owned by Rear-Admiral Cisneros whose flagship at Trafalgar was the *Santísima Trínidad*. Cisneros was wounded but lived to become Spanish Minister of Marine. A Spanish author wrote, 'the figure of Don Balasar, Knight of Cisneros, is one of the most brilliant and glorious in our fleet'. LV

257. French dress sword, *c.* 1800–5

Gilt metal, silver wire, steel and leather
Nelson Museum, Monmouth; sword no. 385

Admiral Villeneuve is thought to have surrendered this sword to Lieutenant Hennah of the *Mars* after the Battle of Trafalgar. This type, with a helmet pommel, was worn by both French army and navy officers in the early nineteenth century. Collingwood, who met Villeneuve three days after the battle, wrote home, 'Admiral Villeneuve is a well-bred man, and I believe a very good officer: he has nothing of the offensive vapouring and boasting which we, perhaps, too often attribute to Frenchmen.' LV

258. Sir Thomas Masterman Hardy, 1769–1839

Domenico Pellegrini (1759–1840)
Oil on canvas
585 x 455mm
Signed and dated 1809
National Maritime Museum, London; BHC2352

This portrait shows Hardy much as he would have appeared at Trafalgar. Born in northern Italy, Pellegrini trained in Venice and Rome before entering the Royal Academy Schools in London in 1793. When the French occupied Portugal in 1807 he found himself in Lisbon where he stayed to paint portraits. This portrait was done there, while Hardy was on the Lisbon station commanding the *Triumph*.   RQ

259. Plan of the Battle of Trafalgar drawn by Lt. (RM) Paul Nicolas
Ink on paper
National Maritime Museum, London; AGC/N/11

Nicolas was a marine lieutenant on the *Belleisle*, a ship which had been captured from the French in 1795. He later remembered the enthusiasm of the crew before the battle, but also their realization that not all of them would survive the action.

During the Battle of Trafalgar, the *Belleisle* was badly damaged in action with the *Fougueux*. Despite being completely dismasted, she refused to surrender. A Union Jack was hung from the end of a pike and held up and an ensign was strapped to the stump of the mainmast to show that she remained unconquered.   DK

260. French account of Trafalgar, 20 January 1806
Ink on paper
National Maritime Museum, London; MON/56

A rare survival in a British archive, this eyewitness account, written by a French sailor known only as Michel, is addressed to '*mon cher Auguste*'. He gives a detailed eyewitness description of the battle, offering a somewhat contrasting view to that given by the victorious British sailors. The letter also mentions Napoleon's land campaigns, in particular the battle at Austerlitz.   AD

261. Captain John Cooke (1763–1805)
Lemuel Francis Abbott (1760–1803)
Oil on canvas
760 x 635mm
National Maritime Museum, London (Greenwich Hospital Collection, presented by Mr and Mrs Christopher Cooke, 1848); BHC2629

Cooke was captain of the *Nymphe* when, together with the *San Fiorenzo*, they captured the French frigates *Résistance* and *Constance* off Brest in March 1797. He was killed at Trafalgar when commanding the *Bellerophon*, the only captain to die

in the battle. Cooke is shown wearing a captain's full-dress uniform (over three years), 1795–1812. Possibly finished by another hand, owing to Abbott's death in 1803.   RQ

262. Light cavalry-type sword, 1800–15
H. Tatham (1770–1835)
Gilt metal, ivory, steel and leather

Inscribed on top locket of scabbard: *Tatham To His Majesty – No 37 Charing Cross, Near The Admiralty*
National Maritime Museum, London (Greenwich Hospital Collection); WPN1001

263. Dirk, 1800–3

H. Tatham (1770–1835)

Gilt metal, ivory, steel and leather
Inscribed on top locket of scabbard: *Tatham Admiralty*
National Maritime Museum, London (Greenwich
    Hospital Collection); WPN1059

264. Flintlock pistol, *c.* 1805

Walnut, brass and gold wire
National Maritime Museum, London (Greenwich
    Hospital Collection); AAA2464

All three weapons were believed to have belonged to
Captain John Cooke who commanded the *Bellerophon* at the
Battle of Trafalgar. It is said that Cooke was reloading the
pistol when he was killed by a French marksman from
L'Aigle. His first lieutenant William Cumby had warned that
his epaulettes would make him conspicuous but Cooke
replied, 'It's too late to take them off. I see my situation. I
can only die like a man.'   LV

265. Book of Common Prayer, *c.* 1800

Leather-bound volume
By descent, Shorthall of Ballylorcan

This book was purchased by Midshipman Henry Parker in
September 1805 and was carried by him at the Battle of
Trafalgar. Parker was seventeen at the time of the battle,
serving in the *Belleisle*. He nailed the colours to the mast
to signify 'No Surrender'. This apparently attracted a hail
of fire as French ships attempted to force the *Belleisle* to
surrender. The entry in his prayer book states that he was

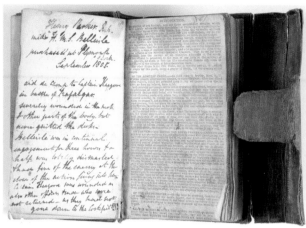

severely wounded (in the neck) but that he did not go down
to the cockpit.   CSW

266. Midshipman Henry Parker

Henry Thomson/Thompson (1773–1843)
Oil on canvas
1140 x 930mm
By descent, Shorthall of Ballylorcan

Henry Parker entered the Navy on 27 January 1801 as a
First Class Volunteer in *Belleisle* and became a midshipman
in June of that year. He served in the ship for six and a half

MS 5141

H: M: Ship Victory 15th Decem[ber]

"About the middle of the Action with the Combined Fleets on the 21 October last, the late Illustrious Commander in Chief Lord Nelson, was mortally wounded in the left breast by a Musquet ball, supposed to be fired from the Mizen top of La Redoutable French Ship of the line, which the Victory fell on board of early in the battle; his Lordship was in the Act of turning on the Quarter Deck with his face towards the enemy, when he received his wound, he instantly fell, and was carried to the Cockpit where he lived about two Hours. —

" On his Lordship being brought below, he complained of Acute pain about the sixth or seventh Dorsal Vertebra, of privation of sense and motion of the body and inferior extremities; his Respiration was short & difficult; Pulse weak small and irregular. he frequently declared his back was shot through; that he felt every instant a gush of blood within his breast; and that he had sensations which indicated to him the approach of death: in the course of an hour his Pulse became indistinct and was gradually lost in the Arm, his extremities and forehead became soon afterwards cold: he retained his wonted energy of mind, and exercise of his faculties until the latest moment of his existence; and when Victory as signal as decisive was announced to him he expressed his pious acknowledgements thereof and heartfelt satisfaction at the glorious event in the most emphatic language, he then delivered his last orders with his usual precision, and in a few Minutes after expired without a struggle

[Course and Site of the Ball ascertained since Death] —
The Ball struck the forepart of his Lordships Epaulette, and entered the left shoulder immediately before the Processus Acromion Scapulae which it slightly fractured, it then descended obliquely into the Thorax, fracturing the [illegible] 2d Ribs; and after penetrating the left lobe of the Lungs and dividing in its passage, a large branch of the Pulmonary Artery it entered the left side of the Spine between the sixth and seventh Dorsal Vertebrae fractured the left transverse Process of the sixth Vertebra, wounded the Medulla Spinalis and fracturing the right transverse Process of the seventh Vertebra, it made its way from the right side of the Spine, directing its course through the Muscles of the back, and lodged therein, about two inches below the inferior angle of the right Scapula. —

" On removing the ball a portion of the Gold lace and Pad of the Epaulette together with a small piece of his Lordships coat were found firmly attached to it " —

W Beatty
Surgeon

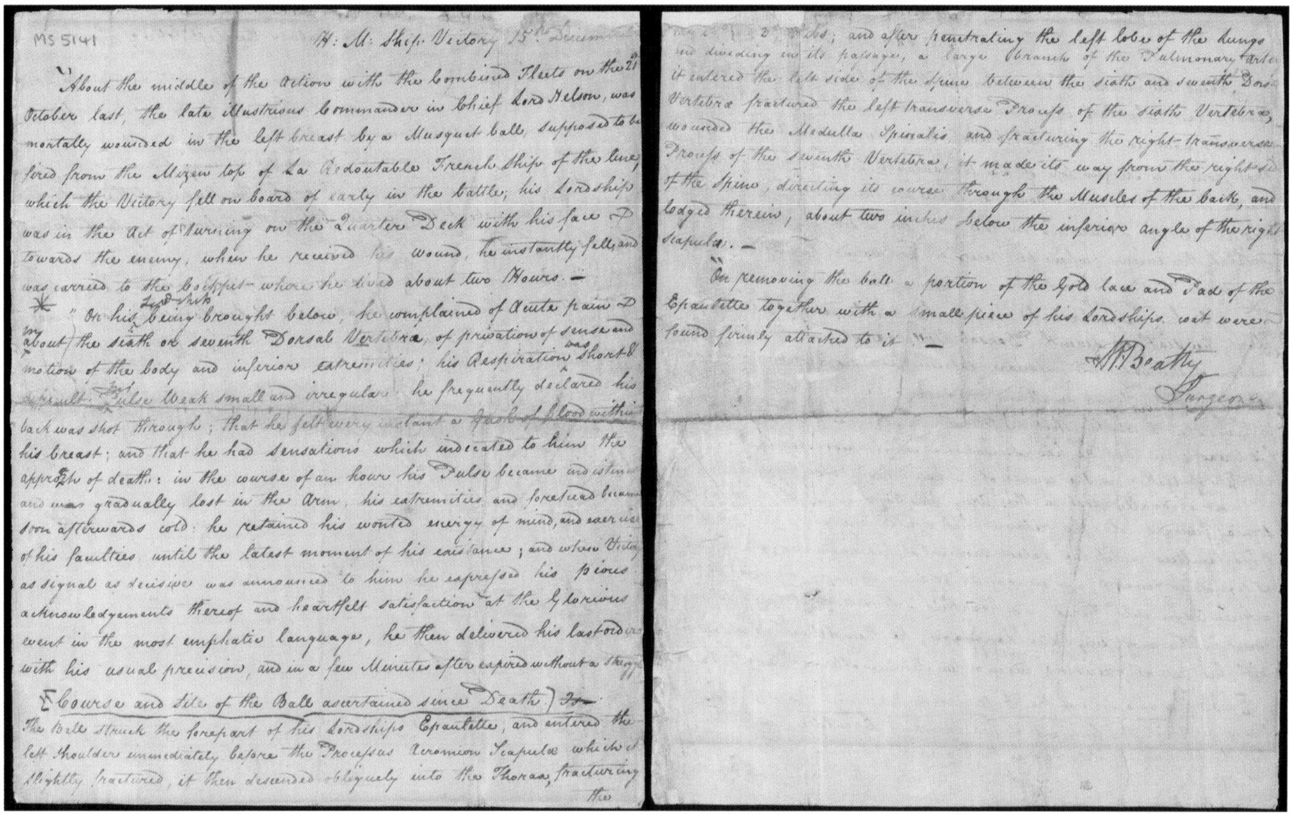

years, at first in the Channel. He later accompanied Nelson to the West Indies and back in pursuit of the combined squadrons of France and Spain and was present at Trafalgar on 21 October 1805. RQ

267. Report on the wounding, death and post-mortem examination of Viscount Nelson, 1805

Sir William Beatty
Ink on paper
Wellcome Library, London; MS 5141

Manuscript report dated 15 December 1805 by William Beatty, surgeon of the *Victory*, describing the mortal wound suffered by Nelson at Trafalgar. Shortly after 1 p.m., Nelson had been struck by a musket ball, fired from the mizzen top of the *Redoutable*. He was carried below to the cockpit, where he was examined by Beatty, who could do nothing to save him, and he died about three hours later. On the day after the battle, Beatty placed Nelson's corpse in a large water cask filled with brandy to preserve it for burial in England. Soon after the ship's return, Beatty carried out a thorough autopsy, removing the fatal musket ball. The cold, clinical nature of Beatty's account emphasizes the horrific nature of the wound, and the agony that Nelson endured before his death:

> The Ball struck the forepart of his Lordship's Epaulette, and entered the left shoulder . . . it then descended obliquely into the Thorax, fracturing the second and third ribs; and after penetrating the left lobe of the lungs and dividing in its passage a large branch of the Pulmonary Artery, it entered the Spine . . . and lodged therein.

JC

Literature: Laurence Brockliss, John Cardwell and Michael Moss, *Nelson's Surgeon: Sir William Beatty, Naval Medicine and the Battle of Trafalgar* (Oxford, 2005).

268. Vice-admiral's epaulettes worn by Nelson at Trafalgar, 1805

Gold alloy, silver, silk, card or sheet metal and cotton wadding
National Maritime Museum, London (Greenwich Hospital Collection); UNI0031
See page 187

Worn on Nelson's Trafalgar uniform, one epaulette has been partially damaged by the shot that killed him. While Nelson lay dying in *Victory*'s cockpit, his coat was placed under the head of Midshipman George Augustus Westphal (1785–1875), who was being treated nearby. Blood from his head wound glued part of the bullions of the epaulettes to

his hair so that it had to be cut away. The fragment of gold lace was retained as a memento by Westphal's family. The epaulettes are made of gold lace mounted over card or sheet metal; the undersides are partially padded and covered with yellow silk. There are two stars, indicating the rank of vice-admiral, worked in metal thread and silver spangles.

BT & AM

269. Nelson's vice-admiral's undress coat worn at Trafalgar, 1805

Wool, silk, metal thread and gold alloy
National Maritime Museum, London (Greenwich
    Hospital Collection); UNI0024

Two hours into the action, at about 1.15 p.m., Hardy, realizing that the Admiral was no longer by his side, turned to see him on his knees, supporting himself on his left arm before this gave way and he collapsed on the spot where John Scott, his secretary, had been killed an hour earlier. Scott's blood can still be seen staining the tails and the left sleeve of the coat. Nelson was one of many casualties caused by marksmen in the rigging of the French *Redoutable*. The hole left by the fatal musket ball can be seen on the left shoulder close to the epaulette damaged by the same shot. Embroidered versions of Nelson's four orders of chivalry are sewn to the front of the coat overlapping the edge of the lapel so that it could not be unbuttoned. They are: the star of the Order of the Bath, the Order of the Crescent awarded by the Sultan of Turkey, the Order of St Ferdinand and of Merit awarded by Ferdinand IV of Naples, and the German Order of St Joachim. Nelson habitually wore them on all his uniform coats. Captain Hardy returned the coat to Emma Hamilton in accordance with Nelson's wishes. A young neighbour, Lionel Goldsmith, was taken to visit Emma towards the end of 1805 and saw it lying on the bed beside her. Nelson's brother William, later 1st Earl Nelson, and his son Horatio wanted to display the relic at their new country residence, Trafalgar House, but a letter found in the pocket agreed that the family should lend it to Lady Hamilton during her lifetime. In the event she surrendered it to Joshua Jonathan Smith to discharge a debt just before she moved to France in 1814 – a few months before her death. HRH Prince Albert, Queen Victoria's husband, purchased the coat for £150 from Smith's widow, through Sir Nicholas Harris Nicolas, editor of Nelson's letters and dispatches, and presented it to Greenwich Hospital in 1845.   BT & AM

270. Musket ball that killed Nelson, 1805

Lead ball; gold, silver and crystal case
HM The Queen, Royal Collection; RCIN 61158

Nelson's death at Trafalgar was recorded in great detail by the *Victory*'s surgeon, Dr William Beatty. This is the musket ball, fired from the mizzen top of the French *Redoutable*, which killed him. Beatty carried out the autopsy in which it was removed on 11 December after the arrival of Nelson's body at Spithead. He records:

> It was at this time that the fatal ball was discovered; it had passed through the spine, and lodged in the muscles of the back, towards the right side, and a little below the shoulder-blade. A very considerable portion of the gold lace, pad, and lining of the epaulette, with a piece of the coat, was found attached to the ball; the lace of the epaulette was as firmly so, as if it had been inserted into the metal while in a state of fusion.

The artist Arthur William Devis, then on board *Victory*, drew the spherical lead musket ball with the portion of

epaulette as it appeared when it was extracted from the body. Sir Thomas Hardy had the ball set in a gold-mounted crystal locket contained in a silver outer case, and presented it to Beatty. Devis's drawing of the ball and his subsequent drawing of the locket were included as engravings in Beatty's published narrative of 1807. Beatty's descendants presented the locket containing the musket ball to Queen Victoria and it has remained in the Royal Collection at Windsor Castle, only occasionally being lent for public display. It was last shown here in 1995, as now, with the coat and epaulette Nelson was wearing, on which the damage can be seen.   RP

LITERATURE: Beatty, *Authentic Narrative of the death of Lord Nelson*; Pugh, *Nelson and his Surgeons.*

271. Stockings worn by Nelson at the Battle of Trafalgar, 1805
Cotton, wool
National Maritime Museum, London (Greenwich
Hospital Collection); UN10067

The stockings are finely knitted using white thread that is a cotton/wool blend. At the top, where they would be

secured with a garter, on both sides of each stocking is the numeral 'II' below an 'N' below a coronet. These laundry marks have been worked in cross-stitch using blue thread. The toes, sole and heel of the stockings have been knitted using a slightly heavier gauge of wool that is also slightly darker in colour. This would serve both to reinforce areas that received heavy wear and provide added warmth. The stockings are heavily bloodstained but the blood is probably that of Nelson's secretary, Scott, killed earlier in the action. The garments were saved as a memento by Lieutenant Lewis Rotely RM (d. 1861).   BT & AM

272. Waistcoat worn by Nelson at the Battle of Trafalgar, 1805
Cotton, linen
National Maritime Museum, London (Greenwich
Hospital Collection); UN10065

The waistcoat is a non-regulation garment of white cotton marsella, woven in a diaper pattern. It is double-breasted with seven self-covered buttons on either side, narrow pockets and a stand-up collar with the reveres folded back. Both the

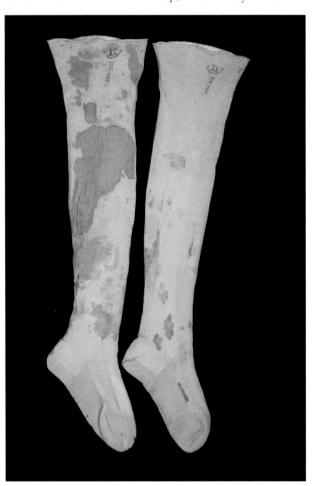

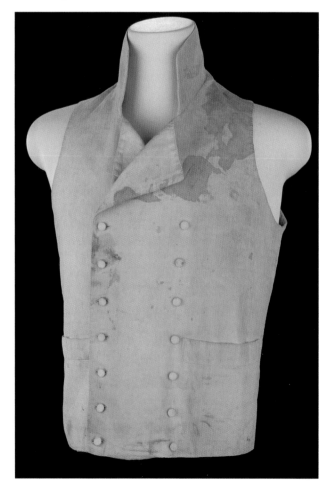

reveres and collar are lined with marsella, while the rest of the waistcoat is lined with white linen. The back of the waistcoat is made of white flannel and has four linen tying tapes to adjust the fit. The left shoulder is heavily bloodstained from the wound in Nelson's shoulder. Nelson is recorded as having habitually worn a marsella waistcoat in undress. This one was obtained from the widow of Alderman J. J. Smith with the associated undress coat in 1845.   BT & AM

273. Uniform breeches worn by Nelson at the Battle of Trafalgar, 1805
Wool, brass and linen
National Maritime Museum, London (Greenwich
    Hospital Collection); UNI0021

Stained on the knees and the seat with the blood of John Scott, Nelson's secretary, who was killed earlier in the battle. The breeches have been cut down the front with scissors by the surgeon so that they could be removed without unnecessarily hurting the patient. They are made of a white twill woven wool fabric with a napped finish and have a flap front. At the back of the breeches is a white linen gusset that was used to adjust the fit by pulling in linen tying tapes that passed through eyelets on either side. The breeches are secured at the knee by four small gilt-brass flag officer's buttons and small brass buckles. The garments were saved as a memento by Lieutenant Lewis Rotely RM of the *Victory* (d. 1861).   BT & AM

274. Nelson's stock, c. 1805
Velvet, silk, gilt metal and linen
National Maritime Museum, London (Greenwich
    Hospital Collection); UNI0066

Stock reputedly worn by Nelson at Trafalgar, an example of the type of non-regulation accessory that was worn with uniform. It is made of black velvet, now faded to brown,

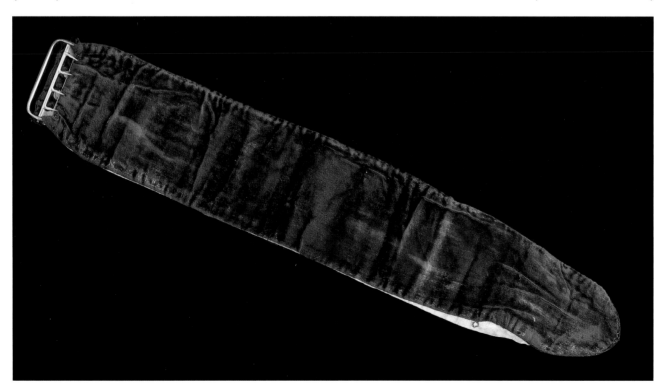

Nelson wore his hair bound into a pigtail or queue, as can be seen in many portraits, and it was cut off when his body was prepared for transport to England. On arrival, Hardy delivered the hair to Emma as Nelson had requested. Some small locks were given to relations and close friends, and some pieces were inserted in special mourning rings and lockets. The pigtail itself was passed on to their daughter Horatia, whose children presented it to Greenwich Hospital in 1881. RP

276. *The Death of Nelson*, 1805–7
Arthur William Devis (1763–1822)
Oil on canvas
1955 x 2615mm
National Maritime Museum, London (Greenwich
   Hospital Collection); BHC2894

When victory . . . was announced to him, he
expressed his pious acknowledgements thereof
. . . delivered his last orders with his usual precision,
and in a few minutes afterwards expired without
a struggle.   *William Beatty*

This is the most famous representation of Nelson's death, in the cockpit of *Victory* at about 4.30 p.m. on 21 October 1805. In painting it Devis was responding to press advertisements of 22 November 1805 from the publisher Josiah Boydell that he would pay 500 guineas for the best 'Death of Nelson' painting, for engraving. Devis may have got aboard *Victory* off Portsmouth with the aid of Nelson's agent, Alexander Davison, to attempt the subject to meet his debts. For this he had been freed from the rules of the King's Bench, where Davison (one of his patrons) had been confined about the same time for electoral fraud, and in which Boydell held an official sinecure. He worked aboard for a week making notes, sketches and portrait studies before sailing with her for the Nore on 11 December, the day he drew Nelson's body (and the fatal bullet) during Dr Beatty's sea-borne autopsy to prepare it for lying-in-state. From this, Beatty commissioned a Nelson portrait – of which Devis made several versions, one shown at the Royal Academy in 1807 – and obtained the illustrations for his own published *Narrative*. Devis's care for accuracy also included making a model of the scene to work from. The group around Nelson are Dr Scott, his chaplain, rubbing his chest to help relieve the pain, and the purser Walter Burke, supporting the pillow. Nelson's steward, William Chevailler, looks towards Beatty, who feels Nelson's pulse and is about to pronounce him dead. Captain Hardy was not present when Nelson died but is shown standing behind him, one of a number of liberties that Devis took to make the work

and is lined with white linen. The stock passed around the front of the neck over the shirt collar and fastened in the back by means of a buckle. The gilt metal buckle has four prongs that secure the stock by means of four corresponding buttonholes. It was presented to Greenwich Hospital by the children of Nelson's daughter Horatia in 1881.
                                 BT & AM

275. Nelson's hair and pigtail, 1805
National Maritime Museum, London (Greenwich
   Hospital Collection); RELO116

William Beatty, *Victory*'s surgeon, recorded Nelson's words as he lay dying, including his request to Captain Hardy, 'Pray let my dear Lady Hamilton have my hair, and all other things belonging to me.'

more than a documentary record and a worthy historical celebration of Nelson's patriotic sacrifice. The 'tween-deck height (in which Hardy, over 6 feet tall, could not stand upright) is exaggerated and the darkness and long outer shadows make Nelson the main source of light – real and symbolic – rather than the three flickering lanterns. Wrapped in a shroud-like white sheet, the wound in his left shoulder covered, he lies at point of death against a massive lodging knee, in a grouping recalling Old Master paintings of Christ's deposition from the Cross. The implication is that the light of this world is dimming and the glory of the next already shining on the hero, with the glitter of earthly rewards redundant at his feet, in the decorations and braid of his discarded uniform coat (cat. no. 269). Those present show a range of emotions – concern, sorrow, resignation, distraction and despair. By contrast, Midshipman Edward Collingwood

and Lieutenant John Yule (rear left and left), with a pile of captured enemy flags being brought in by a seaman, look alertly away, as if towards outer light and the victorious battle just ending above. Gaetano Spedillo, Nelson's Neapolitan valet, stands in right profile in front of Collingwood, holding a glass from which Nelson took his last sips of water. *Victory*'s carpenter, William Bunce, stands on the far right above the dazed and wounded figure of Lieutenant George Miller Bligh, with Assistant Surgeon Neil Smith seated far right.

In 1771 Benjamin West's painting of the death of Nelson's personal idol, General Wolfe, at Quebec in 1759 set a model for those of modern heroes and was best known, including to Nelson, from the print engraved for Josiah Boydell's uncle, John. At the same time as Devis, West began his own *The Death of Lord Nelson* on the Wolfe pattern and for a print to match it, honouring (so he said) an earlier undertaking to Nelson: the print was to be engraved by James Heath and jointly published with West, who finished his picture by May 1806 and immediately displayed it in his own gallery. His version showed Nelson dying where he had fallen, in an 'Epic Composition' on *Victory*'s quarter-deck. In June 1807 he conceded that Devis's version had 'much merit' but thought his factual approach insufficient 'to excite awe and veneration', even though he did an inferior below-deck version himself at that time for Clarke and McArthur's 1809 *Life* of Nelson. 'Wolfe,' he said, 'must not die like a common soldier under a Bush; neither should Nelson be represented dying in the gloomy hold of a ship, like a sick man in a Prison Hole. . . . All should be proportionate to the highest idea conceived of the Hero. . . . A mere matter of fact will never produce this effect.' Devis, however, gained Boydell's patronage and by August 1806 his version was well advanced with 800 subscribers enrolled for the print, though William Bromley was only appointed in December to engrave it – for £800 and in two years. Boydell had the painting shown at the British Institution in 1809 but lost the 'print race' with West, since Bromley's plate was only issued in 1812. Heath's after West was finished and a proof shown at the Royal Academy in 1811, with the original painting, to help promote sales. Both prints were highly successful but Devis's painting became the better known after 1825, when it was presented to the Naval Gallery at Greenwich Hospital by Nicholas Vansittart, Lord Bexley, who had been envoy to the Danes in the events surrounding the Battle of Copenhagen in 1801. (The Hospital had already declined to buy it from Boydell and similarly declined an offer from West's heirs for his 1806 'Epic' version, now in the Walker Art Gallery Liverpool.) By the late nineteenth century Devis's painting was a central image in the Painted Hall's role as a major Nelsonic and naval shrine, which the National Maritime Museum's Nelson displays inevitably inherited with care of the Naval Gallery paintings from 1936. Millions more people came to know the composition from the waxwork tableau based on it that, with some renewal, was a feature of Madame Tussaud's for over a century up to 1992. Queen Victoria paid 500 guineas for Devis's large oil sketch when offered it in 1852 and a smaller replica version has also been shown on *Victory* at Portsmouth, since it was presented to the ship, before 1881, by a group of high-ranking naval officers headed by Admiral of the Fleet Sir James Hope. Despite long-standing tradition that this is

by Devis, its quality suggests it is a copy, perhaps specially commissioned. PvdM

LITERATURE: Joseph Farington, *Diary*, VIII, various esp. 3064 (6 June 1807). Stephen Whittle, *Arthur William Devis* (exh. cat., Harris Museum and Art Gallery, Preston, 1999); Walker, *The Nelson Portraits*; Martyn Downer, *Nelson's Purse* (London, 2004).

277.   Nelson's silk purse, *c.* 1805
Silk, ivory and silver
National Maritime Museum, London (Royal United
     Service Museum Collection); TXT0371

This purse was the one taken from Nelson's pocket by Captain Hardy after his death at Trafalgar. The blue silk mesh 'stocking purse' has a carved ivory and silver collar or 'slider' to close it and metal pins with beads at the open end. When the purse was displayed in the 1891 Royal Naval Exhibition at Chelsea, the catalogue entry explained that it 'belonged to Vice-Admiral Lord Nelson and was constantly used by him. It was removed from his dead body by Captain (afterwards Sir T. M.) Hardy in the cockpit of the Victory immediately after Nelson's death, on October 21st 1805, and was retained by Captain Hardy as a memento. The purse at that time contained a gold guinea, which has since been lost.'

The purse was in the possession of the Hardy family until 1880, when it was purchased by Dr George Williamson, who lent it, together with another yellow and silver purse belonging to Captain Hardy, to the Royal United Service Museum. The National Maritime Museum acquired both these purses through the National Art Collection Fund in 1930. RP

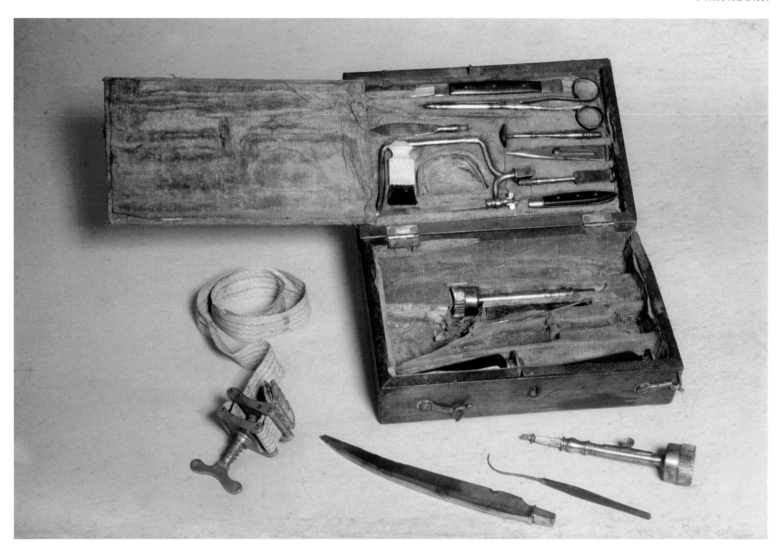

278. Sir William Beatty's surgical instruments, *c.* 1805

Laundy, London

Inscribed on top of the wooden case, *William Beatty, Royal Navy*

Royal College of Physicians and Surgeons of Glasgow

Beatty probably used these instruments to treat the approximately 160 casualties suffered by the *Victory*'s crew at Trafalgar. He and his two assistant surgeons performed eleven amputations in the dimly lit orlop deck during the battle or its aftermath, without the benefit of anaesthetic, and while the ship's hull was shaken by the impact of enemy shot and the concussion of its own gunfire. To qualify as a Royal Navy surgeon, candidates were required to pass oral examinations in surgery and physic. Beatty passed his examination before the Company of Surgeons (which became the Royal College of Surgeons in 1800) on 19 February 1795, earning one of the highest qualifications. At this time, surgeons were required to purchase their instruments themselves, which were inspected and certified by the Company/College. This set includes long and short blade knives, a fine-toothed bow saw, a screw tourniquet, forceps and scissors. Other instruments in the lower compartment include two trephines. Beatty later served as Physician of the Channel Fleet from 1806 to 1815, and was appointed Physician of Greenwich Hospital in 1822.   JC

LITERATURE: Laurence Brockliss, John Cardwell and Michael Moss, *Nelson's Surgeon: Sir William Beatty, Naval Medicine and the Battle of Trafalgar*, (Oxford, 2005)

LAST JOURNEYS

Commemorating Trafalgar: Politics and Naval Patriotism

TIMOTHY JENKS

ELSON'S GREATEST — and last — victory was fought on 21 October 1805, a date subsequently commemorated as 'Trafalgar Day'. Few national victories have remained as resonant in the British national memory as Trafalgar. This was not entirely due to the simple fact that Nelson was a national hero of unprecedented success and celebrity. For at least the first century of its observance, the commemoration of Nelson's death and victory was carefully channelled into calculated celebrations of naval patriotism that had clear political aims. In many senses, commemorations reveal more about the people who practise them than the people they memorialize. Nelson's funeral and the subsequent commemoration of Trafalgar illustrate this truth.

News of Trafalgar arrived in London during the early hours of 6 November 1805 where it delighted those who heard it, whether in the streets of St Giles, the coffee houses of the City, the theatre at Covent Garden, or at the councils of war in Whitehall. For some evenings afterwards, crowds celebrated in the street, fashionable householders illuminated their homes, and theatre companies re-enacted the battle in hastily composed dramatic afterpieces (a short play, often a farce or similar, concluding the two or three pieces that made up an evening at the theatre). A legion of printmakers commemorated the admiral in art. Some of these artists' *œuvres* are now forgotten, those of others — J. M. W. Turner, Benjamin West and William Blake — decidedly *not*. But it is due to all their efforts that a visual record of these events exists. The prints they produced were, like the hastily written biographical sketches and poetic odes to Trafalgar, eagerly consumed by those of the public who could afford them. This is not to say that enthusiasm for Nelson and Trafalgar was narrow in social terms — merely that the visual and literary evidence tends to reflect an elite perspective. This is of central importance, for it requires us to understand the visual and the written records of the funeral as elite representations of an event that was experienced by, and held meaning for, a wide range of groups in Georgian Britain. For the many, Trafalgar represented relief from the prospect of a long-feared invasion; for the cultural elite, it realized the ideal of a heroic 'death in victory'; and for the government of William Pitt it represented a political lifeline, vindicating their conduct of the war and offering — for a short

while — the prospect that a formidable continental coalition could be reconstructed.

That prospect faded by the end of December with the news of the defeat of the Russian and Austrian armies by Napoleon at Austerlitz. But the government's determination to wrest domestic political benefit out of Nelson and his victory continued nonetheless. Nelson's death and victory occurred during a period in which the British government — possibly influenced by the example of France — was increasingly willing to experiment with state spectacle. Within days of news of the battle arriving in Britain, then, the ministry was involved in two projects: planning a state funeral for Nelson and working towards the inauguration of an annually observed 'Trafalgar Day'.

This latter plan — which would have seen 21 October forever celebrated with an investiture ceremony at St Paul's for a new 'Order of Naval and Military Merit' to be founded in Nelson's memory — was eventually shelved and an official state ceremonial for Trafalgar Day never emerged. But Nelson's funeral — advertised as a gift from a grateful George III — did take place, amid great pageantry and public interest. Indeed, the period November 1805–January 1806 can be seen as a lengthy funerary pageant in which Britons engaged with the memory and meaning of both the hero and the battle. This pageant was of long duration for the simple reason that bad weather, and the need to stop in at Portsmouth for repairs, delayed the *Victory*'s conveyance of Nelson's body (which the hero had begged never to be cast into the sea). It was forty-eight days before Nelson's remains (famously preserved in a cask of brandy) arrived at Greenwich. This, as it turned out, allowed plenty of time for competing interests to advance their proposals for the forthcoming funeral.

Those conflicting demands had to be resolved by Lord Hawkesbury, the Cabinet minister charged with responsibility for the funeral. Working in conjunction with the heralds of the College of Arms (the body responsible for official state funerals) it fell to Hawkesbury to determine the formidable logistical details and to resolve the disputes that arose. Central among these were those that broke out between organizers and the representatives of the City. The latter had originally hoped that

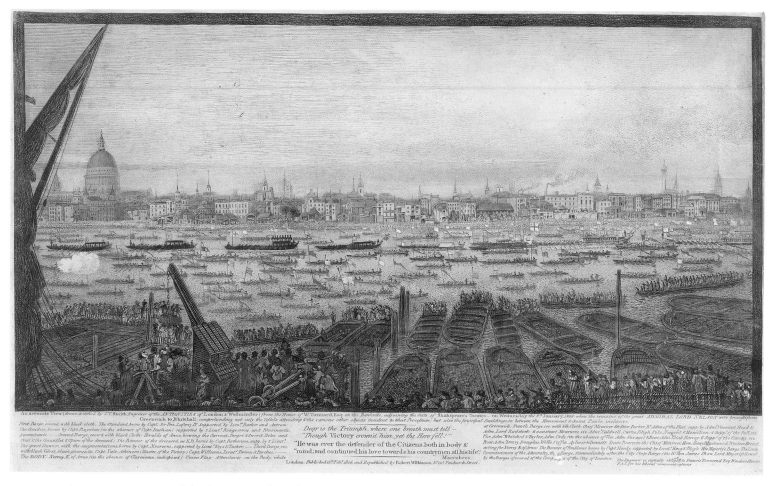

An accurate view . . . of the Antiquities of London & Westminster . . . on Wednesday 8th January 1806 . . . when the remains of the Great Admiral Lord Nelson were brought from Greenwich to Whitehall, drawn and engraved by John Smith (cat. no. 293).

the lying-in-state would take place in the Guildhall. This initial wish was refused, but it proved merely the first in a series of moves designed to ensure that City politicians profited from posthumous association with the dead hero. A greater controversy attended the desire of the Lord Mayor to occupy a more prominent position in the procession. This brought him into conflict with the Prince of Wales, who was similarly interested in insinuating his way into the funeral cortège.

Such impulses on the part of the City and the heir to the throne, however flattering to Nelson, were problematic from the point of view of Pitt's government. In their view, Nelson's funeral had some important work to do. Firstly, in a general sense, it was meant retroactively to endorse the government's conduct of the war. More specifically, it was to emphasize the ongoing nature of British naval supremacy. This latter emphasis was particularly necessary in the post-Trafalgar context, and for two reasons. Firstly, Nelson – the admiral in whom considerable national confidence had been placed – was dead and this had consequences for public morale. Secondly, as became increasingly clear after the allied

defeats at Ulm and Austerlitz, progress on the Continent was going to be so long in coming that domestic support for the war increasingly depended on viewing it with a naval emphasis.

For the funeral to be considered a success, then, it had to articulate these goals. But that was only a preliminary. It also had to be carried off without violence, or disorder, and it had to insulate itself from the possibility of public criticism, or mockery. For all these reasons, Hawkesbury and his assistants had to be attentive to the desires of 'public opinion' – an amorphous and problematic concept for the conservatively minded regime of the day. Gauging and assuaging the public's desire was a major theme of pre-funeral discussion and it must have seriously complicated Hawkesbury's task. He now had to balance concerns of protocol, concerns of politics, with the rising demands of a public – a public that was necessarily fickle and difficult to consult.

The first test of the organizer's success in appeasing the public came at the lying-in-state, held in the Painted Hall at Greenwich, from 5 to 7 January 1806. Three weeks before, when the *Victory* was off Dover, Nelson's remains had been transferred into a plain interior coffin. A week later, as the *Victory* neared Sheerness, undertakers went out and placed this smaller coffin – famously given to Nelson by Captain Hallowell after the Battle of the Nile and constructed out of the remnants of the *L'Orient*, the French flagship destroyed that day – into an elaborate exterior coffin. Black and gold, decorated with naval emblems, heraldic motifs and classical symbols alluding to Nelson's victories and knightly honours, the coffin became the centre-piece of the viewing at Greenwich. A print shows it on display, with the black velvet pall pulled back to permit a viewing by the thousands who flocked to Greenwich. As spectators coursed through, they were presented with a deliberately affecting scene. The Revd Scott, chaplain of the *Victory*, and ten mourners dressed in deep mourning clothes surrounded the body. Heraldic devices and artwork dominated the scene. Prime among these were the Viscount's coronet placed on a pillow on the coffin, and the models of Nelson's shield, gauntlet, sword and helmet. For the first two days, though, the lying-in-state largely failed to satisfy. In part this was a by-product of its popularity. At 11 a.m. on Sunday 5 January, the doors were opened and more than 10,000 people rushed forward to gain entry. In the end, more than 15,000 attended at the lying-in-state, with an uncounted number being turned away. The consequence was tumult and disorder without the gates of Greenwich Hospital, and an unacceptably abbreviated opportunity of viewing within. It was only on the third day that these difficulties were overcome, and that Georgian Britons were treated to a spectacle that fulfilled the expectations of both safety and sensibility. The Volunteer force which had been managing the crowd was replaced by a professional corps – the King's Life Guards – while inside the hall the Revd Scott and the mourners had been rearranged in a more obviously contemplative pose.

If the crowd had threatened the solemnity of the spectacle of the lying-in-state, it was their safe distance, and their apparently tamed nature, which contributed to the perceived success of the next stages of the funerary pageant. First was the procession by water on 8 January 1806, in which Nelson's body was borne from Greenwich, up the Thames, to Whitehall Stairs. Three thousand

Figurehead of Fame from Nelson's funeral carriage, 1806 (cat. no. 299).

people, most notably heralds, naval officers, the Lord Mayor and members of the City livery companies participated in the procession by water. A concourse of spectators flocked to the riverside, with people crowding the windows and roofs of conveniently located homes and buildings. Onlookers pressed up against the banks of the river, and even availed themselves of moored boats from which to view the flotilla. Some prints of this procession concentrate on the identification of the participating personages and barges; but it is interesting to note that others are attentive to the crowd itself, finding considerable comfort in its appropriately interested behaviour. When the body was landed at Whitehall Stairs, a romantic element was introduced. A sudden hail-storm seemed to announce (or resist?) Nelson's arrival on terra firma, which was taken as a pleasing coincidence by all.

Nelson's body spent the night before the funeral at the Admiralty, where it was placed on the funeral car that was to convey it to St Paul's. Funeral cars were a required feature of heraldic funerals and there were strong design precedents for the car that was built. The state funerals for Sir Philip Sidney, Oliver Cromwell, General Monck, Lord Sandwich and the Duke of Marlborough had all used funeral cars. The design of Nelson's funeral car, though, once again reveals that organizers were interested in appealing to popular tastes. For while on the one hand the funeral car's heraldic contexts emphasized Nelson's place in Britain's warrior tradition, on the other the car suggested the popular style of the London stage. As previously mentioned, this was an era in which naval battles were dramatically re-enacted for theatre audiences. Thus, in its broad similarity to the pasteboard models used in London theatres, the funeral car – designed in the image of the *Victory* itself – can be seen as an effort to capitalize upon a popular genre. No doubt this explains its incredible popularity – the funeral car was to become perhaps the iconic image of the funerary spectacle. Dozens of prints testify to the contemporary interest in the car – at the time these would have been purchased by the discriminating as commemorative souvenirs. Many more hundreds, though, would have had to trust to their memories of what they witnessed on the day of the funeral procession.

That procession took place on 9 January 1806, the day of the funeral. Leading up to the 9th, a brisk trade was done renting out window space in buildings that offered views of the procession; the first floor of a building on Ludgate Hill was offered for an astronomical £20, its second and third floors for £15 each. Those willing to pay such prices were caught up in a thirst for viewing that continued throughout the funerary pageant – down to the funeral ceremony itself, in which people precariously perched themselves on corners of the interior edifice of St Paul's. Proximity to the street afforded a better view of the spectacle – this much is obvious to us today. A little less obvious is the importance that Georgian Britons placed on proximity to the body in the procession itself. This had been the subject of controversy for some time. According to the heraldic protocol, the position of highest honour in the procession went to the chief mourner. Customarily, this role would have been taken by the heir of the deceased (in this case Nelson's brother, the newly ennobled Earl Nelson), but for Nelson's funeral protocol was dramatically abrogated. The position normally accorded to the heir and family in the procession was taken instead by admirals – Nelson's fellow naval officers. It was the Admiral of the Fleet, Sir Peter Parker, who was named as chief mourner over the wishes of another rival, the Prince of Wales. Pitt and Hawkesbury were responsible for this decision, which sought national confidence by emphasizing the notion that the Royal Navy itself, and the naval command, were the heirs to Nelson's genius. The government, it is important to understand, was not simply interested in fanning the fires of a generalized naval patriotism, but rather sought a symbolic goal that firmly located the achievement of Trafalgar in relationship to the naval administration. The displacement of Nelson's family in the procession served this purpose.

The contest over the position of chief mourner was followed by the press and so contemporaries were aware of its significance. An even greater level of attention was paid to another naval symbol and the place that it would occupy in the funerary proceedings. This was the crew of the *Victory* – around whom great popular expectations eventually developed. Considerable curiosity attended this crew, primarily because of the paradoxical relationship the Georgian public had with 'Jack Tar' – the common British seaman. Although they were heroic figures, British seamen were viewed by elite and middling ranks as a disturbing and frequently threatening plebeian element. Great fascination, then, surrounded the crew of the *Victory* as it participated in the mourning rituals, particularly when the tars proved capable of the sensibility in which elite opinion placed such importance. This had already been the case at the lying-in-state at Greenwich. Arriving at the close of the last afternoon

to spend quiet moments with their commander's body, the sailors' visit appealed to contemporaries, revealing as it did their susceptibility to the ascendant emotional conventions of polite society. Hopes that the funeral itself would provide similarly appealing incidents explain why the public rallied so strongly to the idea that the crew be assigned a central role in the ceremony. In the end, they marched in two places in the procession – forty-eight of them (one for each year of Nelson's life) marching alongside the Greenwich Pensioners, and a smaller group drawing up the procession into the cathedral with the colours of the *Victory*. But this was taken as disappointing in some quarters, given that many had called for the crew to draw the funeral car itself, or march directly behind the body, or act as pallbearers into the cathedral.

Nelson's body and the funeral car that bore it, the chief mourner, and the crew of the *Victory* were the most symbolically charged elements of the procession from Whitehall to St Paul's. But they shared that processional space with a cavalcade that included innumerable elements, most of which were called for by the esoteric demands of the heraldic form. Close behind the chief mourner was the private coach of Lord Nelson 'empty – with its blinds drawn up'. And it was but one of 106 carriages that participated in the procession. Many of these were required to carry the aristocrats who had decided to attend. Marching in ascending order by rank, these gentlemen, esquires, baronets, barons, viscounts, earls, marquises, dukes and royal princes preceded the coffin. While detachments of Volunteers kept the crowd of 20,000–30,000 at bay, the army regiments quartered near London who had served in the Egyptian campaign were honoured with places in the procession itself. A deputation from the City greeted the procession at Temple Bar, and – as had been arranged by royal warrant – the Lord Mayor, anxious not to lose his place in future state ceremonials, joined the procession in the place of honour alongside the chief mourner. It took two hours for this massive procession – which had left the Admiralty at 10.30 a.m. – fully to enter St Paul's, and at 4 p.m. the funeral service began.

Once inside the confines of the cathedral, it might be thought that spectacle would have given way to liturgy, but – in the reportage of the event, at least – this was not the case. For this vast assemblage of the socially significant, attendance at the cathedral was a statement of their own centrality to the British state. Both attendance and the warmth of the crowd to arriving notables were keenly noted. In this context, there remained opportunities for associational popularity to be dramatically achieved – opportunities taken, not least, by two of the sons of George III. The Prince of Wales, as noted earlier, had twice been

A fragment of the Union flag that covered Nelson's coffin at his funeral, 1805 (cat. no. 296).

foiled in his efforts to benefit from Nelson's posthumous fame. He had been denied the role of chief mourner and he had been pre-empted by the Lord Mayor in the funeral procession. It was only at the cathedral that he was finally able to identify himself with the dead hero. When the crew of the *Victory* came to the communion rail, the Prince specifically instructed that they be 'brought as near to the grave as possible'. By this gesture the Prince both asserted his place as a director of the drama and a sympathizer with the popular wishes circulating around the crew. On seeing his wish carried out, he was affectingly moved to tears. Since his younger brother, the Duke of York, was importantly engaged in the marshalling of military components of the procession, it remained only for his other brother, the Duke of Clarence, to assert a place for himself in the retelling of the day's events. This, in fact, he had already achieved, when the crew of the *Victory* had arrived at the cathedral itself. Clarence had sought them out, and – in an act of considerable condescension – tearfully shook their hands in front of the assembled crowd. The royal princes were not alone in their effort to invest Nelson's funeral with the necessary element of singularity. Even as precedent-bound a person as Sir Isaac Heard, Garter King of Arms, violated the protocol when reading Nelson's titles out over the grave by adding a line about Nelson 'dying in the moment of victory'. And the sailors of the *Victory*, perhaps

responding to the desires that accompanied their presence, tore souvenir scraps of the ensign for themselves before they cast it into the crypt.

The following Sunday, the funeral car was escorted to Greenwich Hospital by the Royal Westminster Volunteers. Greeted by Lord Hood, it was placed in the Painted Hall, and opened to public display. In the years immediately after Trafalgar, Greenwich remained what it had become during the period of the funerary pageant – one of the central memorial sites to Nelson. It had its rivals though – rivals created by the intensive effort to memorialize Nelson in diverse parts of Britain and the Empire. Efforts to construct monuments to Nelson began on receipt of news of Trafalgar. Before the month was out, projects were underway in Liverpool, Edinburgh and Bristol. The years immediately after witnessed a spate of Nelson monuments erected in provincial and imperial locations. So extensive was this impulse that the sculptor Richard Westmacott eventually found himself responsible for three monuments to Nelson erected by 1813 – in Birmingham, Bridgetown, Barbados, and Liverpool.[1] Much of the impetus for these projects came from urban centres wishing to impress themselves (and their compatriots) with their sense of national purpose. To these groups, lasting monuments and columns were suitable displays of local attachment to the national community.[2] Voices were raised elsewhere, though, suggesting various alternative forms of 'living memorials'. Donations to the Patriotic Fund (which dispensed financial assistance to the families of disabled and deceased soldiers and seamen) and the Marine Society (which educated and recruited young men for the naval profession) were frequently suggested in this fashion. Similarly functional was the sylvan memorial suggested by one country gentleman. It proposed that an attempt be made to drain wasteland, where oak trees spelling out the name of Nelson and his victories would later be planted. A national memorial, it would also assist in national defence – the oak being intended for later use in the construction of naval vessels.

When the Napoleonic War ended in 1815, the wish to construct triumphant campaign-concluding memorials was high, and the government attempted to lead the way in the construction of a national memorial. But a wave of proposals between 1814 and 1818 came to nothing, in part because of fundamental disagreements over expense, purpose and form. Perhaps the strongest idea advanced at the time was for a joint monument to the Army and the Navy – the project that eventually became Marble Arch.[3] The original intention was for a national monument that commemorated Nelson and Trafalgar on one side, Wellington and Waterloo on the other. However, parliamentary and public enthusiasm for this project waned considerably once it became attached to the personal ambitions of George IV. By the 1820s, the prince who had been rebuffed at Nelson's funeral was now a king engaged in a series of ambitious and expensive royal building projects. Construction of the arch began, with the intention that it serve as the gateway to a newly renovated Buckingham Palace. Parliamentary resistance to the mounting expense of the King's projects meant that, when George IV died

in 1830, the plans for the arch were radically curtailed and it was consequently divested of its significance as a national monument to Waterloo and Trafalgar.[4] In the same year, though, a long-standing royal project intended to create a square at Charing Cross was completed and renamed 'Trafalgar Square' by an act of William IV. It only remained for a monument to the hero of that battle to be constructed, a project which was launched in 1838, and completed in 1843.[5]

It is interesting, in this sense, to compare the intense desire to construct memorials to Nelson with the desultory nature of the observance of the anniversary of Trafalgar in the years immediately following. During the period of the Revolutionary and Napoleonic Wars, battle anniversaries were primarily celebrated by the officers of the regiments or squadrons involved, or by private gentlemen's clubs and the City livery companies. Occasionally constructed memorials – like that in Birmingham – would be dedicated on a date appropriately proximate to the anniversary of Trafalgar, but it was not until the late Victorian period that Trafalgar Day came to be celebrated on anything approaching a regular basis. The nature of its late-century revival, though, once again reveals the degree to which political considerations were paramount to projects in naval patriotism. For the revived celebration of Trafalgar Day in the 1890s was a deliberate tactic of the Navy League – a special-interest group keen on maximizing imperial naval armament.[6] The 100th anniversary of the battle was celebrated not as the centenary of Trafalgar, but rather as the 'Nelson Centenary', a substitution required by the existence of the new *Entente Cordiale* with France, and a useful indicator of the larger way in which the entire manner of remembrance in both 1905 and 1805 was subordinated to contemporary impulses.

Napoleon's Last Journey

CHRISTOPHER WOODWARD

A MONTH AFTER WATERLOO Napoleon surrendered to the British, handing himself over to Captain Maitland of the *Bellerophon* on the coast of Brittany. A week later the warship sailed into Brixham in Devon. The people of this small port were the first in Britain to discover that the country's greatest enemy had been captured.

Sitting on the quay were three schoolboys, John Smart and Charlie and Dick Puddlecombe.[1] They had been given an extra week's holiday to celebrate the victory. To their generation Napoleon was 'Boney': 'Limb from limb he'll tear you, just as pussy tears a mouse', parents sang to children who refused to go to sleep.

As soon as the *Bellerophon* anchored the three boys joined a local baker rowing out with fresh loaves of bread to sell to the sailors but an officer shouted: 'Sheer off. No boats allowed here . . . if you don't let go I'll sink you'. As they rowed away, however, a sailor in one of the lower gun ports dropped a small black bottle into the water. Inside was a piece of paper bearing the words: 'We have got Bonaparte on board.'

The boys told the town and within hours the ship was surrounded by boats. At three o'clock the enemy appeared on deck, recalled Smart. 'He took off his hat . . . and bowed to the people, who took off their hats and shouted "Hooray!"'. 'How curious these English are,' remarked Napoleon.[2]

The *Bellerophon with Napoleon Aboard at Plymouth (26 July–4 August 1815)*, by John James Chalon (1778–1854).
National Maritime Museum, London; BHC3227.

Napoleon's Tomb, 1821, by Emile-Jean-Horace Vernet (1789–1863). Wallace Collection, London; P575.

Two days later Maitland sailed to Plymouth to join the Commander of the Channel Fleet, Admiral Lord Keith. There – by Maitland's count – a thousand small boats put to sea, each with at least eight sightseers on board, a scene depicted by J-L. Chalons. Several drowned in the mêlée. 'I am worried to death with idle folk coming, even from Glasgow, to see him,' the Admiral wrote to his daughter. 'There is no nation so foolish as we are.'

Keith told the Emperor that the British government had chosen to exile him to St Helena. 'Go to St Helena – no! – no! I prefer death,' he replied.[3] On 7 August he was transferred to the *Northumberland* for his last journey. Nine weeks later the ship dropped anchor at St Helena. General Gourgaud, one of the three French generals who accompanied Napoleon, wrote in his private journal: 'I was in the Emperor's cabin as we approached the island. When he saw it, he exclaimed, "It's not an attractive place. I should have done better to remain in Egypt. By now, I should be Emperor of the East."'[4]

Why St Helena? Lord Liverpool, the Prime Minister, summarized the view of the Admiralty:

> The situation is particularly healthy. There is only one place in the circuit of the island where ships can anchor . . . At such a distance and in such a place, all intrigue would be impossible; and, being withdrawn so far from the European world, he would very soon be forgotten.[5]

The island of bare volcanic rock is 5000 miles from Europe, 1800 miles from Brazil and 1200 miles from Africa. As Julia Blackburn begins her beautiful memoir of a visit, 'St Helena is further away from anywhere than anywhere else in all the world'.[6] Few people could picture its appearance in 1815 but for the next six years until Napoleon's death on 5 May 1821 it became the world's most famous small island. It was the site of the Emperor's last victory: a posthumous conquest over the imagination of posterity.[7]

From the day of his arrival Napoleon had two projects. The

first was to persuade the allied powers to grant his release. He failed. The second was to construct an image of himself for future generations of Frenchmen. To one of his retinue he said, 'If Jesus Christ had not died on the cross, He would never have been worshipped as a God.' And, later: 'Thanks to my martyrdom, [my son] will get back the crown.'[8] The tens of thousands of words he dictated presented him as an egalitarian of liberal and moderate politics. The will he wrote three weeks before he died was a masterpiece of succinct rhetoric, with its famous plea: 'I am dying prematurely murdered by the English oligarchy and its hired assassins . . . I wish my ashes to rest near the banks of the Seine in the midst of the French people I have so dearly loved.'

News of his death reached Paris on 5 July 1821. A few days later Horace Vernet began *The Tomb of Napoleon*. The Emperor's hat and sword are placed on a humble grave dug on a storm-lashed rock; the marshals who died in the Empire's battles wait for him in the clouds.

In Sir Walter Scott's biography of 1827 Napoleon died during a 'hurricane'. In William Hazlitt's biography three years later, he breathed his last during 'a gale [which] uprooted all the plantations of gum-trees'. With each successive book the weather got worse. 'A fearful tempest broke over St Helena, and this fatal island seemed on the verge of being swallowed up by the sea,' wrote one Frenchman in the 1850s. At the beginning of the last century a historian studied the logbooks of the Royal Naval squadron which guarded the island. The weather on the night of 5 May 1821 was noted as 'fine and moderate', with an occasional squall. But in the imaginations of friends and enemies Napoleon could not breathe his last in 'fine and moderate' weather.

Ever since Napoleon's death there have been two St Helenas. In actuality, St Helena was an exposed and rocky tropical island of forty-seven square miles where 3000 people worked in agriculture and trade, planting gum trees and provisioning ships. In the imagination of Europe there is a second St Helena: a lonely and utterly desolate rock in the ocean, dominated by a single figure.

In France in the 1830s and 1840s the two most potent themes in the symbolic representation of Napoleon on St Helena were as Prometheus on the rock – 'They have opened the side of the new Prometheus / The vulture of Albion slowly drinks his blood', as Edgar Quinet wrote in 1835 – and as Christ, awaiting resurrection from the tomb. A popular song was explicit:

> Jesus, by his strength
> Saved the pagan, lost in sin,
> Napoleon saved France;
> Like Jesus he was sold

> After odious sufferings,
> Jesus died on the cross:
> Napoleon at St Helena,
> Has suffered like Jesus.[9]

In 1840 Napoleon's coffin was dug up and returned to France and displayed in the Church of Les Invalides. Six hundred thousand people watched on the last day of the procession, with shouts of '*Vive l'Empereur*' and '*À bas les Anglais!*' His son died as a young man but in 1851 his nephew became Emperor Napoleon III by the vote of the French people. To millions, he was the living embodiment of a memory.

There might have been no second Empire if the first had not ended in martyrdom on St Helena. In 1858 Napoleon III bought from the British government seventeen hectares of land on the island containing his uncle's house and tomb, with a veteran of Waterloo as the first custodian of the shrine. It was rumoured that the American showman P. T. Barnum was about to make a rival bid.

The focus of this essay is on how the British perceived the captivity. No country has been so fascinated by an arch-enemy as the British have been by Napoleon. 'More has been written about Napoleon Bonaparte and his era than any other figure who has ever lived'[10] and no episode in his life has been the subject of such intense scrutiny as the six years of his imprisonment.

For all but the first few months Napoleon lived at Longwood, a single-storey wooden house on a high, windy plateau. 'Here, my dear Las Cases,' he told his secretary six months after arriving, 'you and I already belong to the other world; we are conversing in the Elysian Fields.' It is tempting to picture the last six years as a kind of epilogue to the story of Napoleon, in which the man himself reflected on an epic life from an existence lived in a kind of suspension. On 6 May 1817 General Gourgaud wrote in his journal: 'If he wakes up during the night, he can never go off to sleep again, but turns over in his mind all his mistakes, and compares his present position with the past. Yes, the Emperor is very unhappy.' Napoleon's project that day was to calculate the flow of water in the River Nile but he broke off to ask his retinue at which point in his life he had been happiest. To one courtier it was when he was made First Consul; to a second it was his marriage; to a third, the birth of his son. He was most happy 'after my welcome in Italy in 1796', Napoleon replied. 'What enthusiasm! What cries of "Long live the Liberator of Italy!" At twenty-five years of age! From that time, I foresaw what I could become. I saw the world floating under me, as if I were borne on air.' He stopped and sang an Italian melody.

There are many such episodes in the journals and for five days in a row in June 1816 Gourgaud wrote a single yawning word: 'Ennui.' The Emperor did succumb to days of depression, and endlessly revisited the past. However, this view of the captivity – as an epilogue to the drama – is only possible because we know that Napoleon fell ill and died at the age of fifty-two. To his friends and enemies after Waterloo – and, above all, to the captive himself – there was no reason to think that St Helena would be the final scene. Why should it be? He was forty-six years old, had returned from exile once and inspired a greater devotion in his soldiers than had any general since Alexander the Great.

In Paris the Duc de Richelieu, Chief Minister to Louis XVIII, was haunted by the possibility of a second escape. Were empty barrels leaving Longwood checked? he wrote to the French Commissioner at St Helena. A succession of genuine plots to rescue the Emperor were discovered. In Brazil Colonel Latapie prepared a steamboat but was arrested. In Texas 400 exiled soldiers dug the streets of a town to be named the Champs d'Asile, conceived as a capital for a new Napoleonic Empire. The most remarkable plan was the story of the submarine revealed by Tom Pocock in *The Terror before Trafalgar* (2002). During the war the British government had funded the construction of a prototype submarine in a boatyard on the Thames at Wallingford, Oxfordshire. When the war ended so did the funding and the project's leader sold the vessel to French Bonapartists. In the winter of 1820 the submarine sailed down the Thames to a rendezvous with a merchant ship, to be transported to the South Atlantic and launched off the coast of St Helena. It passed London Bridge but was spotted and destroyed.

Yet Napoleon himself gave no serious consideration to possibilities of escape. He did not wish to live as a fugitive in the deserts of Texas. He placed his hopes for release on the monarchs of Russia, Austria and Prussia – each of whom had been an ally at one time or another – or on public and political opinion in Britain. It is for this reason that his actions on St Helena were determined by how they would be perceived 5000 miles and two months' sailing away.

From the earliest days of his captivity he recognized that he had to be perceived as a victim by the British public, whose celebrated respect for the underdog had been so visible at Brixham and Plymouth. The problem was that he was not a victim. The Duke of Wellington had rejected the Prussian demand to shoot him after Waterloo. The government had chosen St Helena – as opposed to Malta, Gibraltar or fortresses in Britain itself – precisely because its isolation and its impregnable coastline would allow Napoleon to live with the freedom of a country gentleman. It commissioned a large neo-classical villa which was prefabricated in Britain and shipped to the island, with interiors

furnished and decorated by George Bullock, one of the most fashionable and expensive cabinet makers in London. The household would have the best of British luxury manufactures, with Wedgwood porcelain and a Broadwood piano. In deciding the Emperor's accommodation Lord Bathurst, Secretary of State for War and the Colonies, instructed the Governor to 'look first to the security of his person, Secondly to his Comfort . . . and lastly to the Expense'.[11]

Why, then, did Europe imagine Napoleon in a ramshackle bungalow exposed to wind and rain and infested by rats? His tactics were to be seen not to be enjoying the privileges granted by the new government and at the same time to seize any opportunity to present his exile as a brutal imprisonment and the Governor Sir Hudson Lowe as a petty, unchivalrous gaoler. The new house was a typical example. At first he refused the offer because it would indicate to his followers an acceptance of his fate. Later, when the house was constructed, he would not live there because the garden was encircled by a railing. To the Governor every English country house was surrounded by railings. To the French it was an 'iron cage'. He stayed in the old house, with its leaking roof and plague of rats.

When the Governor ordered a reduction in household expenditure Napoleon responded that he would sell his imperial silver to feed the servants and break up his own bed for firewood. Neither was necessary but each propaganda gesture was amplified and distorted in the liberal press in Britain and in Parliament. He told one visitor to Longwood, Lord Amherst, an Ambassador returning from the East, that through Sir Hudson Lowe's actions, 'You have placed on my head, as it was with Jesus Christ, a crown of thorns, and by so doing, you have won me many partisans.'[12]

But how did the prisoner communicate? First, St Helena was less remote than its geographical position might suggest. Every British ship on the journey from China or the Indies stopped there to take on water, and with little else to do passengers would climb to the plateau hoping to catch a glimpse of Napoleon. William Makepeace Thackeray was a boy of six when his ship put in to St Helena and his servant took him to Longwood: 'We saw a man walking . . . "That is he" said the black servant "That is Bonaparte, he eats three sheep every day, and all the children he can lay his hands on".' One indication of the volume of traffic at St Helena in the years before the Suez Canal is a visitors' book for Napoleon's tomb kept at the National Army Museum, London. It begins in February 1836 and by the end of the year more than 4000 people had signed their names.

Napoleon granted interviews to men – such as Lord Amherst – whom he imagined would be listened to in London. Many wrote accounts of their visits, and the majority of these describe

This view of Longwood is a print after watercolour by Louis Marchand, who was Napoleon's valet on St Helena, 1815–21, and an amateur artist. Napoleon is shown in his green uniform. Private collection.

how they are disappointed by their first sight of a short, fat and pale man but are soon magnetized by his intelligence, knowledge and the intensity of his personal attention. The French Commissioner advised Lowe not to permit a single stranger to visit Longwood, because so many left as devotees who protested about his captivity as soon as they reached Europe. The Duc de Richelieu declared, 'This devil of a man exercises an astonishing seduction on all those approach him, witness the crew of the *Northumberland* . . . if the same troops remain on guard for a long time, they will become his supporters.'[13]

A prominent example of a British soldier who converted to Napoleon's cause was Barry O'Meara, the surgeon of the *Bellerophon*. He was chosen to go to St Helena as the Emperor's personal doctor and lived at Longwood until he was expelled by Lowe, on suspicion that he had 'gone native'. It is accepted that not only did O'Meara smuggle letters of protest off the island but that he colluded with his patient in inventing a diagnosis of a dangerous illness of the liver caused by its unhealthy climate.

Napoleon had a genius for understanding what the public wished to read about him. The first of a number of best-selling books was published in 1816 by William Warden, surgeon on the *Northumberland*, who wrote down the Emperor's conversations on the journey. His retinue protested that the book was below the Emperor's dignity: 'Who cares on which sofa you sit and how?' Napoleon agreed that the book was gossipy and inaccurate. But, he continued, the public like to know what a great man 'eats or drinks and are more interested in such nonsense than in studying his good and bad qualities, but as the public is like this we must cater to it and tell it what it wants to be told'. Such images, he recognized, humanized him in the eyes of the British public after fifteen years in which he had been caricatured as a monster.[14]

Napoleon's policy on St Helena was based upon his belief in the sympathy of many British people. In her study of national identity during this period, *Britons: Forging the Nation, 1707–1837*, Linda Colley showed how the resistance to Revolutionary and

Napoleonic France was a phenomenon of genuine patriotism unprecedented in European history. Four hundred thousand men volunteered for the militia in a country which fifty years before had collapsed in the face of Bonnie Prince Charlie's ragged invasion. What was also unprecedented was to the extent to which Napoleon – as opposed to the nation he led – was personalized as the enemy.

At first, therefore, it can seem surprising that Napoleon surrendered to the *Bellerophon* hoping to win over the British people and its rulers. 'London would have been a great opportunity for me', he told Gourgaud at the beginning of his captivity. 'I would have been welcomed there in triumph; all the populace would have been on my side, and my own reasoning would have convinced the Greys and the Grenvilles [leaders of sections of the Whig party].'[15] Why did he place such weight on the working populace and the parliamentary Opposition?

In his early career he had been a hero for many British people, the majority of whom had welcomed the early aspirations of the French Revolution. After his victories in Italy in 1796–97 he was compared by many Whigs and Radicals to George Washington, and welcomed as a general who would end the excesses of the Revolution but preserve its achievements. At the same time he was the liberator of the people of countries such as Italy from despotism and superstition. The expedition to Egypt, for example, was acclaimed by British radicals as the introduction of the Enlightenment to the East. On 18 October 1799 the young poet Robert Southey wrote to the chemist Humphry Davy to share his excitement at General Massena's victories in central Europe and Bonaparte's campaign in Egypt: 'Massena, Buonaparte, Switzerland, Italy, Holland, Egypt, all at once! The very spring-tide of fortune! It was a dose of gaseous oxide for me, whose powerful delight still endures.'[16] 'Gaseous oxide' was an invention of Davy's which Southey had tried that summer and described: 'It made me laugh and tingle in every toe and finger tip. Davy has actually invented a new pleasure, for which language has no name.'[17] The implication is that no existing words could do justice to the exhilarating impact of Napoleon, a handsome young man who was not only the greatest general since antiquity but a liberator of the oppressed, a patron of artists and scientists and an admirer of Rousseau.

During the Peace of Amiens, 5000 English arrived in Paris and police spies reported that the majority were admirers of the First Consul. However, the majority of these – most prominently Charles James Fox – returned disillusioned by their discovery at first hand of his taste for dictatorship at home and war abroad. Southey called him a 'great rascal' and by 1815 was a stout Tory and Poet Laureate. When news of Waterloo reached the Lakes he

and his friend Wordsworth climbed Skiddaw with a cauldron of rum punch and sang 'God Save the King!'

By 1815 very few Britons still retained their respect for Napoleon although the Britons who were profoundly dejected by the news of Waterloo included men as varied as William Hazlitt, Lord Grey, the future Prime Minister; Sir Robert Wilson, the cavalry general; and the 10th Duke of Hamilton, the premier peer of Scotland. British Bonapartism is a complex subject,[18] although it is worth noting that none of these men was a traitor: 'He has been a Héros de Roman of mine – on the Continent; I don't want him here,' wrote another admirer, Lord Byron, in his diary on 17 November 1813. However, the conclusive victory of Waterloo began a new chapter in British attitudes to Napoleon. Captain Maitland of the *Bellerophon* asked his war-hardened sailors what they thought of an enemy who was now their captive: 'Well, they may abuse that man as much as they please; but if the people of England knew him as well as we do, they would not hurt a hair of his head.'[19]

Napoleon had always charmed the rank and file but he also understood the volatility of the wider public who demanded reform in the economic depression after 1815; the British newspapers had been translated for him ever since he was First Consul. Arriving at St Helena he received *The Times*, which in 1818 detailed how a false rumour of his escape had been applauded by spontaneous illuminations in the City of London. *The Times* supported the Tories but Lowe and his master Bathurst did prevent Napoleon reading anti-government publications; he relied upon his doctor O'Meara to slip him copies of the Whig newspaper the *Morning Chronicle*. To Napoleon, a change of ministry was a more immediate hope of release than popular discontent, however.

Many members of the Whig Opposition continued the view of Charles James Fox, who had died in 1806, that it was not the business of Britain to impose a ruler on a foreign country. More than eighty MPs voted against the decision to fight Napoleon after his return from Elba: Trafalgar had saved Britain from invasion, it was argued, but Waterloo only decided whether it was a Bourbon or a Bonaparte who sat in the Tuileries. Three days after the news of the battle the most trenchant representative of the anti-war Whigs, Samuel Whitbread MP, cut his throat. 'The world will point and sniff at me. The populace will pull down my house,' he told a friend as they passed scenes of jubilation on Piccadilly the night before his suicide.[20] It is now thought that Whitbread killed himself because of ill health and financial losses, and that his sudden recognition of being at odds with his own country was only a catalyst. But Napoleon was not to know this when the news came to the *Bellerophon*.

During his exile on St Helena Napoleon received more than 1000 books and pamphlets from Lord and Lady Holland, in addition to daisy seeds for Longwood and prune jam from the gardens at Holland House in Kensington. Holland was the nephew and spiritual heir of Fox and in Parliament the most prominent critic of the government's policy. It was Holland who received clandestine news from the island and accused the government of a slow, underhand assassination of Napoleon by incarcerating him on an unhealthy desert island. It was Holland who welcomed O'Meara to salons at Holland House after his expulsion. In the gardens he mounted a bronze bust by Canova of Napoleon as a heroic First Consul. Inscribed on the pedestal were lines from *The Aeneid*, which he translated elsewhere as:

> He is not dead, he breathes the air
> In lands beyond the deep!
> Some distant sea-girt island, where
> Harsh men the hero keep.

In the years up to 1815 the Whigs' criticism of the Duke of Wellington's campaigns in Spain and France had been unpopular in Britain. However, the handling of the captive became a new cause with which to attack the ministry of 'harsh men' – a cause which was humane, chivalrous and popular. Its significance to Napoleon's last journey is that his exile on St Helena was never a *fait accompli* but, rather, a question of volatile debate. Napoleon's immediate hope for release was that Holland would become Prime Minister; in France the possibility of Holland's appointment was the Duc de Richelieu's greatest fear.

A more belligerent Bonapartist was Admiral Lord Cochrane, one of the great naval heroes of the war. Yet just three years after Waterloo he proposed to take Napoleon from St Helena and establish him as Emperor of South America. Cochrane is an example of how a brave and patriotic but quarrelsome and contrary Briton could become so excluded by the Establishment as to see superior virtues in its greatest enemy. During his career he quarrelled with the Admiralty over prize-money, tactics and recognition. He also became a radical MP, opposing corruption in the Navy. In 1814 he was sentenced to prison after a Stock Exchange scandal, a disgrace that he believed to have been a conspiracy by his enemies in the Admiralty and Parliament. Four years later he left Britain to command the navy of Chile in its war of liberation from Spanish rule, warning Parliament that if it did not reform itself it would be overthrown by the people. When he sailed – recalled Lady Cochrane – it was 'with the intention of making for St Helena, begging for an interview, and ascertaining his Majesty's wishes as regarded placing him on the throne of South America'. During the journey, however, they received news of setbacks in the war in Chile and there was no time to call at St Helena.

British Napoleonists were outsiders, whether by personality, background or a change in circumstances. Their support of Napoleon was more a protest against the Establishment than a call for action, although some of the many people who turned their back on England during this period found a new and more fruitful cause in the wars of liberation in South America and Greece. Lord Byron is the leading example of the outsider who became a Napoleonist, choosing to travel into exile on the Continent in 1816 in a replica of the Emperor's carriage. On 3 March 1820 he wrote from Italy to his friend John Cam Hobhouse, a radical who had been imprisoned in Newgate because of his attack in print on the Prince Regent: 'Brummell – at Calais – Scrope at Bruges [his friends Beau Brummell and Scrope Davies had each fled to the Continent to escape gambling debts] – Buonaparte at St Helena – you in – your new apartments – and I at Ravenna – only think so many great men!'

Ironic, of course, but exiles identified with St Helena – above all, Romantics. Exile was not the only element of Napoleon's captivity that appealed to a movement to which concepts of individualism, persecution, loneliness and flawed genius were so fundamental. St Helena was a dramatic backdrop to paintings by J. M. W. Turner and James Ward, but the artist who became obsessed with Napoleon's rise and fall was Benjamin Robert Haydon. In contrast to Byron – a protégé of Lord Holland in politics – he was a Tory and believed that Napoleon should have been executed for his escape from Elba. To Haydon, however, Napoleon in exile was a character above and beyond politics, time and place. In his journal he wrote about painting heroes: 'Never make Heroes or great characters with the peculiar characteristic of any Nation; they belong to Human Nature.'[21] He began a series of more than forty paintings in which he depicted Napoleon 'musing' in scenes from the pyramids to St Helena. In that same entry he compared his own challenges as an artist to that of his hero: 'A man who has a fixed purpose to which he devotes his powers is invulnerable. Melancholy and misfortune, vice & indolence may surround and beat on him like the waves of the sea [on] a solid rock that juts out into its bosom'. He was writing in 1812, three years before Napoleon's exile; the government could not have chosen a place of exile more inviting to the Romantic imagination than St Helena.

In 1846 Haydon killed himself. That April he hired exhibition space at the Egyptian Hall on Piccadilly to exhibit his canvasses of historical scenes but few people came and no pictures were sold. It was a final blow for a man who had failed to build on his youthful promise as a painter of epic scenes for the edification of the British public. An article published in 2003 suggested that his identification with the flawed, selfish and tragic genius of Napoleon was an element in his suicide on 22 June.[22] In an adjacent room at the Hall P. T. Barnum presented the phenomenon of the dwarf Tom Thumb, who performed impersonations to 12,000 people a week. The title of his most popular act? 'Napoleon Musing on St Helena'. To Haydon the thunderous applause in the adjacent room must have seemed a mockery of everything he had aspired to in his failed career.

Haydon is an extreme illustration of how, in the decades after Napoleon's death in 1821, he became a character whose human interest was not limited by the circumstances of history. When in 1900 Lord Rosebery wrote one of the greatest of the books on St Helena, *The Last Phase*, he concluded that Napoleon was 'the great human problem' and made an observation which explains more than any other the enduring fascination of Napoleon to men of aspiration: 'he enlarged indefinitely the limits of human conception and human possibility'.[23]

It was the years on St Helena which humanized Napoleon in the eyes of the British. As General Bonaparte and First Consul he was a dazzling, enigmatic figure. As Emperor 'he ceased to be human', in Rosebery's words. As the denizen of Longwood he was a man who slept badly, patched up quarrels in the household, struggled to assemble an ice-making machine and sang nursery rhymes to the children of his retinue while talking sadly of his son. He took up gardening, news that appealed to the British; even Lord Bathurst asked if there were any plants that he would like.

News of his death reached London on 4 July, and Paris a day later. The French Minister of Foreign Affairs told his Ambassador in London: 'We see, from the English newspapers, that this event has caused more of a sensation in England than in France.'[24] The following year the royalist Comte de Chateaubriand was appointed the new Ambassador, 'I found that great city immersed in the recollection of Bonaparte: the people had passed from the vilification of "Nick" to a stupid enthusiasm. Memoirs of Bonaparte swarmed; his bust adorned every chimney-piece; his engravings shone in the windows of the picture-dealers.'[25]

Today, each ship calling at St Helena takes pilgrims to the empty tomb. Willows planted from twigs snapped off the trees over the grave flourish across the world, from the courtyard of Les Invalides and the creeks of Australia to the churchyard at Dyrham, near Bath, under which a veteran of Waterloo named Colonel Blathwayt chose to be buried. There will always be the St Helena of Napoleonic legend, 'a catafalque of rock' which saw the last days of a man who was – in the words of Chateaubriand, although an enemy – 'the mightiest breath of life which ever animated human clay'.

The Tomb of Bonaparte Who was Interr'd at his own request under some Willow Trees near a Spring from which | he daily sent for the Water used at his Table | Died May 5 1821, undated, by Captain Frederick Marryat.
National Army Museum, London; 9207-290.

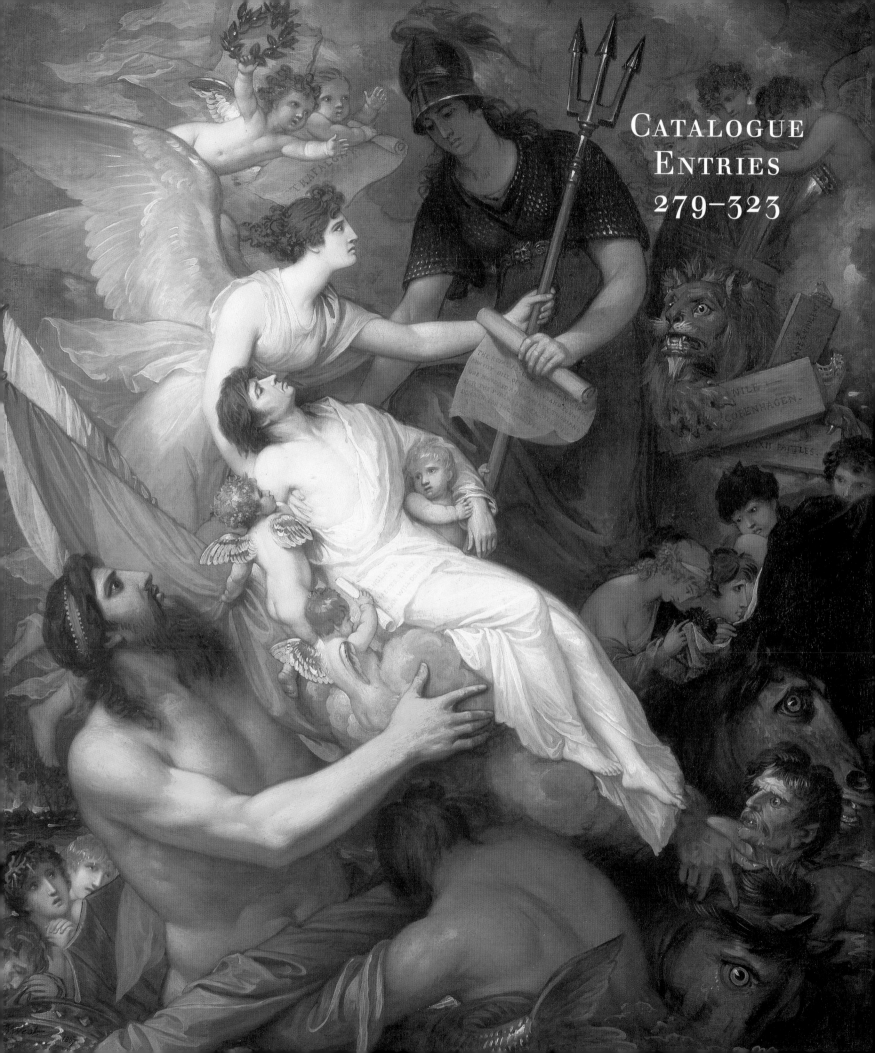

Turner's 'Nelson' sketchbook contains preparatory drawings for the first of his two paintings of Trafalgar, shown in his own gallery in 1806 and, after further work, at the British Institution in 1808. This open page fairly closely foreshadows the finished painting and is based on his deck study of *Victory* (cat. no. 280). She is on the left with a group including the fallen Nelson lightly sketched in by her mainmast. The French 74-gun *Redoutable*, from whose mizzen top Nelson was shot by a sniper, is on the right.   PvdM

279. Study for *The Battle of Trafalgar, as seen from the mizen starboard shrouds of the 'Victory'* in the 'Nelson' sketchbook, *c.* 1805
Joseph Mallord William Turner (1775–1851)
Pencil on paper
114 x 184mm
Provenance: bequeathed by the artist, 1856
Tate, London; D05842 (Finberg no. LXXXIX.26.a)

280. The *Victory*, 1805
Joseph Mallord William Turner (1775–1851)
Pencil on paper
469 x 756mm
Provenance: bequeathed by the artist, 1856
Tate, London; D08243 (Finberg no. CXX.c)

Turner saw *Victory* soon after she arrived off Sheerness with Nelson's body and made pencil notes of her in a small sketchbook. This is one of two larger deck studies which he may have done later at Chatham Dockyard since the other, in ink and wash, shows Captain Hardy's cabin knocked out for refit. The spot where Nelson fell is in the foreground: the viewpoint, looking forward from the break of the poop,

is the one Turner adopted in his 1806–8 painting of *The Battle of Trafalgar, as seen from the mizen starboard shrouds of the 'Victory'* (Tate). PvdM

281. The *Victory* coming up the Channel with the body of Nelson (*c.* 1806–8)

Joseph Mallord William Turner (1775–1851)
Pen and ink and watercolour on paper
200 x 285mm
Provenance: bequeathed by Henry Vaughan, 1900
Tate, London; D08183 (Finberg no. CXVIII.e)

This drawing is a more vigorous treatment of a stately oil of 1806, '*Victory' returning from Trafalgar* (Yale Center for British Art). It was intended for engraving in Turner's *Liber Studiorum* but in the end not included. Both versions pay tribute to Nelson and his flagship by showing *Victory* in three positions (not three different ships) with the distant English coast beyond. This was a traditional formula of contemporary ship portraiture but not one otherwise used by Turner and he presumably consciously adopted it to honour *Victory*, which was already a famous flagship by the time of Trafalgar – forty years after her launch. By contrasting her with the fishing boat getting clear in the foreground Turner also alludes to the humbler aspects of seafaring that underpinned Britain's dominance as a maritime power. PvdM

282. Smart ticket, 3 November 1805

Ink on paper
National Maritime Museum, London; ADL/T/16

This certificate is made out in the name of James Pool, a landsman who served in the *Royal Sovereign* at Trafalgar, as proof that his injury was sustained at sea (Pool's arm had to be amputated). These certificates allowed men to receive a pension from the Chatham Chest, the naval charitable fund set up after the defeat of the Spanish Armada in 1588, to which all seamen contributed sixpence a month from their wages. In 1814 the Chest was amalgamated with the Royal Hospital for Seamen at Greenwich, which also provided pensions and residential care for wounded veterans. The *Royal Sovereign*, as the flagship of Vice-Admiral Collingwood, was the first ship into action at Trafalgar; as a result she was one of the worst-hit vessels on the British side, suffering 141 men killed or wounded. AD

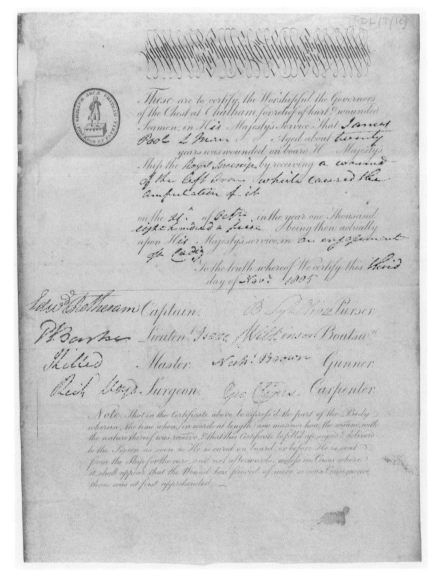

283. *JOHN BULL Exchanging NEWS with the CONTINENT*

[George Woodward], published 11 December 1805
    by S. W. Fores
Hand-coloured etching
229 x 346mm
National Maritime Museum, London; PAF4004

This satirical print indicates the importance to both sides, around the time of the Battles of Trafalgar and Austerlitz, of news bulletins and propaganda offensives. Napoleon and John Bull stand either side of the Channel on cliff-tops, the French side inscribed 'Falsehood', the British side 'Truth'. Against the numerous pamphlets issuing from Napoleon's side pronouncing French progress in the war, John Bull, shown as a plump newsboy, trumpets the news of Trafalgar and 'Total Defeat of the Combin'd Fleets of France and Spain'. In the distance is a naval battle, presumably Trafalgar relocated for the purposes of the print. If it suggests the importance to the war effort of rapid gathering and broadcasting of news, the print also indicates the perceived need for its selective editing: despite the crowing over the victory at Trafalgar, there is no mention anywhere of Nelson's death.   GQ

284. Decrès to Louis Napoleon,
    14 November 1805

Brown ink on paper
One sheet quarto
Provenance: presented 1955
National Maritime Museum, London; AGC/18/24

Days before the destruction of his fleet at Trafalgar, Napoleon had launched the most brilliant year of his career, forcing the Austrian army under General Mack to capitulate at Ulm. Louis Decrès, the French Minister of Marine, received the first report of Trafalgar by courier from Spain. Napoleon was still on campaign, marching towards Austerlitz and perhaps his greatest victory (in December 1805). Decrès therefore wrote to Louis Bonaparte, one of Napoleon's younger brothers, giving the bare outlines of Trafalgar. His major concern was how this should be presented to the French people, and he wanted to publish information in the *Moniteur*, France's official state newspaper. Louis's reply warned against releasing any information until orders were received from Napoleon himself. Further conscripts were then leaving the country for Austria, and he did not want the news to be general knowledge. Famously, the official French account eventually published in the *Moniteur* proclaimed a French victory – 'The English fleet is annihilated . . . our loss was trifling.'   AD

285. Lloyd's Patriotic Fund Certificate, 3 December 1805

Engraving

Lloyd's of London; Nelson Collection

On 3 December 1805 the Lloyd's Patriotic Fund Committee heard the official dispatches from the Battle of Trafalgar. As a result, they agreed that money from the fund would be given to all the wounded survivors.

Officers were to receive sums of between £25 and £100, depending on their rank and on the severity of their wounds. Men in the ranks would receive £40 if their wounds resulted in permanent disability or the loss of a limb, £20 if they were severely wounded and £10 if they were only slightly wounded. Dependants of the dead would be given financial aid 'as soon as their respective situations shall be made known to the committee'.

Each man who was eligible for relief received a certificate, on which his name and rank were handwritten. The certificate is headed with patriotic emblems and includes Collingwood's words 'every Individual appeared a HERO on whom the Glory of his Country depended'. This certificate was awarded to John Deal, one of the 121 casualties on the *Téméraire*.   DK

286. Report of the Battle of Trafalgar from the *Gazette de la Grande-Bretagne*, 8 November 1805

Published by John Lewis Cox, Son and Thomas Baylis

Bodleian Library, Oxford

The *Gazette de la Grande-Bretagne* was a propaganda newspaper, partially sponsored by the British government and distributed to the political elite in continental Europe. It was published in French, the *lingua franca* of European diplomacy and the aristocracy. Here it reports Nelson's victory at Trafalgar almost three weeks earlier, using large headline print, which was still rare. Reports such as this were usually translated from the official *London Gazette*.   SB

287. *EQUITY or a Sailor's PRAYER before BATTLE. Anecdote of the Battle of Trafalgar*

Anonymous, British, nineteenth century

Hand-coloured etching

248 x 350mm

National Maritime Museum, London; PAG8554

A post-Trafalgar satire showing a scene of the deck of a British vessel. It offers an unusually adversarial stance taken from the perspective of the lower-deck sailor. With cannon being prepared, the tar is shown on his knees at prayer. At

this, one of the officers remarks 'Why Starboard! how is this at prayers when the enemy is bearing down upon us; are you afraid of them?' 'Starboard' replies 'Afraid! – NO! I was only praying that the enemys shot may be distributed in the same proportion as the prize money, the greatest part among the Officers.' At one level the print characterizes the tar positively, drawing on stereotypical features attributed to him: his lack of religion, fearlessness, independence and quick wit. However, beneath the joke lies a darker point about the rift between the quarter- and lower decks, above all regarding prize-money and wages, which goes back to the 1797 mutinies at Spithead and the Nore.   GQ

288.   Patriotic Fund vases

The Patriotic Fund was founded at a meeting at Lloyd's Coffee House at the Royal Exchange, London, in July 1803, following the breakdown of the Peace of Amiens. The Fund set up a national subscription, strongly supported by Lloyd's members, which was used to vote money to those wounded in action, and to dependants of those killed, and also to give awards of merit in the form of money, silver and presentation swords. Between 1804 and 1809 sixty-six Patriotic Fund silver vases went to naval and military officers in recognition of distinguished services. Fifteen Patriotic Fund vases were awarded after the Battle of Trafalgar. Most were valued originally at £100, but there was also one larger £200 vase awarded posthumously, one £300 vase, and three magnificent £500 silver-gilt vases on additional plinths.

John Flaxman, the sculptor, produced the final design for the vases, which modified John Shaw's original prize-winning design. They were supplied by the Royal Goldsmiths, Rundell, Bridge and Rundell. The smaller versions have a depiction of Britannia holding Winged Victory in her hand on one side and Hercules slaying the Hydra on the other. All the vases are similar, and based on a classical Greek urn form, but they were crafted by various makers and have slight differences in the design details. They are all surmounted by a lion finial, and the presentation inscription usually appears on the shoulder of the vase.

1)   Patriotic Fund vase
to James Nicoll Morris
By Digby Scott and Benjamin Smith, London, 1806
Silver
National Maritime Museum, London; PLT0091

The Fund presented this £100 silver vase to James Nicoll Morris, captain of the *Colossus*, 'for his Meritorious Services in contributing to the Signal victory obtained over the Combined Fleets of France and Spain, off Cape Trafalgar on the 21st of October 1805'.

2)   Patriotic Fund vase
in memory of John Cooke
By Benjamin and James Smith, London, 1808
Silver
National Maritime Museum, London (Greenwich
   Hospital Collection); PLT0033

John Cooke (1763–1805), captain of the *Bellerophon*, was killed at the Battle of Trafalgar. This £200 silver Trafalgar vase was presented to his widow, Louisa, by the Patriotic Fund.

Cooke had previously served in the American War of Independence, commanded the fire ship *Incendiary* at the Glorious First of June (1794), and, after promotion to captain, took part in Lord Bridport's action near Quiberon. There is a tablet to his memory in St Paul's Cathedral.

3)   Patriotic Fund vase
in memory of Nelson
By Benjamin Smith, London, 1808
Silver-gilt
HM The Queen, Royal Collection; RCIN 60425.1

The Patriotic Fund Committee voted two £500 vases to Nelson's family, the one displayed here presented to his widow, the Viscountess Nelson, and the other to his brother William, who had taken the title of 1st Earl Nelson.

The design of the two Nelson vases was more elaborate than the rest. They are of silver-gilt, rather than silver, and stand on additional plinths, making them larger and heavier than most of the other presentations. The design, though essentially the same as the smaller vases, differs in having Nelson's coat of arms on one side and a long presentation inscription on the other, in English on Lady Nelson's and in Latin on the Earl's, instead of the more usual figures of Britannia and Hercules. The sides of the plinth of both vases are inscribed in recognition of Nelson's victories, and the four corners of the base are supported by mermen blowing on conch shells.

4)   Patriotic Fund vase to Collingwood
By Benjamin Smith, London, 1808
Silver-gilt
HM The Queen, Royal Collection; RCIN 60425.2

This is the third Trafalgar vase originally of £500 value. It was presented to Vice-Admiral Cuthbert Collingwood of the *Royal Sovereign*, second-in-command at Trafalgar. Like the two Nelson vases, it is of silver-gilt and mounted on an additional plinth, with mermen at the corners. The presentation inscription and Collingwood's coat of arms are on the plinth. In 1898, this vase together with Lady Nelson's was purchased by the Prince of Wales, and so became part of the Royal Collection.   RP

LITERATURE: Gawler, *Britons Strike Home*; Leslie Southwick, 'The silver vases awarded by the Patriotic Fund', *Silver Society Journal* (winter 1990), 27–49.

Obverse: Britannia, a spear in her left hand and a shield below, standing on the deck of an antique galley, her right foot resting on a helmet, crowned with a wreath by a winged victory. Reverse inscribed within a wreath of oak and laurel: 'CUTHBERT COLLINGWOOD ESQUIRE, VICE ADMIRAL AND SECOND IN COMMAND. ON THE 21 OCTOBER MDCCCV. THE COMBINED FLEETS OF FRANCE AND SPAIN DEFEATED'. Fitted with a loop and a ring for suspension; the ribbon is missing. Collingwood was also awarded captain's gold medals for his part in the Battles of the Glorious First of June and St Vincent. All three medals are now in the collection of the National Maritime Museum.   BT

289. Flag officer's naval gold medal awarded to Vice-Admiral Cuthbert Collingwood (1750–1810)
Gold
51mm diam.
National Maritime Museum, London; MED0159

Collingwood was Nelson's second-in-command at Trafalgar. He was eight years older than Nelson and the two men had a long professional association. After Nelson's death, Collingwood succeeded him in command of the Mediterranean Fleet but never returned to England alive. He died on board his flagship *Ville de Paris* in 1810, when his body was shipped home, like Nelson's, for burial in St Paul's.

290. Flintlock blunderbuss, late eighteenth century
William Bond (*fl.* 1798–1812)
Brass, wood and steel
Inscribed: *Taken from the French Prize Bucentaure Presentation Thomas Wearing R M in recognition of his accelerty* [sic] *and zeal in the face of the enemy HUZZAH TRUE BRITONS*
John Goldstein, private collection

The blunderbuss, a popular weapon for self-defence, was loaded with buckshot or pistol balls which would scatter over a wide area. This example is fitted with a spring bayonet which was patented about 1781. This weapon, originally taken by the French from an English prize, was retaken at Trafalgar. Thomas Wearing served as a second lieutenant, Royal Marines, in the *Conqueror*.   LV

291. Lloyd's Patriotic Fund £100 Trafalgar sword
R. Teed (1757–1816)
Gilt, ivory, blued steel and leather
Inscribed: FROM THE PATRIOTIC FUND AT LLOYDS
    TO LIEUT. JOHN RICHARD LAPENOTIÈRE OF HM
    SCHOONER PICKLE FOR HIS MERITORIOUS SERVICES
    IN CONTRIBUTING TO THE SIGNAL VICTORY OBTAINED
    OVER THE COMBINED FLEETS OF FRANCE AND SPAIN
    OFF CAPE TRAFALGAR ON THE 21ST OCTOBER 1805
National Maritime Museum, London (Greenwich
    Hospital Collection); WPN1045

Lieutenant Lapenotière is famous for bringing the news of the victory at Trafalgar and Nelson's death back to England after the battle. In command of the schooner *Pickle*, Lapenotière arrived at Falmouth on 4 November 1805 and travelling non-stop by post-chaise reached the Admiralty in London on 6 November. For this service he was promoted to the rank of commander and awarded this sword by the Lloyd's Patriotic Fund. LV

292. **A City of London Trafalgar presentation sword to Captain Thomas Masterman Hardy, 1806**

R. Teed (1757–1816) and J. Prosser (*c.* 1769–1837)

Silver gilt, ivory, steel, leather, shagreen and velvet

Inscribed: T M HARDY NAVIS BRITANNICE VICTORIAE PREFECTO TRAFALGARI XXI OCTR MDCCCV INSIGNITER MERITO CIVITAS LONDINENSIS HOC TESTIMONIUM SUMMAE EXISTINATIONIS MDCCCVI

Lloyd's of London; Nelson Collection

On 28 January 1806, with all of the Trafalgar officers, Hardy received the vote of thanks awarded by both Houses of Parliament. Two days later he was presented with the freedom of the City of London together with this sword of the value of 100 guineas. LV

293. *An accurate view . . . of the ANTIQUITIES of London & Westminster . . . on Wednesday the 8th January 1806 . . . when the remains of the Great ADMIRAL LORD NELSON were brought from Greenwich to Whitehall*

Engraving by and after John Smith, published by R. Wilkinson 15 February 1806

Etching with hand-colouring

270 x 455mm

National Maritime Museum, London; PAG6706

See page 232

Of the many popular depictions of the event this one emphasizes the large numbers of people that thronged the banks of the Thames. Nelson's coffin is carried in the third barge from the left, followed by various barges of the City livery companies. Beyond, the London skyline extends between St Paul's Cathedral and the Monument. RQ

294. The Painted Hall, Greenwich Hospital
Drawn and engraved by Augustus Charles Pugin
and Thomas Rowlandson, published 1 January 1810
by Rudolph Ackermann
Hand-coloured aquatint
200 x 260mm (image)
National Maritime Museum, London; PAF7631

A view of the Painted Hall in Greenwich Hospital, from
the Upper Hall where Nelson lay in state, and where his
funeral carriage was subsequently displayed until it was
dismantled as 'decayed' in 1826 (cat. no. 299). By this time
the Hall had become the 'National Gallery of Naval Art'
(from 1824) and by the middle of the century it was also a
growing Nelsonic shrine of pictures and memorabilia related
to him. This print is no. 97 in the last part of Ackermann's
well-known three-volume *Microcosm of London* (1808–11).

PvdM

GREENWICH HOSPITAL.
THE PAINTED HALL.

London Pub. Jan. 1.1810. at R.Ackermann's Repository of Arts 101. Strand.

295. *Instructions for the yeomanry and
the volunteers: that are to be stationed
on the west side of Temple-Bar, at the
funeral ceremony of the late Lord
Viscount Nelson on the 9th January,
1806*
G. S. Smyth
Printed broadsheet
230 x 144mm
National Maritime Museum, London (Sutcliffe-Smith
Collection); AAB0500

These instructions, by command of His Royal Highness the
Duke of Cambridge, were issued to the volunteer militia
who lined the streets between the Admiralty and St Paul's on
the day of Nelson's funeral. They relate specifically to those
stationed on the west side of Temple Bar – the point at which
the Lord Mayor of London, attended by alderman and
sheriffs, received the procession. They reflect the solemnity
and formality of the occasion, dictating 'muffled drums to
roll' and 'music to play solemn dirges occasionally'. The men
had to stand two deep and wear 'a crape on the left arm
below the elbow' to indicate their responsibilities and also
their respect. They were responsible for ensuring that no
unauthorized individuals joined the procession: 'The troops
are not to suffer any carriage to enter the Grand Route
from the Admiralty to St Paul's, except those following the
procession.'

HP

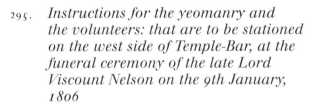

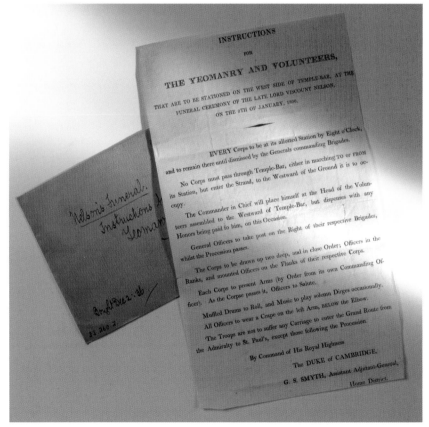

296. Fragment of a Union flag from *Victory*

Wool

406 x 914mm (framed)

National Maritime Museum, London; AAA0924

See page 235

The *Naval Chronicle*, describing Nelson's funeral procession, says, 'The most interesting part of the cavalcade . . .was the exhibition made by the brave Seamen of the Victory, who bore two Union Jacks and the St. George's Ensign, belonging to that Ship. These colours were perforated in various places by the effects of the shot of the Enemy. . . . These parts were particularly exposed to view, and the effect which such a display was calculated to produce may be more easily conceived than described.' At the close of the service, the staves of the officers of Nelson's household were broken and thrown in the grave, symbolizing the end of their authority. The flags from *Victory* were furled by the seaman and also placed there, but 'These brave fellows . . .desirous of retaining some memorials of their great and favourite Commander, had torn off a considerable part of the largest flag, of which most of them obtained a portion'. Although described as part of *Victory*'s Union flag, this could be part of the canton of the white ensign. A label gives the provenance of the item through the family of Sir John Eamer, elected Lord Mayor of London in 1801. The loose weave and hand-sewn construction of the item confirms its authenticity.   BT

297. Ticket to admit John Hoppner RA into the funeral procession from the Admiralty to St Paul's Cathedral, 9 January 1806

Printed ticket

210 x 248mm

National Maritime Museum, London (Sutcliffe-Smith Collection); REL0788

298. Ticket to the funeral in St Paul's Cathedral, 9 January 1806

77 x 117mm

Signed by hand with impressed wax seal

National Maritime Museum, London; REL0143

Two examples of tickets for Nelson's state funeral on 9 January 1806. John Hoppner RA (1758–1810) was a portrait painter. His court connections earned him prestigious sitters, including Nelson. Hoppner would have been able to join the funeral procession as it gathered in Hyde Park. From here the cortège made its way to St Paul's, where the holder of the second ticket would already have

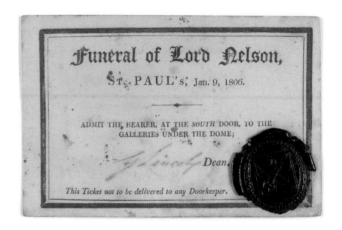

been seated. The wax seal and signature on this item states that it had been issued by the Bishop of Lincoln (Dean of St Paul's).   HP

299. Figurehead of Nelson's funeral carriage, 1806

Painted wood

National Maritime Museum, London; FHD0093

See page 229

This is part of the elaborate funeral carriage on which Nelson's body was conveyed in procession on 9 January 1806 from Whitehall, where it had rested overnight, to St Paul's Cathedral for the entombment. The funeral carriage was modelled on the form of a ship, with a painted wooden figurehead symbolizing Victory (sometimes referred to as Fame) holding her laurel wreath.

After the funeral the carriage was displayed in the Painted Hall at Greenwich Hospital until it decayed and, according to Joseph Allen, a Greenwich Hospital official, was dismantled in 1826. Only this figurehead and a few fragments remain.   RP

300. *The Order to be observed In the Publick Funeral Procession of the late Vice-Admiral Horatio Viscount Nelson*

Ink on paper, printed. Bound volume covered in black velvet

Inscribed: inside front cover: 'Given to Lady Anna Maria Stanhope by the King at Windsor Castle'

National Maritime Museum, London; REC/43

This is a complete order of Nelson's funeral, outlining the route and the ceremony from Greenwich to Whitehall Stairs and then on to the Admiralty on Wednesday 8 January 1806, and also for the following day, when a procession went from the Admiralty to St Paul's Cathedral. It describes the funerary drapes on the coffin at various stages of the proceedings and includes diagrams of where the coffin was to be placed in the cathedral. The funeral was a great occasion of state and the order of state officers and courtiers in attendance of the coffin at various stages of the ceremony are set out. Directions for carriages which were to join the procession are included, with the instruction that the 'Nobility &c in the Carriages cannot alight at the Admiralty'. Also included are directions for mourning dress: 'Servants, who have Silk or Crape Hatbands and Gloves, will be deemed in sufficient Mourning.' A black silk mourning band is preserved in the pages of the volume.

DK

301. Architect's model of Nelson's Column, *c.* 1838

Bath stone, marble and wood
Private collection, on loan to National Maritime
Museum, London; MDL0008

This is believed to be the original model made before Nelson's Column was built in London's Trafalgar Square. In 1838 the Nelson Memorial Committee proposed a General Subscription for the purpose of erecting a national Nelson monument in London. There was a design competition, which was won by William Railton and this model is likely to be the one Railton submitted. It shows features such as the steps, which were part of the original design but changed before the column was built.

The project took many years to complete at a total cost of about £50,000. The column itself was not finished until 1843, Baily's figure of Nelson being erected at the top that November. The bronze bas-reliefs of Nelson's four battles were added to the sides of the base in 1854, and Landseer's bronze lions positioned at the four corners in 1867, nearly thirty years after the first meeting of the Nelson Memorial Committee.

RP

LITERATURE: Mace, *Trafalgar Square.*

302. *Britannia crowning the Bust of our late Hero Lord Nelson*

Engraving by A. R. Burt after T. Baxter, published
5 December 1805
Aquatint with hand colouring
535 x 383mm (sheet)
Dedicated to 'Lord Collingwood the other Admirals,
Captains, Officers and men who Gallantly Fought for
their Country off Trafalgar'
National Maritime Museum, London; PAH7312

Nelson's death generated a flood of commemorative souvenirs and memorabilia, including many engravings. This created an industry of Nelson image-makers among artists and engravers, who drew upon the traditions of

'grand manner' history painting for their representations. Here Britannia is given the features of Emma Hamilton.

RQ

303. *The Immortality of Nelson*, 1807
Benjamin West (1738–1820)
Oil on canvas, signed and dated 1807
908 x 762mm
National Maritime Museum, London (Greenwich Hospital Collection, presented by Jasper de St Croix and others, 1849); BHC2905

A heavily classicized representation of Nelson's apotheosis, showing his body being handed up by Neptune and Victory into the arms of Britannia. This is surrounded by references to his victories and the earthly rewards they brought him, those for Trafalgar mainly benefiting his undistinguished elder brother William, who became 1st Earl Nelson. The painting was exhibited at the Royal Academy in 1807 but became best known in two other forms. It was engraved as frontispiece for the first major *Life* of Nelson (1809) by the Revd J. S. Clarke and John McArthur – a pietistic piece of family-inspired propaganda that has cast a long shadow over later writing. In 1810–12 the design was also converted by West and Joseph Panzetta into a high-relief sculptural version in Coade stone, installed in the King William court-yard pediment at Greenwich Hospital (now the Old Royal Naval College). In fact, West's original idea was that a larger version of the painting should form the central 'altarpiece' of a sculptural wall monument to Nelson – his contribution to the public proposals for such a tribute after Trafalgar. His painted design for the whole thing was also exhibited with this painting at the Royal Academy in 1807, with a detailed catalogue description. That version is now in the Yale Center for British Art, New Haven, Connecticut.

PvdM

*304. The Battle of Trafalgar,
21 October 1805

(displayed in the Queen's House)

Joseph Mallord William Turner (1775–1851)

Oil on canvas, 1822–24

2615 x 3685mm

National Maritime Museum, London (commissioned by
    George IV; Greenwich Hospital Collection from
    1829); BHC0565

This is Turner's only work by 'royal command' and the
largest and most publicly controversial painting of his
career. George IV gave him the commission late in 1822 on
the advice of Sir Thomas Lawrence, President of the Royal
Academy. It was to form a naval pair with Philippe-Jacques
de Loutherbourg's 1795 view of The Battle of the Glorious
First of June 1794, in a patriotic post-war redecoration of the
State Rooms at St James's Palace. Lawrence and George
Jones – both Turner's friends – were also represented, the

former by his portrait of the King and the latter by paintings
of Wellington's victories at Vitoria and Waterloo.

Turner did an unusual amount of practical research for
this work, which is his most complex tribute to Nelson, of
whom he was a great admirer. He already had sketches of
Victory, made on her return to England with Nelson's body
in December 1805 for his earlier The Battle of Trafalgar,
painted in 1806–8 (cat. nos. 279 and 280). For this picture
he borrowed a plan of the ship from the Admiralty and asked
the marine artist J. C. Schetky, at Portsmouth, to make
further sketches of her there. Also unusually, he did two
preparatory oil studies (Tate). The finished work combines a
number of incidents from different times in the action,
within a more symbolic conception. Nelson's presence,
mortally wounded, is only implied in the highlighted
crowd around Victory's mainmast. This powerful absence is
prefigured by the smallness of Nelson's figure, and those
around him, beneath similarly towering masts, in the
1806–8 picture. The small human scale is also a response to

de Loutherbourg's painting, since both in different ways contrast a mass of vulnerable figures with the great floating fortresses in which they are contesting national dominance on a mutually hostile sea. In *The Harbours of England* (1856, p. 16) Ruskin grasped this elemental component when he likened the uncontrollability of the ships' sails, as Turner shows them, to 'as many thunderclouds', most of *Victory's* falling with her foremast and at the same time as Nelson. Also symbolically, the falling mast bears his white vice-admiral's flag, while the code flags spelling 'd-u-t-y' – both the last word of his famous Trafalgar signal and the last coherent thought he spoke ('Thank God I have done my duty') – are coming down from the mainmast. On the right is the French *Redoutable*, from which Nelson was shot, surrendered and sinking, although she in fact went down in the storm after the battle. British seamen in the foreground boats raise a cheer, unaware of the tragedy behind in *Victory*, herself shown on an exaggerated scale as a dominating symbol of British sea power. Other men try to save friends and foes alike from a darkly heaving sea, in which a tangle of floating rigging resembles a monster's head and a Union flag is spread out above, as if to cover the fallen. Below the surface loom fragments of Nelson's motto, *'Palmam qui meruit ferat'*. This can translate as 'Let he who has earned it bear the Palm', or perhaps, in the circumstances, 'the price of glory is death'. That the cost is equal for the common sailor as much as the admiral is thrust into the viewer's face by the dead seaman arching out backwards from the picture plane, in the centre, at what would have been original eye level in St James's Palace. In imposing recession beyond *Victory* on the left are the Spanish four-decker *Santísima Trínidad* and the *Bucentaure*, flagship of Admiral Villeneuve, overall commander of the enemy Combined Fleet. Further left, the French *Achille*, 74 guns, is on fire with the bow of 'the Fighting *Téméraire*' – as Turner called her in his famous 1838 picture (National Gallery) – just coming into the frame.

On delivery in 1824 the painting provoked court criticism for its non-chronological approach to Nelson's victory, and its powerful allusions to the blood price of Britain's triumph, at Trafalgar and more generally in becoming the world's dominant sea power. Ambassadors used to classically heroic treatments are said to have sneered at it and seamen, including Sir Thomas Hardy, *Victory's* captain, have always criticized it on technical grounds. Turner himself later considered the picture spoilt by the eleven unpaid days that he spent at St James's adjusting it to the views of Admiralty men and he credited the King's naval brother, the Duke of Clarence (William IV from 1830), with the only sensible comments, despite a sharp exchange with him at the time. While George IV, when Prince of Wales, had acquired the cooler and more conventionally theatrical de Loutherbourg for Carlton House, Turner's

fierily spectacular but ambivalent pendant proved an embarrassment at St James's. It was also probably mismatched there – at least to the King's polished taste – with the adjacent works by Jones and his favourite portraitist, Lawrence. In late 1829 he presented it, with the de Loutherbourg, as his final gifts to the Naval Gallery at Greenwich Hospital. It has been at Greenwich ever since, and remains to some extent a focus of recurring division between 'sea dogs' and art historians, admirers of Nelson and of Turner.

PvdM

LITERATURE: Martin Butlin and Evelyn Joll, *The Paintings of J. M. W. Turner* (London, 1984, 2nd edition).

*305. Rear-Admiral Sir Horatio Nelson (1758–1805)

(displayed in the Queen's House)
Lemuel Francis Abbott (1760–1803)
Oil on canvas
760 x 635mm
National Maritime Museum, London (Greenwich Hospital Collection, presented by Jasper de St Croix and others, 1849); BHC2889

Following the Battle of St Vincent and the action at Tenerife there was a need for portraits of Nelson, which increased after the Battle of the Nile. The many portraits by Abbott originate from the wish of Nelson's friend William Locker, Lieutenant-Governor of Greenwich Hospital, to have another portrait in addition to Rigaud's of him in 1781 as a captain (cat. no. 69). These were to hang together in Locker's dining room at Greenwich. Nelson gave Abbott two sittings in the autumn of 1797 at about the time that he was staying with Locker, convalescing from his amputation. The story of the production and provenance of the copies that Abbott subsequently produced is complex. The present portrait, however, is a variation of Locker's, probably based on a sketch that Abbott retained in his studio to enable him to make replicas. It was commissioned in 1799 by one of the founders of the *Naval Chronicle*, John McArthur, to be engraved as an illustration. Nelson was then still in the Mediterranean and so the *chelengk* worn on his cocked hat was painted from a drawing and a verbal description. On Nelson's return Abbott repainted and adjusted the orders, but also softened the features to the annoyance of McArthur, who referred to Abbott's tendency 'to adonize'.

RQ

*306. Panorama of the Battle of Trafalgar, c. 1820

(Not on display)
William Heath (1795–1840)
Watercolour and bodycolour on paper, laid on calico;
   signed 'W. H.'
6222 x 10,015mm
National Maritime Museum, London; PAJ3938

This panorama was originally mounted as a complete circle about 10 feet 6 inches (3.2m) across. Only a few spectators at a time would have been able to view it, by stepping up into the centre from below. It was probably lit by daylight from above, round the edges of an inner masking top, with the bottom also masked to create the illusion that the viewer was standing in the middle of the battle. The episodes read from right to left:

— Cadiz harbour, with the combined Franco-Spanish fleet emerging
— A stern view of Nelson's double-column order of battle advancing to intercept the enemy. *Victory* (with three stern galleries) is at the head of the left or weather line
— The French *Achille* on fire, a blaze which started about 4.30 p.m. until the ship blew up about 5.45 p.m. The schooner *Pickle* which brought back news of

the battle is on her left and the panorama as a whole has unusually good representation of the smaller vessels in the fleet
— Nelson shot on the quarterdeck of *Victory*, from the *Redoutable* (seen stern-to on the right) about 1.15 p.m. The individuals around Nelson are intended as portraits, though none are close likenesses. Dr Beatty and Captain Hardy are to his right. The Royal Marine behind and supporting him is Sergeant Secker, with the Revd Scott to the left and two seamen carrying the body of Captain Adair of the Marines, further left.

This is a miniature version of the very large illusionistic circular panoramas invented by Robert Barker, whose son Henry exhibited a version of Trafalgar off Leicester Square, London, in 1806. William Heath was an artist noted for military subjects and 'penny-plain, tuppence-coloured' theatrical prints. He was an illegitimate son of the engraver James Heath and the Nelson scene here is partly based on his father's highly successful print of 1811 from Benjamin West's painting, *The Death of Lord Nelson*. It also owes something to Samuel Drummond's versions. Like West, Heath includes Beatty and Scott, who were not on deck when Nelson was shot. Why this panorama was painted is still unknown. It may have been a promotional attraction in one of London's print shops and is the only known surviving early panorama of Trafalgar.   PvdM

307. *The Empress's wish – or Boney Puzzled!!*

Anonymous, British, published 9 August 1810 by
  J. Johnstone,
Coloured engraving
265 x 378mm
National Maritime Museum, London; PAD4784

A satire on Napoleon's frustration and anger at British superiority and strength in the naval war. Playing, by now very conventionally, upon his diminutive stature, it shows him glowering on the rampart of a coastal fort at the prospect of his fleet at harbour below, blockaded by a single British ship in the distance. The noticeably taller Empress looks down at him, pointing with a spyglass at the British vessel, and says, 'My Dear Little Great Emperor of Kings, Nations & Princes your Majesty has often promised to me – that if ever I longed, or wished, or had a Desire for any thing in all the world, it would be got immeadiatly [*sic*] – I do not wish to put your <u>Highness</u> to such a proof of your Love I only wish you to send out and bring me dat Little <u>Ship</u> with the Blue Flag, that lays at Anchor?' At this Napoleon is perplexed, since it is the one request he is unable to grant.

GQ

308. *The Death of Admiral Lord Nelson – in the moment of Victory*, 1805

James Gillray, published 29 December 1805 by
  H. Humphrey
Hand-coloured etching
410 x 299mm
National Maritime Museum, London; PAF3866

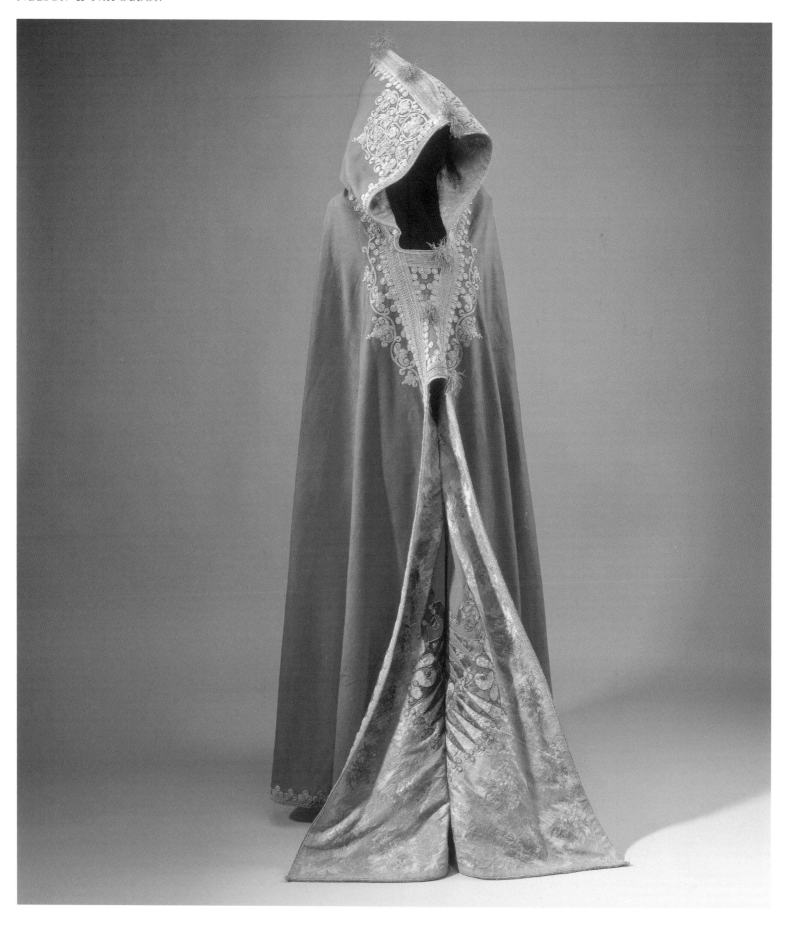

Gillray's response to Nelson's death at Trafalgar was this brilliantly ironic print showing him collapsed on the deck of the *Victory*, eyes rolling upward, embraced by a forlorn Hardy with George III's features. He is cradled by a melo-dramatically tearful Britannia, in a classical 'attitude' of grief: she has the unmistakable features of Emma, Lady Hamilton. The kneeling 'British Tar' is probably intended to be the Duke of Clarence, later William IV. Above, the winged figure of Fame (or Victory) trumpets Nelson's 'Immortality', while the battle rages in the background amid impenetrable billowing smoke. The caption refers to the 'Memorial intended by the City of London to commemorate the Glorious Death of the immortal Nelson', alluding to the spate of proposals for some form of permanent memorial that came almost immediately in the wake of Nelson's death and funeral.   GQ

309. Napoleon's burnous, early nineteenth century

Wool

HM The Queen, Royal Collection; RCIN61156

Based on both Arab and Berber clothing, the burnous is a voluminous, hooded cloak that protects garments; the hood provides additional privacy. This Ottoman Cloak with its scarlet colour of Napoleon's mantle would also have made the wearer instantly recognizable. It was one of the deposed Emperor's personal possessions, abandoned in his carriage after the French defeat at Waterloo, and subsequently claimed as a trophy of war by the Prussians.   AM

310. *Napoleon Buonaparte on board HMS Bellerophon*, 1815

Sir Charles Locke Eastlake (1793–1865)

Oil on canvas

2595 x 1840mm

National Maritime Museum, London (Caird Collection); BHC2876

A full-length portrait of Napoleon on the *Bellerophon*, after he surrendered to Captain Maitland on 15 July 1815 at Rochefort. He arrived at Torbay on 24 July and at Plymouth three days later where he was detained while his fate was decided. Boatloads of sightseers tried to catch a glimpse of him until Maitland was ordered to put to sea, transferring Napoleon to the *Northumberland* three days later for the voyage to St Helena, his final place of exile.

This is the only portrait of Napoleon painted from life by a British artist. He stands at the gangway of the

Bellerophon leaning on a bulwark wearing the uniform of colonel of *chasseurs à cheval* of the Imperial Guard. He holds an opera glass and surveys the crowd. Behind Napoleon to the left is the full-face portrait of Captain Piontkowski, one of Napoleon's personal troops, in the uniform of the Polish Guard. Not permitted to remain with Napoleon, he was landed at Plymouth where he sat for Eastlake's portrait. Behind Napoleon to the right, with balding head turned away, is General Bertrand. In profile, in front of Bertrand, a British marine stands guard, while below Napoleon a sailor looks upwards. They guard Napoleon yet show respect for the vanquished Emperor. The sailor removes ropes from the ship's side placed there to prevent sightseers scrambling aboard.

Napoleon dominates this portrait, recognized by the *Art Union* as 'of great historical importance'. Admired for its innovative composition, sentiment and veracity, it reveals a man who, though defeated, retained his charisma. Evoking Renaissance *Ecce Homo* imagery, the incongruous composition is finely balanced, like Napoleon's fate at the time. His positioning, underneath the unconquered ensign, underscores the British victory and his defeat. The powerful vertical mainmast, the height of the marine's rifle and the upright sailor's hammock emphasize the dramatic effect.

Among thousands who rowed out to glimpse Napoleon, Eastlake was able to draw him from life. Noticing him

263

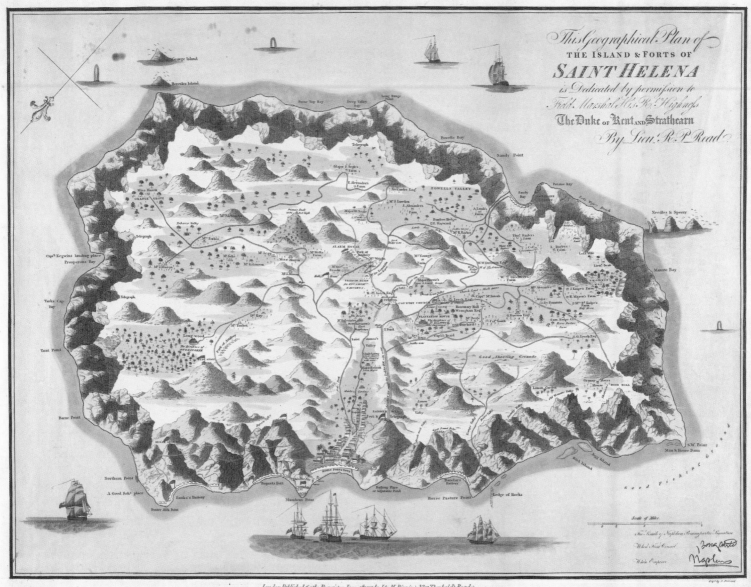

sketching, Napoleon reportedly cooperated by posing on the gangway. Eastlake painted three versions, a full-length portrait, a small full-length from which the mezzotint by Charles Turner was made and this life-size version. Enormously popular, it helped establish Eastlake's reputation and was exhibited in Plymouth at the Picture Gallery, Frankfort Place, from 23 December 1815. The painting then moved to No. 236 Piccadilly, London, together with two certificates authenticating its resemblance to Napoleon. Purchased by five Plymouth citizens, it was bought by the National Maritime Museum from Lord Clinton whose grandfather acquired it from Plymouth Library in 1824.　　GY

LITERATURE: *Connoisseur*, Oct. 1950; Robertson, *Sir Charles Eastlake and the Victorian Art World*; *Annals of the Fine Arts*, vol. I (London, 1816), p. 91.

311. *This geographical plan of the Island of Saint Helena is dedicated by permission to Field Marshal His Royal Highness the Duke of Kent and Strathearn*, 1817 (2nd edition)

Lieut. R. P. Read

Hand coloured engraving

545 x 755mm

National Maritime Museum, London; G214:25/2

This pictorial map was first published in 1815 to capitalize on the public celebration and curiosity surrounding Napoleon's surrender and exile to the extremely remote island of St Helena in the South Atlantic. The voyage out on the *Northumberland* took ten weeks. The map portrays how small the island is, only 47 square miles (122 sq. km), and suggests that the seas around it were well covered by British shipping. In 1817 Napoleon was moved to a different house on the island, prompting the publication of this second edition of the map. It shows the position of Napoleon's first residence in the centre of the island and Longwood, his new residence to the west. Napoleon spent the last five years of his life on St Helena and used the time to write his memoirs.

Facsimiles of Napoleon's signature, as First Consul and as Emperor, are added. GH

312. Death mask of Napoleon, 1901
Moulded by Colliot Jaffret
Bronze
Musée de la Marine, Paris; 7 SO 157

This is a later bronze copy of one of the death masks of Napoleon which came from a private collection. Considerable controversy surrounds the provenance of surviving Napoleon death masks. On 5 May 1821 at 5.49 p.m. Dr Francesco Antommarchi, Napoleon's personal physician, proclaimed him dead. The plaster to make a death mask was not immediately available on St Helena, and it was some forty hours before the procedure could be carried out. This delay, together with the painful death Napoleon had endured, may serve to explain the appearance of the masks. In 1824 Dr Antommarchi obtained a royal mandate to the French mint to make three bronze castings of the

death mask, of which one went to New Orleans and two stayed in Paris, one going to Les Invalides.

Dr Francis Burton, an English army surgeon posted to St Helena, was one of the five medical officers present at the autopsy and has a good claim to have participated in making the death mask. He later wrote, 'Bonaparte's countenance was then certainly the most striking that I had ever beheld. The sensation I experienced I can never forget, viewing him thus laid low, who had once ruled the greater part of the civilised world with an iron hand.' Another death mask was the property of a Scottish army doctor, Archibald Arnott, who was also present at the death. That one is thought to be one of only five masks made on St Helena. Copies of these original masks may now be seen in many museum and private collections. RP

LITERATURE: Louise Linden, *Histoire des masques de l'Empereur Napoleon*. (See www.napoleon.org).

313. Letter written by Barry O'Meara to Hudson Lowe, 28 January 1817
Ink on paper
British Library, London; Add. MS 20214 77r.-80v.

Barry O'Meara was Bonaparte's first doctor while he was in exile on St Helena. This letter, written to the Governor of St Helena from Longwood, Bonaparte's residence on the island, is particularly interesting as, according to the Fondation Napoléon, it is one of the only known records of what Napoleon's plans were to have been if his invasion of Britain had been successful. In conversation with O'Meara, undoubtedly embellishing, streamlining and improving his thoughts with the benefit of hindsight, Bonaparte stated that he wished 'to render [the English nation] free and to relieve them from an obnoxious and despotical Aristocracy'. He would have proclaimed a republic, which he would have led, and would have abolished monarchical government, the nobility and the House of Lords, keeping the House of Commons only after significant reforms. When challenged by O'Meara, who noted that 'all parties would unite in expelling and annihilating the French', Bonaparte claimed that London would have been the key, its capture providing him with a substantial economic base, and that, in his appeals to the lower classes, he would have emphasized the restoration of their rights and a redistribution of property – 'I would have made rich promises'. If possible, he said, he would have annexed England to France; if not, he would have established a government 'as would be most consonant to my views'. 'I might have succeeded,' he said, had the invasion plans devised to get him to England in the first place not failed. CLW

314. **Napoleon's English lessons from Longwood** [Longwood, 1816–17]
Autograph manuscript
Fondation Napoléon, Paris; inv. 1153

Brought back by the General Bertrand from St Helena, Napoleon's island of confinement and death in 1821, these scraps of paper bear witness to Napoleon's attempts to learn English. During the long voyage of banishment from Europe in 1815, the fallen Emperor had received two English lessons from Comte Emmanuel de Las Cases, but since most of the ship's officers spoke French, the experiment was to be interrupted until the beginning of the following year. Desperate to keep up to date with world events, and receiving only the very occasional English newspaper, Napoleon was an impatient pupil. On Wednesday 17 January 1816, he had his first lesson. He asked Las Cases to dictate to him some sentences in French, which he would then translate into English (with the help of a table of auxiliary verbs and a dictionary, which Las Cases made Napoleon use for himself). The words are indicative of Napoleon's attitude to his confinement. '*Quand serez vous sage?* – When will you be wise / *jamais tant que je suis dans cette isle*. Never as long as I should be in this isle / *Mais je le deviendrai après avoir passé la ligne* / But I shall become wise after having passed the line / *Lorsque je débarquerai en France je serai très content* – When I shall land in France I shall be very content.' There are also some moving fragments concerning women, his son and his last pleasures, 'my wife shall come near to me, my son shall be great and strong if he will be able to trink [*sic*] a bottle of wine at dinner I shall [toast] with him . . . / The women believe they [are] ever prety [*sic*] / The time has not wings / When you shall come, you shall see that I have ever loved you.' After about twenty

lessons Napoleon was apparently able to hold a conversation and, most importantly of all, to read the news.　　PH

LITERATURE: B. Chevallier, K. Huguenaud, *Trésors de la Fondation Napoléon, Dans l'intimité de la Cour impériale* (Paris, 2004), pp. 176–7.

315. **Napoleon's star of the Légion d'honneur**, *c.* 1802–14
Silver, silver thread and sequins.
HM The Queen, Royal Collection; RCIN 441 475

This embroidered star of the Légion d'honneur was intended to be worn sewn to clothing, at a time when such orders were worn constantly. This example was one of Napoleon's own stars, presented to Quartermaster Sergeant Stevens of the 66th Regiment of Foot, which had formed part of the garrison at St Helena during Bonaparte's exile there. The star has five double points and the centre shows an imperial eagle facing right with thunderbolts in its claws, within the motto *Honneur et Patrie* (For honour and the fatherland).

All existing French orders of chivalry had been abolished at the time of the Revolution in 1789. In 1802 Napoleon founded a completely new order, the Légion d'honneur, to reward civil and military service to France. His idea was to create a new aristocracy based on merit rather than birth. The design is attributed to the painter Jacques-Louis David, and the statute decreed that the insignia should be made in gold and enamel, with the head of the Emperor on one side and the French eagle on the other, to be worn suspended from a red ribbon. The first awards were made in 1804 at the Church of Les Invalides, and later at a ceremony at the Boulogne camp. This star is framed with other artefacts from Napoleon's exile on St Helena including his letter of surrender to the Prince Regent of 13 July 1815.　　RP

LITERATURE: Stephen J. Patterson, *Royal Insignia: British and Foreign Orders of Chivalry from the Royal Collection* (London, 1996).

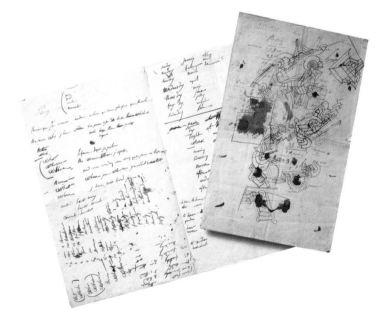

316. *SKETCH OF BONAPARTE. As laid out on his Austerlitz Camp Bed, taken by Captn Marryat R.N, 14 hours after his Decease, at the request of Sir Hudson Lowe, Governor of St Helena. & with the permission of Count Montholon & General Bertrand*

Captain Frederick Marryat (1792–1848)

Lithograph published 16 July 1821 by S. & J. Fuller

347 x 489mm

National Maritime Museum, London; PAF3523

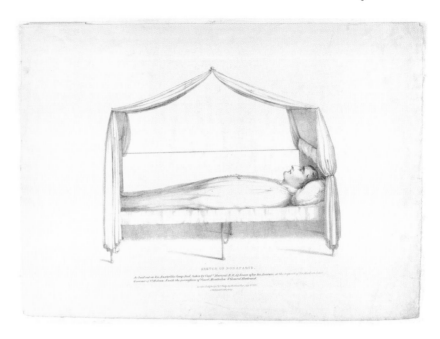

Marryat was a naval officer and later the author of *Peter Simple*, *Mr Midshipman Easy* and other popular seafaring novels, and later children's books. He was also a competent amateur draughtsman. At the time of Napoleon's death he commanded the sloop *Beaver*, guard ship at St Helena. When the ex-Emperor died he carried the dispatches announcing the death back to England. RQ

317. **Three imperial eagles from the *Belle-Poule*, 1840**

Anonymous

Gilded walnut

Musée de la Marine, Paris; 7 SO 10.3 (No. Inv. Chaillot 2726); 7 SO 10.4 (No. Inv. Chaillot 2727); 7 SO 10.7 (No. Inv. Chaillot 2730)

The *Belle-Poule* was the French naval frigate which brought Napoleon's remains back to France from St Helena in 1840, under command of the Prince de Joinville. She had been laid down at Cherbourg in 1828 but not launched until 1834. In recognition of having performed this last duty for Napoleon, the *Belle-Poule*'s upper works were afterwards painted entirely black, and remained so until the end of her service career.

These fine gilded eagle carvings are part of the seven surviving eagles which had formed part of the *Belle-Poule*'s ornamentation during the voyage bringing back Napoleon's coffin. Carved eagles were also on the floating catafalque which bore the body along the Seine on the final stage of the journey. The eagle emblem was a prominent element of imperial symbolism during the Napoleonic period. The eagle carvings are all slightly different. Two of those on display have one foot resting on a sphere, perhaps different feet for port and starboard positions. The third eagle, which stands with both feet on a scroll, is probably from the bow. The eagles were acquired by the Musée de la Marine from the State Arsenal of Cherbourg in 1931. RP

LITERATURE: *Les Génies de la Mer: chefs d'œuvres de la sculpture navale du Musée national de la Marine à Paris* (Quebec, 2001), pp. 121-2, 162.

(2)

318. Translation of the body of Napoleon,
nineteenth century
Brioude after Charles-Nicolas Lemercier (1797–1859)
Panorama in nine lithographs
265 x 370mm each
Fondation Napoléon, Paris; Bibliothèque Martial
    Lapeyre, inv. 00593

On what would have been Napoleon's fifty-second birthday, 15 August 1821, his mother, Madame Mère, wrote to Lord Londonderry begging for the body of her son. No reply was forthcoming until Napoleon's companions on St Helena, Bertrand and Montholon, sent a formal application to Lord Liverpool in September of the same year. The British government declared itself merely the guardians of the body and stated that they would hand it over to France if a formal request were made by the French government – something which Louis XVIII's government was never likely to do. The death in 1832 of Napoleon's son, the Duc de Reichstadt, unblocked the stalemate. With the direct successor to the Bonapartist crown gone, Louis-Philippe, 'King of the French' (as he styled himself), felt less threatened by Napoleon's mortal remains. So in 1840 the then head of the government and author of a monumental history of the

Consulate and Empire, Adolphe Thiers, proposed to the French government that they should ask the British for the Emperor's body in order that Napoleon's last wishes should be respected, namely that his body should 'rest near the banks of the Seine, in the midst of the French people I have so dearly loved'. Palmerston replied positively, hoping that British willingness would be interpreted as a 'desire to efface every trace of those national animosities . . . which engaged the two nations in war'. The body was exhumed and taken back to France on the *Belle-Poule*, a vessel that had seen active service during the Empire period. The festivities that took place when the body arrived in Paris were remarkable. 'It was greater than a Roman triumph,' noted Balzac the day after the event. Indeed there was nothing funereal about the occasion: an immense crowd lined the streets, delighted despite the freezing weather on that winter's day, 15 December 1840. Empire veterans in their uniforms were enthusiastically acclaimed. The monumental bier reached the Hôtel des Invalides at 1.50 p.m., where King Louis-Philippe received it 'in the name of France'. As Norwood Young remarked in 1915, 'No name was placed upon the slabs of white stone at St. Helena [of Napoleon's grave]. It was unnecessary to inscribe any name on the sarcophagus at Paris.' Napoleon's immortality was assured.   PH

319. Pall from Napoleon's coffin, 1840
Velvet
Pierre-Jean Chalençon, private collection

This fragment of fabric, embellished with laurel leaves and imperial motifs was part of the pall that covered Napoleon's coffin during the ceremony of repatriation for the Emperor's remains on 15 December 1840. The coffin, covered in a purple velvet pall decorated with bees and eagles, had been transported from St Helena to France in the *Belle-Poule*, arriving at Cherbourg on 30 November. There the crowds viewed the catafalque before it proceeded to Paris. Still covered by the velvet pall, the coffin was transported up the Seine by a black-painted boat. On the morning of 15 December sailors from the *Belle-Poule* transferred the coffin to an elaborate hearse for the procession to Les Invalides via the Arc de Triomphe. After the ceremony the church was opened to the public to file past the coffin, more than 100,000 people viewing it in three weeks.   RP

LITERATURE: Martineau, *Napoleon's Last Journey*.

320. Sketch for the painting of the *Belle-Poule* carrying the remains of Napoleon
Jean-Baptiste Isabey (1765–1855)
Pierre-Jean Chalençon, private collection

This sketch is a compositional study for Isabey's large painting, commissioned by King Louis-Philippe in 1840 to be placed in the Galerie des Batailles at Versailles. Isabey would have been an obvious choice for the commission; he had produced many portraits of Napoleon and members of the imperial household during the days of glory. Napoleon died on St Helena in the afternoon of 5 May 1821. On the orders of Louis-Philippe, the *Belle-Poule* would convey Napoleon's remains back to France and, in accordance with Napoleon's wishes, he was buried on the banks of the Seine, among the French people.

The final painting faithfully follows the outlines of the ship in this sketch, as it advances diagonally towards the spectator, filling the space of the canvas. It also follows the lines of the masts and rigging and the emphatic black and white drapes over Napoleon's coffin as it is hoisted on to the *Belle-Poule*. Isabey has indicated the positioning of the small boats in the foreground, the raised oars, the flags and even the splashes of colour for the uniforms of those who attended this solemn ceremony. These included his generals and advisers, Bertrand and Gourgaud, and Napoleon's former valet, Marchand. Two months later the coffin arrived in Paris and was carried under the Arc de Triomphe, the monument that had been built to commemorate Napoleon's many victories. It was accompanied by the veterans of the Imperial Guard and laid to rest in the chapel of the Church of Les Invalides.   HW

321. Miniature coffin, 1840
M. Le Marchand
Ebony
Inscribed on the lid: *Napoleon*
Musée de l'Armée, Paris, Ca. 106

This model of Napoleon's coffin bears his name on the lid in gilt letters and a capital N on the side, between ornamental handles. It is one of three models made from the ebony used for the actual coffin.

When Napoleon was buried at Sane Valley, in St Helena, after his death in 1821, his body was placed within four coffins, one inside the other; first tinplate, then mahogany, lead and an outer mahogany layer, all buried under flagstones. After his body was exhumed nineteen years later in 1840, it was reported to be in a remarkable state of preservation and still recognizable as Napoleon. The coffins were then

resealed, except for the outer mahogany coffin, which was sawn up and turned into mementos. The coffins were placed in a large lead-lined ebony casket, which had been brought from France on board the *Belle-Poule*. The ebony was polished to look like black marble, and the coffin ornamented with bronze-gilt handles and initial 'N's, and 'Napoleon' in copper-gilt. A final outer layer of oak protected the fine sarcophagus and its gilding during the journey. RP

AJACCIO 1769 MORT A STE HÉLÈNE 1821' (left). Signed 'E . ROGAT' below truncation on the obverse. Reverse: *Belle Poule*, frigate, under sail, the castle of St Helena (right), tower of Les Invalides (left). Legend: 'IL NE TRAHIT JAMAIS LA FRANCE ELLE REND HOMMAGE A SON GÉNIE MILITAIRE' (He never betrayed France, she pays homage to his military genius) '16 OC. TRANSLATION A BORD DE LA FRTE. LA BELLE POULE. DU CORPS DE NAPOLÉON DE STE. HÉLÈNE AUX INVALIDES 15 DÉC. 1840' (The body of Napoleon carried from St Helena to Les Invalides on board the frigate the *Belle-Poule*). BT

322. Medal commemorating the translation of the body of Napoleon from St Helena to Les Invalides, 1840

Emile Rogat (1770–c.1850)

Bronze, 51mm diam., signed

National Maritime Museum, London; MEC0789

Obverse: head of the Emperor Napoleon I, laureate (left).
Inscription: 'NAPOLÉON EMPEREUR ET ROI' (right); 'NÉ A

323. *The Apotheosis of Napoleon I*, 1859

Jean-Auguste-Dominique Ingres (1780–1867)

Brown wash pencil drawing

428 x 380mm

Inscribed lower left: *Ingres 1821*

British Museum, London; PD 1949-2-12-6

1821 is the date of Napoleon's death and the start of his apotheosis, but the design for this imperial cameo is based on Ingres's ceiling painting for the Salon de l'Empereur in the Hôtel de Ville in Paris, which dates from 1853. The ceiling was destroyed by fire in 1871, but a sketch exists in the Musée Carnavalet, and there are photographs of the painting as it appeared in the Ingres Gallery at the Exposition Universelle in 1855. In 1859 Bonaparte's nephew Napoleon III commissioned the sculptor Adolphe David (1826–96) to carve a cameo to be a companion piece to the largest surviving cameo from classical antiquity: the

Grande Camée de la Chapelle Royale (Bibliothèque Nationale, Paris). The sculptor worked on the commission for thirteen years but, unfortunately, no suitable stone was found to complete it.

As in the print of Bonaparte's arrival in Egypt (cat. no. 52), Napoleon is here crowned by a winged figure of Victory. The imperial eagle flies above, and beneath the chariot a Nemesis figure pursues Crime and Anarchy. The painting was harshly criticized by Charles Baudelaire in 1855; he accused Ingres of having failed to harness the 'supernatural' horses to their chariots and of being unable to give some hint of the 'epic and fatal beauty' of the Emperor. Far from suggesting an ascent towards the heavens, this apotheosis, for Baudelaire, was falling fast, like a hot-air balloon without gas to keep it airborne. HW

LITERATURE: Rowlands, *Master Drawings and Watercolours in the British Museum*, no. 132.

APPENDICES

Nelson Chronology

1758 29 September: Horatio Nelson born at Burnham Thorpe, Norfolk

1767 26 December: Catherine Nelson, Nelson's mother, dies

1771 Joins *Raisonnable* as a midshipman

August: sails to West Indies in a merchant ship

1773 June–September: joins Captain Phipps' Arctic expedition in the *Carcasse* under Captain Lutwidge

Joins *Seahorse* and sails to East Indies

1775 Invalided from his ship suffering from malaria. Returns to England

American War of Independence begins

1777 April: passes examination for lieutenant

Appointed to the frigate *Lowestoft* under Captain Locker

1778 September: appointed first lieutenant of the *Bristol*

December: appointed commander of the *Badger* brig

1779 June: promoted to post captain, appointed to command the frigate *Hinchinbroke*

1780 Takes part in the Nicaraguan expedition (capture of Fort San Juan)

Falls ill and returns home to England

1781 Appointed to command the frigate *Albemarle*

1782 Joins North American Squadron. Visits Quebec and New York

1783 American War of Independence ends. Returns home. Visits France

1784 Appointed to command the frigate *Boreas*. Sails for West Indies

1785 May: meets Frances Nisbet

1787 11 March: marries Frances Nisbet at Nevis

Returns to England. Placed on half-pay. Lives at Burnham Thorpe

1793 Beginning of the French Revolutionary War

26 January: appointed to command the *Agamemnon*

June: sails for the Mediterranean

September: visits Naples. Meets Sir William and Lady Hamilton

1794 January–August, Corsican campaign

12 July, wounded in right eye at Calvi

1796 March: appointed commodore. Joins the *Captain*

1797 14 February: Battle of St Vincent. Created Knight of the Bath

Promoted to rear-admiral. Hoists flag in the *Theseus*

24 July: failed attack on Santa Cruz, Tenerife. Loses right arm

Returns home and goes to Bath to recover

1798 March: hoists flag in the *Vanguard* and joins fleet off Cadiz

April: enters Mediterranean in command of a detached squadron

1 August: destroys French fleet at Aboukir Bay, Battle of the Nile, badly wounded in the head

Created Baron Nelson of the Nile

22 September: arrives at Naples

23–26 December: rescues Neapolitan royal family from advancing French army and takes them to Palermo

1799 23 January: French capture Naples

Begins relationship with Emma Hamilton

8 June: transfers his flag to the *Foudroyant*

June: assists in the recapture of Naples. Orders execution of Commodore Caracciolo

Created Duke of Bronte by King of Naples

1800 June: recalled home, returns overland with the Hamiltons

6 November: arrives at Great Yarmouth

1801 Separates from his wife

1 January: promoted to vice-admiral

13 January: hoists flag in the *San Josef*

c. 30 January: Emma Hamilton gives birth to their daughter Horatia

12 March: sails with Hyde Parker to the Baltic

2 April: Battle of Copenhagen. Flies flag in the *Elephant*

Created viscount

6 May: succeeds Parker as commander in chief

June: returns home

27 July: appointed to command anti-invasion forces in the Channel, hoists flag in the *Medusa*

15 August: failure of attack on Boulogne

September: buys Merton Place, Surrey

1 October: armistice signed between Britain and France

22 October: returns home to Merton Place

1802 25 March: Treaty of Amiens ends French Revolutionary War

26 April: Revd Edmund Nelson, Nelson's father, dies

July–August: tours South Wales and the Midlands with the Hamiltons

1803 6 April: Sir William Hamilton dies

16 May: Napoleonic War begins. Appointed commander in chief in the Mediterranean

18 May: hoists flag in the *Victory*

6 July: joins the fleet off Toulon

1804 Blockades French in Toulon

1805 April–July: chases French fleet to West Indies and back

18 August, arrives back in England. To Merton Place on leave

14 September: rejoins the *Victory* at Portsmouth

28 September: takes command of the fleet off Cadiz

21 October: Battle of Trafalgar and Nelson's death

6 November: news of Trafalgar reaches England

4 December: *Victory* arrives at Portsmouth bearing Nelson's body

5 December: Day of Thanksgiving for Trafalgar

1806 8 January: funeral procession on the River Thames

9 January: funeral service in St Paul's Cathedral

Effigy by Catherine Andras installed in Westminster Abbey

Napoleon Chronology

1769 15 August: birth of Napoleon Bonaparte in Ajaccio, Corsica

1779 15 May: enters the Brienne military school

1784 17 (or 30) October: leaves Brienne for the Royal Military School in Paris

1785 28 October: leaves the military school, forty-second of the fifty-eight graduates taken annually into artillery from all French schools; is garrisoned in Valence

1786 15 September: receives leave of absence; goes to Corsica

1787 9 November: returns to Paris

1788 1 January–June: second stay in Corsica

1789 September–February 1791: third stay in Corsica. Involves himself in Corsican political struggles

1791 September–May 1792: fourth stay in Corsica

1792 10 August: present at the siege of the Tuileries
October: fifth stay in Corsica

1793 11 June: quarrel with Paoli; Bonaparte forced to leave Corsica with his family. Goes to Toulon

1793 18 December: the English leave Toulon. Town representatives make Bonaparte head of a battalion at the rank of brigadier general
Beginning of the French Revolutionary War

1794 11 July: mission to Genoa on the orders of the younger Robespierre
9 August: arrested after fall of Robespierre brothers, but cleared on all counts

1795 13 June: promoted to General of the Army of the West
15 September: struck off the list of generals employed by the Committee of Public Safety. Period of financial difficulty
15 October: meets Josephine de Beauharnais
16 October: promoted to divisional general of the Army of the Interior
26 October: made commander-in-chief

1796 9 March: marries Josephine
11 March: leaves to become head of the Army of Italy
Victories at Montenotte (12 April), Mondovi (21 April); Lodi (10 May)
15 May: enters Milan
Victories at Castiglione (5 August); Bassano (8 September); Arcole (17 November)

1797 14 January: victory at Rivoli
2 February: capitulation of Mantua
4 September: anti-royalist *coup d'état*. Bonaparte sends Augereau to support the Directory
25 December: Bonaparte elected to the French Institute, in the section 'Physical and Mathematical Sciences, sub-section Mechanical Arts'

1798 19 May: sets sail for Egypt
11 June: takes Malta
2 July: takes Alexandria
21 July: victory at the Battle of the Pyramids
24 July: enters Cairo
1 August: Nelson destroys the French fleet at the Battle of the Nile
22 August: foundation of the Egyptian Institute
21 October: revolt of Cairo against French domination

1799 7 March: taking of Jaffa
19 July: discovery of the Rosetta stone
25 July: victory at Aboukir
23 August: leaves Egypt
16 October: reaches Paris
9–10 November, *coup d'état*. Bonaparte provisional consul with Sieyès and Roger Duclos

1800 19 February: Bonaparte moves to the Tuileries Palace
20 May: crosses the Saint Bernard Pass
14 June: victory at Marengo

1802 25 March: Treaty of Amiens ends war with England
10 May: proposal for a national vote to grant Napoleon Bonaparte consulship for life (first official use of his Christian name), which he wins
20 May: reinstitution of slavery in the French colonies

1803 16 May: war resumes with England

1804 18 May: Napoleon Bonaparte proclaimed Emperor of the French
2 December: Napoleon's coronation

1805 17 March: Napoleon crowned King of Italy
19 October: victory at Ulm
21 October: defeat of the Franco-Spanish fleet at Trafalgar
2 December: victory at Austerlitz

1806 14 October: victories at Jena and Auerstädt
27 October: enters Berlin
21 November: declares the Continental Blockade

1807 8 February: difficult victory at Eylau
14 June: victory at Friedland
25 June: meeting of Napoleon and Tsar Alexander I on the Niemen
7 July: signing of the Treaty of Tilsit between France and Russia

1808 27 September: meeting between Napoleon and Tsar Alexander I at Erfurt
4 December: surrender of Madrid before Napoleon

1809 Victories at Eckmühl (22 April); Essling (22 May); Wagram (6 July)
15 December: the Senate pronounces Napoleon's divorce from Josephine

1810 2 April: church marriage of Napoleon and Marie-Louise of Austria

1811 20 March: birth of their son, the King of Rome

1812 8 April: Alexander sends an ultimatum to Napoleon
18 May: conference in Dresden
24 June: Napoleon crosses the Niemen
14 September: enters Moscow
18 October: decides to retreat
5 December: Napoleon leaves his retreating army

1813 17 March: Prussia declares war on France
Victories at Lützen (2 May); Bautzen (20 May)
21 June: Wellington's victory at Vitoria. Spain lost to the empire
16–19 October: Battle of the Nations (Leipzig). The fall of Napoleonic Germany
30 October: victory at Hanau

1814 Victories at Brienne (29 January); Champaubert (10 February); Montmirail (11 February); Montereau (18 February); Rheims (13 March)
30–31 March: fall of Paris
6 April: Napoleon's unconditional abdication
4 May: sets sail for the island of Elba
30 June: Treaty of Paris
1 November: Congress of Vienna assembles (until June 1815)

1815 26 February: Napoleon escapes from Elba
20 March: Napoleon in Paris
12 June: leaves for Belgium
16 June: victory at Ligny
18 June: defeat at Waterloo
22 June: Napoleon abdicates
15 July: surrenders to Captain Maitland on board *Bellerophon* off Rochefort. Sails to Plymouth
7 August: transferred to the *Northumberland*
16 October: Napoleon arrives on Saint Helena. Moves into 'The Briars'
10 December: moves to Longwood

1821 5 May: death of Napoleon. His last words: '*à la tête de l'armée*' (to the head of the army).

1840 Napoleon's remains returned to France and entombed at Les Invalides

Footnotes and Further Reading

NELSON AND NAPOLEON:
AN INTRODUCTION

Pages 3 – 7

1. General Kléber, quoted by Alistair Horne, *How Far from Austerlitz? Napoleon 1805–1815* (London, 1996), p. 12.
2. Sir Nicholas Harris Nicolas, ed., *The Dispatches and Letters of Lord Nelson*, 7 vols (London, 1844–46), V, 438.
3. Philippe Masson and José Muracciole, *Napoléon et la Marine* (Paris, 1968), pp. 188–90; Philippe Masson, *Histoire de la Marine*, 2nd edn, 2 vols (Paris, 1992), I, 360–62. Cf. Martine Acerra and Jean Meyer, *Marines et Révolution* (Rennes, 1988), p. 254; Maurice Dupont, *L'amiral Decrès et Napoléon* (Paris, 1991), pp. 9, 275.

Doyle, William, *The French Revolution: A Very Short Introduction* (Oxford, 2001); Meyer, Jean, André Corvisier and Jean-Pierre Poussou, *La Révolution Française*, 2 vols (Paris, 1991); Schama, S., *Citizens: A Chronicle of the French Revolution* (London, 1989).

IMAGES OF NAPOLEON:
A NATIONAL HERO FOR FRANCE?

Pages 35 – 41

1. E. J. Delécluze, *Louis David, son école et son temps* (Paris, 1983), pp. 200–202.
2. A. Dayot, *Napoléon raconté par l'image* (Paris, 1902), pp. 182–3.
3. The name given to Napoleon Bonaparte's *coup d'état* of 9–10 November 1799 when, on his return from his Egyptian campaign, he put an end to the government of the Directory and established himself as First Consul.
4. Both paintings are now housed in the Musée de Malmaison.
5. Moreover, these images are testimony to the literary culture of the hero, who ought not to be confused with a common soldier.
6. The Gauls described by Julius Caesar actually included those of Belgium, the left bank of the Rhine, the Cisalpine and the Transalpine regions. One needs to be aware of this to fully understand frequent French references to 'the Empire of the Gauls' when talking about the new France.
7. In depicting the Civil Code, the register of civil and private laws, Girodet attributes the whole of its production to Napoleon and moreover, he keeps quiet about the constitutional oath that was supposed to protect civil and political liberties.
8. C. Brifaut, *Souvenirs d'un Académicien*, 2 vols (Paris, 1921), II, 1–2.

Crow, Thomas, *Emulation: Making Artists for Revolutionary France* (New Haven, 1995); Jourdan, A., *Mythes et légendes de Napoléon* (Toulouse, 2004); Lentz, T., ed., *Le Sacre de Napoléon* (Paris, 2003); McLynn, Frank, *Napoleon. A Biography* (London, 1998); Wilson-Smith, Timothy, *Napoleon and his Artists* (London, 1996).

THE BATTLE OF THE NILE
AND ITS CULTURAL AFTERMATH

Pages 65 – 71

1. Nelson to Lord Howe, Palermo, 8 Jan. 1799, in Sir Nicholas Harris Nicolas, ed., *The Dispatches and Letters of Lord Nelson*, 7 vols (London, 1997), III, 230. See Lavery, *Nelson and the Nile*, for a full account of the battle.
2. Cooper Willyams, *A Voyage up the Mediterranean* (London, 1802), p. 54.
3. Nicholas, Tracy, ed., *Naval Chronicle*, I, 253.
4. British Museum, *Acts and Votes* (London, 1805), p. 83.
5. BL Add. MS 34907, fos 144f.
6. *Monthly Magazine*, IX (1799), 237.
7. *Naval Chronicle*, I (1799), 309–12; 237f.
8. Nicolas, ed., *Dispatches*, III, 55, 89.

Jenkins, Ian, *Archaeologists and Aesthetes: The Sculpture Galleries of the British Museum 1800–1939* (London, 1992); Lavery, B., *Nelson and the Nile: The Naval War against Bonaparte, 1798* (London, 1998); Walker, Richard, *The Nelson Portraits: An Iconography of Horatio, Viscount Nelson, K.B. Vice Admiral of the White* (Portsmouth, 1998).

EGYPTOMANIA:
THE IMPACT OF NELSON, NAPOLEON
AND THE NILE ON MATERIAL
CULTURE IN FRANCE AND BRITAIN

Pages 105 – 110

1. C. de la Jonquière, *L'Expédition d'Égypte, 1798–1801*, 5 vols (Paris, 1899–1907), I, 62, quoted in Alan Schom, *Napoleon Bonaparte* (London, 1997), p. 111.
2. James Stevens Curl, *Egyptomania: The Egyptian Revival, a Recurring Theme in the History of Taste* (Manchester, 1994), p. 174.
3. *The Lady's Monthly Museum* (November 1798), p. 376.
4. Robert Southey, *Letters from England: by Don Manuel Alvarez Espriella. Translated from the Spanish* (London, 1807).
5. *Mirroir de la Mode* (March 1803), Figure IV.

6. Luigi Ficacci, *Piranesi: The Complete Etchings* (Cologne, 2000).
7. Dominique-Vivant Denon, *Travels in Upper and Lower Egypt during the campaigns of General Bonaparte*, 2 vols (Ridgeway, 1802), volume I, p. 5.
8. *Ibid.*, p. 9.
9. *The Lady's Monthly Museum* (January 1802), p. 69.
10. Thomas Hope, *Household furniture and interior decoration executed from designs by T.H.* (London, 1807), p. 32.
11. *Ibid.*, p. 26.
12. *Ibid.*, p. 27.
13. *Ibid.* p. 6.

'History of the Légion d'Honneur', www.legiond-honneur.fr/shared/us/histoire/hisolh.html
Ribiero, Aileen, *The Art of Dress: Fashion in England and France, 1750–1820* (London, 1995).

BRITISH PROPAGANDA
AND ANTI-NAPOLEONIC FEELING
IN THE INVASION CRISIS OF 1803

Pages 125 – 130

1. Estimating the size and social composition of the audience for written texts is fraught with difficulties for the historian, especially as the standard measure, the ability to sign a marriage licence, measures only one ability among a spectrum of skills. As late as 1850, half the population still could not sign, but this should not obscure the existence of something approaching mass literacy. In many urban areas, basic literacy was the norm among males, and in London, as early as 1750, 92 per cent of grooms and 74 per cent of brides could sign their names. While many editions of printed books (for which average print-runs were around 1000) were the preserve of an educated and social elite, pamphlets and ephemeral forms of print could reach a large audience, including the illiterate, for reading works aloud was not uncommon. If each copy of Paine's work reached five people, it is not inconceivable that it reached 20 per cent of the adult population. According to the 1801 census, the British population numbered 10.7 million, not including Ireland.
2. On popular loyalism see especially the collection of essays by Mark Philp, ed., *The French Revolution and British Popular Politics* (Cambridge, 1991).

Burrows, Simon, *French Exile Journalism and European Politics, 1792–1814* (Woodbridge, 2000); Franklin, Alexander and Mark Philp, *Napoleon and the Invasion of Britain* (Oxford, 2003).

THE ROYAL NAVY IN 1803

Pages 149 – 152

1. Jedediah Stevens Tucker, *Memoirs of Admiral the Right Hon. Earl of St. Vincent*, 2 vols (London, 1844), I, 423.
2. *Memoirs of the Administration of the Board of Admiralty under the Presidency of the Earl St. Vincent* (London, [1805] never issued), p. 2.
3. David Bonner Smith, ed., *Letters of the fleet the Earl of St Vincent whilst First Lord of the Admiralty, 1801–1806*, 2 vols (Navy Records Society, 1922–7), II, 320, of 21 Aug. 1803.
4. Sir Nicholas Harris Nicolas, *The Dispatches and Letters of Lord Nelson*, 7 vols (London, 1844–46), V, 396.
5. Edward Hughes, ed., *The Private Correspondence of Admiral Lord Collingwood* (NRS, vol. 98, 1957), p. 149.

Dickinson, H. T., *Britain and the French Revolution* (Basingstoke, 1989); Duffy, Michael, *Soldiers, Sugar and Seapower: The British Expedition to the West Indies and the War against Revolutionary France* (Oxford, 1987); Rodger, N. A. M., *The Command of the Ocean: A Naval History of Britain, 1699–1815* (London, 2004).

THE IMPACT OF NELSON AND NAVAL WARFARE ON WOMEN IN BRITAIN, 1795–1805

Pages 173 – 178

1. Amelia Opie, *Poems by Mrs. Opie* (London, 1802), p. 150.
2. Henry F. Chorley, *Memorials of Mrs. Hemans. With Illustrations of Her Literary Character from Her Private Correspondence*, 2 vols (London 1836), II, 172–73. Others thought that women had a right to fame. Cf. Lucy Aikin, *Epistles on Women, clarifying the Character and Condition in Various Ages and Nations with Miscellaneous Poems* (London, 1810), p. 80. 'Epistle the Fourth', l. 485.
3. Frances Nelson to Davison, NMM DAV/2/41 (1 May 1801).
4. [Lady Anne Hamilton], *The Epics of the Ton; or, The Glories of the Great World: A Poem*, 2nd edn (London, 1807), Book I, ll. 69–96.
5. E.g., National Maritime Museum samplers: TXT0057 and TXT0058.
6. Laurence Sterne, *A Sentimental Journey, Travels through France and Italy*, ed. G. Petrie (Harmondsworth, 1967), p. 137.
7. Ernest de Selincourt, ed., *The Early Letters of William and Dorothy Wordsworth (1787–1805)* (Oxford, 1935), p. 547.

Elmsley, Clive, *British Society and the French Wars* (London, 1979); Fraser, Flora, *Beloved Emma: The Life of Emma Lady Hamilton* (London, 1986); Lincoln, Margarette, *Representing the Royal Navy. British Sea Power, 1750–1815* (Aldershot, 2002).

TRAFALGAR

Pages 189 – 196

1. Quotations from Nelson's letters are taken from the material recently discovered by 'The Nelson Letters Project' and published in Colin White: *Nelson: The New Letters* (Woodbridge, 2005).
2. Quotations by Napoleon and other French participants are taken from: E. D. Desbrière, *The Naval Campaign of 1805* (Oxford, 1933).
3. For a full examination of this discovery, and the evidence for its dating, see C. White, 'Nelson's 1805 Battle Plan', *Journal of Maritime Research*, May 2002, www.jmr.nmm.ac.uk.
4. Clive Richards Collection, CRC/91.
5. Quotations by British sailors come from Stuart Legg, *Trafalgar: An Eyewitness Account of a Great Battle* (London, 1966).
6. Sir Nicholas Harris Nicolas, *The Dispatches and Letters of Lord Nelson,* 7 vols (London, 1844–46), VII, 226.

Gardiner, Robert, ed., *The Campaign of Trafalgar 1803–1805* (London, 1997); Schom, Alan, *Trafalgar: Countdown to Battle* (London, 1990); White, Colin, ed., *The Nelson Companion* (Stroud, 1995).

COMMEMORATING TRAFALGAR: POLITICS AND NAVAL PATRIOTISM

Pages 231 – 236

1. Marie Busco, *Sir Richard Westmacott: Sculptor* (Cambridge, 1994), pp. 43–51.
2. See Alison Yarrington, 'Nelson the Citizen Hero: state and public patronage of monumental sculpture, 1805–18', *Art History* 6 (3) (1983), 315–29.
3. Alison Yarrington, *The Commemoration of the Hero: Monuments to the British Victors of the Napoleonic Wars* (New York, 1988), p. 218.
4. Busco, *Sir Richard Westmacott*, pp. 57–61.
5. For which see Rodney Mace, *Trafalgar Square: Emblem of Empire* (London, 1976).
6. W. Mark Hamilton, 'The 'New Navalism' and the British Navy League, 1895–1914', *Mariner's Mirror*, 64 (1) (1978) 37–44.

NAPOLEON'S LAST JOURNEY

Pages 237 – 244

1. John Smart's memoir in Clement Shorter, *Napoleon and his Fellow Travellers* (London, 1908), p. 305. The best modern account of this episode is in David Cordingley, *Billy Ruffian* (London, 2002), pp. 254–79.
2. Account by Lieutenant Bowerbank, quoted in Shorter, p. 312.
3. Lord Keith's letter to his daughter quoted in the Earl of Kerry, *The First Napoleon* (London, 1925), p. 163.
4. Sydney Gillard, ed., *The St Helena Journal of General Baron Gourgaud* (London, 1932), p. 1.
5. Letter to the Foreign Secretary, 21 July 1815, quoted in Cordingley, p. 267.
6. Julia Blackburn, *The Emperor's Last Island* (London, 1991), p. 5.
7. I am indebted to G. L. de St M. Watson, *The Story of Napoleon's Death Mask* (London, 1915), p. 6.
8. De Montholon, *Récits de la captivité de l'Empereur*, 2 vols (Paris, 1847), I, 286.
9. See Michael Driskell, *As Befits a Legend: Building a Tomb for Napoleon* (Kent State University Press, Ohio, 1995), Chapter 1.
10. Donald Howard, 'Introduction to Napoleonic Research' in Donald Howard, ed., *Napoleonic Military History: A Bibliography* (London, 1986), p. 1.
11. See Martin Levy, 'Houses and Furniture for Napoleon on St Helena', in *Furniture History*, 1998, 2–212; Bathurst's letter to the Governor is on p. 39.
12. Gillard, ed., *The St Helena Journal*, entry for 23 July 1817, p. 245.
13. J. Lucas-Dubreton, *La Culte de Napoléon 1815–48* (Paris, 1860), p. 97.
14. Philippe Gonnard, *The Exile of St Helena* (London, 1909), p. 13; Sudhir Hazareesingh, *The Legend of Napoleon* (London, 2004) was published after this essay was written.
15. Gillard, ed., *The St Helena Journal*, entry for 11 January 1816.
16. Simon Bainbridge, *Napoleon and English Romanticism* (Cambridge, 1995), p. 22.
17. *Ibid.*
18. The most important single study is E. Tangye Lean, *The Napoleonists* (London, 1973); Stuart Semmel, *Napoleon and the British* (London, 2004) was published after this essay was written.
19. Captain Maitland, *Narrative of the Surrender of Buonaparte and of his residence on board H.M.S. Bellerophon* (London, 1826), p. 220.
20. Roger Fulford, *Samuel Whitbread* (London, 1967).
21. William Bissell Pope, ed., *The Diary of Benjamin Robert Haydon*, 5 vols (Cambridge, MA, 1960–63), I, 253.
22. 'Landseer and the Lion Tamer' by Stephen Duffy, in *British Art Journal*, III (2003), no. 3.
23. Lord Rosebery, *The Last Phase* (London, 1900), p. 252.
24. Lucas-Dubreton, *La Culte de Napoléon*, p. 176.
25. Chateaubriand, *Memoirs d'Outre-Tombe* (London, 1902), vol. 17, 112.

Cookson, J. E., *The British Armed Nation 1793–1815* (Oxford, 1997).

Select Bibliography

Acerra, Martine, José Merino and Jean Meyer, eds, *Les Marines de guerre européens, XVII–XVIIIe siècles* (Paris, 1985)

Acerra, Martine and Jean Meyer, *Marines et Révolution* (Rennes, 1988)

Alexander, Louis [of Battenberg], Prince, afterwards Mountbatten, Louis Alexander, Marquis of Milford Haven, *Naval Medals: commemorative medals, naval rewards, war medals, naval tokens etc of France, the Netherlands, Spain, and Portugal*, 2 vols (London, 1921)

Ashton, John, *English Caricature and Satire against Napoleon I* (London, 1888, reprinted 1968)

Bainbridge, Simon, *Napoleon and English Romanticism* (Cambridge, 1995)

Banerji, Christianne and Diana Donald, eds, *Gillray Observed: The Earliest Accounts of His Caricatures in London und Paris* (Cambridge, 1999)

Battesti, Michèle, 'L'expédition d'Égypte et Aboukir', in *Napoléon et la mer. Un rêve d'empire*, sous la direction de Jean-Marcel Humbert et Bruno Ponsonnet (Paris, 2004)

Beatty, William, *Authentic Narrative of the death of Lord Nelson* (London, 1807)

Bennett, George G., *The St Helena Reminiscences*, ed. T. Hearl (Cheltenham, 1989)

Bertaud, Jean-Paul, *The Army of the French Revolution: From Citizen-Soldiers to Instrument of Power*, trans. R. R. Palmer (Princeton, NJ, 1988)

Bindman, David, with contributions by Aileen Dawson and Mark Jones, *Shadow of the Guillotine: Britain and the French Revolution* (London, 1989)

Black, Jeremy and Philip Woodfine, eds, *The British Navy and the Use of Naval Power in the Eighteenth Century* (Leicester, 1988)

Blanning, T. C. W., *The Origins of the French Revolutionary Wars* (London, 1986)

Bourguet, Marie-Noëlle, 'Science and Memory: The Stakes of the Expedition to Egypt (1798–1801)', in Howard G. Brown and Judith A. Miller, eds, *Taking Liberties: Problems of a New Order from the French Revolution to Napoleon* (Manchester and New York, 2002)

Bramsen, Ludwig Ernst, *Médailler Napoléon le Grand; ou Description des Médailles, clichés, repoussés, et médailles-décorations relatives aux affaires de la France pendant le consulat et l'empire*, 3 vols (Paris, 1904–13)

Bregeon, Jean-Joël, *L'Égypte française au jour de la jour, 1798–1801* (Paris, 1991)

Bret, P., *L'expédition d'Égypte, une entreprise des Lumieres 1798–1801* (Paris, 1999)

Brifaut, Ch., *Souvenirs d'un académicien*, 2 vols (Paris, 1921)

Broadley, A. M., *Napoleon in Caricature, 1795–1821* (London, 1911)

Bruce, Evangeline, *Napoleon and Josephine* (London, 1995)

Lord Burke, Sir Bernard, *Book of Orders of Knighthood & Decorations of Honour of all nations* (London, 1858)

Burton, J. K., *Napoleon and Clio: Historical Writing, Teaching and Thinking during the First Empire* (Durham, NC, 1979)

Chandler, David, *The Campaigns of Napoleon* (London, 1966)

Chastenay, Victorine de, Comtesse, *Mémoires, 1771–1815* (Paris, 1987)

Clarke, John D. *The Men of HMS Victory at Trafalgar including the Muster Roll of HMS Victory* (Dallington, 1999)

Clayton, Peter A., *The Rediscovery of Ancient Egypt: Artists and Travellers in the Nineteenth Century* (London, 1982)

Clerc, Catherine, *La Caricature contre Napoléon* (Paris, 1985)

Connelly, Owen, *Blundering to Glory: Napoleon's Military Campaigns* (Wilmington, Del., 1987)

Cordingley, David, *Billy Ruffian* (London, 2002)

Crouzet, F., *L'Économie britannique et le Blocus continental* (Paris, 1959)

Czisnik, Marianne, 'Nelson and the Nile: the Creation of Admiral Nelson's Public Image', *Mariner's Mirror*, LXXX (2002)

Dawson, Warren R., *The Nelson Collection at Lloyd's* (London, 1932)

Dayot, A., *Napoléon raconté par l'image* (Paris, 1902)

Delécluze, E. J., *Louis David, son école et son temps* (Paris, 1983)

Deschamps, J., 'Les défenseurs de Napoléon en Grande-Bretagne de 1815 à 1830', *Revue de l'Institut Napoléon* (1955)

Donald, Diana, *The Age of Caricature: Satirical Prints in the Reign of George III* (London, 1996)

Doyle, William, *The Oxford History of the French Revolution* (Oxford, 1989)

Drakard, David, *Printed English Pottery: History and Humour in the Reign of George III 1760–1820* (London, 1992)

Driskell, Michael, *As Befits a Legend: Building a Tomb for Napoleon* (Kent State University Press, OH, 1995)

Duggleby, Vincent, *English Paper Money* (Stroud, 2002)

Ellis, Geoffrey, *Napoleon* (Harlow, 1997)

Elting, John R., *Swords around a Throne: Napoleon's Grande Armée* (New York, 1988)

Fedorak, Charles John, 'The French Capitulation in Egypt and the Preliminary Anglo-French Treaty of Peace in October 1801: A Note', *International History Review*, 15 (1993)

Fraser, Edward, *The Enemy at Trafalgar* (London, 1906)

Gardiner, Robert, ed., *Nelson against Napoleon: From the Nile to Copenhagen 1798–1801* (London, 1997)

—, *Frigates of the Napoleonic Wars* (London, 2000)

Gawler, Jim, *Britons Strike Home: A History of Lloyd's Patriotic Fund 1803–1988* (Sanderstead: Pittot, c. 1993)

Gee, Austin, *The British Volunteer Movement 1794–1815* (Oxford, 2003)

George, M. Dorothy, *English Political Caricature: A Study of Opinion and Propaganda*, 2 vols (London, 1959)

—, and Frederick George Stephens, *Catalogue of Political and Personal Satires Preserved in the Department of Prints and Drawings in the British Museum*, 11 vols (London, 1952)

Gonnard, Philippe, *The Exile of St Helena* (London, 1909)

Grainger, John D., *The Amiens Truce: Britain and Bonaparte, 1801–1803* (Woodbridge, 2004)

Gutteridge, H. C., ed., *Nelson and the Neapolitan Jacobins: Documents Relating to the Suppression of the Jacobin Revolution at Naples, June 1799* (NRS, vol. 25, 1903)

Hall, Christopher, *British Strategy in the Napoleonic War, 1803–15* (Manchester, 1992)

Harbron, John D., *Trafalgar and the Spanish Navy* (London, 1988)

Harding, Richard, *Seapower and Naval Warfare 1650–1830* (London, 1999)

Harland, John, *Seamanship in the Age of Sail* (London, 1984)

Haskell, Francis, *History and its Images: Art and the Interpretation of the Past* (London and New Haven, Conn., 1993)

Herold, J. Christopher, *The Age of Napoleon* (London, 1963),

—, *Bonaparte in Egypt* (London, 1963)

Hibbert, Christopher, *The French Revolution* (London, 1980)

Hill, Draper, *Mr. Gillray, The Caricaturist* (London, 1965)

Holmes, T. W., *The Semaphore* (Ilfracombe, 1983)

Holtman, Robert B., *Napoleonic Propaganda* (Baton Rouge, La., 1950)

Humbert, Jean-Marcel, Michael Pantazzi and Christiane Ziegler, *Egyptomania: Egypt in Western Art 1730–1930* (Ottawa and Paris, 1994)

—, and Bruno Ponsonnet, eds, *Napoléon et la mer: un rêve d'empire* (Paris: Seuil and the Musée de la Marine, 2004)

Huskisson, Thomas, *Eyewitness to Trafalgar: Thomas Huskisson RN, 1800–1808*, ed., D. B. Ellison (Royston, 1985)

In Aid of the 'Save the "Victory"' Fund Loan Exhibition of Nelson Relics Catalogue (London, 1928)

Janowitz, A., ed., *Romanticism and Gender*, Essays and Studies 1998 (Cambridge, 1998)

Jenks, Timothy, 'Contesting the Hero: The Funeral of Admiral Lord Nelson', *Journal of British Studies*, XXXIX (2000)

—, '"Naval Engagements": Patriotism, Cultural Politics, and the Royal Navy, 1793–1815', unpublished Ph.D. thesis (Toronto, 2001)

Jones, Mark, *The Art of the Medal* (London, 1979)

Jonquière, C. de la, *L'expédition de l'Égypte*, 5 vols (Paris, 1900–1907)

Jourdan, A., *Napoléon. Héros, Imperator, Mécène* (Paris, 1998)

—, 'Le Sacre de Napoléon ou le Pacte social', in *Napoléon. Le Sacre* (Ajaccio, 2004)

Knight, R. J. B., *Nelson* (London, 2005)

Laird Clowes, W. *et al.*, *The Royal Navy. A history from the earliest times to the present*, 7 vols (London, 1897–1903)

Lambert, Andrew, *Nelson: Britannia's God of War* (Faber, 2002)

Lapthorne, W. H., 'The City of London River Fencibles', *Coast and Country*, 8 (1979)

Lavery, B., *Nelson's Navy. The Ships, Men and Organisation, 1793–1815* (London, 1989)

—, *Shipboard Life and Organisation, 1711–1815* (NRS, vol. 138, 1998)

—, *Nelson's Fleet at Trafalgar* (London, 2004)

Lean, E. Tangye, *The Napoleonists: A Study in Political Disaffection, 1760–1960* (London, 1973)

Lefebvre, Georges, *Napoleon: From 18 Brumaire to Tilsit, 1799–1807* (London, 1969)

Le Fevre, Peter and Richard Harding, eds, *Precursors of Nelson: British Admirals of the Eighteenth Century* (London, 2000)

Leech, S., *Thirty Years from Home, or A Voice from the Main Deck* (Boston, Mass., 1843), reissued as *A Voice from the Main Deck. Being a Record of the Thirty Years Adventures of Samuel Leech* (London, 1999)

Linkin, H. K. and S. C. Behrendt, eds, *Romanticism and Women Poets* (Lexington, Ky., 1999)

Lloyd, Christopher, *The Nile Campaign: Nelson and Napoleon in Egypt* (Newton Abbot and New York, 1973)

Loveday, Arthur F., *Sir Hilgrove Turner, 1764–1843, Soldier and Courtier under the Georges* (Alkham, 1964)

McCunn, F. J., *The Contemporary English View of Napoleon* (London, 1914)

Mace, Rodney, *Trafalgar Square: Emblem of Empire* (London, 1976)

Mackesy, Piers, *British Victory in Egypt* (London and New York, 1995)

Macleod, Emma Vincent, *A War of Ideas: British Attitudes to the Wars Against Revolutionary France, 1792–1802* (Aldershot, 1998)

Mansel, Philip, *The Eagle in Splendour: The Court of France 1789–1830* (Cambridge, 1988)

Marshall, P. J., ed., *The Oxford History of the British Empire*, Vol. II: *The Eighteenth Century* (Oxford, 1998)

Martineau, Gilbert, *Napoleon's Last Journey*, trans. Frances Partridge (London, 1976)

—, *Le Retour des Cendres* (Paris, 1990)

Mathis, H-P., ed., *Napoleon in the Mirror of the Caricature* (Arenenberg/Zurich, NZZ, 1998)

May, Cdr W. E. A., RN, and P. G. W. Annis, *Swords for Sea Service*, 2 vols (London, 1970)

Morriss, Roger and Richard Saxby, eds, *The Channel Fleet and the Blockade of Brest, 1793–1801* (NRS, vol. 141, 2001)

Muir, Rory, *Britain and the Defeat of Napoleon 1807–1815* (London and New Haven, Conn., 1996)

Nash, Michael, ed., *The Nelson Masks* (Hoylake, 1993)

O'Brien, Patrick K., 'The Impact of the Revolutionary and Napoleonic Wars, 1793–1815, on the Long-Run Growth of the British Economy', *Review of the Fernand Braudel Center*, XII (1989), 335–95

Oman, Carola, *Nelson* (London, 1947)

O'Meara, Barry E., *Napoleon in Exile; or a Voice from St Helena* (London, 1888)

Parkinson, C. N., *The Trade Winds: A Study of British Overseas Trade during the French Wars 1793–1815* (London, 1948)

Parkinson, Richard, with contributions by Diffie, W., Fischer, M. and Simpson, R. S., *Cracking Codes: The Rosetta Stone and Decipherment* (London, 1999)

Penzer, N. M., *Paul Storr 1771–1844 Silversmith and Goldsmith* (Feltham, 1954, 1971)

Percier, Charles and Pierre-François-Léonard Fontaine, *Description des cérémonies et des fêtes qui ont eu lieu pour le couronnement de leurs majestés Napoléon, empereur des Français et roi d'Italie, et Joséphine, son auguste épouse: recueil de decorations executes dans l'église de Notre-Dame de Paris et au Champ de Mars, d'après les dessins et sous la conduite de C. Percier et P.F.L. Fontaine, architectes de l'empereur* (Paris, 1807)

Philp, Mark, *The French Revolution and British Popular Politics* (Cambridge, 1991)

Pratt, Stephen, *The French Revolution and Napoleon* (London, 1992)

Pocock, Tom, *Horatio Nelson* (London, 1987)

—, *The Terror before Trafalgar: Nelson, Napoleon and the Secret War* (London, 2002)

Porter, Andrew, ed., *The Oxford History of the British Empire*, Vol. III: *The Nineteenth Century* (Oxford, 1999)

Prentice, Rina, *A Celebration of the Sea* (London, 1994)

Pugh, Gordon, P. D., *Nelson and his Surgeons* (Edinburgh and London, 1968)

Pyke, E. J., *A Biographical Dictionary of Wax Modellers* (Oxford, 1973)

Rawson, G., ed., *Nelson's Letters* (London, 1960)

Reilly, Robin and George Savage, *Wedgwood: The Portrait Medallions* (London, 1973)

—, *The Dictionary of Wedgwood* (Woodbridge, 1980)

Risk, James, *The History of the Order of the Bath and its Insignia* (London, 1972)

Robertson, David, *Sir Charles Eastlake and the Victorian Art World* (Princeton, NJ, 1978)

Rodger, N. A. M., *The Wooden World: Anatomy of the Georgian Navy* (London. 1988)

—, 'Image and Reality in Eighteenth-century Naval Tactics', *Mariner's Mirror*, LXXXIX (2003), 349–64

—, *The Command of the Ocean: A Naval History of Britain, 1699–1815* (London, 2004)

Rowlands, J., *Master Drawings and Watercolours in the British Museum* (London, 1984)

Schama, Simon, *Citizens: A Chronicle of the French Revolution* (London, 1984)

Schnapper, A., ed., *David* (Paris, 1989)

Semmel, Stuart, *Napoleon and the British* (London and New Haven, Conn., 2004)

Shiner Wilson, Carol and Joel Haefner, eds, *Re-Visioning Romanticism: British Women Writers, 1776–1837* (Philadelphia, Pa., 1994)

Shorter, Clement, *Napoleon and his Fellow Travellers* (London, 1908)

Sipe, Thomas, *Beethoven: Eroica Symphony* (Cambridge, 1998)

Soboul, Albert, *The French Revolution 1787–1799: From the Storming of the Bastille to Napoleon*, trans. A. Forrest and C. Jones (London, 1989)

Sparrow, Elizabeth, *Secret Service: British Agents in France 1792–1815* (Woodbridge, 1999)

Thompson, J. M., *Napoleon Bonaparte* (Stroud, 2002)

Tracy, Nicholas, ed., 'Sir Robert Calder's Action', *Mariner's Mirror*, LXXVII (1991), 259–70

—, *Nelson's Battles: The Art of Victory in the Age of Sail* (London, 1996)

—, *The Naval Chronicle* [consolidated edition], 7 vols (London, 1998–9)

Tulard, Jean, *Napoléon à Sainte-Hélène* (Paris, 1981)

—, *Napoleon: The Myth of the Saviour*, trans. T. Waugh (London, 1984)

Tunstall, Brian, *Naval Warfare in the Age of Sail: The Evolution of Fighting Tactics 1650–1815*, ed. Nicholas Tracey (London, 1990)

Tussaud, Marie, *Memoirs of Madame Tussaud: her eventful history*, ed. R. M. Hayley (London and New York, 1878)

Walker, Richard, 'Nelson's masks – life or death', *Mariner's Mirror*, LXVI (1980), 319–27

—, *The Nelson Portraits* (Portsmouth, 1998)

Wareham, Tom, *The Star Captains: Frigate Command in the Napoleonic Wars* (London, 2001)

Warner, Oliver, *A Portrait of Lord Nelson* (London, 1958)

Watson, G. L. de St M., *The Story of Napoleon's Death Mask* (London, 1915)

White, Colin, *1797 Nelson's Year of Destiny: Cape St Vincent and Santa Cruz de Tenerife* (Stroud, 1998)

—, 'Nelson's 1805 Battle Plan', *Journal of Maritime Research* (May 2002)

—, *Nelson: The New Letters* (Woodbridge, 2005)

www.jmr.nmm.ac.uk

Wilson, G., *The Old Telegraphs* (Chichester, 1976)

Wilson-Smith, T., *Napoleon and his Artists* (London, 1996)

Woodman, Richard, *The Victory of Seapower: Winning the Napoleonic Wars 1806–1814* (London, 1998)

Woolf, Stuart, *Napoleon's Integration of Europe* (London, 1991)

Yarrington, Alison, *The Commemoration of the Hero: Monuments to the British Victors of the Napoleonic Wars* (New York, 1988)

Zuleta, Julian de, 'Trafalgar – The Spanish View', *Mariner's Mirror*, LXVI (1980)

Picture Credits

Illustrations in the catalogue appear by kind permission of the following:

Apsley House/Victoria & Albert Museum © V&A Images: 120 (bottom right), 121 (top left)

Archiv der Gesellschaft der Musikfreunde in Wien: p.62

Ashmolean Museum, Oxford: p.117 (bottom)

The Bodleian Library, University of Oxford: pp.115 (top), 142 (right), 144 (top)

The British Library, London: pp.49 (left), 76, 77, 89 (bottom), 103, 108, 111, 118, 119, 121 (right), 207,

Château de Fontainbleau/© RMN Photo – droits réservés: p.39

Copyright © British Museum, London: pp.17 (all), 18 (both), 20, 21, 22 (top), 58 (bottom), 61 (bottom), 114 (top), 147 (top), 199 (top), 270

Courtesy of the Trustees of Sir John Soane's Museum, London: pp.4; 47

Courtesy the Spode Museum Trust: p.122 (both)

The Drapers' Company, London: p.96 (left)

Fitzwilliam Museum, Cambridge: p.120 (left)

The Faringdon Collection Trust, Buscot Park, Oxfordshire: p.109

Fondation Napoléon, Paris – Patrice Maurice Berthier: p.46, 266 (left), 268

The Governor and Company of The Bank of England: pp.164 (bottom), 168 (top), 169(left)

Lloyd's of London, London, UK: pp.7 (top), 74, 82, (bottom), 97 (right), 98 (right), 160 (right), 169 (right), 182 (right), 249 (top); 252 (bottom)

Madame Tussaud's Archives, London: p.14 (right), 24 (above - photo © National Maritime Museum)

Musée Carnavalet, Paris: © P.M.V.P./Trocay p.10; © P.M.V.P./Ladet/Pignol/Claire: pp.12 (right), 13 (all), 14 (left), 22 (bottom); © P.M.V.P./Svartz: p.11 (bottom); © P.M.V.P./Degraces: pp.202 (left), 205 (both)

Musée d'Armes de Liège: pp.36, 56,

Musée de l'Armée, Paris: pp.1, 15 (all), 16, 26 (left), 43, 48 (both), 50, 57, 58 (top), 59 (bottom); 137 (left), 270

Musée de la Révolution française: p.24 (bottom)

Musée de Malmaison, France/© RMN Photo: pp.52 (right), 53 (right)

Musée du Louvre, Paris/© Photo RMN – droits reserves: pp.61 (top)

Museo del Tessuto, Prato: p.53 (left)

Museo Napoleonico, Rome: pp.123, 133,

Musée national de la Lègion d'honneur et des orders de la chevalerie, Paris: p.136 (right)

Musée national de la Marine, Paris: © P. Dantec pp.55, 131, 135, 215 (top), 267; © A. Fux: p.132 (top), 134, 165

Museum of London: pp.73, 75 (bottom), 81 (top)

The National Archives, Kew (PRO) ADM/52/3711: p.211 (bottom)

National Army Museum, London: pp.165 (both), 166 (both), 244

National Gallery of Art, Washington. Samuel Kress Collection/Bridgeman Art Library: p.40

National Portrait Gallery, London: pp.27 (bottom); 95, 128, 129, 154 (all)

Nelson Museum, Monmouth: p.216 (top right); p.216 (bottom left)

Osterreichische Nationalbibliothek, Vienna: p.94

Platt Hall, Manchester City Galleries: p.113

Photograph © 2005 Museum of Fine Arts, Boston: p.37

Private collection, UK– photo George Skipper © NMM: p.216 (top left)

Private collection, UK – photo Tim Williams © NMM: pp.9; 11 (top), 25, 52 (left), 167 (top), 251 (top

Private collection, France © Photos12.com: pp.19, 45, 49 (right), 59 (top), 60, 63 (both), 117 (top left), 125, 148 (bottom), 269

Private collection, UK – photo © NMM: pp.97 (both), 198 (both)

Private collection, UK: p.241

Royal Astronomical Society, London: p.114 (bottom)

The Royal Collection © 2005 Her Majesty Queen Elizabeth II: p.221, 262, 266 (right)

Royal College of Physicians and Surgeons of Glasgow: p.227

Royal Naval Museum, Portsmouth: pp.75 (top), 178, 182 (centre), 184 (top)

Shortall of Ballylorcan: pp.218 (top right) 218 (bottom right)

© Tate, London 2004: pp.33, 70, 78, 115 (bottom), 156, 157 (top), 246 (both), 247 (top)

Victoria & Albert Museum © V&A Images: pp.106, 176

Wallace Collection, London/Bridgeman Art Library: p.238

The Wellcome Trust, London: p.219 (top)

Computer model of Napoleon's Coronation, courtesy of Vaughan Hart, Joe Robson, Peter Hicks (University of Bath, UK, and Fondation Napoléon, France).

National Maritime Museum, Greenwich
Reproduction references for pictures in the collection of the National Maritime Museum are listed below. These may be ordered from the Picture Library, National Maritime Museum, Greenwich, London SE10 9NF or online at www.nmm.ac.uk

Copyright © National Maritime Museum, London: PU4050 p.ii; 1806 p.1; A4288 p.3; D5481 p.5; PY0129 p.12 (left); E3538-1,-2 p.26 (right); D5481 p.28; PAF3899 p.29; F3699 p.30; A3700-2 p.31; F3665 p.44; PW3964 p.51; PW3965 p.54; PU3879 p.66; PW3893 p.67; E3376-2 p.71; E3376-1 p.81 (bottom); D5541 p.83; E3377-1,2 p.84 (bottom), PW3888 p.85; E5828 p.86; PU3221 p.87 (left), F3692 p.87 (right); E1916 p.88 (top); PW3876 p.90 ; F3564 p.91 (top); 1806 p.93 (top); A4288 p.93 (bottom); B3197-2 p.98 (top); D7649 p.100; PW3864 p.107; F3663/F3664 p.116; C586 p.136 (left); E3061 p.138 (top); PW3967 p.138 (bottom); PY7246 p.139; PU4060 p.140 (top); C1463 p.140 (bottom); PU4783 p.141 (top); PU4797 p.141 (bottom); F3654 p.142 (left); A5505 p.143; PY7437 p.144 (bottom); PW3949 p.145; PW4005 p.146; PY7338 p.147 (bottom); PW3950 p.148 (top); PAF3899 p.149; BHC2901 p.150; A929 p.153, 155; D4080-1 p.157 (bottom); PU1358 p.158; D4547 p. 159 (top); D9880-1 p.159 (bottom); POU3881 p.160 (left); D7562 p.161; F3705 p.162; F3683 p.163 (left); PU1621 p.163 (right); F3682 p.164 (top); F3642 p.167 (bottom); PZ7124 p.168 (bottom); E5868 p.170; BHC0539 p.171; 8252A p.181 (bottom); PW3866 p.175; F3644 p.177 (top); PW3874 p.178; H4822 p.177 (bottom); E1990 p.180 (top right); F3693 p.181 (top); F3869-1 p.183; F4242-1 p.184; (bottom); F3675 p.185 (top); PW5885 p.190; BHC0539 p.192; E7102 p.193; BHC0548 p.195; PU4050 p.197; D4717 p.199 (bottom); F0074 p.200; F2847-2 p.201 (top); PU4792 p.201 (bottom); F3706 p.202 (right); F3676 p.204; F3681 p.206 (left); F3672 p.209 (left); PU4050 p.209 (right); E3685 p.210 (top); D7566 p.211 (top); F2881-1 p.212; D7561 p.213 (bottom); E1066 p.215 (bottom); BHC2352 p.216 (bottom right); D5510 p.229; PX6706 p.232; D5510 p.233; F3673 p.235; BHC3227 p.237; F3674 p.247 (bottom), PW4004 p.248; PX8554 p.249 (bottom); D4925-2 p.250; D5056 p.251 (bottom); PW7631 p.253 (left); F3680-1 p.254; E5362-1 p.255; PY7312 p.256 (left); D3481-6 p.260; PU4784 p.261 (top); PW3866 p.261 (bottom); PW3523 p.267 (top); E3604-1,2 p.270 (bottom)

Caird Collection: BHC2736 pp.88 (bottom); BHC2876 p.263; F3702 p.264;

Girdlestone Collection: D6112 p.186

Greenwich Hospital Collection: F2148-1 p.79; BHC2905 p.80; F3646 p.99; F3655 p.99 (top); F3656 p.99 (centre); F3657 p.99 (bottom); F2161-2 p.187; BHC2593 p.206 (right); F4077-1 p.213 (top); BHC2629 p.217 (top); F3685 p.217 (bottom); E1118 p.218 (top left); E8578 p.218 (bottom); F2160-5 p.220; F2163-2 p.222 (left); F2159-1 p.222 (right); F2162 p.223 (top); F2164 p.224 (bottom); D3210 p.224; BHC2894 p.225; BHC2905 p.245; F3707 p.252 (top); BHC2905 p.256 (right); BHC0565 p.257; BHC2889 p.259

Nelson-Ward Collection: D5717 pp.89 (top); 4933 p.91 (bottom); D6591-2 p.92; D5575-4 p.182 (left); E2055 p.185 (bottom); F0908 p.203 (left); E6068 p.203 (right)

Royal United Service Museum Collection: D6813 p.23; F3678; p.132 (bottom); D7563-2 p.210 (bottom); F3701 p.226

Stopford Collection: E3376-1,2 p.84 (top)

Sutcliffe-Smith Collection: D5447-1 p.112; E2022 p.180 (top left); E1872 p.180 (centre left); E1879 p.180 (bottom left); E1873 p.180 (bottom right); F3679 p.253 (right)

Trafalgar House Collection: D7555 p.208

Walter Collection: F3661 p.117 (top right); E1844 p.137 (right); F3661 p.151; E2014 p.180 (centre right);

Supporters of the National Maritime Museum

The Museum gratefully acknowledges the assistance of those listed below:

The Department for Culture Media and Sport
The Heritage Lottery Fund
The Department for Education and Skills

Major Donors

The DCMS/Wolfson Foundation Gallery
Refurbishment Fund
The Millennium Commission
Particle Physics and Astronomy Research Council
(PPARC)
ReDiscover
Swiss Re
Trinity House
The Weston Foundation
The Wolfson Foundation
The Zvi and Ofra Meitar Family Fund

Donors

Chamber of Shipping
David Gestetner
Institute of Chartered Shipbrokers
John Mitchell and Son
Morgan Stanley International Foundation
National Art Collections Fund
Society for Nautical Research
The Arts Council
The Basil Samuel Charitable Trust
The Cowley Charitable Foundation
The Donald Forrester Trust
The Edinburgh Number 2 Charity Trust
The Elephant Trust
The Friends of the National Maritime Museum
The Headley Trust
The Inchcape Foundation
The Inverforth Charitable Trust
The J S F Pollitzer Charitable Trust
The Leathersellers' Company
The Linbury Trust
The MacRobert Trust
The Met Office
The Raymond and Blanche Lawson Trust
The Royal Society/COPUS
The Sir John Fisher Foundation
The Worshipful Company of Builders Merchants

And all those other donors who wish to
remain anonymous

Donors to 'A Universal Appeal' to redevelop the Royal Observatory Greenwich

CHH Owen
JMR Sharman
Lady Hardy
Mr Maxi Gainza
NJ Squibb
Patricia Rothman
Reeves Charitable Trust
Sir David Hardy
The Quarmby Fund
W Oelsner
David Wells

And all those other individuals, too numerous to
mention, who have supported the campaign.

Supporters of the American Fund of the National Maritime Museum and the Royal Observatory Greenwich (EIN 30-0190984)

C Richard Carlson
Lee MacCormack Edwards PhD
John W Oelsner
The Carlson Family Trust
The Dmitro Foundation
The Gladys Kreible Delmas Foundation
The Hubbard Broadcasting Foundation
The Kelton Foundation
Susan T Zetkus

Major Sponsors

BP Shipping
Morgan Stanley and Co International
P&O

Sponsors

Accurist Watches
National Physical Laboratory
The Crown Estate
The Maritime Coastguard Agency (MCA)

Nelson's Fleet

HMS *Victory* – The Zvi and Ofra Meitar Family Fund
HMS *Téméraire* – Greenwich Inc
HMS *Dreadnought* – Pusser's Rum
HMS *Colossus* – Mr Clive Richards OBE
HMS *Sirius* – Walpoles of Greenwich
HM Schooner *Pickle* – Warwick Leadley Gallery
HM Cutter *Entreprenante* – Mr John C. Bogle

Corporate Members

Accor UK
Braemar Seascope
Cheeswrights
Evergreen (UK) Ltd
General Maritime Corporation
HSBC Insurance Brokers Ltd
Kipling – part of the Vanity Fair Group
Liberty Syndicates
Lloyd's Register
Lloyds of London
Morgan Stanley and Co International
National Physical Laboratory
Shell International Trading and Shipping Co. Ltd
Swiss Re
The Baltic Exchange

Corporate Loan Holders

AVIVA plc
Jupiter Asset Management
Lloyd's of London
Mandarin Oriental Hyde Park Hotel
Pemberton Greenish
Rathbone Brothers plc
Simpson, Spence and Young Ltd
The Leathersellers' Company
The Orrery Restaurant – Conran Holdings plc
Wellington Underwriting

BP Shipping is the corporate sponsor of the *Nelson & Napoléon* exhibition

Index